TALES
OF THE
TUNGSTEN MINE

TRUE STORIES OF THE PASAYTEN WILDERNESS

TALES
OF THE
TUNGSTEN MINE

TRUE STORIES OF THE PASAYTEN WILDERNESS

G.A. HENDERSON

Tales of the Tungsten Mine
Copyright © 2021 by G.A. Henderson.

All rights reserved. No part of this publication may be reproduced, distributed, or transmitted in any form or by any means, including photocopying, recording, or other electronic or mechanical methods, without the prior written permission of the copyright holder, except in the case of brief quotations embodied in critical reviews and certain other noncommercial uses permitted by copyright law. For permission requests, write to the publisher, addressed "Attention: Permissions Coordinator," at the address below.

ISBN: Soft Cover – 978-1-64318-039-7

Imperium Publishing
1097 N. 400th Rd
Baldwin City, KS, 66006

www.imperiumpublishing.com

INTRODUCTION

THIS IS THE SWEET AND bitter story of the Tungsten Mine. The story takes in the amazing life of Frank Arnold, the long-time caretaker who made the Tungsten Mine his home for 20 years. Arnold wandered the vast eastern Cascades in what we now call the "Pasayten Wilderness" until his untimely death in the winter of 1934-35, while out scouting his trap lines. *Pasayten* is a French word meaning the "land of Satan." The area is as beautiful as an angel but can be cruel as its namesake! Indeed, the mystery surrounding Frank's death, how he was found by a mental patient and all the stories that boiled out of that strange event are appropriate for a land called Satan and enough to move a statue of stone.

Frank Arnold himself was unique, a riddle. As one man who knew him said, he was "not your average human being." He was an extremely intelligent man and in every way a curiosity. Fortunately, there are those from whom one can glimpse a fading shadow of this little-big man and gather the threads of the mystery of his sad death at the mouth of Horseshoe Creek. The legend of Frank Arnold is one with the tale of the Tungsten Mine. The stories about this intriguing man and the history of the Tungsten mine are so interwoven into the history of the high mountain land called the Pasayten that they must be told together.

History is good and bad, sad and happy. This story too is both happy and sad. The eventual fate of the Tungsten Mine rests no longer with the miners, but in the hands of a government organization known as the Forest Service, which has had a track record of destroying old historical cabins. How Frank died is still open to the imagination of the reader… But…This is the story of the Tungsten Mine on which all imaginings can rest. The story was written, for the most part, in the late 1980's.

Note: In some instances, the names in this book have been changed.

ACKNOWLEDGMENTS

I WOULD LIKE TO EXPRESS his thanks and appreciation to each and every person who helped, with their time and their interest in the high country, to tell this story of the Tungsten Mine.

A special thanks to: Bob Curtis, Paula Curtis, Jim McDaniel, Harry Sherling, George Honey, Omar Smith, Albert Smith, Emmet Smith, George Miller, Clara Northcott Miller, Francis Lufkin, Roland and Doris Darling, "Dutch" Wasiforth, Carl Gibbons, Jimmy Steves, Leonard Honey, Doug Loudon, Ann Briley, Leland Thrasher, Lloyd Ford, Bill Ford, Jim Ford, Bob Irwin, Billy Cohens, Gint Cawsten, Harold MacWilliams, Foss Creveling, Frank Dammann, Hay Hill, C.C. Ditzel, Don Zellweger, Della Northcott, Opal Cook Kennisten, Mrs. Ralph Miller, "Tick" Hill, Ted Boland, George Williams, Alice Tweedle, Jim Glanders, and Bruce McPherson. The story is woven from their recollections.

The pictures in this book were kindly donated by: Bob Curtis, Harry Sherling, George Honey, Bob Irwin, Harold MacWilliams, Foss Creveling, Oren Dodd, Jay Hill, Della Northcott, Opal Kennisten,

TALES OF THE TUNGSTEN MINE

Bruce McPherson, Billy Cohens, and The New Brunswick Provincial Archives. And, for these, we are thankful.

My father, Art Henderson, enjoyed his many trips into that faraway "high country," where the charm of the Tungsten Mine took hold of him every year from the mid-fifties, through and into, the sixties, seventies, eighties, and nineties. His cause, in a large part, in the early years, and later, was picked up by many local horsemen, too many to number. They determined to keep the mine cabins roofed, repaired and cleaned, doing whatever was needed to save them from the hands of time. Because of the determination and hard work of the local horsemen—and only because of it—the Tungsten Mine still exerts its strange "magnetic" pull, and the mine cabins are still standing and can be enjoyed by you and me today.

And last, to my editor, Margo Thompson (who still wants to "slap" my hand), whose many hours of work has helped make this story what it is.

This book is dedicated to each and every person ever stricken by the Fever of the Tungsten Mine

TABLE OF CONTENTS

CHAPTER NAME
1. A Mental Patient Finds a Mental Case. 13
2. A Tungsten of a Find. 31
3. The Deputy Sheriff Makes His Investigation 41
4. Herb Curtis, Bill McDaniel, George Loudon
   Get the Tungsten Mine. 57
5. The Queens Guard and Trouble
   (Speculation and Conjecture) 69
6. A Trapper is Kicked off the Train. 77
7. $275,000 for a Mine & $24,000 for a Ton of Tungsten. 93
8. A Frozen Foot and an Infected Eye 109
9. The Great Era of the Tungsten Mine 123
10. Wild Times. 145
11. Down with the Germans — Down went the Tungsten 165
12. High Prices, High Country and Fine Furs. 175
13. Fire and Destruction 197
14. 30 Tons in 1936 209
15. Lost Stories of Frank Arnold 223

16.	Frank's Lost Gold Mine	259
17.	Don Zellweger on the Hatfield Claims & Foss's Missed $100,000	265
18.	In All Fairness, Was It Really Suicide?	273
19.	The Boom of 1951	287
20.	A Mouth Full of Teeth	303
21.	The Rogue Trapper and The Wandering Prospector	313
22.	How George Miller and Pete Found Frank Arnold	331
23.	Foul Play on Horseshoe Creek	349
24.	Hopefully Not the Closing Chapter on the Tungsten Mine	385

The Story Begins

Our story begins with the tale told by Clyde Paul as it was told to him by a man called Iron.

"**WE FIGURED THAT SLED THERE** was left by that renegade trapper. We found it in here the next spring, and that was the first time we had ever seen it. That killer must have run out of snow and left it right here. I figure he was the one who killed Arnold. He was a stranger to this country for we had never heard of him before and figured he was just traveling through…didn't know if he was a Canadian or where he had come from. We're sure he was the same man who came into the Len Easle Tavern in Oroville on……that noisy Saturday night.

The music was playing non-stop in the smoke-filled tavern. In 1935, Oroville was every bit the rip-roaring border town that called miner, lumberjack, apple-knocker, saw-miller, cowboy and a lot of Indians to its fun-loving night life. Yes, it was Saturday night at Len Easle Tavern.

The tavern sat right below Ben Prince's grocery store on Main Street, and everybody in town knew Ben Prince, including the bartender pulling on the beer tap that Saturday night. The dark, smoke-filled tavern didn't help the looks of the unshaven, wild-eyed mountain man who sat himself at the bar and asked for a beer.

It was the heavy wool clothes and the wild looks (he threw) around the room that made the man next to him take note. This wild-eyed man seemed to stand all by himself in this noisy tavern with too many people in it. He was cold, while everybody else was warm and having a good time. He was different that's all there was to it! Even the bartender sensed it, but he couldn't stop to give him any more than a second look, and a beer, and another. The big man must have sat there for close to an hour, and seemed to drink beer as fast as the bartender could keep his glass filled, but what got both Joe and the bartender was on the man's last beer, instead of a greenback coming out of the man's pocket, there was a check written out to Bud Shaffer! The check was from Ben Prince for $350.00! The bartender had never in his life seen this man before. He stood there in a quandary of befuddlement trying to figure out what he should do with the man's $350.00 check that lay in his hands. He turned it over, looked, turned it over again, looked at the big 'Ben Prince Groceries' in bold lettering across the front. He knew that the check was probably good.

"Are you Bud Shaffer?" he asked in the strongest tone he could muster.

"Ya D-D rights I am," he roared. "Ben Prince wrote me that check just an hour ago when I sold him my ##**@@ FURS!"

Now that was something that made sense, Joe thought as he sat there listening in. The bartender walked over to the cash register machine and popped open the till. It made sense to him, too. It was Ben's signature, and it had to be as good as the groceries upstairs.

Bud Shaffer picked up his change, three hundred forty-nine dollars and so many cents. He turned and was gone before Joe could take another look. But the image of this big, cold man stayed in Joe's mind for years. It was two days later that the story got back to him about the trapper with the Ben Prince check. Bud Shaffer was wanted by the Law."

CHAPTER 1

A Mental Patient Finds a Mental Case

This tale is true, as true as Frank Arnold. The story was told to Loy and Jim McDaniel a number of times over the years that followed Frank Maron's death in the 1950's. Pete, who plays the part in the story, also told the same story of Maron finding Frank Arnold. His young sons remembered Maron leaving their home with their dad to search for Frank Arnold and hearing the strange story when they returned from the trip with Frank Arnold hung, and just all bones. The story was also repeated by Pete in their presence as the years rolled by. Bob Curtis, Al Smith and George Honey were others that also heard the story from Pete. But Bob Curtis and Jim McDaniel also spoke of the body being just bones in suit of coveralls with the stocking hat, gloves, and boots tied on, even wired on. The story has not been fantasized or exaggerated. Frank E. Maron, himself, told the story as it is described here...

FRANK E. MARON WAS ESCORTED out the doors of Medical Lake Mental Hospital. He had been committed to the Washington

State Mental Hospital in late 1934. About the same time, the tough old mountain man, Frank Arnold, turned up missing. He was still missing during the winter of 1934/1935 and through most of 1936. If he had not been confined around all those doctors in white coats at a hospital with white-tiled walls and floors, he surely would have gone looking for his old acquaintance long before 1936. Frank Arnold, it seemed, had just vanished up in those high mountains, the rugged and timbered Cascades of north central Washington. As the Medical Lake Hospital doors closed behind Frank Maron, the man who had signed his release walked at his side.

Maron was still a young man in 1936 (25 or 30 years old, I'm guessing). He was thinking that if nothing else could be said about the place he was walking away from, at least he could say that life had been easy there at the hospital with hot meals three times a day and a soft bed to sleep on for the last 2 years. This was not something by any means that he had always had. These were the depression years, hard times, and life on the "outside" was not easy.

The man at Maron's side was Pete. In the year 1936, Pete drove 140 miles in his new, bright red, 1935 Dodge to the Medical Lake Hospital just to get Frank Maron. Pete needed him to go into those high mountains to look for the missing Frank Arnold. Pete knew that if anyone was going to find the old trapper, after so many failures, it was going to be Frank Maron, Frank Arnold's old friend and Pete's last good hope.

A few years before, when he was healthy and not in a mental hospital, Maron was a friend of the missing Frank Arnold. He was even more than a friend for he had lived and trapped with the old mountain man just a few years before. It was the same year that he drifted into Loomis, a small mining town not very far from the Canadian border; the town was so small, it hardly found a place on the map. That summer, as Maron soon saw, the Loomis valley and its mountains to the west were dry, hot and

A Mental Patient Finds a Mental Case

on fire! The residents needed help. As he rode into town that day with hopes of obliging that call for help, smoke was everywhere. He couldn't see into the heavy gray and black fog for more than a quarter of a mile. The mountains to the west were burning up — it was the unstoppable fire of 1929, and Frank Maron had come to town to help put it out.

Now, Maron was no auto man in this new age of cars. His cowboy hat had the trademark loosened brown sweat band; it was pulled down low over his brow. His boots hung in their leather stirrups. The white horse he rode down the busy Loomis main street on led a pretty sorrel that carried all his "personables." Loomis was abuzz, like a stirred bees' nest, because the fire to the west demanded to be put out, and that was not an easy thing to do. Dozens of men milled about the town that was on the verge of panic.

In the years before, he arrived in Loomis, Maron had been trying to make a living in the gold placers on the Columbia River, but without much success. His family had a homestead on the Colville Indian Reservation, which is where he got his excellent horsemanship skills. This is also why he still use horses 15 years past their useful place in history. Maron spent most of his youth in Kettle Falls. And though he had no way of knowing it at the time, he was going to become an important witness to the events about to unfold in the dark mountains he was riding into.

He was a cowboy, and now as he had hoped, he had become a Forest Service employee. Maron did soon get a job firefighting in those woods. He had become friendly with his big boss, "Pete," whose name has been changed here and in the rest of this true story, to protect, as they say, "the innocent." While working on the mad fire that year, Pete, a Forest Service man himself, was more than helpful to Fronk Maron because he had all kinds of things going on in those days, and he needed Frank Maron's help as much as Maron could use his. Pete had a small ranch that put up hay and pastured horses. Maron took advantage of this by boarding his own horses there. Pete was also a packer for the Forest Service and for government surveyors working in the mountains at the time. And being a packer, he furnished horses, for not only the government, but also for a local, summer "dude" ranch. This was about half of what Pete had going on. So, Maron was a needed man and stayed on at Pete's ranch after fighting the huge forest fire that year. And, now, 7 years after that 1929 fire, Pete had another reason for needing Maron's help, and that is how he came to be walking out of the Medical Lake Hospital beside Frank Maron.

Maron knew that there had to be a good reason for him to be released from the hospital, and he was thankful that Pete, in needing his help, had provided it.

"Boy, I'm sure glad Pete came and got me out of those tiled rooms with those white-coated doctors...whooo...what a place...crazy people screaming, laughing..."

Then, Pete, with Maron in the passenger seat, pointed his new car away from Medical Lake Hospital and back the many miles to what was now his home in Okanogan, Washington. Pete had just moved there after selling his Loomis ranch a few months before. While Pete drove, Maron had plenty of time to reflect on his days with the now missing Frank Arnold.

He remembered that Frank Arnold and Pete had also been friends. Arnold, the Englishman turned mountain man had long been living deep in the high mountains at the non-operative Tungsten Mine 40 miles west, high up the mountains from Loomis.

"Heck, It was Pete who took me into the Tungsten Mine late that fall, after the snows had finally put out the 1929 fire, to meet Frank Arnold, the legendary old Englishman. I guess Pete felt kind of sorry for me being out of work and all. It wasn't easy getting through that burn, but we packed Frank a few groceries."

A Mental Patient Finds a Mental Case

Maron ended up spending 2 years with Frank Arnold, from the late fall of 1929, through and until the summer of 1931. And because of that extended time, traveling hundreds of miles with Arnold, Pete figured that Frank Maron would know, if anyone did, all Arnold's old trapping haunts. And while Maron was away with his health problems for 2 years, Pete gathered what information he could about where Frank Arnold was not. The old trapper had not been found in Long Swamp nor in the Horseshoe Basin, nor the Windy Mountain region. These were areas of high mountains where Arnold had commonly traveled, both summer and winter. These places had all been searched in the last two summers and were the most natural places to look first. Even so, there was still a lot of country to cover and walking and looking that Maron could yet do. He knew, all too well, that Frank's total trap-line could have covered at least 100, maybe 150 miles in those later years, perhaps even more. Who could really know how far south Frank Arnold went or how far north into Canada he trapped? That 1929 fire had changed the hunting grounds and much of the old, burnt regions were no good now for fur. Maron knew that he could walk all fall, and next summer, too, in those mountains and never cover all of Frank's old haunts, let alone any new game areas Frank Arnold had explored. Arnold had always been free, like the wind, and as powerful. He went where he wanted to go, stopped only by the lowlands and the people who filled them. Still, Maron has committed to giving the search a try. Pete wanted him to look, so he would. This was the very reason he was now free again.

What happened to Frank Arnold? Maron wondered. *Darn, he had been okay the last time I saw him. Except for his bad teeth, Frank was in perfect health, and he was tough as nails 2 years ago. Shoot! Frank was too level-headed. He was for sure woods-wise. Too woods-wise to have messed up so bad that he got himself into a jam he couldn't get out of. Or was he? The man was getting up in years, there's no doubt about that. Well, he was gone. That seemed for sure. He would have come out of that high-country months ago if he were alive, or if he was still in this area. Maybe that's what happened. He pulled out. He just left, the same way he had come into this country years before. But no, he had friends, and his home for 20 years had been the Tungsten Mine. There was no reason to move out, the mine was his home, and we were his friends. Surely, he wouldn't have gone back to England or wherever he came from after all these years. No, Frank would have told somebody. Something bad has happened to Frank. I know it! I'll sure try to find him if I can. He won't be alive, but if Pete wants me to look, I'll look! Maybe there's still a chance...*

Maron, like Arnold, was a bachelor, and he had as much in common with that lone bird as a man was going to have. But it was now September, and another summer had gone by. Maron was the last on the list of several men who had gone out to look for this watchman of the Tungsten Mine.

Missing

Frank Arnold hadn't come out of the high country to the town of Loomis that winter of 1934 or in the spring of 1935 either. Word was out that he was missing. The spring of 1935 was like all springs, and Emmet Smith was driving his band of sheep up from the Pine Creek wintering grounds to stay for a few days just outside of Loomis, at the Ford/Reeder ranch, before heading the white sheep into the high mountain grasslands of the Pasayten Wilderness. Pete came to Smith's camp and had a talk with Emmet that bright spring day. He spoke of the worrisome news that Arnold hadn't come out of the mountains that year and asked if he would ride back to the Tungsten Mine and see what had happened to the old trapper. Acting on Pete's worries, it was sometime, around a week later, from the mountainside called Deer Park that Emmet finally shook loose from the thousand curly-haired sheep and spurred his horse toward the Tungsten Mine to the west. He knew that this could be serious. If Pete was worried, so was he.

A Mental Patient Finds a Mental Case

Emmet was also a man who had spent many summers alone in those high mountains, watching his sheep. He knew that a man didn't just stop coming out of the mountain to town like that for no good reason. It was now the end of June and leaving the thousand head of sheep in the hands of Lloyd Campbell, his herder, Emmet rode hard for the mine, 25 miles away to the west. He wondered why Frank did not come out that spring. He wondered what could have befallen him. The possibilities were many, and his mind wandered over the options as his trusty horse slowly put the miles behind him. The horse was in a lather of white when Emmet reined in at the doors of the Tungsten Mine.

He told me how he agonized over what he might see when he opened the door of the trapper's cabin that strange day. Pete had warned him that he was the first one back to the Tungsten Mine that spring. *Would there be a dead man stretched out on his bunk?* Emmet trembled at the thought. He did not know Arnold well. Frank Arnold and Emmet had crossed paths only twice in 17 years. They had shared a hot meal over an open campfire and some badly needed conversation in that lonesome land. They had met at Emmet's sheep camps in the Horseshoe Basin. Once Frank had stayed for two days with him and Ed Grounds just to talk.

"We did have fun talking...I really thought he would stop in more often, Emmet recalled, but he never did. (Frank was like that). The last time I saw Frank Arnold was at our camp in the Horseshoe Basin. It was the same time that Roosevelt (Coolidge?) died," mused Emmet. "Arnold had heard the news of the President's death on his radio."

Emmet did not hear the radio playing when he rode in among the mine cabins. His heart pounded in his chest as he jumped up on the porch steps of the upper rustic log structure where he knew Frank stayed. The solid wood door swung on its squeaky hinges and opened into a dark, unlit, one-room cabin. Emmet's eyes struggled to adjust to the dimness as he stepped through the door and onto the brown wood-planked floor. Outside the bright sun hung in the west in a blue sky. Inside, it was cold, dark and silent. Emmet stood there, cocked his hat and scratched his head. His eyes scanned the room. It was the first time he had been in the cabin. It looked unlike a bachelor's, or even a trapper's home to him. The cabin was empty! Of all life... and of all death!

The small 15-by-15-foot home had somehow, for some strange reason, been cleaned out. There was nothing in there. Not only was Frank Arnold not there, but neither were any of his belongings. There were no pictures, bedding, clothing or shoes. There were no dishes, pots or pans, and no food, either. Emmet was puzzled. He found no traps, no radio, no guns, or any of the cameras or radio equipment Frank was notorious for owning. Strangely, the one-room cabin was completely empty, not razed, just empty. From the looks of it, Frank Arnold hadn't been there...EVER! The only hint of past intelligence was a mound of salt on the table and a couple of small radio parts, which Emmet ran through his hands. There was a rusty coffee can on the floor with a little water in it, set there to catch the melting snow from a leaky roof. Emmet wrote all this down like this in a record of his early days in the Pasayten.

Lloyd Campbell was waiting with the sheep when Emmet rode back into the Deer Park camp very late that night. After Emmet told Lloyd what he found, which was nothing, Lloyd, too, was soon off to see what he could find of the lost trapper. Lloyd rode around the woods for several days, checking all the trapping cabins that he and Emmet knew of, and he rode back to the Tungsten Mine again, just to take a better look. He exhausted all the places he could think to look. Frank Arnold was just not to be found. Although they did not find Frank Arnold, there is a persistent rumor that Emmet or Lloyd found a number of Frank's things in his scattered trapping cabins, one of which was one of Frank's guns, a 303 Savage rifle.

When word got around that Frank had not come out of the high country, the few cattlemen, prospectors, trappers and others traveling through the high Pasayten wilderness kept an eye out for the lone

A Mental Patient Finds a Mental Case

trapper during the years 1935 and 1936. Doug Loudon, whose family ran cattle on the mountain ranges, can remember being with his dad, Paul, in the Horseshoe Basin and running into Clarence Landergreen, a friend of both Frank Arnold's and Pete's, in 1935. Doug wasn't very old, but he remembers that Clarence had been hired by Pete to search the mountain country for the missing man. Clarence probably looked in all the known layouts on Frank's trapping grounds, but despite his best efforts, Clarence couldn't help Pete find the missing trapper.

Now "Shorty," also known as Lester Fairbrother, was a finer trapper. If a better trapper could be found, it would boil down and shake out to be Frank Arnold. Shorty trapped beside Frank for over 10 years, and it was more than once that they spent a cold winter night beside a hot wood stove, sharing stories. Shorty's last year of trapping was the winter of 1935/1936, and it was that fall of 1935 when Shorty went back in to stock his winter cabins. Shorty said he looked for Frank at that time. He searched Windy Mountain, he looked in Long Swamp, Thirty Mile Meadows, and all along the Chewack River. But Shorty could not find his old friend at any of his known camps.

The Loudon's must have also looked for Frank Arnold, and Pete was said to have asked Johnny Bell (Beal) to make a search. Johnny thought he knew about a cabin up Horseshoe Creek, at its headwaters somewhere, that Frank used. Loy McDaniel, Mickey Kinchelo, Ross Woodard and his cowboys, and George Miller, the Methow packer, must have looked around the lower mountains for the old trapper.

We can well assume that all the local men who went back into the high country in those summers of 1935 and 1936 kept their eyes open for any sign of Frank. The sheepmen, cattlemen, miners, trappers, hunters, and the Forest Service personnel all knew about the possibility of running into the remains of the lost trapper. The vast land would not hold its secrets indefinitely.

Found

It was early in the morning when Pete and Maron left from Pete's home in Okanogan and bounced up the new dirt road that wound over the dangerous Loup Loup Pass and on through the small towns of Twisp and then Winthrop, Washington. From the little mountain town of Winthrop, Pete took Maron up a long, rough dirt road that followed the beautiful Chewack River, up a deep valley to a ranger station called "Thirty Mile" because it was 30 miles north into the woods from the little town. This road, the house, the ranger station, and the road going on up the river a half mile past the station was being built by a crew of the Civilian Conservation Corps (the C.C.C's). The CCC crew was being run and bossed by Pete. From the ranger station (a ways further than you can drive today), Pete dropped Maron off as deep as you could go into the wildwoods of Washington State and by doing so saved him from the drudgery of that mental hospital. Pete gave Maron a pat on my back and a slap on my shoulder to set me off on a quest to find their lost old friend, Frank Arnold. It was now 2 years since Frank Arnold had last been seen. Maron was Pete's last card to play.

It was probably the weekend of the 4th and 5th of September 1936, when Maron found himself in the deep woods and suddenly on his own after so many days in the "funny farm." As he walked, Frank Maron mumbled to himself,

"Something bad has happened to Frank, I know it! Frank was one level-headed man. He didn't get excited; and he always, I mean ALWAYS, seemed to have it together. He was like me, somewhat, but woods-wise as an old coyote. There'll probably never be another like him. Boy, I sure would like to see the old man come walking out from those trees right now!"

Maron knew he was indeed Pete's last good hope of finding Frank Arnold because he was the only one who had spent two winters with Frank Arnold, back and forth across the big bum. They had trapped the

A Mental Patient Finds a Mental Case

wide, blackened country of Windy Mountain, Thirty Mile Meadows, and the Ashnola River trying to catch a few martens.

"Yaa-h, it was that cold winter of 1929/1930 and the summer of the next year, 'cause I stayed with him those 2 years. That summer, Clyde Andrews, Frank and I staked mining claims at the Tungsten Mine. Clyde Andrews got a part. I got a part. Frank Arnold got a part. I never did really get much out of old Frank as to where he was from… other than he had been in the Queen's Guard in England, I think. He just didn't like to talk of his past and that's all there was to it."

So, Maron hiked up the trail from the Thirty Mile Ranger Station. It was a nice late summer day.

"It might have been summer, but BOYEE, how this country can get cold; I mean cold!"

Maron was remembering that time in January 1930, when the blue cold blew in from the north and didn't go away? Nothing moved in these woods for darn near a month. Nothing! What game was alive was too smart to be out in that frigid weather. The traps just kept coming up empty. It started with that week-long blizzard that blew in the heavy snow from the north. Finally, it quit blowing and snowing, but it didn't quit getting cold. It was a blue cold northerner that sapped the breath and what little heat you could get up like ice water on a fire. Frank Arnold and Frank Maron couldn't work their trap-lines even if they wanted to. The land was locked up in a cage of deadly cold. The bait was no good for the alcohol that had kept it from freezing froze. The ungodly cold mist that covered the land seemed to make their mountain home another world, a world in which no living thing belonged. As the cold gripped the wilds, they became desperate for food, solid food! They needed meat! It was meat that would keep them going strong all day.

Frank Arnold had tried to teach Maron to live on the animals they caught in the traps. That idea worked just fine in most winters, but they weren't catching a thing this winter. It was just too darn cold to even try. It would kill a person if they ventured out. The venison had been gone for days, but the cold, of course, stayed on day after day after day. Arnold knew he wasn't going out until the weather changed, and Maron knew he wasn't going to last that long. The temperature had been down to -50 and then -60 degrees below the big zero for two weeks. Maron could take it no longer. He stepped out in the bitter weather and put on his snowshoes.

He remembered telling Arnold, "I'm going to run the line, Frank. I'll be back tomorrow evening. Maybe I can find something in a trap to eat."

The old trapper advised, "Well, if you must, but you have got to keep moving in this weather just keep moving and don't stop!" I tromped out of sight through the deep powder snow into the silent and bitter-cold wilderness.

Maron had been gone for 3 days, with barely enough food for 2 days. So Frank Arnold, out of meat and with little flour, reluctantly put on his snowshoes and followed after Maron toward the high western Cathedral Peaks and the distant Ashnola River. They got a break that day. Frank Arnold was following Maron's snowshoe tracks like ugly following a moose. His long snowshoes cut a deep furrow in the soft, crystalline powder snow. A thick cold frost, so thick you could cut it with a knife, hung over the mountains. He had been traveling on an empty stomach for the better part of the day when his eyes caught movement ahead. He saw Frank Maron. Maron was moving toward him. He squinted his eyes. He could tell Maron was carrying something.

"Why, Frank, what in the billy-dickens have you got there on your shoulders, and where in the world have you been in this cold?" he yelled

A Mental Patient Finds a Mental Case

as he walked up. His breath, a cloud of icy frost trailed out behind him, gathering on his long mustache and beard. He was looking at Maron's shoulder where the hindquarter of a large game animal was resting. "Well, I hear the music playing young man! Where did you get that be-a-u-ti-ful side of meat?"

Maron dropped the heavy hunk of meat in the snow and they sat down on the trail so Maron could tell Frank Arnold his story.

"Frank, I was all tired out and weak with hunger after I made the rim. I was looking down into the river. I found nothing but a damn weasel in the traps. That's all. Nothing is alive in this country! There're no tracks or anything! Anyway, I came back to your trapping camp and spent the night and ate the damn Weasel, I was so hungry. Then I made the loop, and was coming back just like I said I was gonna do. I was about a mile out of camp when what do you think dropped out of heaven right in front of me? Standing just off my old trail was this big buck...standing there like he was frozen, as surprised to see me, as I was to see him. And look at the size of this hindquarter. Well, you better believe I didn't give him time to unfreeze! I had my rifle up and a bullet through his back faster than I can tell you about it. I thought I was dreaming. But I sure wasn't, because here I am! Well anyway, by the time I got some meat cut off him and hiked back to the line cabin and cooked up the meat,...I ate so much I couldn't move. So, I didn't want to try for the Tungsten, I just took it easy and ate some more."

"Maron, it's 4 miles back to the mine, and it's 2 miles if we go back to my line-camp where you just came from. I'm so damn hungry, and getting hungrier listening to you. I'm making a fire right here under this tree and cooking me up a meal right now, sixty below be damned!"

So, right there in the gray, misty fog, on that cold snowy trail, Frank Arnold and Frank Maron cooked a hot meal of venison. Arnold had never needed a meal so badly as he did then. What that big mountain buck was doing up there in the middle of winter, only a big mountain buck would know, but the deer saved Arnold and Maron from near starvation.

The Chewack River and the trees swept by as Maron marched on up the river recalling the past. It wasn't always venison that Frank and Maron sat down to eat. Nothing could ever make Maron forget that winter day when he stepped into camp at dinner time with a marten hide in his hands. Arnold was busy cooking their dinner and had a big iron kettle bubbling over the fire. Maron walked over to the steaming pot on the hot stove for a peek at the sweet-smelling stew that was boiling.

"What's cooking, Frank?" Maron asked, as he lifted the lid off the big pot.

"Some of the best!" Arnold said.

There in the big cooking pot, floating in the green boiling water, were two big, wet, yellow eyes looking back at Maron. A large "CAT HEAD" floated in the green soup!

"Tonight, we are having Lynx for supper!" Frank said. At that very instant, the big cat head rolled over and then "jumped" in the boiling water!

Maron quickly slammed the lid closed. He stood there holding the lid down on the wet cat head with both hands. Suddenly Maron wasn't hungry anymore. A sickening feeling crept over his body, and his face turned white.

A Mental Patient Finds a Mental Case

Maron felt good to be out of the hospital and into the fresh, clean air. He knew this was a good place to start looking for Arnold, here along the Chewack River, because Frank Arnold had trapped on and around the river for years. Thinking the old trap-line over in his mind, Maron knew the old trapper had a camp on up ahead that the two men had slept at four, five, maybe six times at least. It was halfway to the Tungsten Mine from Thirty Mile Station, and if Maron did not find Frank at that camp, he would go on into the mine to look for him. As it turned out, Maron would not have to go to the Tungsten Mine.

Pete had sent Frank Maron to look along Arnold's old trapping trails and past camps and layovers that he had used for years and years because the high country is so extensive, wide and long, that you could not look everywhere. You had to concentrate on some area. Frank could be laying 20 feet off any trail and probably be missed by a passer-by. Pete thought Maron would know of some places, one camp in particular, along the Chewack River, that no one else knew about or could find. Pete had heard Maron talk of a number of trapping camps. Maron told Pete about this one camp on Horseshoe Creek just above where the creek runs into the Chewack River. He thought there could be a camp in that area but didn't know if anyone had looked there or not. This camp was on the edge of Frank's trap-line, an eighth of a mile off the trail. In the early days, the camp had bordered another trapper's line. That trapper was Joe Baker, one of the Pasayten Wilderness' earliest trappers. Both men's trap lines ran along the Chewack River. Joe had built a cabin at the mouth of Tungsten Creek that Arnold often used until the big 1929 Rummel-Lake forest fire burned it down. After that, he just used the simple, make-shift camp, that Maron was heading for, there on Horseshoe Creek.

The day was well along when Maron finally saw the sheep bridge crossing the river that he was looking for. Then he saw the open, green meadow at the mouth of the creek that he remembered. There he found the old trail going up the east side of the creek. Maron was now 6 miles or so from where Pete had let him off at the end of the road.

How many people have looked over this camp? he wondered. *Perhaps no one.* He thought. *Heck, the camp laid right off the old trail going to the Tungsten Mine, and dozens of people must have gone up and down this trail in the last two summers.*

Maron knew that Pete and his crew were working on a new trail across the creek from here that Pete had lined out for the Forest Service and C.C.C. to build. Pete said he was working on the trail now, running a work crew that has been working on the trail for several days. Pete wasn't very far from the old camp that he wanted Maron to check out.

As he walked towards the camp, Maron thought about Pete saying he would get him on the new trail job, too. *I sure need the work*, Maron thought.

Maron eased himself along the tree-lined bank over the old trail and the thick brush into the dark camp he remembered from 5 years earlier. This was the first place he wanted to look; and really, it was the central focus of Pete's hopes too. This is Frank Arnold's last undiscovered layout. But I'll tell you, Maron was not prepared for what came next as he stumbled into the lost trapper's camp. He stopped dead in his tracks!

"Hoo...!"

"Fear and fright grabbed me like a giant hand!" Maron would say later. "My body turned to ice, petrified like stone, at the scene that was suddenly before my eyes."

"What in God's world could that be?" Maron shouted to no one.

Is that Frank Arnold? He wondered. *How in the Devil's eye could he be like THAT?"*

The sight before his poor eyes was almost beyond belief. Yet there it was, strange as a wizard's trick, scary as a scene from a horror picture show. An apparition? Truly a more weird and frightening sight would have been hard to put before a man, any man! Let alone a man just out

A Mental Patient Finds a Mental Case

of the mental hospital! For there was a strange hanging body! A corpse! A body hanging from a tree!

"But..but...but it's hanging like a mummy," Maron whispered.

He felt like a vibrating, frightened squirrel looking at this strange sight before him. Should he run, fight, fall or what? His eyes must be telling him a lie! He shook himself, thought about checking himself back into the mental hospital, and started to turn away and run back down the trail to get Pete. Get Pete and some help! However, he stopped.

He hesitated. "The scene held me like a magnet," Maron remembered. "The scene was very real. Of all the ways I expected to find Frank Arnold, this was not in any one of the books. But there he was...."

The body hung over a small earthen bank off the ground about a foot, maybe two, from a rope that was tied high up around a tree. The rope was around the man's neck. The strange part of it all was that the body was in coveralls and wore a black stocking cap that was pulled down over the head, covering the face. The stocking cap was tucked into the neck of the coveralls and then tied with a light rope in the back. The hands, too, had gloves on that were tied to the wrists, and both hands were tied the same and tied together. On the feet were rubber boots. One leg bone stuck out of a rubber boot that had come undone and lay on the ground under the body. The other rubber boot was tied to the other leg bone and hung off the ground. There was a big, iron 5-to-7-gallon pot off to the side on the bank. *Did Frank stand on this pot?* Maron wondered. *His hands are tied together? A stocking cap covers the dead man's face?*

What could have happened to Frank Arnold? Maron tried to comprehend. "Is this even Frank Arnold?" He wondered aloud. He thought it had to be but had some doubts too. All did not look right with this man in the tree.

I need to know more. Maron thought. He knew there was only one way to find that out.

So with a dizzy head and shaking hands and against his fearful judgment, Maron found a stick and slowly walked up to the hanging corpse. Sweat ran down his face. Fighting the fear to break and run, he knew he had to look at the face of this hanging man. He reached up and pried at the stocking cap tucked into the coveralls. The dark mask came up quickly. White bone flashed where the face should be and white teeth grinned. Empty eye sockets stared down at Maron. He cringed.

Suddenly out popped a long, dark, hairy SOMETHING! Like a large, furry winged bug, it came from under the stocking cap and seemingly winged it for his face... "I-EEEEEEE!" Maron yelled, arms slapping, jumping into the air, stampeding back down the trail toward civilization. The long, hairy, dark mustache fluttered, circled, and twisted to the ground behind him; Frank Arnold had been found!

CHAPTER 2

A Tungsten of a Find

The following account is based on Herb Curtis's manuscripts and stories from Bob Curtis and Jim McDaniel along with numerous reports.

IT WAS IN THE LATE 1850's that Canada and the United States figured they had better mark their boundary lines and mark them well, so as to end the petty differences that kept arising between the citizens of the two countries. Now that they had settled down to a peaceful coexistence, both countries needed to keep their 49th Meridian marked on the land, and not just on a map that hung from some governor's wall. So off was sent a team of surveyors and trail cutters, to mark and cut a 60-foot-wide blaze between Canada and the United States.

This work on the border line seemed to go on for years and years, and in the 1890's the boundary line was still being "fine-tuned." The year was 1893 when a boundary crew of hardy men crossed the high, rugged peaks on top of the world, the land that was called by the French trappers and mountain men "Pasayten," or "Devil's land!" They came up a Canadian River, called the Ashnola, following the Indian trails that were maintained by the constant movements of wild animals. Into the high mountains they went to find the cut ribbon that ran like the wind over this high, rugged land. Yes, in 1893, with their Indian guide and a small pack string, the surveyors snaked their way up the Ashnola River, where at the headwaters of the South Fork, they found the boundary line with the glorious high mountain peaks. It was over one of these endless mountains that one of the surveyors found some interesting mineralized quartz and made a note of it in one of his journals. The International Boundary ran on the north side of this mountain marked by quartz, but it was a 1,000-foot rock wall, the south side barely offering footing for man or beast. But a good man, with a good horse, could, with some work, get around this mountain on an old trail cut probably by an earlier boundary crew. For the trees were big and the downed timber sparse.

These first men were not miners, and when their journals were closed, the quartz ledge was forgotten. Still, in the years ahead, there was much work to be done on this boundary, and the men coming after were not of the same cut of cloth as the government surveyors. These men knew that quartz could mean money.

Herbert Curtis was born in a nice little town called Cobourg, just east of Toronto, Canada. This is Herb Curtis's own account of 1903 from his old manuscripts:

"I was in an oil spree just on the North-Fork of the Flathead River. It petered out and my partner, Pearl Snow, joined the Canadian and U.S. Boundary team in 1902. We finished at Port Hill, Idaho, in the spring of 1903, and we came to Wenatchee the same year, taking the river boat to Riverside in the Okanogan Country. There was no transportation for us, only for our baggage, which the officials took care of, so we walked

A Tungsten of a Find

to Loomis that hot, sunny day. We struck out through the foothills until we came to Lloyd Bell's place, and there we got something to eat, flapjacks, fried eggs and bacon for twenty-five cents. He didn't make anything on that deal. We left his place for Loomis just about sundown and got to the town about midnight. As luck would have it, Jimmie Callahan's saloon was still open, and the crowd of us were asked to take a drink, which we did, and had another besides. We started looking for our bedrolls but couldn't find them. The hotels were all full, so we just laid down! Anywhere was just fine that night.

The next morning, word came to us that we were to go to William McDaniel's ranch about 1 mile from town because our bedrolls were there. It was a fine camp, and we spent several days enjoying the fine cooking of Mrs. McDaniel. We moved from there to the Horseshoe Basin. I was packing for Mr. Heflin sometimes, and when not packing, I was busy cutting out trail as far as convenient, both ways from camp. Then we moved to what is called "the Mail Box" (Scheelite Pass), and I was given a crew to open up the trail to the Skagit River. While on the trail between the Mail Box Camp and the Cathedral Mountains, I found some Tungsten ore and sent it out to be assayed."

This was 1903 (possibly 1904), and a trail was needed so brass monuments could be brought in and erected on the boundary line by Herb Curtis and the boys. Three thousand miles of this work would take a number of years, to be sure. The monuments were to be placed randomly on the boundary line, the 49th parallel, roughly, so a man standing at one marker could see, or almost see, the next monument in the distance as the surveyor's scope told. And so, it was done, but not easily; the make-up of the heavy brass monuments that stood 4 feet high and must have weighed 75 pounds each, had to be hauled on the shoulders of two stout men, for miles. If the way wasn't up, it was down. Many dozens of times, the brass monuments were carried up, almost straight up to the top of some unnamed mountain. Then, the monuments were carried down into some dark spruce forest, crisscrossed by a thousand fallen trees, where the stumbling men would plunge over and into deep lost canyons surrounded by walls of rock. Again, the monuments would be hauled up to the next peak of some unnamed pinnacle, thousands of feet above the valley floor where only the eagles had ever set foot before.

With the marker monuments came trails, men with horses, packers, cooks, laborers, surveyors, and all their gear, all working their way west to the blue Pacific. At 6,950 feet, on this obscure 8,200-foot granite mountain, and at the edge of the United States of America, the boundary trail cut right through a rich out-cropping of mineralized quartz rock. The name of the one man who found this rock first has been debated for years in the town of Loomis where there are four names spoken, each seeming to have taken credit for the basic discovery. Johnny Bell (Beal) had this to say at 82 years of age, and still trapping furs in the 1950's.

"In 1904, I started an eight-year job with the Coast and Geodetic Survey, running the line on the boundary, and that same year Dan Davenspike, a packer, found the ledge. It was then located by Bill Johnson and a fellow by the name of Chombes."

William, Loy and Jim McDaniel told the story of Bill Johnson making the discovery; the story is similar to the basic one told by Herb Curtis verbally to his son, Bob, and backed up by a November 11, 1906, engineering report. But it does have some variation. A local newspaper speaks of the tungsten discovery being made in August 1904. The fact is, the trail went right over that mineralized quartz and therefore the work crew, each one of them, walked right over the white and black rock. The loaded quartz rock looked too good to just walk right over and forget about. It was probably Bill Johnson along with Herb Curtis, who were the first ones though to cut out parts of this old wild sheep and deer trail. Herb and Bill, who were good friends by this time after covering hundreds of miles together. They were not likely to walk over a gold mine just to build the government a trail and erect bronze monuments. They knew the find could be valuable. So, later on that fall, as Herb told his son, Bob, years later, a week or two after they had crossed the quartz, over on Sheep Mountain, 20 miles away, Bill Johnson got himself fired by the job foreman, Mr. Heflin, because he went back to stake the quartz outcropping. It didn't take a mining engineer to recognize the rock was mineralized, though some of the crew working on the trail laughed at him, thinking the rock was only coal. The miners who saw it down in Loomis called it plain "black-jack," (whatever that was). But Herb and Bill knew that there was a good chance it was a silver or gold ore. The more the men looked at the quartz samples that summer, the more gold they thought they could see. The rock was also unusually heavy.

Bill Johnson threw up some claim posts on the vein for Herb and himself and was off to the assayer's office in Loomis. The assayer's office sat on a hill on the south side of the town. J.E. Beaton was well known and respected as an assayer in Loomis, and his reports could be relied upon to be as good as you could get. So, after that fateful day when Bill Johnson stumbled into his Loomis office after his 60-mile hike, it was clear these rocks would have repercussions for Loomis.

Johnson walked for three days just to dump his sack of rocks on the table of Mr. J.E. Beaton. The quartz rock looked good, even to Beaton, but Beaton had been an assayer too long to get excited over a sack of quartz rocks. He took out his ten-power magnifier and took a close look at what Johnson had brought in. It was well mineralized, the mineral being a dark gray-black color that appeared to be rusted when scratched. Although he thought the rock interesting, look as he did, he saw no visible gold; he didn't want to build false hope in Bill. He was only sure of one thing; it was heavy and mineralized with some kind mineral, and that is what he told Bill Johnson.

Johnson paid the assay fee, and Beaton fired up the kiln, worked over the ore and slapped it in the 2000-degree heat of the oven. Bill

Johnson was at the office the first thing the next day hoping the assay results would lead to a trip to the courthouse in Conconully to register his and Herb's rich gold claim.

It cost Bill and Herb Curtis $5.00 dollars to read the assayer's report, and one loud "DAMN" could be heard clear down to Jimmie Callahan's saloon! The quartz contained no gold and almost no silver. The 1905 Engineering Report told it like this:

"...In 1904, they returned to the place of discovery along in the winter and staked a claim and took samples of rock to Loomis, Washington, to be assayed. The result was disappointing and the locators, subsequently, relinquished their right to the claim."

With that report, Bill Johnson turned right back around and headed back into the Cascades to try to talk his way back into his old job with Herb after that disappointing assay. Neither one of them, at that point, gave a "hoot" about that black stuff that had let them down. But Beaton, the assayer, continued to try to get a handle on the ore he knew was in the rock. The prospectors had looked no further than for gold or silver, but Beaton knew that the granular, dark gray, brownish-black rock was not iron, and the heavy white-yellow rock at the bottom of the pan was not quartz. He was a good assayer, and it took the better part of the winter of 1904-1905 to get his curiosity satisfied: "TUNGSTEN!" Tungsten was in that ore. The dark gray, black rock was "Wolframite" and the white heavy rock at the bottom of the pan was "Scheelite," both high grade tungsten ores.

Beaton had sent the ore to Edgar C. Riebe of New York. He also sent some to the Primos Chemical Company of Primos, Pennsylvania. The analysis, which was a concentrate gave a reading of 72.8% WO_3 tungsten acid with 13% manganese, 14% iron, an analysis that would make any German metallurgist do a jig.

A Tungsten of a Find

Herb Curtis, and Bill Johnson were back in the mountains in the early spring of 1905 and Herb said, "...they could not find out what it was..." (the ore). "We located the property, I think, in April, 1905. William (Bill) Johnson, William McDaniel, Clayton Baldwin and I were packing monuments and along came Clayton Baldwin and said the mineral was Tungsten."

Who even knew what "tungsten" was in 1904? It was a new metal selling for about a dollar a pound and made good filament for the bright new light bulbs that were starting to light up cities. But some men knew it had other properties, and it would be men in far-away Germany who would put it to a much more strategic and sinister use.

According to the November 11, 1905, report:

"Clayton Baldwin, an old prospector, who had grub-staked the surveyors and became interested with them, discovered vein cropping and later on took Henry Bahrs, a mining man of Loomis, to see the ground. Mr. Bahrs recently located on it seven claims as follows: The Elizabeth, Henrietta, Marie, Wolframite, Cathedral, Tungsten, and Armor Plate."

Henry Bahrs located claims October 12, 1905, in the Courthouse in Conconully and was the first person to register a Tungsten Mine claim. Herb Curtis tells it like this:

(Clayton to Herb) "Henry Bahrs wants to stock. And he (Bahrs is) give(ing) Bill Johnson and myself $200.00 and a nice bunch of stock."

"Are you going to take the same?" I (Curtis) ask Clayton Baldwin.

"McDaniel and I are going to help in the stock proposition and will take all stock:" I said (Curtis said to Clayton) "I will take it (all stock) if Johnson would." I told him where Johnson could be found. When we came back that fall (from setting monuments), we camped in a meadow near the Tungsten property and packed out the next morning. Just a little way from the meadow we ran into a cabin and Clayton Baldwin and his crew were standing there." (At the new Tungsten Mine!)

TALES OF THE TUNGSTEN MINE

The Tungsten Mine era had begun; It appears that Bill Johnson, Herb Curtis, Billy McDaniel, and Clayton Baldwin were all friends because to be legal, Herb and Bill Johnson had to let their claims slip so that Henry Bahrs, through Clayton Baldwin's hands, could locate the claim. Bahrs had the money!

"When Johnson and I got to Loomis, we were handed $200.00 apiece."

Bahrs said, "Herb, they want you to snowshoe to the mine and take in the mail and any other little articles they may need. You can work there a week or two and bring in any samples and reports. I will give you better than miner's wages and pay hotel expenses as long as you wish to stay in."

Herb had a winter job and the mining journal, Engineering Report, November 1905 reports,

"At present the surface is covered with new snow 2 feet deep, but a camp has been established and six men are employed exploiting the main vein. It has been stripped 60 feet in length and an incline shaft has been sunk in 30 feet deep. It is thought the ore will concentrate ten to one or better. Suitable log buildings have been erected for mess and bunk houses, a cellar, blacksmith shop, etc., and ample provisions and mining supplies for the winter sufficient to last for eight months, have been sent to the camp."

Henry Bahrs called his company "Tungsten Consolidated Mining and Milling Co." The Trustees for the company were Dr. A.M. Polk, Henry Bahrs, Wm. H. McDaniel, Bill Johnson, and F.M. Dallum. The Trustees elected a President and General Manager, who was none other than Henry Bahrs. The Vice President was Dallum; Treasurer; McDaniel and the Secretary, well, the assayer; Mr. J.E. Beaton. Beaton wasn't going to miss out on his new strike! (For after all, again, it was Mr. Beaton who had through the Primos Chemical Company discovered the ore was tungsten.)

A Tungsten of a Find

The original blowout was exceptionally rich. It was 5 feet wide and traceable for at least 500 feet. A lot of it was almost pure Wolframite and would concentrate ten parts Wolframite to one part waste. If it would just hold, it would make them all rich!

CHAPTER 3

The Deputy Sheriff Makes His Investigation

The story is true, as true as Frank Arnold. The story was told to Loy and Jim McDaniel by Frank E. Maron himself in the years to follow. The story was also told by Pete to family and friends as time went by. Pete's son heard the story from his dad and was there when the deputy sheriff came back to Pete's house in Okanogan that September weekend. Pete's son can remember Art Mitchell and Frank Maron when they left late, as he said, that evening of the 11th, and when they returned. He can still remember them sitting around the kitchen table talking of the strange trip to find and bury the lost Frank Arnold.

FRANK MARON, ALMOST IN PANIC, hurried back down the river to the Thirty Mile Ranger Station that same day, He believed it was Friday or Saturday. The mental patient had found the man Pete had sent him out to find, and Maron was shaken! Pete had stayed over that day at the Ranger Station, so when Maron came walking back out of the mountains he saw him. He was sure glad to see him and hear the sad, but good, news that Frank Arnold had finally been found. It sure didn't take long with the right man. He listened over and over again as Maron told and retold the strange sight he had seen. It was a strange story indeed. What could have happened to Frank Arnold that he would be found in such a bizarre way? Pete said it was undoubtedly suicide. But Maron was not so sure. Was this suicide? Did that cover all the facts and questions? In Maron's mind, though one mystery had been solved, another mystery was hanging by a rope! But surely not for long, for this should be something that any competent person or lawman could clear up because, after all, a dead man was hanging in a tree.

Ironically, Pete did not go right back into Horseshoe Creek, and the reason was he was tied up with work. There were the Civilian Conservation Corps (C.C.C.) and the Forest Service jobs he had to oversee. The C.C.C. was quite active in providing jobs during the Great Depression years. The group was organized by the Army and supervised by the Forest Service. It was a place to go for work from 1933 through 1937 in the Okanogan.

So, it took the better part of a week for him to organize a trip into the mountains again. He timed it so that there was a horse at the Thirty Mile Ranger Station that he could use to pack needed items back into Frank's camp; and of course, pack the poor hanging trapper out. When the day came that Pete could leave, it took Pete all day to get everything together for that trip. The trip itself would only take two- or three-hours to cover the 6 miles in, and then the easier down-hill 6-mile walk back out. It was a late in the day when the three men finally left Pete's house in Okanogan. It had taken Pete until evening to get everything organized, and Art Mitchell had been waiting all day for him when Pete finally pulled up.

Art was a new deputy for the Deputy Sheriff for Okanogan County at the time. He had been at his job in law enforcement only a few months. Nevertheless, Art thought he had an idea of what lay ahead of him as

The Deputy Sheriff Makes His Investigation

Pete picked him up. But not all factors were in his control that Friday night, the 11th day of September 1936. Pete and Art were acquaintances only. Okanogan was a small town and both men worked for the people. Pete did not think the trip would take too long when he stopped by the Sheriff's office earlier. He had told him the basics of the story about his old friend Frank Arnold, and he felt that the law should be there when they brought the old trapper out.

"I suppose we could bury him right there, Frank would sure like that. He always did love those mountains. But I've got a horse up at the station to help us pack him out," Pete told Art. "The darned old foreigner just wouldn't come and live in town. Hell, he smelled too bad for one thing, and probably smells now. But every time he came over to our house, mother would always take care of him. We liked him a lot just the same. Heck, I'm surprised he made it as long as he did the poor old man. That last winter he didn't take in much food with him. Trapping, he said, had been real poor after the bad fire a few years ago, and was low on money to buy food, I would guess. Yah, I think he was real low on food that last winter. His health couldn't have been that good either. From the sounds of it, he decided to cash it all in. Those cold, long winters had to have been hard on him. He was probably starving to death! That's no doubt what happened."

Pete went on. "Knowing him the way I did, he would not have wanted to be on the ground where the animals could get him! You know they will eat all the meat off of you if you're lying on the ground. Sounds like he did a real good job of hanging himself, getting up off the ground like he did. But I think the martens ate on him anyway. Yeah, the old Englishman was smart, alright. I just wish I could have gotten him into town before this happened. But ya know, Art, that guy Maron who found him is just a bit crazy. I had to go clear to Medical Lake Hospital to get him, for he was the only one who could find the old trapper. I hope he knows what he's talking about!"

Pete filled the deputy in on his old friend, and the arrangements were made to take the deputy into the far reaches of the wild Pasayten Wilderness.

Going In to Get Arnold Out

That Friday evening, the red Dodge that belonged to Pete rambled over the narrow dirt road outside the town of Okanoganto, heading for the Loup Loup Pass. Pete, Art Mitchell and Frank E. Maron, their guide were the occupants of the car. Pete continued to talk about Frank Arnold, what he knew about him, acknowledging how little was really known about Arnold's reclusive life in the mountains. Maron didn't have much to say except a grunt here, and a "ya" there. He was a hard man to judge. The man was troubled. Art could see that, He must have wondered if Maron had maybe a "screw" or two loose, as Pete had told him, having just come out of Medical Lake Hospital. Was his story even 100%, Art wondered?

Maron would have acknowledged that he was indeed troubled over that weird sight he now had to go back to. There were things to think about that Pete didn't seem to grasp.

At about 8:30 P.M., the car made it to that small, back-woods town of Winthrop, Washington. The next 35 miles would be very rough and slow.

Pete was still talking, filling up the time.

"He must have killed himself, being times are so tough, Art. He spent the better part of his life up there and he was getting mighty old. He told a friend he had gone snow-blind last year for a good week, and I guess he almost died then. He had a tough life, the old man... few friends... and nobody knew where he was from. I always figured he was on the run... didn't you Frank, Frank? Well, anyway, I always worried about him living up there by himself. I even had to grubstake the old man the last few years, for he would just make it, trapping furs

The Deputy Sheriff Makes His Investigation

from year to year and all. He would barely have enough money to buy groceries. Maron and I were just about as close to Arnold as anybody got. Worked with him 2 years in the twenties for the Geodetic Survey crew. He and I were the packers, and I slept in the same tent with him. The wife cooked him many a good meal over the years, and he came by our place every time he came to town. He

No one at this Sheriff's office has ever heard of Frank Arnold, let alone heard he was missing for one and a half years, thought Art Mitchell, as he ran the facts through his mind. *Obviously, he didn't come from this part of the country and if Pete and Maron had guessed it right, he was a foreigner, perhaps a Canadian, or even from England? He was known as just Frank Arnold, with no middle initial. A lone trapper, poor as a coyote, with no family — country's in a hell of a depression — lived way hell-and-gone-back in the woods, right along the Canadian border. It's a good guess he came from Canada. I hope I don't have to get the Mounties involved in this. An odd recluse who probably hurt himself and got in one "hell-of-ah-jam," and rather than starve to death, killed himself — Now he is just bones hanging from a tree. Yes, just an old trapper that stayed one too many years in the woods. Sounds like another suicide, alright. I would have done the same.*

Art stepped out of the car at the Thirty Mile Ranger Station as Pete turned off the lights. It was dark as he put on his coat and looked at his clock. It said 9:45 P.M. Maron stumbled out of the back seat. He had been like a clam for most all of the trip, and now that he was out of the car, he was uneasy and nervous as he walked back and forth and around the car.

The man's a mental case, alright! I hope he can find his way back into these mountains and that corpse, Art fretted.

Pete had vanished into the blackness as Art and Maron stood there in the dark.

The guy's not wrapped-too-tight. Hardly out of Medical Lake. I'm glad Pete knows something about these woods, cause I don't trust this man to take me across the street, thinks Art.

"I guess Pete's been working up here, huh, Frank?" Art asked.

"You too?"

"And you're going to start Monday!"

"You start Monday with the C.C.C.? Or, is it the Forest Service?"

"That's good!" Art says as he carries on a one way conversation with Maron for the half hour or so Pete was gone.

Finally, Pete walked up leading a pack horse with a few supplies on its back.

"We are...er...not...not going in tonight, are we, Pete?" asked Maron.

"Yah, hell, it's only a few miles up there, and I hate to waste another day on this project. Let's get it over with! Besides, I didn't come prepared to spend the night and there's not enough blankets in the Ranger cabin for all of us. You lead the way, Frank, and we'll follow. It's not that far and look at Art here, tough as nails. Ha-ha! From what I can gather, my trail crew was working not very far from where you found Frank," Pete goes on.

"Maron here is an old Forest Service, C.C.C. hand and has been up this trail many, many times himself. Hell, I think I know every rock on that trail by now, too. Been going up it for three weeks and 7 years or so. So, come on Frank. Let's go! You're going to be working on this trail next week."

So, they were off — three men and one gentle packhorse. Away they went, Frank Maron in the lead, following the splashing Chewack River in the black of that September night. Their mission: to bury or bring back one old dead trapper.

They spooked a deer as they walked along the dark trail. Dead tree limbs snapped, and bush and timber popped in the darkness as the deer made its escape.

The Deputy Sheriff Makes His Investigation

"There's plenty of bears in here too, Art," Pete volunteered. "It wouldn't hurt to keep the talk up just to keep them away from the trail."

Art did not need to hear that. He had already seen at least a *DOZEN* move in the black woods! Every shadow seemed to take the shape and the look of some kind of bear. Art put his hand down on the gun that was strapped at his side. *It was still there, and that was good*, he thought.

Time passed, and Art's feet began to hurt, his flashlight had quit long ago, and it didn't take him long to throw it into the Chewack River. *How had he let himself get into this mess?* he began to wonder as he stumbled along behind the horse. *Here he was, 30 miles from the nearest light, with a mental patient leading them deeper and deeper into the wilds. And God only knew where else. What am I going to find when I get there? Pete doesn't even know! Seems like we have gone 10 miles already, and boy, it's black as a gun-barrel out here, and me stumbling behind a horse's rear end! Was that a bear that made that noise? Probably a Grizzly or Wild-Cat! The woods are full of them! Boy!*

Art, to be sure, was out of his element and not having fun. Aloud he grumbles, "The old man is just all bones now, huh? Some old recluse who committed suicide 2 years ago and all dried-up bones. #@*!" he cussed. "I wish Sheriff Hilderbrand had gone on this bear hunt and not me! Yeah, he would fit right in on this trip; he's even a cougar hunter... a cougar-hunting sheriff! Shoot, he could have brought home a bear, maybe even a cougar, and one old trapper all on one trip."

Frank Maron bravely marched on; he was in the lead, and Pete had to holler at him to stop now and again to give Art and himself some air. Maron set a fast pace. On and on he went. After close to three hours, from the time the men had started, Maron stopped cold and took a look around, a look into the darkness.

"The trail goes on and crosses the river here. See? That's Horseshoe Creek Bridge right there. See the bridge?" Maron pointed. "We have got to stay on this side of Horseshoe Creek here and go up this side."

"Where-are-we?" puffed Art. He had just found the tail of the horse, and it had been pulling him along for the last ten minutes.

"I think we're almost there," Pete said. "Go ahead, Frank, you know the way from here. I've never been to Frank's camp on this creek before. Are you sure it's up there?" asked Pete.

"Yes. Here's the bridge, and Arnold's old camp is just up from the mouth. He's right up there about a quarter of mile," said Maron.

"Well, okay then. But hold on, let me get out the lantern."

After Pete tied up the horse to a tree and retrieved the light from the pack, and after a strategic battle with the wind, the lantern was lit and casting some welcome light as the three men moved on out through the trees towards some sort of dead body. Maron slowed the pace to near a crawl as they worked their way through the brush, bushes, standing trees and downed logs that lined the rocky black bank of Horseshoe Creek. The trail was faint and hard to follow in the dark.

Boy, I'll be glad when this trip is over with. My feet are so sore in these @#^*shoes. If I stop again, I'll never get them moving again, Art thought. "*Must be 1:00 or 2:00 A.M.*," Art mused. It had been a long, miserable night for Art so far, and it wasn't over yet! The chilly September wind gusting through the trees didn't help as the three men made their way along the noisy creek.

The light of the lantern flickered and danced through the trees and made strange shadows in the hands of Pete as he walked along behind Maron. It wasn't a pleasant early morning by this hour, and the moon gave little light as the clouds ran across its silver beam, running like horses across the mountain tops on a never-ending race to nowhere. Art pulled his coat closed again as the wind cut into him, and Pete tried

The Deputy Sheriff Makes His Investigation

to adjust the lantern that flickered and smoked in his hands. Maron shuffled nervously in the spooky light that faintly revealed their tired, cold faces. He turned and pressed on.

"OUCH! DAMN IT!" Art shouted as he stumbled and scratched his face… "Damn, this is torture, Pete. How much further is it, anyway. This is a jungle along here. I hope we're not lost."

"Ask Maron," Pete said. "Frank, how much further?"

"We're getting close, I think." came the reply.

"He's making me as nervous as he is," hissed Art.

The three men fought on and beat their way through the trees in the dim shadows of the light. The high mountain banks moved in around them as they turned into mountains, like giant arms, squeezing, squeezing them into a dark abyss.

"Why didn't we stay at the Ranger Station until tomorrow? I mean today! Shoot. I don't know what I mean. It sure would have made it a whole lot easier, Pete, I'm telling you that! And this old guy is nothing but dead bones?" complained Art.

Maron's mumblings were getting louder as if Art needed anything else to shake him! Suddenly, Maron again stopped in his tracks.

"What is it?" Art shouted.

"I hear something." Maron hissed.

"Hear what, Frank?" Pete asked.

"Do you hear it? There it goes again!" Maron said as a puff of wind again blew down the black creek draw.

"Yah-hh. I heard something too!" Art said as his hand moved over the grip of his gun.

All three men stood frozen on the black creek bank, trying to sort out the strange sounds that they were hearing. The wind kicked up again and they strained to hear the noise. There was definitely a strange knocking sound filtering through the trees ahead of them.

"What's that noise, Pete?" Art asked, his heart racing. "There it is again!" he cried out as the wind blew through the trees.

"KNOCK... knock-knock... KNOCK!"

"Th-at-t-t's Frank-k!" Maron stuttered in a raspy, scared voice.

"Are you crazy, Maron? What the hell are you talking about?" Art asked in a rush.

"KNOCK.... KNOCK... RATTLE... RATTLE!" came the sound once again.

Art unsnapped his gun holster, "Something is sure as hell up there making a strange sound!"

"That's coming from Frank!" Maron rasped again.

His mumbling and squirming increased.

Pete stepped forward, his light flashing through the trees as he held the lantern up high, hoping for a better look.

"Sure as hell there is something rattling and making noise up there! You guys hold here for a minute, and I'll go have a look," Pete volunteered.

The rattling began again as another cold gust of wind blew through the trees.

"Frank's up there, I tell you! Frank's up there making that noise!" Maron screeched at Pete in a wild voice, trying to make himself heard over the wind.

Now Art was coiled like a snake ready for quick action. His hand was on his gun half out of its holster. He was ready for whatever it was: ghost, bear, boogeyman,

Pete's lantern danced twenty, thirty, perhaps 40 feet ahead of them.

"Yah see anything, Pete?" Art shouted. "Yah see anything?"

"That's Frank Arnold up there, I tell you! Frank's up there and his bones are shaking!" Maron yelled as he danced back and forth and wouldn't shut up or stand still.

The Deputy Sheriff Makes His Investigation

Finally, a shout came from Pete. "Well, we found him, Art! And I'll be damned! Come look at this!"

The deputy bolted like a rabbit up to Pete with Maron on his heels. There was Pete standing back from the hanging body, and it was moving, swinging, and rattling with the blowing wind. The light of the lantern cast a spooky glow over the strange, gruesome, swinging body that hung from a rope in mid-air. There before them, a foot or so off the ground, in a dark suit of clothes, swayed a hooded, one legged man, with dark gloves covering his hands. Part of the man's skull and jawbone showed from under the hood, a hood that once had covered all his face. And, as the wind gusted, the swinging body (more like just a sack of bones), hanging by a rope, would rattle and knock... rattle and knock!

It was easy to imagine that the dead man was calling out in his morbid way!

"The weirdest darn thing I have ever seen!" Art said in a choked voice as he turned his head away from the dangling, swaying, hanging man.

"We sure as hell found him, or he found us. Maron wasn't stretching things one bit! No - not one darn bit at all! I got to admit, it's a spooky, spooky sight to behold!"

"Well, we found him and a whole lot harder than I thought, too." voiced Pete. "Let's go back to where the horse is tied and build a fire and warm up. Maybe we can get some rest and take care of poor Frank in the light of morning. Boy, I'm glad we found him. He's sure been missing a long time." There was no argument with that statement.

The fire put life in the woods as the three men sat down beside its warm glow that late night, or early morning, far out in the wilderness on a grassy flat beside the splashing Chewack River. The noisy waters slapped the rocks and rushed on by as a tired and overworked deputy sheriff's head nodded and slowly slipped into a deep sleep. Pete and Frank Maron were not far behind him. The quiet horse was tied to a near-by tree. It picked up a foot and set it down again, turned its eye over to three men by a fire, and let its head sag too, one eye open, one eye closed.

Not many hours later, as the gray light of day glistened over the high eastern mountains, Pete got up and gently set some more wood on the fire.

"Maron...Maron?" he called softly. "Come on," he whispered as his foot woke his friend. "Let's go take care of Frank. I can't sleep. It's too cold, damn it!"

"Let' s bury Frank and get the hell out of here," Pete ordered in a low voice. "We'll let Art sleep for a while."

Maron staggered to his feet and walked behind Pete into the woods. After stumbling up the dark creek one more time, Pete stepped up to the hanging corpse and started digging below it with a shovel and then using a pick; both tools he had found at the site.

In a few short minutes, he handed the shovel to Maron and said; "Frank Maron dug the grave of Frank Arnold."

When they set out, it was the 12th and then the 13th of September, very early Saturday morning.

Maron had been digging for about a half hour, working under the body, trying not to touch it, when Art Mitchell, came stumbling into Frank Arnold's river camp. It was just getting light, and Art could see the body much better this time. Maron had told no exaggerations. The bones he could see were in a suit of coveralls; and, as said, there was a stocking cap pulled partly down over a bony white skull. The hands were covered with gloves, and there was one rubber —so the grave could be dug. A big seven-gallon pot was set over to the side also. A 7- or 8-inch tree hung over a small bank like a bow and held the hanging body in the air.

"I think he must have stood on the pot and this block of wood and then jumped over the bank." Pete suggested. "Look what I found here. It was hanging over there in the tree, over by his lean-to."

The Deputy Sheriff Makes His Investigation

Pete handed Art a knapsack, and Art took a look inside. It held a gun, a .22 Woodsman Automatic Colt, that had been wrapped in a well-oiled sock.

"That's Frank's handgun there, and I'd sure like to keep that as a remembrance," Pete said.

There was also a notebook with the date January 1935. In addition, there was an assortment of small items such as matches, one sharp knife, wax, and string in the bottom of the pack. In the camp itself, there were lots of things laying around: there was a small table standing with a few traps on it, a Sears catalog, and a small pick. The camp held an ax, saw, pots and pans. Art walked toward the only structure, a small, low lean-to where the trapper had slept, but stopped at an old 30-30 Winchester rifle that was leaning against a tree. It was rusted up a bit. Art picked it up and looked it over. The stock was somewhat weathered, and Art could see it had been there for many months — *but it was worth taking home*, he thought. He held the rifle in his hand as he stuck his head inside the open-sided lean-to and looked in at the old blankets covering the ground.

"Did you sleep in here, too, Frank?" Art asked Maron, as he backed out and stood up.

He took a look around the steep-sided canyon that hid the old trapper's camp. It was a lonesome, cold, damp place that Frank Arnold had chosen for this winter layout. Art shook his head. *It was not a place he wanted to leave his blue blood or white bones to rest.*

"That's deep enough, Frank." Pete said. "Let's put poor Frank Arnold to the rest he deserves and get the hell back to town. This place is creepy and cold and is making wrecks out of all of us. He's just all bones, and I don't want to touch him! We'll never get him out in one piece anyway. Damn, this place gives me the creeps!"

There wasn't any argument with that statement as Pete pulled out a sharp pocketknife he had found in Frank's pack and opened the blade.

"Give me that shovel, Frank!"

He had some string in his hand and tied the knife to the handle of the shovel and walked over to the hanging body. Reaching up high with the shovel over his head, Pete laid the knife across the heavy 1/2 to 3/4 inch rope that held the body in the air. With a couple of quick slices from the razor-sharp knife, the body of the hanging man fell into a heap in the shallow hole. There was one last loud rattle from the old trapper's bones as the body hit the dark brown earth. Frank Arnold it seemed, was finally laid to rest.

The dirt fell on the old clothes and bones of a man that slowly faded from sight, as Maron's shovel went back and forth with each load of soft dirt. But, something wasn't right to Maron's way of thinking, and it would stay with him for a long, long time. He was reaching conclusions on his own from the body he slowly covered there that September day on the gray, windy banks of Horseshoe Creek.

The Deputy Sheriff Makes His Investigation

Chapter 3 Notes

Art Mitchell, as he told in the newspaper, spoke of a "swinging body" hanging from a limb, (amongst other things), in the only written report to ever be found in this case.

Jim Vandiver, who had worked as a deputy under Art Mitchell in 1938, when Art became county sheriff, remembered hearing, even then, the story of the hanging man of bones. Art had brought out Frank Arnold's old 30-30 rifle, and Jim couldn't resist shooting Frank's rusty old gun one day but wished he hadn't. It kicked him like a mule, almost blowing him and the gun up as he told the story. He also painted-in the fact that Art was not much of the outdoor type; he was an office man, "hardly getting out of the office," Jim said.

George Honey of Winthrop, who worked with Pete and many others in this story, also heard this story of finding Frank Arnold from Pete.

Omak-Okanogan County Chronicle, 1936, A newspaper account was found in the Okanogan paper of September 15, 1936. It told of the suicide death of Frank Arnold. A search was made of the Sheriff's records at the Okanogan Courthouse in the 1950's. A card was found with the name "Frank Arnold" and nothing else. No death records can be found in Okanogan or Olympia.

Note: Just how Pete came to get Art Mitchell, and not Boyd Hilderbrand, the elected county sheriff up on that mountain, is a guess. If Art was the poorest of woodsmen, as Jim Vandiver indicated, Boyd Hilderbrand, on the other hand, was one "hell-of-a-good one," and should have been the one to go in for Frank Arnold. Boyd loved the mountains and was truly a real cougar hunter. Pete might have just run into town with this amazing find and grabbed Art Mitchell off the street or out of the sheriff's office, but Art did little to solve, or clear the mystery of Frank's death.

Bob Curtis said that Pete packed in the shovel and pick on Pete's horse, but taking into account the number of mining things and tools already in this camp that night, the story was written as such.

Author: A body is still today buried in the sands of Horseshoe Creek, under a fir tree.

Omak Chronicle, September 15, 1936. Swinging Body Clears Mystery of Missing Man: Frank Arnold, 65-Year-Old Trapper Dropped from Sight a Year and A Half Ago. Date: January 1935.

Notebook Found in Suicide's Pocket Indicates Time He Hanged Self

Discovery of a year and a half old suicide was reported to the county sheriff's office after forestry trail crews found the body of Frank Arnold, 65-year-old trapper in the upper Methow district hanging from a limb of a tree at an unfrequented spot near the Canadian border last Saturday. Arnold had been missing for more than a year and a half, but residents believed that he was out tending to his trap lines which were far removed from civilization. The old trapper had been in the country for over 30 years.

Nearby was found an iron kettle on which he had stood before he apparently kicked it out from under himself, springing his own deathtrap. He is believed to have been dead since January 1935 from an inscription in his notebook bearing the date, several circles, and the inscription "Tl" "SC", which officers believe may be his traps or the location of a mine.

CHAPTER 4

Herb Curtis, Bill McDaniel, George Loudon Get the Tungsten Mine

The following tales are based on several sources, old newspaper accounts, family records, Herb Curtis's manuscripts, Bob Curtis's stories, and McDaniel's memoirs, with Jay Hill's account, and Dick Loudon's stories.

IT WAS STILL THE "GOLDEN age of mining" in 1905, when every other man on the street was a miner. Henry Bahrs and his mining men had made a good showing that winter of 1905-06 up at the Tungsten. Henry was on the go all over the country promoting stock in his seven claims: The Elizabeth, Henrietta, Marie, Wolframite, Cathedral, Tungsten, and Armor Plate. However, Bahrs was not having much success in raising the necessary capital to keep everybody happy. The old saying has never been truer than in the mining industry, "It takes money to make money." If Bahrs shipped any ore to help pay the bills, it is difficult to say, but he just might have. However, it wasn't enough to turn the needed profit.

Bahrs himself did little in the way of work at the mine. He accomplished the things that he did by the hard work of his right-hand man, Clayton Baldwin. Clayton was quite a man in 1905. He stood somewhere around 6 feet, 4 inches tall, and had just come back down from the gold fields in Alaska and the Yukon. He was a hardened traveler, and there were few men who could keep up with him on a set of snowshoes, or anytime, for that matter. It was said that he could go from the mouth of Toats Coulee to the Tungsten Mine in one winter day: a distance of over 35 miles up, up steep mountains. He would strip down to his long-johns, his "union-suit," put on his snowshoes and take off flying. The sweat would just roll off in streams, and he wouldn't stop until he got where he wanted to go. He was as tough as they came, and more than once cleared the tavern in Loomis. His hands were as quick as lightning, and he was the fastest single-jack man around. Nobody could beat him.

Clayton Baldwin was originally from Loomis. He came back from the Yukon, the story goes, with three large fruit jars full of gold, and three notches on his pistol. His sister was the town's schoolteacher. She later married Billy McDaniel and became mother to Loy and grandmother to Jim. Clayton Baldwin was a hell of a man, good or bad, and a good friend of Herb Curtis. But one day in 1918, the year after Billy McDaniel died and received the large paycheck from the sale of the Tungsten Mine, Clayton got "drunked-up," and probably because of hurt feelings and disgust over being cut out of any money, took off with young Loy McDaniel's best team of horses, never to return. Word was he lived into his nineties in California and died in the 1950's, and created a rift in the family that never was healed.

Clayton played a very important role in the early development of the Tungsten Mine. It was he who staked the mine for Henry Bahrs after first getting his interest in the rich deposit. This, while his friends Herb and Bill Johnson were out cutting trail. He ran the crew that built the first

Herb Curtis, Bill McDaniel, George Loudon Get the Tungsten Mine

cabin at the mine that winter in 1905. It was called the "Baldwin Cabin" until it was blown up and burned to the ground by Frank Arnold's liquor still in the early 1920's. Clayton was one of the packers with the first surveying team in 1904 and was definitely in on the earliest discovery of the ore body. It is believed that he grub-staked the packers in those early years until the government came up with some money. It was he who brought Henry Bahrs into the deposit to look at it in 1905 on his horses, and later helped him promote the mine. But Henry Bahrs lost grace with Clayton when things got tight and he couldn't pay his bills. Clayton had been ram-rodding the crew up on the mountain. Herb Curtis was running messages. Herb put it like this:

"Well, we stayed on the job (winter of 1905-1906) and on payday we all came out in March. I believe the miners and Mrs. Baldwin got some money, but I believe that McDaniel, Clayton, and myself did not get any pay. I do not think that my partners ever got a cent, and that McDaniel's was a heavy loser. This ended the first try at the Tungsten. We next located in 1908."

It is not known what was done in 1906-1907, but it looks like very little, if anything happened up there on that mountain. Henry Bahrs quite possibly was trying to raise money to erect a small mill to treat his own ore. Word was out he was broke! He must have had trouble getting money and help to keep his assessment work up. Clayton Baldwin was the one who had been recording Bahr's assessment work in Conconully at the courthouse for the years 1905 and 1906, but he didn't go down in 1907 because he hadn't gotten paid! Bahrs, thanks to Clayton, let his claims slip on the mine. The claims were open. Bahrs was trying to get some Canadians to snowshoe in and stake the mine again. Herb tells it this way:

"George Loudon had to be at his daughter's place at Keremeos, British Columbia. And he came to me and said that he heard in Keremeos that Henry Bahrs was trying to get some Canadians to go up and locate the Tungsten."

There's a story about how Clayton slipped into the Tungsten Mine (or somewhere) and left a red flag tied to a tree to signal Herb and Bill Johnson that the claims were open for staking. "It was a claim jumping type of deal," as Bob Curtis put it years later. And Herb Curtis, still repeating George Loudon, put it like this:

> "Mac, as you know, packed us to Snowshoe Camp by Sunny Pass and Johnson and I started on the trail. Johnson was getting along in years, so I broke trail. The snow was soft, and we didn't get more than halfway that day. We got a large pine that had blown over and had pitchy roots, and we used our snowshoes to clear a place then set a fire. And it was not long before we were down to bare ground and a big hole in the snow. It must have been 4 feet deep after the fire had burned down. We had a little bacon and rice and a couple of cans. Johnson held the bacon on a stick, and I made some tea. The heat melted the snow off a small tree, so I cut it down and made a bed that was nice and warm. Johnson soon went to sleep and stayed that way most of the night. We got to the old Baldwin cabin the second day at dusk. We had blankets and provisions wrapped in a tarp. The cabin was full of pack rats and they stayed awake all night and so did I. We Stayed there till the first of the year, 1908, and located the claims."

Herb Curtis

Herb had two partners: George Loudon and Billy McDaniels (Mac). But a trip to the courthouse would tell you Herb Curtis was the sole owner of the mine because George, Billy McDaniel, and Bill Johnson's names are not on the location notes filed. George and Billy need not have worried, though, if ever they even knew. But for some reason, in these years, Bill Johnson fades out of the story.

Herb Curtis, Bill McDaniel, George Loudon Get the Tungsten Mine

Herb Curtis, however, spends these years prospecting and building at the mine. The lower cabin at the Tungsten Mine, the big one, is built in four sections, and each section represents an era of mining, 1908, 1915, 1916, and 1952. The east end of the cabin, the old, big log section was built by Herb Curtis and Johnny that summer of 1908. These activities generated several of the stories, including the story of the whipsaw incident that occurred when Johnny Bell and Curtis were building the roof on the big cabin.

Now if there was a tool invented to cause division, the whipsaw was it. Sourdoughs claimed it ended more good friendships than any institution except marriage. "It should be suppressed!" said one. "No character is strong enough to withstand it! Two angels could not saw their first log with one of these things without getting into a fight."

Herb Curtis and Johnny Bell were no exceptions to this rule. Johnny told the story of Herb and him working the old "tool-of-the-devil" up on the mountain at the mine.

Herb and Johnny built the hanger for the logs, skidded in some big spruce up on the hanger, peeled them, snapped a line down the log and then commenced to saw. The saw bowed, the arms strained, and the sawdust and cuss words flew to the twang of the bending, bowing whipsaw. Herb was on the top, standing on the scaffolding and straddling the log. Johnny was on the bottom, spitting and pulling and cussing in the sawdust, the two managed to cut maybe half a board when Herb had a bright idea. "John, damn it! Let's you and I change places!"

"Well, that's the best damned idea I've heard from you yet," said Johnny as he quickly let go of the saw and jumped out from under the log. He didn't give his partner two seconds to change his mind. Johnny laughed about that for years after, thinking about Herb down in the pit being buried in sawdust, and pulling down on the saw, board after board after board. To him it was the closest place to "Misery Street" he could think of. Once down there, Herb was just too proud to admit he hadn't gained a thing; and was, in fact, worse off than before (unless you liked sawdust). But, he toughed it out, and never suggested a swap of positions again.

In another story, Herb's staunch, "matter of fact" proudness almost got him to quit using tobacco one year at the mine. This time it was he and Paul Loudon who were spending some time together in the high, far-away mine. Both men were proud, "be-reasonable-do-it-my-way" type of people and were rubbing each other the wrong way for the whole duration of their long stay. By the end of their partnership at the mine, patience had grown as short as a quick fuse on a dynamite stick and so had their supplies. Herb was flat out of tobacco and had been for days, but Paul, on the other hand, had lots of the badly needed stuff, and every time he took a bite off a plug, Herb's mouth would start watering. Herb, of course, would not ask for any, and Paul was just mad enough not to give him any if he had. So, Herb suffered. He almost made it.

Finally, the boys had finished their work at the Tungsten and were on their horses heading down the trail for home. Paul and Herb rode along, not saying more than was necessary, while Paul kept rolling his tobacco in his mouth, and then spitting it in a big wad on the ground beside his friend. He had been, day by day, slowly torturing his companion by these antics. Herb, not being able to escape, or overcome his yearning with hard work as he usually did, had to sit on his horse and watch Paul play with his tobacco. Now that life was easier, Herb could not take any more and rode up to the silent Paul mouthing his tobacco.

"Paul, I sure would like a pull on that tobacco!" said Herb in a sheepish way.

Paul never looked up at his partner as he let Herb ride along beside him for more than a few feet. Then, without a word or a look, he reached into his pocket and pulled out his pack of tobacco, took another mouthful, looked Herb in the eye, and slowly handed over the tobacco. Herb was saved, but Paul got the last tease on his partner and still laughed about it, years later.

Except for times when he had help from his friends, it was just about a one-man operation for Herb at the mine from 1908 through, say 1914. Herb shares a look into conditions in those years:

"I stayed there alone one summer excepting a dog for company. Well, he took sick, and he looked at me so mournful out of his eyes and wagged his tail. I think he was trying to tell me the grub was not cooked right, but I gave him the same as I had. He lingered along for a day or two then died. Poor dog! Then I went to Loomis and got another dog. I fed him the same as myself, but he only stayed a day or two, then went back to McDaniel's."

The next year, I was there alone and did a lot of prospecting. I uncovered a fine bunch of Tungsten... about a ton that I mined in one day. McDaniels came in and brought a jar of strawberries and said the girls, Grace McDaniels and Cassie Hobert, sent them in. I took William down and showed him the ore I had found. My, he was pleased. We went to camp, built a fire, and visited. Then he said, 'The Spokane Fair is on... you could go with a piece of ore.' We picked a piece about 60 pounds of nearly pure ore. We went to Oroville and took a description of the claim to a lawyer and gave him the money to record it. You will hear of this later on. I got a write-up about it in the Spokesman-Review."

It was in one of these years that Herb was supposed to have found a rich deposit of scheelite ore also. It was never mined in those early years. And years later, Loy McDaniel and Paul Loudon spent some time looking for it, but it eluded them and was never found. It may still be there waiting for the next big boom.

TALES OF THE TUNGSTEN MINE

Billy McDaniel

Billy McDaniel was not a young man in 1914. He had been a miner and a cowboy for most of his life. "Once a miner, always a miner," they say, and he was no different. He hailed from eastern Canada and was therefore considered "kin" to Herb. Billy had headed for California in the later gold rush era, 1876, but was too late for the good strikes. He found work in San Francisco, but it didn't last long. From there the winds of fate blew him to Portland, Oregon, then south to Arizona and New Mexico, and on to the rich gold fields of Sonora, Mexico.

Billy worked in a gold mine in Sonora that ran $40,000.00 to the ton at 1880 prices. Few young miners stayed at one mine for very long, so by 1882 or 1883, Billy was at the North Fork of the Coeur d'Alene River in Idaho, panning for gold. Then in May of 1883, he came riding into the sparsely populated, and newly opened Okanogan country to do some cowboying. He found a job with one of the first settlers in the upper valley, Mr. Henry Wellington, a Harvard graduate who was raising cattle south of the little town of Oroville on the Canadian border. Billy also engaged in some freighting business back and forth from Oroville to Spokane, almost a 350-mile trip. Mr. Wellington must have thought a lot of the hard-working young man, for when he died a few years later, he willed his Oroville ranch over to Billy. Billy was now a rancher.

By 1884, Billy had a place in Loomis, Washington, and was married to Harriet Baldwin in 1896. Billy had fallen in love with both Miss Baldwin and the Okanogan country, and too, there was mining all around him. The government had just taken the land away from the Indians and opened it to mining and homesteading. Billy filed on 160 acres below the mouth of Toats Coulee Creek. Later his brother-in-law, Clayton Baldwin, filed beside him.

With his powder horn, or more properly his "panning-horn" in his hand, Billy would take off over the hills and up the Similkameen River. He panned the many creeks he would cross in this vast new land he found himself in. "Stick the half-horn in the water, scoop-up some sand, work out the lights, and the gold stayed behind in the bowl." Billy never used a gold pan; he used his Mexican bull horn.

Being a miner, Billy got curious about some custom jewelry that the local Indians were wearing. It was made of an interesting mineral that was a glassy, a smoky sheet of translucent soft stone called "Isinglass" or "sheet mica." It was a substance that the Indians had always placed high value on. The white man had a commercial use for it, too, on his stoves and oven doors. You could look through it and watch the fire blaze away, but the mineral would not melt. The Indians had big sheets of the glassy stuff and were proud of it. But none of the white men knew where it came from or where the Indians were finding it. And when asked, the Indians would just point toward the high western mountains, the land called "Passayten."

Billy finally talked an Indian into taking him back into this wild, unexplored country to look for the mica sheets of Isinglass, but where they went and how they got there even Bill had trouble figuring out. They probably went up the old Indian trail on the Ashnola River. It is rumored that the Isinglass came from the Sheep Mountain area, but Billy didn't really know what mountain he found himself on when the Indian finally brought him to a tall mountain with a slide-scree.

"No more!" said the Indian. "No more... snow come and rock over stone!" There apparently had been a big slide, and Billy figured it had covered the Isinglass deposit; at least that is the story the Indian told him, and the deposit hasn't been found to this day.

In time, Billy and his wife had a hearty son named Loy and a girl named Grace. Billy passed away August 10, 1916, in the middle of the glory days of the Tungsten Mine. But Loy, his son, would pick up the reins, and play no small role in the Tungsten Mine story in the years to come.

George Loudon

George Loudon, the third partner, also helped keep Herb Curtis and the mine afloat in the early years before the great First World War. George was born August 8, 1855, in the city of Philadelphia. His mother died at an early age, and though it hurt his father deeply, George was "bounded-out" at the tender age of seven. At fourteen he was bought back from servitude and worked in Pennsylvania until he was about eighteen, when he shucked it all and went west. He landed in Virginia City, Nevada, and there found a special young girl to marry. With a lot of determination and through many hardships, they arrived in the Okanogan in 1890 with little money and seven children. Yet, if George had learned one thing in life, it was how to work! And he knew work has its rewards though it may take some time. The Okanogan was going to be his home, but maybe not the river bottomlands below Oroville. A tremendous flood in 1894 made that clear. It was called a 1000-year flood, for not even the Indians could recall one of its magnitude, and such water has not been seen since. It wiped out the Loudon's Ranch on the Okanogan River, and everybody else's too, flooding all the way to the Columbia River. It pushed the Loudons up the mountain to the Loomis area to start all over again. This time he would become one of the big ranchers in the Okanogan Valley.

George Loudon, Herb Curtis and Billy McDaniel knew they had a good mine, but was it good enough to risk the big investment (the one from their own pockets) needed to develop it? It would take all the money the three men could gather to bring the Tungsten into production. Herb didn't have anywhere near the money needed, and if George and Billy had it, or could get it, they weren't going to put their life's work all on the Tungsten Mine barrelhead! They needed men with more money than they had to take the chances.

From 1908 to 1913, Herb did all the physical work. He was probably working at the mine at least part of every summer. It is a good bet that

Herb Curtis, Bill McDaniel, George Loudon Get the Tungsten Mine

George and Billy grub-staked him most of that time. Dick Loudon, George's last son (still alive at this writing in 1988), had this to say years later about his dad and Herb Curtis, who, by and by, married his sister Mae. I quote from his family book:

> "About a thousand feet up the mountainside above our Similkameen Valley home was the Mountain Sheep Mine. The annual assessment work had to be done. The owner supplied the necessary funds and had my father hire the miners and manage the work… Each year my father recruited skilled miners from the Loomis area. Among them I remember were Joe McMillian, Rory Cameron, Claude Guyton, and Herb Curtis. All boarded with my parents and lived in the bunkhouses nearby… During those years, Herb had been a friend of the family and a partner of my father in the Tungsten Mine for years… He was a good miner and his work ethic was his most prominent characteristic. He worked hard and he believed those around him should do likewise."

George Loudon came out well on the Tungsten, though just how well is not really clear when the big money was divvied up. He died in 1931, leaving ten children to carry on the family name. A few of the children would go on to play their part in the story of the famous mine.

Herb and Mae Loudon Curtis had a hearty son by the name of Bob. Bob Curtis too would play no little part in this written story. For he, too, became bitten by the high country mine bug, and got the fever of the Tungsten Mine.

CHAPTER 5

The Wolf that Ate the Sheep

This tale of the early years at the Tungsten mine were accounted by Herb Curtis at the mine as related by his son Bob Curtis. The history of mining is full of stories of riches, but more often than not, stories of "hard knocks." The story of Tungsten as it relates to the first world war is based on research done at the University of Washington.

A GREAT WAR WAS FOUGHT a hundred years ago during the years 1914 to 1918. Many thought this war could be won in just a few weeks when they picked up their rifles and sailed across the dark blue sea for the shores of Europe. But the warriors on the losing side fought so "hard" that it took many powerful nations, and millions of men to stop them. The country that fought so "hard"—with a powerful modern innovation—was Germany. The war was World War I, and if the old middle-aged parable of the 'lost-horseshoe-nail can be applied to the Allied Powers of World War I, that being: "Because of the loss of a horseshoe nail, the shoe was lost, and because the shoe was lost, the horse and Calvary-man was lost, and because of the loss of the Calvary-man, the battle was lost, and because the battle was lost, the war was (almost) lost!" The reason the metaphorical nail was lost by the Allies was because it was not made with *tungsten*!

There are many reasons why this European country could take on the whole of modern Europe, with the U.S.A. thrown in for good measure, and almost win. A quick scenario being that Kaiser Wilhelm simply worked himself into a dogfight with too many dogs in it. But this doesn't answer the question of how he gained territory and held off four powerful nations for 4 years. To this question of "how?" we must add to his arsenal and warring skill a new materiel called *tungsten*! For it was the highly intelligent German chemists who had learned that if they added refined tungsten to steel, it made it much, much harder and many times stronger than any steel made before. Steel, in lieu of iron, had only been developed a few decades before this. Even though this hardening and strengthening effect was known to many industrialized countries, these other nations had a problem — they were at a loss as to how to refine and work this strange rock. This fact being so, their steel and iron, made like it always was in their blast refineries across the world, was, as a fact, far inferior to the super hard tungsten steel of their adversary, the Germans. It was only the energetic Germans who could refine this black ore and turn out a steel harder than all others, and that on a production scale. It was this method of smelting and refining tungsten ore that gave them their surpassing advantage over all other nations of power, for now they alone had far superior hardened steel weapons, tools, bearings, gun barrels, and, most important, armor plating.

Yet the metal tungsten had been known for centuries. The English tin miners had gotten quite disgusted with this awful metal. The " wolf," they called it, for like the black wolf that would rob and eat their sheep at night, this treacherous black mineral would seemingly eat their white tin; the tin they worked so diligently to mine for their Roman tin buyers. So, they named it "Wolframite" — "the wolf."

The Wolf that Ate the Sheep

If you had a nugget in your hand of pure tungsten and a nugget of pure gold, both the same size, you would have two stones so close to the same weight that you could not tell the difference by weight alone. It is said that pure tungsten is just a little heavier than gold. Of course, neither pure tungsten nor pure gold occur in nature, but few elements in nature are heavier. The Scandinavians gave the metal its present name, "tungsten," meaning "heavy stone."

Why did it take the clever German metallurgists to discover the hardening effects of this strange stone? The reason lies in this stone's amazing ability to withstand the assayer's kiln. It be-deviled the wisest of assayers for centuries. They could not build a furnace that would get hot enough to melt this ore. It seemingly couldn't be done. The kiln would get hotter and hotter until it melted out. But the strange rock would sit there, unchanged in the highest of heat. No man could even come up with a crucible to mix in some fluxes, let alone have a furnace that would not melt-out long before this perplexingly unbeatable rock melted. It appears to be a metal with no earthly use. And yet, the metal's very unbeatable qualities held such great potential, if only one could break it down and unlock its secrets.

If 6000° Fahrenheit sounds hot, it is! That is what it takes to melt tungsten. Most furnaces go to about 2500 to 3000°, and even the best are burn out by anything over 3000° Fahrenheit. No kiln could get hot enough to melt this heavy, strange stone until the Germans put together one that did. The kiln was called the "Electric Arc Furnace." If you add to your tungsten ore the right fluxes and put this in your new Electric Arc Furnace, you become not only the leader in super hard steel production, but also the leader in the game of war. As the Germans found out, this stone was not only extremely heavy and impossibly infusible but also proved to be the strongest metal known to man. At just under 500,000 pounds per square inch of tensile strength, tungsten ran far ahead of all other metals. Basic steel was really quite soft until tungsten was added;

only the diamond is harder. So, the Germans alone put a very high value and wanton demand on this wonderfully useful heavy metal.

In 1912, Herb Curtis, George Loudon and Billy McDaniel had tungsten. In 1912, the best and only real market for tungsten ore was Hamburg, Germany. If you wanted top dollar you got your tungsten ore to Hamburg. In fact, all tungsten, for all practical purposes, went to Germany. This was a "cut and dried" fact. If you had a tungsten mine before the World War I, one way or another the Germans got your ore. They were simply the only ones who could work it on any kind of tonnage scale.

If the Germans had the monopoly on treating tungsten. However, it was the British who controlled the countries with the few existing tungsten mines. For this was still the era when it could be said that "the sun never set on the British Empire." The U.S. produced a little tungsten, but if the U.S. wanted any tungsten steel or "ferro-tungstate" as it was called by the chemists, they knocked on a door in Hamburg. New York was the big marketing point for U.S. tungsten and from there it was loaded on ships and sent to Germany. Of course, there were buyers and sellers, brokers and shippers, and they all took a little cut off the top. But the biggest cut of all was taken by the mills, the mills that crushed and concentrated, sacked and shipped the high-grade ore.

Tungsten comes from the ground in mainly two types of commercial ore: one is called "The Wolf," Wolframite, the other is named "Scheelite." Both minerals run about 80% tungsten, (WO_3) in their highest natural form. The buyers of the metal learned quickly from the steel mills that they did not want to mess with any ore that wasn't at least 60% WO_3, that is, high grade scheelite or wolframite. So, if you came up to them with a bag of rocks that was half quartz and half scheelite, they would tell you to go home and separate the scheelite from the quartz, come back with your bag of scheelite, which meant you had high-graded it to 60% or better tungsten ore, worth about $1.00 or maybe $2.00 a pound in 1912. Of course, the higher the percentage of tungsten in your ore the better you and the Germans liked it, and the more money the broker would pay.

Tungsten ore did not occur naturally in Germany, and because of their great demand for the metal, it became customary for the Germans to buy all available bags of the concentrated ore. A half ton of wolframite was bought up as quickly as 100 tons. All the miner had to do was put the 60% ore in a bag, in about 20-pound increments, (60 to 90-pound sacks were common) and ship it to the buyer, who was probably in New York City. One bag or a 1000, it didn't matter; the Germans wanted it!

The high German demand for Tungsten ore is one reason Herb Curtis, Billy McDaniel and George Loudon would have liked to have gotten that 73% black Wolframite ore off Wolframite Mountain and over to New York. It was the highest of all grades, and the finest ore to be had. It is difficult to say today if the boys fully understood the marketing procedures, but they sure knew that the percentage of tungsten had to be 60% or greater, at least by 1916, but maybe not in 1912.

The First Ore Shipped

Herb swung the pick at the black and white ore and pulled it back to him. Again, he swung and pulled the black and white quartz rock from the overhanging ledge. He shoveled it up with a quick movement, put it into the canvas ore bag, and then started on another. There were thirteen bags setting outside the mouth of the shaft; some of the bags contained high-grade wolframite of 73%. Herb then shoveled the remainder into a sack and dragged it towards the daylight and open air. The panoramic view of Apex Mountain overshadowed him as he sat down on a rock and looked out over the beautiful mountains. "It might be hard work, but you can't complain about the scenery," Herb said out loud. The little dog at his side wagged his tail. This was Herb's fourth year at the Tungsten Mine, and this year he was going to ship some ore.

Hours later Herb had three more bags of what he knew was good ore. The furry dog shot out from his side as he walked up the hill to make some coffee and eat some of the sheep jerky that hung in the log cabin. The dog darted around, trying to catch the little chipmunk that flew over the rocks and into a big fir tree that stood a few feet away. "You're going to have to learn to run a bit faster, there boy, if you're going to catch that little thing." The chipmunk chattered and scolded the dog as Herb stepped into his cabin and lit a fire in the stove. He soon had the coffee boiling and a cup in his hand. Fourteen sacks of high-grade ore sat over the hill in 60-pound bags. "I can get two more bags with another shot, and then we'll get this black gold off this mountain and over to Montana. If you'd just learn to hold that hammer down there instead of chasing squirrels, we'd have had this done days ago." The dog wagged his tail and looked up into Herb's eyes.

In a few minutes, Herb was back down the mountain in the black hole with his hammer in one hand and his drill steel in the other. Herb would get another round off tomorrow, but then he would have to timber up the loose granite that hung over him from the ceiling of the shaft. There were better types of rock to mine; this granite geology was dangerous.

Herb shot the vein and got his two more sacks of quartz ore. The vein narrowed a little to about 4 feet. Sixteen sacks of ore sat outside the shaft as Herb picked up his backpack and started down the trail for Loomis. It was time to ship some ore to Butte, Montana. In a few days, walking, the miner was back down, and then back up on the mountain again with Billy McDaniel and a string of pack horses. From that point, it took three days to get the ore to the siding at Nighthawk, Washington. It took three weeks for the ore to get to Butte, Montana, and it took three months for the mill in Butte to run the sixteen sacks of tungsten-quartz ore through their ball-mill.

The Wolf that Ate the Sheep

Now there has never been born a hardened miner yet, that has trusted an ore mill. To some the mills held a bunch of wizards and alchemists; to others, slipshod mechanics and incompetent fools. But to most, they were just plain thieves, and the mill roofs covered a den of robbers. In reality, this was the truth in a few cases, but surely not all. The trouble was, once the ore was dumped into the machinery at the mill, you were at the mercy of the mill-man. Something like giving a stranger your money to count because you can't, then hoping he can count or will count right. The principle was about the same, and at times, so were the results.

The only rough dollar value for the ore was the owner's assay report from the chemist. The problem with this was that few, very few, miners wanted to, or knew how to, sample an ore vein correctly, for the better they high-graded their ore vein, the better the assay report, and the better the assay report, the better the next buyer would like it. The buyer of the mine, that is, for every miner wants to sell his mine for the right price, and it was always better to own a good mine rather than a bad one. So, the formula went like this: the poorer the sampling, the better the assay; the better the assay, the better the mine; and the better the mine, the better the money from the future buyer of the mine. Or, the better the mine owner felt, in any case. Of course, it all collapsed when the mill report was received, but that could wait.

Still again, the temptation for a struggling ore mill to be on the long end of the return was strong. Even an honest mill had to charge a lot of money to keep the machinery running. Too many times the poor miner only got back a little pocket change because the ore in the shipment barely covered the shipping and the milling cost.

But Herb was there in Butte, Montana, when the first tungsten ore bag was dumped into the crusher. He kept a close watch on it as it went through the milling stages. No mill was going to "lose" his ore. But had this mill ever run tungsten ore before? You can't crush wolframite ore too fine. The mill had their problems. It was said that they couldn't separate the scheelite from the quartz through the flotation process because most the tungsten was lost. An expensive lesson for the miners, to say the least, but they were learning. If any more ore was going to be shipped from their mine in the high mountains, the 40+ miles from town, it was going to be high grade 60% or better ore, and not a grade run just as it came out of the ground. If 1912 was a disappointing year, 1913 would be a lot better. The three miners, Herb, Billy and George, knew that there was some pure, rich black wolframite ore to be found; they could see lots of it in the rock, but there was also a lot of white scheelite ore that was tied in with the white quartz rock that they could not see, and it could only be gotten out by some heavy duty milling equipment. They needed their own mill. However, this heavy, costly equipment was beyond the means of the three would-be miners. The very fact that the mine was 40 miles of mountainous forest from the nearest road was in itself a large obstacle to overcome. The best they could hope for was some high-grade wolframite now and again and forget about the scheelite and smaller grains of black wolframite scattered throughout the vein of quartz. Still the miners had another option, go prospecting to find some money. And the green money came not from up on that wilderness mountain, but from the big city.

CHAPTER 6

A Trapper is Kicked off the Train

Frank Arnold's biography and mountain stories from Bob Curtis, Jay Hill, Bill Higgenbothoam, Frank Zackerman, Harry Sherling, Harold MacWilliams, and a few others.

THE WHISTLE BLEW AND THE ground shook as the train pulled into the small town of Molson, Washington. The noise and shaking of the ground woke any who were still asleep in their beds. It was 6:00 o'clock in the morning. The steam blew loudly from the big wheel pistons as the coachman hollered, "Molson Stop... end of the line!" Four or five people stepped off the coach and onto the siding of the train station. It wasn't much of a station compared to Spokane, but Molson was glad it was there. The line had just been finished, snaking its way up the steep mountain from the town of Oroville in the valley below, and it looked mighty good to the businessmen of town. Molson was a thriving mining and farming town in 1910. It was the end of the line for the Great Northern on the Molson run, 200 miles from Spokane.

The conductor walked back down the aisle of the car to check and make sure the passenger coach was empty. Something told him the drunk who was put on in Spokane hadn't gotten off at any of the stops on the way, and he was right. He looked into one of the back seats; "COME ON, MOVE IT! THIS IS THE END OF THE LINE MISTER!" The conductor had no patience for drunks as he reached down and grabbed a fist full of clothes. The sleeping man was yanked to his feet! "NOW GET OFF THE TRAIN!" The man staggered through and into the seats as the conductor pushed him down the aisle. He stumbled down the steps and onto the wood platform of the train station. He stood there dizzily, stepping from side to side, trying to plant his feet underneath his body, trying to pull himself together from the effects of way too much "red-eye.'

The man stood 5 feet 10 inches with his shoes on. He was 40 years old, not particularly husky but was a solid 170 pounds. He had long arms and big hands that clenched a wrinkled felt city hat. He had heavy legs with light English shoulders. His hair was of a sandy, red-brown color and his weathered tan complexion contrasted with his white neckline, exposed by a loose wool plaid Mackinaw shirt. He wore farmer blue bib-overalls that matched his blue eyes, which squared off with his straight brow and jaw. The upper lip sported a long bushy "cooky-duster" mustache. The man, other than his staggering steps, would not have stood out in a crowd, but the small town of Molsen gathered no crowds.

The new man in town weaved over to the end of the platform and read the sign on the wall of the station: "MOLSON." He scratched his head and looked up again, and again, "Where in the world is Molson at?" he muttered to himself. This was Frank Arnold's grand entrance into the Okanogan country.

Once One of Ten Thousand

Frank Arnold was born in Yorkshire, England in 1870. He was an active, healthy and a strong little man; his mother was diligent in raising

A Trapper is Kicked off the Train

and bringing up the boy in a right and proper manner. He was given the best schooling with what money his father sent to her, being that his dad and mother separated when Frank was just a little fellow.

His mother married again when Frank was twelve, and his new father moved them to Canada. The stubborn lad did not get along well with his new father, and that same year the young man found himself in a military school. Through discipline and hard work, the lad became an outstanding student and a good soldier. He joined the English military at seventeen and by nineteen was an officer. The young man's superior strategic skills quickly became noticed and this in itself might have gotten the man into the special services. Yet the young man had another talent that put him before all others. He could drive a nail in a board with a bullet at 100 yards. His marksmanship skills were without equal in the Queen's Army. A man with such ability was needed in special places, and he was promoted to the elite guard in Buckingham Palace to her Majesty, the Queen: The Queen of England, certainly a place of high honor and service.

Frank struck a fine figure on his white thoroughbred horse with sword and handgun at his side, rifle slung handily over his shoulder. Decked out in his bright uniform of red and blue, one of ten thousand, he was called. He served the Queen well - at least for a while.

For Arnold, at the age of nineteen, life seemed never to have been brighter. At this time, he fell in love with the girl of his dreams, a striking young aristocrat. They were soon married after a dizzy romance, and life seemed, for a time, that it could not have been better. But, the young girl was difficult to satisfy. The military man found her high living and partying much too expensive for his simple military salary. Sadly, the bright young soldier could not keep his new, fast-living wife happy, and she did not stay with her military man long.

Frank Arnold was crushed. His best friend became Mr. Whiskey Bottle, and a bottle of whiskey on a parade day before the Queen does not mix well with a thoroughbred horse, a firecracker, or a poorly placed spur. For whatever reason it was, the hot-blooded horse jump out from under the man in the saddle; and suddenly, Frank found himself laying on the cobblestone street, dead to the world. Horses danced sideways as his comrades rode around him. The crowd gasped, stared and laughed while the Queen had a short talk with a disgusted general. This incident cost Frank six months in the brig and a berth on a steamer bound for Hong Kong. Frank had been demoted to a simple infantryman in the service of his Queen. From Buckingham Palace to a simple barrack in China went Frank.

But this did not solve his problem. He still could not keep himself out of trouble. The brig was too often his home. Many, many a night he sweltered in the oven of filth and cockroaches. No amount of punishment could break the young man from the bottle, and nobody but the military would put up with him. And so, on one of his better drunks, he sold his soul to his past master, the military. With a bottle under his coat, a pen in his hand, and a slap on his back, he signed: "For a life term in the service of Her Majesty, The Queen!"

Now when sober, Frank amazed his officers by his thoroughness, his energy and his high intelligence. However, it was still his marksmanship that won Frank many an early release from the brig to shoot for his regiment. Drunk or sober he could outshoot anybody in Hong Kong - hands down he was the best.

Forty years old and long parted with the Queen, Frank Arnold had most recently been working for a fur buyer in Spokane until they put him on the train and bought him a free ride out of town — just as far as the train would take him. Frank was just too good of a drinker, and

A Trapper is Kicked off the Train

if it hadn't been for prohibition 6 years later to slow him down a notch, the man would have probably died long before his time.

It was Will Turner of Molson who remembered Frank in town. He said that Frank and another fellow trapped together that first year between Molson, Chesaw and the Canadian border. In the summer months, Frank worked at odd jobs found in the area: sawmills, farming, maybe the mines, and it is said that he worked for a short time in an apple-box factory in Oroville.

Frank Arnold while living in the Oroville area met Fred Manwiller. Fred had quite a bunch of sheep that ran west of the town of Oroville. They wintered at a lake called Wannacut, 6 miles out. Frank was in his second year or so in the Okanogan, and he had put together a small dog team to run his trap-line faster. Fred Manweller was having a big problem keeping the coyotes and wolves from taking the top fifteen percent of his sheep. So, in a conversation with Frank, he worked out a deal with the new trapper to come over and work the Wannacut Lake area that winter of 1911 or 1912.

It was a good winter for both Fred and Frank. Frank piled up quite a stack of nice coyote pelts, but it cost him more than he had bargained for. One night his dog team got loose and found the dead sheep-carcass laced with poison meat, set for the mouths of coyotes. The sheep bait was full of deadly "strychnine," and Frank Arnold lost every one of his dogs to the poison! They were the last pets he ever owned. Trapping, strychnine, steel-leg-traps and pet dogs just do not work well together.

The new trapper to the Okanogan seemed to trap for reasons beyond his need for just an income. Though in the cut of life, the occupation of trapper seemed to fit him. His personality and conversation seemed to reflect one of education, and above average schooling. Yet he had no problem with solitude and independence. He was an obvious foreigner in a country that was made up of foreigners, yet he guarded his past from all who ever knew him. Nobody knew for sure if he ever had a home, or where that home might be. His reclusive life did one thing for Frank Arnold, it kept him away from the "watering-holes" and the kind of trouble that had removed him from prestigious service in a faraway land. He was friendly and conversational when he came to town but could spend months alone in those mountains. He was soon looked upon as a rough, tough, lone mountain man; the kind that were getting fewer and fewer in a changing world.

The man in bib-overalls, after thinning out the coyotes, doing-in the wolves at Wannacut Lake, and trapping around the small gold mining towns of Golden, We-hes-ville and Wanicut, found some new and less-civilized country some 15 to 20 miles away. Looking from the tops of the smaller mountains, he could often see these high-country mountains from the tops of the low mountains above Wannacut Lake. It was a big, not-well-explored land to the west across the Loomis, Sinlahekin Valley and over to the Douglas Mountain area, at the edge of a rugged land called the "Pasayten."

Into this high, wild and free wilderness Frank ventured, trapping for two winters up and down Redman Creek and over Douglas Mountain. He found the trapping very good in this high, lodge-pole tree country. Even today, if a person knows where to look, they say you can find old Frank's "log cabin" on Redman Creek, which wasn't a log cabin at all, but it gives a good look at the resoluteness and ruggedness of the 45-year-old trapper.

Old timers say his "cabin" consisted of just a bunch of logs laid up against a large rock with a crawl space underneath. That's it. Frank would spend the winter underneath the logs. Even though Frank might have been soft spoken and unpretentious when he came to town, outside in the elements he was as tough as the stones he walked over. The man amazingly withstood the coldest days and the longest bitter cold nights that winter could throw at him. Just a blanket or two, with little shelter, stretching the word shelter to its limits, was all the man seemed to need

A Trapper is Kicked off the Train

to live through those long, bitterly cold nights, days and months in the high country of North Central Washington. Yes, this new mysterious man who came into the country was hardened and tough. In fact, he made hardened and tough men take a second look — and wonder how he could live like a wild animal in the wild woods.

Today it is difficult for any of us "softies" to comprehend how this man lived; for more than one person spoke of Frank as living like an "animal," and certainly, by today's standards, no truer statement could have been made. For there were times in his life, lots of times, when he did live like an animal. He was somewhat dirty, grubby and had a "wild" smell most all of the time — as did all mountain men. Still, most often when in town, he was clean shaven and presentable.

Mrs. Herb Curtis would shudder when her daughter would come running in, shouting, "Frank Arnold's coming!" Mrs. Ford would shiver too, but she would quickly cover her furniture and order Frank into the washroom for a good bath and scrubbing, sending in a change of clothes for him to come out in. Frank would stay for days with the Fords, but he never slept in the house, but in the barn. He would sleep in the tack room. It never seemed to bother this resolute Englishman, though in afterthought, it could have been a bit of a put-down to this educated man of the mountains. Still, if there was any pride in him, it had long since been washed out by booze, solitude, rain and snow.

If Frank lived a rough, animal like life in the mountains, it sure wasn't a deterrent to his health. He was "the picture of health" and my was he tough!" said Frank Zackerman. Frank's eyes were clear and his shaven face seemed to glow. He came through Frank Zackermen's camp at the high Horseshoe Basin one morning in 1927. Arnold was then 57.

"I was herding sheep for Omar and Emmet Smith and here comes this man down the trail. I got him to stop and talk for a short while. In a way, I had to force him to talk to me. Company was few and far between in those days in the high mountains. Of course, I was just a kid at the time (about 20.) He was a nice man, pleasant and mild mannered, but he wasn't one to talk much. Maybe he was in a hurry. He said he was going to town, (Loomis) and had just left the Tungsten Mine (14 miles away.) It was about 7:30 in the morning then."

"You're not going to Loomis today, are you?" Frank Zackerman asked the city-hatted Englishman in a surprised voice.

"Oh, that's no chore," Frank Arnold said. "I'll be into town today (close to 30 miles away) and back up to spend the night at the Duncan James cabin. I'm going to town for a few supplies, and if you're here tomorrow I'll stop and see you."

Sure enough, at about 8:00 the next morning, Frank came through Horseshoe Basin with a heavy pack on his shoulders. Now from the mine to Loomis was all of 40 miles as the old trails ran, and from there back up the Toats Coulee River to Duncan James cabin is another 11 miles added on. Frank covered a cool 50+ plus miles that day and 80 miles in 2 days. Bob Curtis, Al Smith, Lloyd Ford and Ted Boland all knew and told stories about how Frank was capable of walking, and often did walk, thirty, forty, even 50 miles at a given time, and this was no young man in 1927.

Jay Hill of Loomis remembered when he was a young boy, Frank throwing a cool 100-pound bag of sugar on his back at the Loomis store and stepping out for the Toats Coulee Creek drainage. "He rigged it up with a headband where the weight was carried from his forehead, Indian style. I watched him walk out of town with this heavy 100-pound bag of sugar on his back and shook my head in disbelief as he faded out of sight." The sixty-some-year old man (at that time) had at least 25 miles to go with that sugar on his back before he came to his first line cabin.

Shorty Fairbrother, who trapped beside Frank for a good number of years, remembered him coming to his cabin (more than once), for a visit on a cold, wind-blown winter day, and staying till way late at night talking. When conversation slowed and it was time to think about

A Trapper is Kicked off the Train

bedding down in Shorty's warm log cabin, Frank would put on his coat and just walk out into the darkness of a cold, windy, snow-whipped winter night, out into 4 feet of snow, disappearing into the winter darkness. "Just got up and left!" said Shorty. "He would move through the woods for miles like an animal." Even the tough, wiry, little woodsman, Lester Fairbrother was awed by the unbelievably strange hardiness of the reclusive mountain man that trapped beside his line.

His Fellow Contemporaries

The tungsten miner, Harry Sherling, remembered the story about Frank making big money one year and then traveling overseas to Ireland. It must have been after his first or second year on Douglas Mountain that Frank made enough money to make a trip back to Ireland. Now why he went to Ireland when it was said he was an Englishman, is an unanswered question. Almost surely it was to see some past family member. However, the question will have to remain unanswered for now. It was said, and still remembered, that he made $1,800 that year trapping. Now the average wage in town in those days was somewhere around $500 dollar-a-year, making this $1,800 quite a handful of money for one man. It would have been enough spending money to get Frank across the ocean and back in 1913.

And after Frank got back from his trip over the ocean, (or wherever he went) he again trapped for coyotes, but not in the lower valley. This time he trapped for the sheepherder up in the Horseshoe Basin, said to be Webber, but more likely James Lynch, who ran sheep there between 1905 and 1917. Frank would have used a small cabin that was just around Rock Mountain from Loudon Lake. The little cabin was said to have been built by some earlier woodsman or perhaps the sheepherders. Here the Englishman found himself in a beautiful, high, open grassland with pointed peaks and rolling grass-covered mountains in every direction — and it was here that he would stay.

This new land that stretched out before him was prime fur grounds and all but endless. He might or might not have been the first trapper to find and trap the area in 1914 but being that it was the sheepherders who asked him to come over and trap the Horseshoe Basin, most likely he was the first. Other trappers might come and go in this fair land, but Frank Arnold would not. He would stay the longest, by far, of any trapper before or after. The land running along the Canadian border in this high country called Pasayten would become Frank's for the next twenty some years.

The list of his contemporaries who came and went, sharing his mountains and valleys at the same time is rather long: Elvert Lynch, an early patriarch of the Lynch family in Oroville; Clyde Andrews, an early explorer of the Pasayten pre-1900, whose history is mostly lost, but he became a friend of Frank's, and a sharer in a mining claim there, and has a creek drainage named after him; then there was a trapper named Zasrow, who was considered one of the best coyote trappers out there, and that because of some secret "hot coyote" bait that no coyote could pass up. In those days, there was a five-dollar bounty on all coyotes. He would sell you the recipe, or most of it, for $50.00. Lester Fairbrother pushed and wedged in next to Frank in the twenties and trapped besides him for some 10 years. Frank split his line, and gave him some of his fur grounds, namely parts of Windy Mountain, including Big Horn Creek and Coleman Ridge. Then there was Pat Carr, a long-time mountain man who stayed at Billy Goat Corrals, up Eight Mile Creek from the Methow Valley where he held a copper mine for many years. Others included Sy Walter, a Methow trapper; and Jim Dodd, a noted trapper and Winthrop, Washington entrepreneur, a man that trapped more because he loved those high mountains than one who needed an income. His ground was Sheep Mountain and would have bordered Frank's along the Ashnola River. There are still one or two of Dodd's cabins standing.

A Trapper is Kicked off the Train

Earl Erwin joined Jim Dodd for a short time in those years. Also, Charley C. Johnson was a Winthrop trapper and later a Forest Service employee who owned a restaurant for a while in the thirties, and then turned logger, whose trap-line would have bordered on the south of Frank's. Francis Lufkin was also a Winthrop trapper and Forest Service employee who trapped with Charley Johnson up Lake Creek and along the Chewack River, becoming somewhat famous for being one of the first smoke-jumpers in the U.S. George Dunkin trapped the North Fork of the Toats Coulee. His cabin was at the foot of Snowshoe Mountain and strangely, he too, like Frank Arnold went missing, after selling his winter fur catch. His line also would have bordered Frank's on the southeast side, and later this area was taken over by Johnny Bell.

George Bowers was a long-time mountain man living at 3,000 feet on Chapaka Mountain, above Chapaka Lake in a small cabin where he lived for years. An interesting story is told about this old man and shows how the mind can often twist things around for an old, lone, recluse. On year, the old man kept walking the ten very steep miles down off that mountain into the town of Loomis, just to buy a few more rifle shells for his gun.

"What the hell are you shooting at up there, George, that once a week you're coming to town and buying more rifle shells? You have a war going on up there? What the hell are you shooting at that you need so many shells?" asked Jack Richman of the Loomis General Store after George's third trip down in that many weeks.

"Those damned GHOSTS! — Those damned white ghosts keep coming by my cabin at night, Jack, and the only way I can keep them back is to shoot the hell out of them and scare them away!"

"Ok," said Jack, "I can understand that. You don't want "ghosts" around your place; no one does."

Jack now knew that the mountains had finally "cracked" the old mountain man. And after one more trip down off the mountain for more shells, Jack sent someone up to see what the old man was really shooting at. And wouldn't you know it! There were indeed white things behind his cabin — Dead White Mountain Goats lay "hither" and "thither" beyond his humble log cabin. At night, who could tell the difference, "ghost" or "goat?"

The list of trappers goes on: Frank E. Maron, mentioned previously, trapped with Frank Arnold for 2 years; Romeo Johnson and Clint Hanks worked the Hidden Lakes region together for years, but were on the C.C.C. job that winter of 1934/1935 when a supposed crazy-man named "Bud Shaffer" hit their cabin and stole their traps. Their cabin is the one called the Hidden Lakes cabin today, and it is still used by the Forest Service. These two trapped out of Winthrop, Washington, coming over the 7,000-foot Hart's Pass, dropping down into the Pasayten River at a 4,000-foot elevation. Their lines would have covered the Pasayten River drainage.

Joe Baker a pre-1900 trapper, ran a line up the Chewack River at least as far as the mouth of Cathedral Creek. He gave up the line only many years later, probably in the late teens or the early twenties. His cabin stood at the mouth of Tungsten Creek until the 1929 fire burnt it up. Johnny Bell was a well-known Loomisite who trapped the lower Toats Coulee, up the North Fork and over and around Snowshoe Mountain to the Canadian border. Like Jim Dodd, Johnny Bell trapped until he couldn't move his feet anymore, well into his eighties. He left a small, crawl-in-on-your-knees cabin on Corduroy Creek, and trapped from about 1920 until, about 1960 — forty or more years. His fur grounds bordered Arnold's on the east side.

To the north in Canada, there were at least three names that came up as Pasayten trappers. One, a man named Dennis, an Ashnola Native Indian, who trapped marten way into Easygoing Creek, a creek running west from the Ashnola River, to Trapper Lake. His family lives in Kerameos, British Columbia today. They have traded traps for cattle,

A Trapper is Kicked off the Train

but the cattle cover the same range. A relative of theirs, Art Hayword, also an American Indian, made his home in Oroville, south of the Canadian American border. Art was related not only to the Dennis's, but also to Bob Irwin, a life-time resident of Oroville, the Postmaster, as well as historian. Art Hayword trapped off his horse for as long as the snows would let him and then put on snowshoes. He went into the high Pasayten in the late 1920's and early 1930's to trap, but just where he found open fur ground is the question. It almost had to have been on the Canadian side, and if the dotted lines can be connected, he is one of the Canadian Indians in the winter of 1930-1931 who pushed Frank out of his northern fur grounds, as the other tribal Indians probably did as well.

There was also a Canadian trapper by the name of Armstrong who also worked the Ashnola River. All of these named and probably a few more including Joe Baker and Clyde Andrews, two of the very earliest trappers in the eastern half of the Pasayten. Clyde Andrews, the namesake of Andrew's Creek, was walking those mountains as early as the 1890's, maybe much earlier.

Barker and Brown were two men who were probably early trappers as well as miners in the area. They built a small miner's cabin on the open top of Sheep Mountain on the south, sunny side that was covered in the summer by a perfusion of wildflowers. Pat Carr, who we have mentioned before, was also in the same area. If Frank Arnold had a rival in the Pasayten, it was Pat Carr. For years and years, Pat stayed on a mining claim at the head waters of Eight-Mile Creek, some 30 miles from Winthrop.

Though the Pasayten was young in perspective, it must be remembered that by 1907, all the major mountains, creeks, and lakes had been given names, showing the mountains early use. Horseshoe Mt., Windy Mt., Remmel Mt., Cathedral Mt., Bauerman Mt. , Bald Mt., Billygoat Mt., Dollar Watch Mt., Black Lake, Corral Lake, Diamond

Creek, Eight-mile Creek, Lake Creek., Andrews Creek, Windy Creek, to name some of the geographical features that were all named and on a map by 1907, or before. The gold mining rush into Canada in the 1860's put all the passes through the northern mountains into use. The miners went up the Columbia River, then up the Methow River, up the Chewack River, and up Lake Creek drainage, over Ashnola Pass, north down the Ashnola River, down to the Similkmeen River, then up the Similkmeen River. The alternative was the Hart's Pass route to the high mining town of Barron. The miners travelled over the high 7,000-foot Hart's pass then downhill to the Pasayten River; but this trail had the advantage of going due north to the Canadian gold fields.

Harold MacWilliams, "Mac," a Winthrop packer at the time, ran into Frank more than once up in the high country. He was a Methow packer into the Pasayten from about 1929 to 1940. He lived out his life in Cle Elum.

"For you see, I packed into all those lookouts." Mac reported. "I supplied Dollar Watch Mountain, Monument #83, Dome Mountain, Bunker Hill, Point Defiance Mountain, and maybe one or two others. That reminds me of the time I packed in some 24-foot, 24-foot mind-you - 2 by 6's (some 20 to 30 miles in, to be sure) into one of the 'lookouts' for the Forest Service, and when I got them up there on top of that mountain, with much cussin' and swearin', tree cutting and straitening trail, on and off my horse hundreds of times all the way up that @#*% mountain, the dirty buggers that were building the lookout, sawed them in half right in front of me!

"I also met a big silver-tip coming down off Point Defiance in about 1934. A hell of a big grizzly he was, too! He must have been 1350 pounds, for he was bigger than any of my horses. He just stood there and looked at me. I pulled out my .38 caliber pistol, looked at the bear, looked at my gun, and put it back in the holster. He was much bigger than any of my horses and they were going crazy, so I let the pack horses

A Trapper is Kicked off the Train

stampede back up the trail, which got the big bear slowly moving on his way. Later, by a day or two, one of the Forest Service rangers walked up the trail and measured the track; it went 11 ½ inches. They had run a bunch of sheep up on the mountain and I figured he was following them," said Mac.

Mac remembered seeing Arnold all the way over on the Pasayten River.

"It was always interesting to run into the man," Mac said, "Quite a prospector he was, traveled all through that country. Ran into him a number of times on the trail. One time, I think it was at the Hidden Lakes, I was resting my horses when the trapper came walking up. Talked for a good while."

Mac was coming back from packing fish into the lake for the Fish and Game Department. "Wonderful man he was. Knew more about that country than the Forest Service did by a long shot.

It was on one of these meetings with Frank that young Mac was told of the two moose Frank had raised from young calves and had taught them to pull a wagon. Two moose domesticated to pull a wagon? Mac was truly impressed with this strange "Canadian" he found in the back woods of Washington. Frank Arnold was "a fascinating man," and spice to the new land he wandered.

CHAPTER 7

$275,000 for a Mine & $24,000 for a Ton of Tungsten

Many tales have been told about the rush for the tungsten, and many stories have been lost. The accounts that follow are based on fragments from many who were there, and taken from numerous newspaper accounts, verbal reports, and courthouse records. The long stories were told by Bob Curtis, Jim McDaniel, Harry Sherling, Doug Loudon, and the short stories were told by the late Paul Loudon.

TALES OF THE TUNGSTEN MINE

"Tungsten Mine Sold"

Oroville Gazette   **October 8, 1915**

"*Word has been received here that Herbert Curtis of Loomis has sold his Tungsten Mine property, located in the vastness of the mountains, some distance west of Loomis, to Seattle investors. No authentic word has been received as to the consideration in transfer, but it is hoped that Mr. Curtis has received sufficient to make him comfortable for life, as he has fairly earned a substantial reward for the hardships he has undergone…*"

Herb pocketed a thousand dollars and had a real deal this time. The best thing Herb and Billy McDaniel could have done was to go to the Spokane Fair and show off that 60 pounds of solid tungsten ore. The write-up in the Oroville Gazette was like a home-run hit, and the three claim holders quickly found out who had the money. Kaiser Wilhelm wanted Europe, and to get it he needed tungsten. The price of tungsten jumped to $4.00 a pound, which meant that just one of Herb's 60-pound bags of rocks, was worth $240 dollars, and he had them in number. A ton was worth $8,000.00. Indeed, the mine was a source of wealth, and Herb goes on to relate:

"Finally, I got Judge Albert Allen to come in to see the property. He took an option for $1,000.00 and brought in August Paulson and a German. He said he would take it — only it was winter, and he had to have it right away. This was the year before the war…"

Judge Allen knew a good thing when he saw it; Herb had wolframite laying all over the place. The Judge got excited and got out pen and paperwork; he wrote up a lease option on the property and gave Herb a handful of cash, $1,000, and a ten-thousand-dollar contract option. The judge leased it for enough time to find and bring in the right men with enough money to develop the hot, but far away mine.

$275,000 for a Mine & $24,000 for a Ton of Tungsten

The man he found was August Paulson, of the famous *Paulson Building* of Spokane. Paulson was already a mining man from the Coeur D' Alene, a silver man who had money enough from the rich mines of northern Idaho. He had contacts, and it didn't take him long from the time Judge Allen talked to him to run down a German mining man whom he knew would want a good tungsten mine - Baron von Alvensleben.

With the Baron rounding-up a few other west coast German investors, things started to jump. There was a lot of business going on over Herb's head, as the big boys promoted and shuffled the lease option Judge Allen had written up. All of 1914 and most of 1915 went by before a man named "Sylvester" from British Columbia finally got it all together. Herb said he "took over." (This part is not clear: Sylvester and a man named "Shouty" might not have come into the scene until the summer of 1916.)

Paulson stepped into the saddle of "Wildfire," Billy McDaniel's best horse. Von Alvensleben sat on another of Billy's better riding horses waiting, but Herb was already moving up the trail to the far distant Wolframite Mountain, 35 or 40 miles away to the west. Paulsen and Baron von Alvenslevben didn't like the rough horse ride into the mine, but they did like all the tungsten ore Herb had laying around. The rich wolframite was as good as gold to the German Baron, and it laid in a beautiful vein almost 5 feet wide. All they had to do was come up with enough money, machinery and men, and the tungsten would be theirs.

By this time, things had gotten awfully crazy on the world scene. All the countries of Europe were involved in a fight either with or against the German war machine. Germany had been cut off from most of its supplies of tungsten by the British, (and any other metal they could stop), but the United States was trying to keep a neutral stand and still had an open market with the Germans. Germany was paying a lot for all metals, but especially tungsten. Rumor was, and it was true, that if a person could get tungsten ore 60% into Germany, he could ask his own price in gold! There was never a better time in history to own a tungsten mine. In 1915, it was selling for $12.00 a pound, $240 a unit (20 lb.), a cool $24,000 a ton in U.S. dollars. The 60-lb. rock Herb showed off at the Spokane fair was worth a cool $600.00, probably equivalent to about $60,000.00 today.

The miners lost a few months of high prices, but by the end of 1915 August Paulson, J.R. Marshell, W.H. Rowe, Mr. Messier, and Baron von Alvensleben had it together. A new lease option was drawn up September 29, 1915, and Herb Curtis was handed just short by $40, a cool $200,000.00 - two hundred thousand cold cash. The local newspaper wrote it like this:

SOLD BIG TUNKSTEN MINE AT LOOMIS
Rowe & Marshell of Seattle Pay $100,000 for Property
Loomis, Wash., Oct 2, 1915:
Herbert Curtis who owns the Tunksten mine back in the Horseshoe Basin west of Loomis, has sold same to Messrs, Rowe, and Marshall. Mining men of Seattle for $100,000. Mr. Curtis has held and worked this property for ten years and has had it bonded several time for that sum, and from first to last, considerable work has been done on the property and it is demonstrated beyond all doubts that it is one of the largest and richest deposits of Tunksten ore in the United States. Mr. Curtis started yesterday with about a dozen men with provisions and supplies preparatory to starting work and working all winter. Owing to the war tunksten ores are very high and it is the intention of the gentlemen who have bought the property to work and extract ore just as fast as men and machinery can do it.

Just how the money was split up, that is, the amount going to Billy McDaniel and George Loudon, Herb's partners, is not really clear. It has always been a little shadowy and probably of some debate, but

$275,000 for a Mine & $24,000 for a Ton of Tungsten

the clear fact is, Herb Curtis was never a poor Loomisite again. If the October 2, 1915, newspaper report above can be speculated on, Herb took $100,000 for his share, and McDaniel and Loudon probably split the other $100,000. The *Option Agreement* is interesting and puts light on just what went on up there for the next few years. In Appendix I, their Option Agreement is reprinted in its entirety, so one can judge for himself. (To note, Jacob Kast was Herb's lawyer.)

Once the paperwork was signed, the action started. Speed was now the all-important word because winter was coming on, and a war was to be fought, but most important of all, tungsten ore was worth a staggering high price.

Herb expeditiously made a trip over to Spokane to oversee the loading of all the mining and milling machinery, the tons of supplies needed to sustain life 40 miles from life, in a mine tucked away in absolute remoteness. The supplies filled two train boxcars. The supply list was for sure, extensive; besides the heavy mining equipment, there was a commissary list that could outfit a small army, and that for years. All the menagerie of things that it takes to make up a town had to be toted into the mine and toted in quickly. Clothes, shirts, pants up to size 48 were on the list, as well as boots, rubber boots, blankets and bedding, socks and gloves, tobacco and pipes, brimmed hats and stocking hats. The list went on and on; nothing could be overlooked. Crushers, compressors, boilers, drills, hammers, jack hammers, horses' harnesses, picks, shovels, iron pipe, conveyors, nuts and bolts, dynamite, blasting caps and lighting fuses. It was said there was enough dynamite fuse to run from Loomis to the mine and back again. Ten thousand and one commodities had to go into those boxcars. The items needed to put the cook to work themselves must have made up tons of supplies. (Some wise man, probably Herb, foresaw the need for boxes and boxes of mouse traps. A few of the boxes were found years later, with dozens of traps still in working condition.) This was now "no small operation."

Eighty tons of supplies and equipment were stuffed into the train cars in Spokane and sent to the Nighthawk siding. The mad rush for the "black gold" was on!

J.R. Marshell was the man's name who would also see that it all got done in an "expeditious manner," and he was in Loomis long before the two boxcars showed up in Nighthawk. Marshell was the overseer and had a big investment in the project. He was back into the mine as early as October of 1915, putting a crew of men to work on a road and improving the living conditions at the mine. Marshell had also found a teamster to contract the hauling of the supplies from Nighthawk to Loomis: Frank Shell. But before Frank Shell could load his wagons, the rainy fall weather made them realize the need for tents. Three or four big tents, giant tents, such as a circus would have, were used to cover the goods. The tents were erected in Loomis, right where the church stands today. And when the boxcars arrived, Frank's wagons rolled steadily for weeks on end, bringing in the Nighthawk goods.

J.R. Marshell no sooner got Frank Shell going, than he contracted out to a freighter by the name of Joe Hall. Joe Hall would move the equipment and supplies into those steep, high western mountains, as far in as the men could beat out a road. Winter had already reached the high country, and Joe Hall had his work cut out for him. But, by the time the first heavy snows of winter hit, Frank Shell and Joe Hall had transported by wagon a few tons of goods as far as the Middle Fork of the Toats Coulee River. This was as far as a wagon could go. Marshell's new road, just up above, was being built as quickly as the men could move the dirt and clear the trees. In the meantime, a steady stream of goods went on past them, packed on the back of pack horses and headed across the tops of the mountains to the mine, 30 long miles of twisting trail away.

$275,000 for a Mine & $24,000 for a Ton of Tungsten

On the Middle Fork, 11 miles from town, was 160 acres of deeded land. It was homesteaded by Duncan James, a single man that wanted nothing more than to carve out his place on earth at 4,200 feet of elevation against a steep mountain with 200 miles of wilderness to his west. He built a small cabin on his claim in about 1912, and it was there that all the equipment was brought that October 1915. This could be called stage two of the big shuffle, and it was a good place for a stop, not because it was almost level, because it was not. Nor could it be said that the spot was the right distance from town. The fact was, it was the end of the road and there was a cabin there. The added fact that Duncan James was the best cook around certainly could not have hurt the cause for making it a stopping place. It was said Duncan James could put out a meal on an open campfire that would rival a French chef. They finally got him up at the mine in one of those years as chief cook. A man with such talent was appreciated. Tents were set up around his cabin, and all the equipment and supplies that arrived had to be wrapped, tarped and placed in tents. A hundred tons of supplies came by wagon up the Toats Coulee to Duncan James' front door that winter; it was truly a busy by-way.

Paul Loudon, Al Cerew, Joe Mills, Ed Renne, Ceciel Hutchins, and Happy Dunn were all used as horse packers from there on in. Like ants on the move, these horsemen kept a steady line of beasts-of-burden coming and going to the Tungsten. On one of those strings coming back out, Marshell got out a fine bunch of pure tungsten ore, Black Wolframite! They didn't take any chances with this commodity; it was put under armed guard in Loomis until it was well on its way out of town. This made all the people in Loomis see the light. They now understood just how badly some people in the world wanted this rock they called "Black-Jack," the stuff that had been called "coal" and laughed at 10 years before.

TALES OF THE TUNGSTEN MINE

The Hardest Winter Ever

The weather had surprisingly been in the miners' favor well into December. But nobody was prepared for one of the hardest winters to hit these mountains in many hundreds of years. Uncannily, the winter of 1915/1916 was the year of the "Big Snow." The snow started in late December — 5 feet — then 9 feet by January — 14 feet in February, and finally, in March, by the time it was all said and done, 20 feet of snow had piled up on the cabin roof at the Tungsten Mine. No one could believe it. This was also the winter of the big kill-off. Hundreds of deer and sheep sadly got caught in the mountain draws, and it looked like the bone yard of a slaughterhouse the next spring when Joe Hall brought in his young nephews, the Dietzel boys from Oroville, into the mine for a look-see. It was a scene of carnage the boys would never forget. Deer on top of deer on top of deer filling up the draws. Some of the bloated carcasses were that of big-horned sheep that, the year before, ran over the high mountains in the hundreds. It would be 20 years before the deer population would make a comeback, but the wild sheep herds never would, not in their former numbers. Not as Clyde Andrews saw them anyway. Clyde said he saw huge herds of wild sheep, up to 400 in number, on Windy Mountain alone before that winter of 1915/1916. Emmet Smith, the sheepherder, said: "There were almost no deer in 1918. I saw my first deer in 1922 after spending four summers in the Horseshoe Basin." And Paul Loudon spoke of 30-foot snow drifts on the mountain tops that winter; snow that made the perfect deer trap.

Joe Hall stopped at the fork of the South and North Creek junction of the Toats Coulee at the foot of a steep mountain slope. He unbuckled

$275,000 for a Mine & $24,000 for a Ton of Tungsten

the four-horse team from one of his wagons. With reins in his hands, he pulled the team to the front of the wagon driven by his wife, Rosey. She helped him pull the big team in place. "Back! Back boys! Back!" Rosey and Joe worked the two teams together. With cross trees, tugs, and reins sorted out, Rosey put her cat on the wagon seat besides Joe, then went over and climbed on the back of the left lead "pull" horse. "Head-em-up boys!" Joe hollered as he cracked the reins over the backs of his eight big black Percheron crosses. The big horses jumped into action as Rosey kicked the black she was riding in the flanks. The calico cat sunk his claws into the seat besides Joe and the 4,000 pounds of machinery started to pull the 45% bank that loomed before them. For

twenty minutes Joe Hall stood in the wagon and hollered, shouted, and screamed out of fear and necessity to keep his big team moving. Their big muscles bulging, the horses strained and blew and coughed in the dirt and dust that flew high in the air from the hooves of his bolting, snorting and staggering black team. They fought to keep their feet under them as the leather collars dug deep into their shoulders. Rosey sounded like a bullhorn as she shouted, slapped and kicked the rump of her powerful Percheron, trying to keep him lined out straight, and pointed up. The wagon wheels bounced, jumped, and then sank into the loose sand. Four thousand pounds of freight moved up the mountain in a cloud of dust, sweat, and fear. The big team never turned because of Rosey's kicking and pulling on the leaders, demanding that they go just one way - up! And none too soon, Rosey, Joe, eight big black horses, and one little calico cat found themselves on a bench of land above the forks of the Toats Coulee River. Joe set the brake on the wagon and stepped off and pulled the pin that held the sweating horses to the two tons of wagon. Rosey picked up the feed bags and put a load of grain in each one of the horses. An hour or so later, Rosey and Joe had eight big black Percherons and one calico cat back down the steep mountain and the horses hooked-up again, to another two tons of four wheels and dead weight.

The big sandy hill at the forks of the Toats Coulee River was one of the worst pulls on the trail into the Tungsten Mine. It was long, steep and sandy, but by no means the only mountain on the 40-mile stretch. It seemed that it was all mountain! Time and again Joe had to hitch teams of horses together to pull the mountain grade. However, Duncan James' cabin was the end of the road that fall. But in the next year, 1916, wagons pulled as far as "Wagon Camp," and as far as Rock and then Haig Mountain later that year.

If Loomis was stage one, and Duncan James cabin was stage two, then Wagon Camp was stage three of the big shuffle. Today, we call it the Old Iron Gate, about 6 miles on up from James cabin door, and again it was a "hellish" steep pull to get there. Just down on the ridge from Iron Gate, off the Deer Park Trail, is a small clearing that still shows where Joe Hall, the foreman Marshell, Paul Loudon, and a dozen other men set up big tents for bunking, cooking, and covering the tons of supplies and horses that landed there that winter. And what was too big for a horse to pack in on its back would wait for a winter sled ride. Old timers said it was Paul Loudon who spearheaded the coming of a great snow road that ran for 30 miles. And for Paul Loudon of Oroville, a more difficult winter could not have been chosen for the robust young man to challenge. But Paulson and Baron von Alvensleben couldn't sit on $24,000.00, a ton of tungsten. Spring was too far away, and snow could not be a deterrent to this operation. The pay was accordingly high. So Paul Loudon with his team of horses and crew of men embarked from Duncan James cabin to make a passable snow trail over the last 6 miles and another 1,500 feet of elevation to a pass that would put them in a big open basin, and 15 miles from the Tungsten Mine.

$275,000 for a Mine & $24,000 for a Ton of Tungsten

❦❦❦❦❦❦❦

Herb Curtis stood at the entrance of the cookhouse tent. He looked at the thermometer nailed to a post. It said six degrees above zero. It had been a productive fall at the mine. Herb and Johnny Bell with a crew of men had managed to set up a commissary building, a blacksmith shop, a couple of small log cabins and added onto their original bunk house. Now, the snow was coming down heavy and in big flakes. Paul Loudon and his crew of men were somewhere out there on snowshoes tromping down snow and dragging a heavy drag-float behind them, making a roadbed that had to hold up horses and tons of freight. Herb had snowshoed out from the mine that day to make a mail run.

A new superintendent, a man by the name of Harold Savage, had driven in none too soon with two teams of beautiful, matched mules from Cour D'Alene in Idaho. He had also found five Yukon sleds, 3 feet wide and 7 feet long, to use on the new snow road — for this road was not for wheels. Savage came over and looked out at the falling snow from the big tents at Wagon Camp.

"I don't think this is going to be one of your easy and mild winters I've heard so much about, Herb," he said.

Herb started rattling on about only 3 1/2 feet of snow last year, snow that didn't fall till the end of January. Harold just laughed and walked back over to the red hot stove that stood in the middle of the tent, pumping out heat. He was already looking at 3 feet of snow on the ground.

The snows fell from the heavens like a huge white wall, and once the snows started, they wouldn't quit. How deep was it? Well Paul Loudon simply walked over and nailed a sign to a tree where the trail cut across Daisy Creek. Some years later, the 6-foot-2-inch Emmet Smith, standing on top of his saddle horse and saddle could just barely read it, stretched out at his tallest. It said: "March 10, 1916, 10 feet of snow. Making last trip with hay. Four eight-horse teams, 10,000 pounds each."

So, from Nighthawk to Loomis, stage #1: 10 miles. From Loomis to Duncan James homestead, stage #2: 11 miles. From Duncan James cabin to "Wagon Camp," today's "Iron Gate," stage #3: 8 miles. And then on to stage #4, which would be their last hard pull and put them on the back side of Rock Mountain at the northwest side of Horseshoe Basin. It became known as "Tungsten Camp:" 9 miles. At Tungsten Camp there was a log cabin that came in handy for the travelers going to and from the mine. It was from here that the snow road crew hammered out 7 more tough miles of road, adding one more camp called "Big Horn Camp," stage #5: 7 miles. This last camp lay right below Bauerman Ridge at the foot of Teapot Dome. From here, the snow-road turned north and took a precarious route around the northern side of the big mountain called Bauerman Ridge. Then the snow road went past the "Mailbox Camp," now called "Sheelite Pass," and then finally crossed the last 2 miles to the Tungsten Mine, 7 miles from the Big Horn Camp, and over 50 hard miles from Nighthawk, the start of the process.

Tents again were erected to protect the supplies and workers. The fine team of mules from Coeur D' Alene made a striking picture, dancing in tandem over the new snow road as their driver sat on the load of supplies bundled up in his winter garb. The high, white pointed peaks in the background stood guard over this winter wonderland. If there was a good part about this venture, it was the beauty of the high mountains covered in a blanket of white, rolling snow. The worst part was six cold months of terrible hardship. Five hundred pounds to five tons would be loaded on the Yukon sleds and pulled to a new tent camp. Here is how Paul Loudon described the long, difficult winter job:

"Here's what was put aboard the horse-drawn sleighs: six steam engines, an electric light plant, a complete sawmill, a complete ore mill,

$275,000 for a Mine & $24,000 for a Ton of Tungsten

a giant old range which, with its complement of pots and pans, weighed 1,800 pounds, a complete camp for the packers, a four-month supply of food for them, and hay and grain for the horses.

Two dozen men would build roads — digging a swath in the deep snows or falling trees and boughs for a roadbed. In steep winding country, they fashioned a remarkable road along hillsides, riprapping the road fills with snow and timbers and underbrush. The party would stop and set up a complete camp. The road party the next day would move out to build perhaps 4 miles of road. Then the caravan, with horses in tandem pulling the sleigh, would push on until they ran out of road. Then another camp, another stretch of road.

That turned out to be one of the worst winters we've ever had around here."

As many as eight horses were hooked, one in front of the other to pull the heavy loads over this steep winding grade. It was a dangerous undertaking, calling for alert drivers. Paul Loudon once described the impossible situation that horses, men and mules could get into when a sled or horse would step or slide off into the unpacked snow. Thinking about eight horses in 20 feet of snow — it would literally bury all — animals, men, and the sled under hundreds of pounds of powder snow. The horses would flounder hopelessly until they became so tangled in the rigging and snow they couldn't move. Then it would take hours to dig out the sled, horses, and supplies from the white grave that held them trapped. More than one horse stumbled off the new snow road or busted through the packed snow that made up the hard surface of the road to flounder for their lives. Much snow and ice had to be thawed and then poured onto the road to harden into ice to fill the bad spots. Many were the trees that were cut off 15 feet in the air, but level with the snow, to make an unobstructed straight road.

The stage camps looked like small winter tent cities, 6 to 9 miles apart. One of the tents was always set aside and filled with tons of hay and oats for the horses. Paul Loudon said his horses actually came out in better condition in the spring than when they went in that winter. Another big tent at the camp held the cooking and mess hall. Yet another held the sleeping quarters for the men, and three more held the tons of mining supplies all wrapped nicely and tarped and safe from the winter weather.

The snow road, the freighting, the snow 20 feet deep, the short winter days of freezing cold, the determined, hard working men that were there to perform this feat, all were not be forgotten or repeated again. Somewhere between 70 and 300 tons of supplies were freighted into the mine over that narrow, slippery, icy trail called a road. There were horses and mules hurt and lost. There were frostbitten hands and frozen feet and too many ice-burned eyes and faces to count. There were sleepless, bitter cold nights that winter of 1915/1916 suffered by the men sent in to make a mine. Though Herb made it sound easy:

"I think it was the fall of 1915 we started the mine and they built a snow road to haul in seventy or a hundred tons of material. (*Paul Loudon said 300 tons) In the fall of 1915, we went in and in October built a bunkhouse, cellar, and blacksmith house. It was during this winter that I broke up rock and there was a lot of tungsten in it. I sacked it, also. I think there was about ten sacks of awful rich tungsten and among the first sleds that came in, we shipped the ore. Never did hear what it was worth. We worked the mine by hand, and with homemade wheelbarrows..."

Such was the mad push for tungsten when the Germans would pay anything for 60% pure.

$275,000 for a Mine & $24,000 for a Ton of Tungsten

Chapter 7 Notes

Loomis Notes from the Oroville Gazette

Senator C.E. Myers, Sam Griswold, Dick Phillips, Dr. Good, and A.J. Pretty John of Davenport are in the hills west of Loomis in quest of big game. So far, they met with poor success, not having bagged a single deer... October 21, 1915.

It has been raining here steadily for three or four days; our road supervisor is preparing to get out and drag the roads in his district and get them in shape for fall and winter. The roads are fearfully cut up all over the county and if they are harrowed or dragged after this rain, they will be in fine shape all fall... October 21, 1915.

Henry Bahrs, a mining man of Golden, was in town today shaking hands with his many acquaintances here... October 21, 1915.

Cecil White, Lon and ?.F. Gadberry and George Burge, who have been working on the government trail back in the Horse Shoe basin for some time came in last evening. They reported considerable snow back there... October 21, 1915.

Mr. Marshall, the gentleman who bought the Tunksten mine of Herb Curtis, has a string of fifty pack horses taking in provisions and supplies to his mine and bringing out ore. It is reported that the mine is showing up well and they expect to pack and rewhiddle out ore all winter... October 21, 1915.

Mr. Marshall, the man who purchased the Tungsten Mine, (editor finally learned how to spell tunksten - tungsten) has returned from Seattle and has a force of men surveying a road to the mine... January 7, 1916.

TALES OF THE TUNGSTEN MINE

Herb Curtis, one of the owners of the Tungsten Mine, came in Friday from the mine and in company of his brother, left for Chopaka Saturday morning... January 14, 1916.

J.R. Marshall, superintendent of the Tungsten Mine, has gone to the mine for the purpose of taking immediate charge of the construction of the mill... April 14, 1916.

Manager Marshall is working some 60 men at the Tungsten Mine. A ton of ore has been delivered at Loomis and there are two or three tons at the mine to be freighted out. The ore in the tunnel is looking better than at any time since the mine was opened... May 12, 1916.

CHAPTER 8

A Frozen Foot and an Infected Eye

This is a hunting story based on a true account told by Jay Hill and Loy McDaniel with the hunters telling about Frank Arnold passing out in the creek and freezing his foot and hurting his eye. Herb Curtis told the story of Frank hearing the blasting on Windy Mountain and coming into the Tungsten Mine in late November with "a badly infected eye, and a frozen foot." Bob Curtis and Harry Sherling painted a picture of life at the Tungsten Mine that Year, and they spoke of Frank "living on a sack of flour and a bear" before coming to the mine in 1915.

"WHOA. YOU WORTHLESS NAG!" THE cowboy hollered as he pulled back on the reigns of his horse. "This is as far as we want to go. Looks like a good place to camp to me. What about you, Chuck? Ah, what do you know about camping? You can't even tell what end of that gun the bullet comes out of."

"Fred, you just keep it up; but $5.00 says I have my six-point buck hanging in that tree over there before you, before you even roll out of that sleeping bag tomorrow, you saddle-bum," Chuck answered as he swung off his horse.

"I may be a saddle-bum, but you'll never live long enough to beat me when it comes to hunting! My mother fed me on gunpowder and lead when you were drinking milk," said the cowboy, Fred.

"You both lie like the water in the Deep Blue Sea, but I'm tired of sitting on this four-legged, long eared excuse for a horse you gave me. Let's make camp and eat something," said the third hunter, Ted.

The three hunters were in Long Swamp, on the edge of the Pasayten Wilderness. The time was fall 1915. The tent was soon up, the horses hobbled, and the fire crackled as supper was on, and the light of day faded into darkness.

"You boys aren't going to shoot all my deer, are you?" came a deep voice out in the darkness.

Fred, leaning over the fire cooking, jumped like a scared fawn at the new voice that came from nowhere, spilling the potatoes into the fire at the same time. A hissing steam sputtered from the hot coals. Chuck, just as startled, jumped up in surprise, spilling his coffee on himself. Ted reached for his gun as if there might be an Indian raid.

"Where the hell did you come from, mister?" Fred asked the stranger that came walking out of the darkness in a surprised voice. "I didn't think there was another person within 20 miles of here!"

"Name's Frank Arnold. I live right up the hill a little way. Heard you laughing about an hour ago."

"Hell, yes! I heard of you, 'Frank Arnold!' I work for Woodard down in Loomis. I heard you lived up here somewhere! Glad you came over. You're Just in time for the best dinner you could ever eat! Of course, Chuck here, he's no judge. And well,...Ted, he wouldn't know good cooking from dog food, but set down and have a drink!"

"Ted. Chuck. Frank here's the best shot this side of the Atlantic Coast. Can shoot the eye out of a gnat at 1000 yards, if he can at two.

A Frozen Foot and an Infected Eye

Damn rights, I'm not lying and I'm not dying! Frank here was shooting his gun one day at the Woodard place last summer and shot three black birds right out of the air in three shots! And that's not all! He kept a tin beer can spinning in the air for five minutes or more! I'm not lying either. No kidding, Ted!" Fred looked Frank in the eye and bragged up the new man at the fire.

And so, the night got started. The hunters were well supplied with firewater and stories of interesting things that happened long ago. Hours spun out, the night wore on, the whiskey bottle-cap was thrown to the wind. Frank told them of deer and bear, caribou and Canada. He kept them spellbound for hours with his mountain stories, and the boys talked of girls, guns, and getting the big one.

"Well, just where in the hell do you come from, Frank?" asked Ted as he poured the last of the second bottle of whiskey into Frank's glass.

"Well, you go walking... just keep walking over that mountain until you come to saltwater, and... until..." Frank, suddenly got up and staggered away from the fire, into the black of the night!

"Now where in the billy-hell is…is he going in the middle of his s-story?" slurred Fred, as he looked at his empty bottle of whiskey. The boys waited. They waited some more, but Frank didn't come back.

"Guess the guy went home. It's getting way too, too, too cold for me anyways. I think I am going to find a warm blanket and get some sheep, too."

The next day, the sun hadn't broken over the mountain yet when Ted kicked the heavy frost off the frying pan. His throat was as dry as desert sand, and worse yet, he felt like he had been dragged through a knot hole!

"Sure as hell got cold last night!" he griped.

The fire slowly started from the cold ashes. He dumped a solid block of ice from the water bucket.

"Get up, you saddle bums, there's a big buck out here with ten points on one side and one on the other! Get up or I'll warm you up with this block of ice from the water bucket. Buck—shoot! Look who's coming down the creek! It's Frank Arnold! Hell boys, and he's hobbling on a broken leg... from the looks of it!" Frank stumbled into the hunter's camp and pulled up next to the fire.

"I didn't do my foot any good last night," he said as his shaking hands pulled off his boot and sock. "I passed out next to the creek last night, and I'll be damned if it doesn't look like my foot got in the water and froze!" Ted looked at the tops of Frank's black toes.

"You sure as hell did. Frank." Chuck said as he pulled on his coat and walked out of the tent and over to the fire, looking at the dark red foot with black toes, all swollen to nearly double their normal size. "Hell, Frank, don't fry it in the fire now." He pushed the foot away from the edge of the flame with his knee.

"Ted, get some water warmed up. Here Frank, rub the black things in your hands, don't fry them. Looks like you hurt your eye, too." Frank's eye poured water down his check. The left side of Frank's face was bloody and swollen.

"Yes, I did. I must have poked it on a tree, but it will be alright," Frank said confidently. But the cowboys knew otherwise. And, when the hunters pulled out of Long Swamp, they had three big deer and no whiskey, and Frank had a badly frozen foot and a swollen, injured eye he couldn't see out of. He could barely hobble up to his small cabin, quarter mile away, with his over-sized foot. Frank's black and blue foot was a lot worse than he thought. There was pain, pain, and more pain. Added to that, he was stuck in the mountains, not even being able to hunt to get in his needed winter deer supply. He was cabin bound. His trapping season was ruined. The early mountain winter was too soon upon him, and he was forced to eat flour and bannock, bannock, and more bannock, slowly starving on the poor rations. Frank was in a world of hurt, and he knew it for sure now. His foot and eye were not getting any better and were maybe getting worse. He was not only out of all food but flour, but out of grease to cook his water-cakes with. Life was now again, hanging on the edge for Frank. And this called for some extra desperate effort and mountain skill as he forced himself under heart-stopping pain and suffering to do a little hunting around his cabin. Using every skill, he possessed, Frank felled that little fat bear that came nosing by his camp on those black quiet nights. From then on, for a month and a half, Frank "lived on a sack of flour and a bear."

Frank Arnold's Old Home in Long Swamp

After 6 weeks and still suffering from the effects of that rough night in Long Swamp, with 2 feet of snow on the ground, the Frank started snowshoeing slowly about. One day he was on the open top of a west ridge on Windy Mountain, when a clear "Boom. Boom." caught his attention. The second boom rang out a second later than the first.

That's not too far away, Frank thought. *Those hunters did say something about the Tungsten Mine opening up. Better make a go and see what's going on over there.*

It was the first of December 1915, when Frank Arnold came hobbling into the Tungsten Mine with a badly frozen foot and an infected eye. The miners were flat-out taken back at Frank's troubled and sorry condition. His foot was still swollen and badly damaged by the freeze. His eye was not at all pretty to look at, either. It was red, closed, and infected.

"Frank, you should have walked the other way weeks ago. You've gotta see a doctor and now!"

"Well, you're right, I know, but I usually heal up quickly and can take care of myself."

"Ya, but not this time. We're putting you on a sled and you're going to Loomis, pronto!"

So, that is what they did. The first sled to arrive had Frank on it going back out to Loomis.

The horses moved quickly down the mountain into town. The Loomis doctor soon had the sorry trapper patched up and on his way again with a school kid's scolding. After a few days in town, catching up on the latest news and visiting friends, Frank caught a ride back up the mountain to the busy Tungsten Mine. Since trapping was out of the question for him, he thought he could make himself useful around the new mine. At the least, their food supply was much better than his.

His First Moonshine Still

It was soon the end of December, and Herb, his brother Frank, Bill Lightner, Melsure, and all the rest of the fifteen or so miners at the Tungsten Mine, were quitting the mountain and heading to town for the holidays,

"Frank! Take care of the place and think about us once in a while; we'll be back in a week," the miners yelled.

The boys went on home for their short break, and Frank had the run of the place. He was all by himself. Like a kid turned loose in a candy store without a person around, he realized he was in hog heaven. With just a little English ingenuity and some free-wheeling talent, he could put his time to good use. First he lined out a big pot and filled it with all the dried fruit he could find. Next came 20 pounds of sugar, backed up with some water and flour. He rounded it all out by going down to the horse barn, digging up some oats and slapping the oats into the big pot. He next threw in a whole lot of yeast. With that done, he worked up a copper condenser coil with some copper pipe that didn't have a good use, screwed the lid on the big pot down nice and tight, lit the fire that was under the whole conglomeration, and then stood back admiringly, watching the fire crackle under the big pot of mush. Just as sure as little stars sigh at night, Frank had himself the best little

A Frozen Foot and an Infected Eye

moonshine still that anyone could make in a day and a half. Frank sat up there on the mountain that Christmas and had his own celebration.

When the boys came back in a matter of days, Frank was found "three sheets to the wind" and "feeling no pain in foot or eye." It absolutely amazed Herb how Frank could have thrown together a still from nothing, and then gotten the booze to ferment so quickly. But they couldn't use his obviously working still, because Marshall allowed no drinking. Frank could only clownishly look on as the men dismantled his neat little factory throwing out his alcoholic brew.

Frank's adventure put him in line for an unexpected job. The miners had a lot of good men at the mine, but the one thing they didn't have that winter was a cook.

"Well, Frank, if you can keep from burning the hot-cakes, you got yourself a job cooking in this camp."

Frank, knowing his trapping season was off, took the job at the mine that winter.

"He sure wasn't the best cook in the world, but then he wasn't the worst, either," Herb said years later. He put the food on the table. The miners ate it and lived to talk about it.

Many a lonely winter night, the fire crackled in the stove on that snow-clad 8,000-foot mountain, as a small handful of miners sat around killing the wintertime because there was little they could do in such a harsh environment. A few hours of work a day was all they could handle. A stove oil lantern sat on the table and gave but dim light over the cards that would fall to the greasy wood table. Candles flickered in the breezy cabin over another game played, the game of chess. The two combatants at the board on this night had been playing for two hours and there were still a lot of pieces being shuffled around. The two chess players were Herb Curtis and Frank Arnold. If a man could beat the Englishman at a game of chess, he was an exception. It was all Herb could do to whip the man, and he was not able to do it often.

The poker players kept after Frank to sit down and play a hand or two. And after beating Herb in too many games of chess, poker became the only other game to play on the long winter nights at the Tungsten.

"Ok, I'll sit in for a while," Frank said after dodging the card games for weeks.

The boys' eyes looked like silver dollars as Frank put a new meaning into shuffling a deck of cards. The cards came to life and seemed to dance in his hands as he put them in order.

"Hell, Frank, I'm not so sure we want you to play after all!" one of the boys said to the sore-footed trapper.

It was really no contest, but he made the game last two or three hours.

"Gal-dang-it, Frank! Where did you learn to run a deck of cards like that? You sure you're not from Monte Carlo?"

Frank just smiled as the coins piled up on his side. He wasn't asked to play much after that, and Frank's legend continued to progress, along with the mystery of his distant past.

If Frank Arnold was just another grubby trapper, certainly his conversation gave no clue, for he was noticeably intelligent to talk to. "He was schooled," they all said, but he didn't care much for long conversations, and yet was often caught talking to himself. He had been alone for so long before coming to the Tungsten that he found himself his own best company. Still, Herb and Frank Arnold spent many a long night playing cribbage, chess, checkers, and a game or two of poker. They ate together, slept together, smoked together and worked together. No drinking was allowed at the mine, so they didn't do much drinking together. The men got to know Frank well, but they didn't get to know him that well. His trapping on the Flathead River, at its headwaters in Montana, was all the further back Frank's stories got.

"He had to have been there," Herb used to say, "because I was there, too, and we would talk about the same places where we had both been."

A Frozen Foot and an Infected Eye

The men being gentlemen of the west, with their code of ethics, didn't pry into a man's past. You just didn't do it in 1915. Yes, Arnold was different and unusual; he walked to his own drummer and nobody did the things he did.

One time, Herb's pipe lost its fire and it was time to repack it with some fresh tobacco. Herb dug out his pocketknife and scraped out the bowl of his pipe.

"Yo, Yo-o Herb... don't throw out that spent tobacco!" Frank said, as he hustled over to Herb with his hand out. "Here, give that to me."

Herb stood there a minute looking questionably at the Englishman. He shrugged his shoulders and palmed the spent tobacco over to Frank. "What the hell ya want that for?"

"It's Good for you," Frank said as he dropped the spent, black, dry, charcoal tobacco into his mouth.

"Why you crazy fool, Frank! That stuff is put in your mouth before it's burnt, not after... just in case you didn't know it!"

"It's better this way, Herb," Frank replied as he turned and walked away.

"Now there's a first," Herb said as he refilled his pipe, struck a match, and took a pull, filling the room with smoke. "Frank, you had better give up tobacco or we will have to pack you out of here again!"

If sucking on spent pipe tobacco sounds lip puckering, try a bit of strychnine. Herb Curtis was not the only one that talked about seeing Frank masterfully avoid death by taking a wee bit of the strychnine, a deadly poison. Loy McDaniel and Frank Maron had seen Frank often take a wisp of the stuff. All the trappers used it, mainly to kill coyotes and wolves, for it was a deadly poison; however, strychnine, taken in very small quantities, like tenths-of-a-milligram, can have a medical benefit. And Frank, the town doctor, and a few crazy bartenders knew that strychnine could be used as a great stimulant.

"What are you doing now, Frank?" Herb said as he watched the trapper dig out some white powder from a small vial with his knife and tap it all back in again.

"Medicine," he said.

"Medicine? What's wrong with you?" Herb asked.

"Just gets everything working good again," was his answer as Herb watched Frank tap all but the tiniest bit of white dust off his narrow-bladed knife.

"There's nothing on the knife," Herb growled, as Frank put the blade under his tongue.

"Doesn't take much!" Frank mumbled back.

"Hell, it doesn't take any!" charge Herb. "What is that medicine?"

"Strychnine," Frank replied dryly, as he turned and walked away. Herb's mouth dropped open and his ears started wiggling.

By the spring of 1916, the Tungsten Mine was in high gear; somewhere around twenty or more men were crawling over the south side of Wolframite Mountain, and more would come. The mine had found a new cook too, so Frank became the "roust-about," a handyman. He still helped the cooks, and he piled firewood. He ran messages to the various men as needed, and he was there to help the packers load and unload their horses. He might have butchered the chickens and turkeys or helped out in the commissary. He worked in the blacksmith shop, and we know he got in a fight with Johnny Bell, probably over at the charcoal pit. All the men could get time off from Harold Savage to go hunting. Those like Frank, who had guns, would hunt often. Big deer, sheep and goats ran wild in those early years at the mine. It is said that

A Frozen Foot and an Infected Eye

Bauerman Ridge was a "blanket of ptarmigan." Not tens, not hundreds, but thousands blanketed the tops of the peaks in 1916. Even Frank, handicapped with a bad foot, was in his element when he hunted for camp meat. Frank brought in deer, sheep, goats, bear and birds. He was a hunter and steady worker, not expecting much from anyone. He never did want to work in the diggings themselves and was content just being a helper with a sore foot. Chickens and turkeys were brought in live and kept in cages. The beef was brought in by way of Canada and the Ashnola River. Along with the beef came vegetables and fruit grown in Keremeos, British Columbia.

The men at the mine ate well — really well. One cook came out of Arizona and was only a young man, but a "hell of a good cook," they said. There was always a string of pack horses coming through with a load of food and supplies; at times there were more pack horses tied up to the hitching rails, trees and in the corral than men at the mine. It was a vigorous and busy place full of hard working, active men with a job to do, a job accomplished with strong men, tough horses, and plenty of money. Though only the farsighted knew it, it was the closing of an era, and few, if any mines would ever be developed in the same way again. The scene played out that summer in 1916 would echo off the mountains of the High Country for years and years to come.

By fall of the year, Frank Arnold had moved out of a tent and into a cabin of his own, possibly Joe Bazano's or one of the others who had lost a worker. The move was alright with the boys he bunked with, "cause old Frank was talkin all the time to himself."

"He'd just start telling himself a hunting story about a bear he killed or a big cat he caught or something on that order. A good storyteller, except he told them all to himself! You would ask him what he was talking about, or what he had said, and he paid no attention to you until he had finished his story. Then when he was done, he would ask what you had wanted," said Harry Sherling about his three months in the same tent with Frank.

Harry felt that after Frank had been around the mine for a while, he tired of the life and just kept to himself as the year of 1916 rolled by. Harry just didn't see much of him. He was around, but not very often, then again, he said that Frank did work nights also for a while.

Harry Sherling, the youngest man at the Tungsten Mine, landed the job of working a team of fine horses that were skidding in logs for the sawmill. The skid trail went right by the bunkhouse Frank was trying to sleep in. The hollering at the horses and the banging of the logs would wake poor Frank from a sound sleep. He never complained to young Harry but mentioned it to his bunkmates. This might have contributed to his moving to another bunkhouse. And in summing up his dealings with Frank, Harry had nothing but good to say about this mild-mannered man who chose to live in the mountains. Harry, from that time on, always had an interest in the man.

But if Frank was mild and friendly, it was not to be taken for a weakness. Frank was made of steel and stone and he had no use for unjust treatment. Sometime in 1916, or perhaps in the years after, Frank had a big "set-to" with Johnny Bell. It wasn't clear what it was all about, but whatever happened, Frank came out of it with a deep dislike for the man, and Johnny got himself fired over the blow up. The "set-to" was no petty argument, the 5-foot-9-inch Englishman could get mad, and Johnny must have done him wrong.

By the first of December of 1916, the cold winter had again put the clamps on Wolframite Mountain. They couldn't keep the boilers running and had to shut the works down. A skeleton crew worked until the last of December and then Frank Arnold was left again to take care of the mine. "Watch the place Frank, and no moonshine this year! We'll see you in a week or two," Herb Curtis said and the miners pulled out for the holidays, again, on yet another year.

A Frozen Foot and an Infected Eye

CHAPTER 9

The Great Era of the Tungsten Mine

Based on many newspaper articles and accounts by Bob Curtis, Harry Sherling, Billy Cohens, Paul Loudon, Jim Glanders, and Ann Briley's stories.

IT WAS THE FIRST OF June 1916. The snow lay in big piles around the Tungsten Mine. Road crews were busy working on the lower portion of the snow free road, 29 miles away above the Duncan James homestead and the upper snow road was still packed tightly over the high mountains and would remain so through much of the summer. The horses that packed in the equipment, over both the dirt road and the snow road, were bringing out the rich ore that Herb Curtis, Frank Curtis, Bill Lightner, Meisner, and the rest of the coal miners had mined, chipped off the quartz, and sacked-up that winter. Al Cerew, a packer who later moved over into the Methow Valley, often talked about the rich tungsten ore brought out that summer, "Chunks of tungsten (wolframite} as big as a man's head," said Al Cerew to George Honey years later.

TALES OF THE TUNGSTEN MINE

J.R. Marshall put the hard-working Herb Curtis on the ore mill to work with Abby Jorgenson and the other millwrights. The men had dug down through the snow in early April to put in the foundation for the ore mill and sawmill that laid in pieces at the door of the cabins on the south side of Wolframite Mountain. Marshall and Savage had a hundred tons of supplies and equipment to put to use as the snow melted away in the spring sun. Every time J.R. Marshall came out to town, he hired more men: carpenters, plumbers, miners, millwrights, and general laborers. By the end of June, Marshall had a good sixty men at the mine. All had picks, hammers, saws, wrenches, shovels, jacks, axes, and frying pans in their hands. Harry Sherling of Oroville said in July when he came in that altogether eighty men worked that year, including the packers. He counted them. They had constructed a much larger cookhouse that measured 30 feet long by 12 feet wide. It had a raised roof over the stove to pull the heat out in the summer and let in the light through the long deep snows of winter. Six feet of snow was all too common in those early years, but this year had been the amazing exception — over 15 feet of snow fell.

The first on the list of most important items needed was the boiler. The Tungsten mine would have three (if not four), before they got it right. No modern mill could run without a boiler because it made steam, and steam made all sorts of good things run. The boiler was the heart of the whole mine. The men in the hole needed steam to run their compressors and therefore their drills. The sawmill and ore mill needed steam to run the steam engines that cut the lumber and crushed the rock. Everything ran on steam. Steam is made by two things: water and fire.

The first boiler sat right above the sawmill, not far from the cabins. It seemed, to their frustration, that no matter how much wood the miners could throw under the tank, they just could not keep the cold mountain water steaming. With the sawmill soon going, and the air compressors sucking up the H2-0 gas, the little boiler just could not cut it. A new one was eventually brought in and set up about the same time the ore mill started going strong. The new boiler looked real good setting there, but the problem that soon materialized was the fact that both boilers took all the water in the little stream east of the cabin. There just wasn't enough water to keep both water eaters producing to anywhere near their full potential. It didn't really matter much, because no matter how fast they threw wood under the two tanks, the 7,000-foot-high elevation was against them, and the water (when they did have enough} was difficult to bring to a boil.

It didn't help matters, either, when Harold Savage's son got all " wipped-up" one night on some Canadian whiskey and decided he needed to see if his .45 caliber Colt still worked. Slam! Slam! Slam! Blam! The gun went, as the tipsy young Savage took aim with his "shooting-iron." Water poured through the first little boiler like a cook's sieve.

"Wasn't any good anyway!" he cried out the next day, trying to reason with Marshall and his dad as they chased him around the leaking, lead-filled tank.

J.R Marshall had one more option left to try to solve his steam shortage. He put a crew of men splitting and ricking wood in a 20-by-10-foot hole west of the main cabin. After the wood was ricked high in the hole, the pile of wood was lit to make a slow fire, then covered with dirt. In a few days the wood was exposed again, and if done right, had turned to charcoal. It was their best chance of a hotter fire, and in turn, more steam. It worked, but again, only to a degree. The boiler, with its big water tank was still having its problems. As the season turned to summer, their little creek got smaller and smaller. Soon, with all the machinery going, not only did the boiler not give enough steam, but the little creek did not give enough water. With the sawmill engines running full blast, the ore mill engines, two compressors and possibly, as one report said, an air-consuming flotation tank, it was quite obvious that the second boiler was not going to be adequate, and neither was the little creek. So, the miners became engineers as they pursued their quest. They found a grade over to the horse pasture to the west, at the head of Tungsten Creek, where they built a dam to give a flume some headwater. A flume running over from Tungsten Creek would at last be their answer to the water shortage. The sawmill slapped out 1 x 8 and 1 x 10 boards as fast as the head-saw could cut them, and men put the boards together just as fast. The new, tarred-up flume ran for half mile from the creek to the boilers and was soon pouring water into the second boiler in great quantities. Finally, they now had all the water they needed; but alas, the second steam-maker, the new boiler from down below, just set up, was still short of H2-0 in the gas form at their 7,000-foot elevation. Getting enough steam was a never-ending problem in one form or another.

After 150 years of boilers being built in a particular way, a stranger put together a boiler that worked better than them all, and the Tungsten Mine would become the first place to try out a new type of process to boil water. Whoever found the clever designer who would solve the miners' steam problem, and how he was found, is lost to history, but the third boiler was a new experimental "pipe boiler," and it was an oddity that was reported to be the first of its kind, created just as steam power was going out of style in lieu of gasoline motors. The new boiler was simple in its principle, being just a mass of piping running above the raging charcoal fire. It worked well. It could bring water to a boil much faster than the standard tank-type design and the designer; (whose name is unknown), arrived riding his own horse into the mine to set-up the pipe boiler himself. He promised Marshall and Savage the best boiler in the world, and it was! In fact, the first pipe-boiler worked so well that the miners built their own design out of rock and mortar. The two pipe boilers stand today as a rusty, lonesome reminder and a proud memorial to a wise designer and builder, whose name has died along with the early mine itself.

The Great Era of the Tungsten Mine

The sawmill was probably the best-running piece of machinery in the Tungsten mine. It was a neat setup with its steam powered motors and pistons, spinning sawblades and gear-pulled chains, and hand levers and shafts giving control. It would have made any sawmill-man happy even today. At least a hundred thousand board feet of timber went through that little mill that summer, and every board was in demand. It was the first plant up and running , and soon made the little mine on the mountain look like a small city. There were at least ten buildings built out of sawed lumber, not counting the ore bins, scaffolding and timbers for the mine, plus decks, landings, and the flume. The sawmill worked and worked well.

The ore mill was a different story. First, Marshall and his men were coal miners from the coast, and apparently there was a lot of machinery brought in that year that was just no good for hard rock mining. If the Tungsten Mine was ever going to be the quality mine expected, the mill men were going to have to come up with the best process for treating the kind of ore found on Wolframite Mountain. They needed nothing short of 60% Tungsten acid. Supposedly, said one, the mill was a flotation process, but this is highly debatable and not likely because the flotation process was in its infancy in 1916 and not really the right system for tungsten. What is known is that there was a jaw crusher working, brought in over the snow road that winter. Then a roller crusher came in later that summer, over Bauerman Ridge in pieces, on a wagon. These are the only pieces of milling equipment that were known to have been used in that first big push of 1915/1916. The equipment is still there today. The present setup, though, was done in 1939. It was said by another that the mill had a ten-ton stamp mill, but there was not a stamp mill up there. This statement could have been misunderstood and the speaker meant the jaw crusher. It was good for processing around ten tons a day. There is evidence that a type of ore concentrator called a "jig" was used at the mine, and there could have been a number of these on the site to gravity-concentrate the scheelite and wolframite. These ore concentrators may have been confused with flotation equipment. The mill was almost certainly just a small "jig-mill." But the way the Germans were throwing money at the operation, it's hard to say just what was in use up there in those years.

Since a significant part of the machinery has been salvaged through the years, it makes exact details a difficult call. What is known is that in about September of 1916 they decided they needed finer ore crushing capability, so the roller crusher was ordered in, and Harry Sherling remembers the thrilling trip made bringing in the roller crusher on the only two wagons that made it into the mine in those years, until the 1953 road was constructed. The two heavy, steel rollers snaked over the mountains in two trips, and each weighed a ton. Four trips were made over the high, steep, rugged, nearly impassable 8,000-foot mountains - Bauerman Ridge being the most challenging. Over the very top was the only way!

Harry and five or six other men had to cut down poles and tie them onto the uphill side of the wagon. With two or three men on each of the swinging poles on the uphill side, the artful teamster Joe Hall, was "just able" to keep the wagon right-side-up. It was a bold and tricky stunt that Joe pulled off — dangerous to say the least — and shows that he was truly a master teamster. After riding over the mountain, myself, I would have said it just could not be done. It is an ungodly steep mountain that only a Billy goat could climb with any degree of confidence. I do not see how they did it. But men have been known to do the impossible, and Harry has the pictures to prove the feat, with Herb Curtis' word for verification. It took six head of horses to pull each of the one-ton rollers up a mountain side that few horses and riders would even want to climb, and then "side-hilling" it along the 45% grade of the mountainside for a mile.

The Great Era of the Tungsten Mine

Then, it came time to point the wagon down the other steep, west side; a place where rocks roll for hundreds of feet. The brakes on the wagon were locked at Joe's instructions. This time the six or seven men cut 6 or 7-inch trees and laid them out behind the wagon as "drag-trees." They were tied at the end with ropes and made fast to the wagon. Sailors call these types of things "anchors." The men sat on the fan of trees behind the wagon, like kids at play, hitching a ride, and with the wheels locked on the wagon (and Joe praying they would stay that way), he cracked the reins over the backs of his six black horses. Diving over the edge of the mountain, Joe Hall braced and leaned back in the wagon seat like he had rigor-mortis, shouting out of the side of his mouth, "Drag your feet boys, or we'll never make it down in one piece!"

The wagon slid into the back feet of the horses, pushing their collars loose and the back-leather breeching to the point of breaking. The tried and true horses sensed the danger they faced on that steep hill and sat back on their hind legs and skidded down the hill themselves. The young men clenched tree branches and dug their heels into the dirt, the friction factor could not have been figured any closer against the pull of gravity, as the team of horses and men was just able to keep the wagon from breaking loose and making a fast trip to the hostile bottom.

After all this effort, the time, trips to the outside, set-up labor, and engineering, it turned out, for some reason, that the new roller crusher still wasn't the total answer to the mine's ore-crushing dilemma. If a flotation mill was in use, it called for some fine grinding that would come from only a ball or rod mill. There does appear to be evidence of a kind of home-made, small, rod mill laying up there today, but it isn't one that would inspire confidence in any kind of a flotation mill. Whatever the workings of the mill were, they were never satisfied with the return from the ore. Some old millwrights who were there working on the mill said that as much tungsten went over the sides of the operation as went into the ore sacks for shipping. Even Herb Curtis said that "much more high-grade ore came straight out of the ground and down the trail, than ever went through the mill." So it was, like so many things tied in with this story, the true workings of the mill are lost in time, and anything more than the two crushers is speculation.

The wagon crew that brought in the 4000-pound roller crusher in 1916 included Kid Aimsley of Spokane; Fred Stevens of Tonasket; Frank Reeder son of an early freighter and store owner from the ghost-town of Kipling; young 16-year-old Herry Sherling, the youngest man in camp; one Mr. Morton from an unknown place; Jim Weed of Molson; Joe Hall, master teamster; and Rosey Hall.

Mining the Vein

In the spring of 1916, the high-grade ore was there by the sack-full, as pure as God made it. Most of it, with just a little chipping here and there, would run close to 70% tungstic acid, worth every bit of $12.00 a pound to a German steelmaker.

The underground vein of rich ore lay like a blanket covered by tons of granite rock above and below. The miners worked eight and ten hours a day to get it to the surface. Two eight-hour shifts were kept busy drilling, blasting and mucking. The men had to work in narrow quarters: the distance between the ceiling and the floor being 4 feet or less. They worked like moles across the blanket of quartz, stooped over on their knees, trying to make themselves half their size to fit in the wide but low, space. The mined face was called a "stoop," or "stope." After they drilled all day, they would load the drill holes with dynamite, cut the fuse to the right systematic lengths, light two cigarettes, holler, "Fire-in-The-Hole!" and then one man would light all the fuses, turn, and crawl out like the devil was after him! The earth would shake with a muffled boom from deep in the ground and shift one was over. When the air cleared and the dust settled, the next crew of miners would enter the shaft and the job of separating the quartz from the country rock

The Great Era of the Tungsten Mine

began. The quartz rock was all that was wanted; it was hand-picked and separated from the granite and put into small wooden boxes measuring 16 by 20 by 12 inches.

Harry Sherling told the story of how he went from skidding logs with a team of horses at $2.00 a day to pulling out wooden boxes from the black, underground shafts, with just 4 feet of clearance for his 6-foot frame, for $2.50 a day. He always questioned his wisdom about making the switch. Once the quartz rock was hand-separated along the face, the quartz ore was put into the boxes, the waste rock was thrown into "stall s" behind them. Miners called this a "post and stall" procedure. The stall was merely a running series of wooden posts and support timbering caps that made a framework a few feet back from the blasted rock. The "posts and caps" were driven up tight against the ceiling to keep it from collapsing on the miners. The caps and posts were cut 5-inch by 5-inch timbers, and through this support, the waste rock was thrown away from the face of the vein into the stalls. The quartz ore was hand sorted all the time while "mucking-out." Ninety percent of the blasted rock never saw daylight. It was just moved about. The high-grade ore in the boxes was drug out of the smaller shafts and set to the sides of a larger side shaft. The side shafts and main shaft to the outside were much higher than the vein shaft, about 7 feet high, by 5 feet wide, giving the miners standing room in these areas. In this larger shaft, a wheeled ore car ran on tracks. The ore cart stood ready for the quartz to be dumped into it by the young Harry Sherling, whose job it was to empty the boxes of quartz into the ore cart. After the cart was filled, Harry took the boxes back to the miners working against the stope (vein). The rich quartz ore that filled the ore car was pushed on the track to the outside of the mine by Harry who dumped the quartz ore into the ore bins outside above the grinding mill. Mining was not a job for the faint of heart because the ground was always "talking" to the miners as it settled on newfound ground and green cut timbers. In the stope, the upper level of ground would settle down on the green posts and caps with tons of pressure, compressing the cap timber from 5 inches to only 3 compressed inches of wood. The ceiling would just keep settling until it rested on the back-filled rocks in the stalls. The work was truly dangerous and claimed the life of "Vic" and almost killed Clayton Baldwin in the early summer of 1916.

There were three main tunnels, called adits, worked in those years. They went as deep, and long as 700 feet, with 1,500 feet of side workings, a 350-foot adit with 500 feet of side workings, and a 200-foot tunnel with 300 feet of side-workings. Mining engineers of the past, Culver and Broughton, describe the two deepest and most obvious workings at the mine saying:

> "This (largest adit) is the principal adit of the Wolframite Mountain area, as it produced most of the ore shipped. An 8-inch vein with three narrow splits below is exposed in the main adit at 130 feet back. It carries some Wolframite here, but the mineral is particularly blades of Wolframite 1 to 3 inches long and are inclined to the plane of the vein. At 200 feet the vein retains a 6-to 7-inch wide

> "Between 240 and 280 feet, the vein widens to 1 foot in one place then starts to narrow, finally splitting into two parts that terminate beyond the final side drift. At one place there is a relatively high tenor in Wolframite with 22 clusters of crystals along 10 feet of surface. At some 330 feet one portal has four veins each 1 to 2 1/2 inches wide and 6 to 8 inches apart are visible, and the remainder of the adit shows no vein of greater width. Another vein or a faulted segment appears at the head of the 35-degree incline, which leaves the main adit at 340 feet from the portal. Its width is only 5 to 6 inches, but the Wolframite reaches a maximum estimated at 4 to 5 percent of the volume of the vein. The stope on the northeast side of the third drift shows three veins that are 6 ½ and 7 inches wide. The southeast side of the stope shows the vein widening to 10 inches close to the surface. The vein

in this stope shows considerable Wolframite, particularly next to the adit, together with Scheelite."

Harry Sherling, C. C. Ditzel and Dewade Creveling all found through the years some beautiful crystals in the mine. They describe the vein in the 350 lower adit as such:

"The vein is first seen at about 70 feet from the portal where it is cut by one or more dikes. Wolframite occurs in the vein where it lies close to the floor of the first drift southeast. At 115 feet from the portal, in the main adit, the vein is faulted up 3 feet above the floor and shows a width of 6 to 7 inches with considerable Wolframite. It strikes north and dips 15 degrees west. In the second side drift southeast there is sparse mineralization of Wolframite and Pyrite. The width remains at 6 to 8 inches along the adit up to the northwest ward drift along which the vein decreases 2 or 3 inches until faulted out close to the face of adit. In general, Wolframite occurs as occasional blades from 1 to 2 inches long in both the main vein and splits there from."

In the "Mineral Resources of the Pasayten," 1965, the upper 200-foot adit, east of the cabins is described:

"Faulting has displaced the vein in places and changed the strike. The vein is exposed for 200 feet along the strike in the walls of the adit. A 21-foot-long lateral to the east and a 45-foot-long lateral to the west provide exposures for 71 feet along the dip. Width of the vein ranges from 4.5 to 12 inches thick. Wolframite is scattered through the vein, and a small amount of Scheelite was observed at one point in the adit and at another point in the cast lateral…Sample ####, taken from the north side of the west lateral and near the face, yielded a trace of gold, 0.5 ounce of silver per ton, and 2.76% Tungsten {3.50% Wolframite}."

TALES OF THE TUNGSTEN MINE

Many stopes and drifts went off the sides of these three main shafts. The two longest tunnels were down below the main cabins. The other was east of the cabins. It was reported that six rail carloads of high-grade ore were shipped between 1915 and 1920. Carloads, in this case, would only be small shipments of ore.

Summer was in full swing. Horses and men were on the trails coming and going all day and all night long. Strings and strings of horses pulled into the Tungsten Mine and tied up to the hitching rail. They packed from Loomis and they packed from Keremeos, British Columbia. As many as 150 horses, said one, were either coming or going from the mine at any one time that summer. At times, twenty to thirty horses were packed and herded down the trail like a bunch of goats. One cowboy led a belled pack horse and yelled, "Look-out, here they come!" in front of the herd. Another cowboy pulled up the rear, shouting at the string of thirty horses, keeping them from turning back. There were only the two packers with thirty loaded horses.

A big bathtub was on one of the loads that came in that early spring, and it was meant for only one person — Mrs. Harold Savage. She was the only woman on the grounds, and the only person apparently needing to keep clean. Paul Loudon was given the job of finding a way to pack the 250-pound tub in. He knew he had one beast of burden that could carry it, but how could he keep it on its back? A camel would have worked great! Instead, he threw a bed mattress over the back of his best mule, turned the big tub over, and with the help of six good men, he put the bathtub on the mule's back. He then commenced to try to lash down the round cast iron hunk of metal. When he was all done lashing and roping, the nose of the big mule was 6 inches off the ground. With a "Hidey-ho!" and "Away-we-go," from Paul, the funny looking mule crossed the high mountain trail with its head just skimming the ground. Only four legs, two big ears, and one big nose stuck out from under

The Great Era of the Tungsten Mine

the white tub. The tub and mule made it to the mine, and like a lot of the heavy material that crossed those mountains, it is still there waiting for the next bather.

Before the snow melted off the snow road, Marshall had the packers bring in one of the largest stoves ever seen by a cook. It took five tandem horses to get it to the mine, one in front of the other. It was close to 20 feet long and held more pancakes than sixty miners could eat in one setting. "It was big enough to roller skate on," said one man who saw it. And in later years, it became as famous as the mine itself. If you ever saw it, it was not easily forgotten. It seems to have disappeared, possibly in the forties. It ended up burnt and ruined in an old house fire in Loomis. It was a grand old stove, a spectacle to behold. (This is not the same very big, 4 by 8-foot, old stove in the log cook house that was used by later day visitors, which was big and famous also.)

Tungsten Mine Company Sells Out

Carpenters sawed and hammered all day long on the many building projects that Savage and Marshall laid before them. By the end of July, a large cookhouse had been constructed on the west end of the existing 12-by-30-foot log cookhouse. It was big by Tungsten Mine standards and measured somewhere around 25 feet wide and 40 feet long. It was made entirely of sawed lumber. The cookhouse stood for years and fed many a hungry miner with the help of its 20-foot cook stove. As the years went past, the big building was used as a horse barn and stood until about 1949 or 1950, when weather and snow finally put it down.

"Tungsten Mines Company" sold out to, or brought in, "Grandby Mines," a British Columbia Copper Company. Sylvester and Shouty might have come into the story at this point. The British Columbia Copper Company was a very important mining company and carried a lot of weight. They had property all over the northwest and possibly the world; the company may still be running today. With a big Canadian company now at the reins, the ore was no longer going to go out the Loomis side of the border. It was said that the first ore from the mine under the new owner went to the Tacoma smelter, but after a search of the records from the smelter, no tungsten ore milling could be found to have ever been done in this time period. Also, in thinking about it, 60-70% tungsten does not need to be processed further. The German company was concentrating quartz rock themselves, up on Wolframite Mountain, so why send 60% tungsten acid to another mill.

Grandby wanted the ore out the shortest way, and the shortest way was due north into Canada. The road being built from Loomis was put on hold. Herb and a crew of road builders were given shovels and a walk-behind plow and were pointed north from the mine down the South Fork of the Ashnola River. In the meantime, Grandby Mines talked the Canadian government into starting a road also. This road was begun at the town of Keremeos, British Columbia, which was at the mouth of the Ashnola River. Grandby had a crew going from both ends and hoped to meet in the middle, halfway up the South Fork of the fast flowing Ashnola River.

With the change of companies, Harold Savage, the superintendent, was, in time, also, to be replaced by a man named "Eisman," who must have been foreman down at the mill, or the underground diggings. Harry Sherling, having worked for Eisman in the black hole, did not care at all to see him in charge, and said it took all the fun out of working at the mine; well, almost. Another problem that sprung out of this change of ownership that was more serious had to do with the paychecks. For some time during that summer, the paychecks didn't come through. The men were still willing to work and had put their trust in Harold Savage to see that they were taken care of with regards to their hard-earned money. Harold Savage, the salt of the earth, didn't let them down. The paychecks hadn't come through in weeks, and there was a nice bunch of

The Great Era of the Tungsten Mine

high-grade ore sacked, stacked and ready for shipment from the mine. The horse packers came in with orders to bring it out.

Savage made a bold stand by saying, "Hold on men! That ore doesn't move until these men get a paycheck in their hands!"

The packers shrugged their shoulders and left with the message, but sure enough came back in a few days with the men's checks in their saddle bags. Savage came through and the ore went out. But, it cost him his job, and he was replaced by Mr. Eisman. Herb had this

to say about 1916:

"It was not long before we had two power drills going. Remember the time we gave the location of the Mountain Dew Mining Claim to the lawyer in Oroville and he did not record the claims. A man looking over the records found it and offered me a lot of money if I would leave the property. I said I would think it over and he started down towards what we called "the Park." I went to my tent and got a blank and located the claim. A wagon was in and I sent it out to McDaniel to be put on record. (The wagon being the Joe Hall wagon with the roller crusher on it.) If I had taken the money, I would have broken the contract. Where would the man who was putting up the money and my partners be? There was not enough money in the U.S. for me to do that. Everything was going fine..."

It was the hey-day of the Tungsten Mine, with the pack trains coming and going loaded with food — potatoes, chickens, oats, beef, flour, parts, equipment, tools, and more tools. The sunny days and beautiful scenery gave the place a spirit of gaiety and fun. Harry Sherling said it was "...a great experience, one not to be forgotten, and he was the one that should have paid them for the great times he had..." Harry, too, got the fever from the far-away mine. To Herb Curtis, the Tungsten Mine became part of him and he couldn't shake it. Tungsten ran in his blood and it dominated his whole life. He helped make 1916 the greatest year the Tungsten Mine would ever know! Yes, the sunny days of 1916!

It was a nice fall that year, and the heavy freezes didn't start until into November, but when they did, they put an end to the mill works. They certainly needed steam from the water boiler to run a compressor. The boiler needed water, and the water was freezing. So, they decided to box in the flume that ran the half mile to the meadow and pack it with sawdust all around for insulation, hoping that this would keep the line from freezing. With a lot of boards and a lot of nails, a half mile of flume was boxed in. This trick worked great for another few days, until the temperature dropped 15° more and again, the water froze solid.

"Well, hell then, we'll run steam up the darn flume! That ought to keep the water from freezing!" the mill men reasoned. And when this was done, it also worked great for another few days, until the temperature dropped another 15°. By this time there was 2 feet of snow on the ground, the creek was frozen over, and the half-mile of steam pipe, well, it just wasn't steam at the far end. The water flume and the steam pipe froze solid!

All the mill men had to be sent home along with the road crew and packers. Four or five men stayed behind at the mine, along with Clayton Baldwin and Herb Curtis. It's hard to mine when the temperature dips to -40 and there is 6 feet of snow on the ground, but tungsten was still worth $24,000 a ton in the U.S. Herb tells about it like this:

> "...The farther in we went, the poorer the ore and we were not making much money. The flume carrying the water froze up, and not being able to run things, the mine closed down, leaving me and three others to do what we could. So, we drilled one day, mucked the next and sharpened steel.
>
> We had started a road down the South Fork of the Ashnola. When we got within 3 miles of the road coming up the North Fork of the Ashnola, we got word to shut down. We all went out for Christmas excepting the cook (Frank Arnold). When we came back in, we sent

The Great Era of the Tungsten Mine

the teamster with mules and horses to bring the beef and other things from the old camp (on the Ashnola). They got in a day or two before New Year's Day, which was the latest any horse had ever gotten into the mine. The road was in a valley though, so they got in fairly easy. We three worked till March and the ore looked so bad. I said we would go out, and at Keremeos British Columbia, we got a letter... The Mine was in... THE HANDS OF THE RECIEVER!"

It was March of 1917! Months later in September 1917, the Oroville paper had this to say under the title, "Tungsten Mine Idle:"

"Herb Curtis of Loomis was a weekend visitor in Oroville... For a time, considerable work was done on these claims. Large ore deposits uncovered and much machinery hauled and packed into the mine at much trouble and expense. The operator ran short of funds and work has been suspended for a number of months. Mr. Curtis has reason to believe that the mine will be operated again next spring as soon as work can commence at the altitude of the mine..."

Next spring would have been 1918. The article said the Tungsten Mine had been idle "for a number of months," since March of 1917 through September of the same year. One can't say the Tungsten Mine shut down completely and never ran again after March 1917, but history is just about blank for the next few years. Several questions cannot be answered because of this blank spot in the history of the mine: Did it start up again in the spring of 1918? When was electric power produced at the mine? The early pictures don't show the power lines, but some later ones do.

Harry Sherling said they didn't have electric power at the mine while he was there though Harry Canfield, who worked at the mine in 1916, was both kitchen help and electrician. Electric power seems to have come to the mine after the winter of 1916. Harry is also sure that there was no ore shipped into Canada down the South Fork of the Ashnola while he was up there. Yet, despite what he says, some people claim today that quite a bit of ore went out through Canada. It's true, they never finished the road completely, but it was almost complete. In one of those years, they shipped a whole lot of ore out into Canada. They put it on sleds in the winter and shipped it down the South Fork of the Ashnola to the Similkameen River railroad siding, 20 miles from the mine.

Harry Sherling remembers some ore sacked and laying at the mine when he went out in the first few days of December. Herb mentions working through the winter until March. What did he do with the ore they mined that winter of 1916-1917 until March?

Every Canadian I talked to, who felt he knew something about the Tungsten Mine, said that they thought a lot of ore was brought down the Ashnola River. But it was Billy Cohens, the young packer for Harry Tweddle of Keremeos, who truly remembered the ore laying at the siding at the mouth of the Ashnola River. He even recalled the two men who hauled it out. He knew them: their names were Floyd Brewer and Tommy Smithers. They hauled the ore out that winter on sleds into Canada. "It laid piled at the siding for quite a while before they shipped it," Billy recalled. He thought it was the winter of 1916 or 1917, or both. An old article clipped from a local paper, written by historian Ann Briley, had this to say:

"The ore was brought out in the wintertime by sleds down the Ashnola on the Canadian side. Ed Klobucher who knows the mountains well, tells of a trip he and Tom Bean made some 15 years ago over the old ore train route. There were still a couple of old abandoned sleds along the trail at that time. You could see trees in the center of the trail cut off 20 feet in the air, where they had been cut during the winter when drifts were sometimes that high. There had once been stations along the route where each night the trains could wait over. (The old stations are still there.) The sleds were long and narrow, they drove horses tandem taking the ore out."

The Great Era of the Tungsten Mine

There truly is no doubt that ore went out by the South Fork of the Ashnola River. Gent Cawsten of Cawsten, British Columbia, who traveled the South fork trail, also remembers the trees being cut off in the winter above the ground where they "beat his horses' legs up bad," and made a difficult trip out of it when going in to see Frank Arnold in the 1920's. And what about the old ore sled left on the trail in Canada? I understand that if you go to the museum in Keremeos, British Columbia, you will find a pair of runners that were found on the trail on the South Fork of the Ashnola by a local trapper, Jim Glanders,. He said the sleds still had ore on them, too. This is Strange. Why were the sleds abandoned along the trail? Was Grandby Mines buying the ore? How much tungsten ore was really piled on the railroad siding at the Similkameen River? Was it just a coincidence that in one of those years the U.S. Government seemed to get interested in the Tungsten Mine? The Forest Service went in to finish the road/trail to the Tungsten Mine from Loomis, and Herb didn't like the route it was taking-because it didn't make sense to him.

"There's only one way to put that road in!" Herb bellowed. "And that's around on the North side of Bauerman Ridge."

"Well now, just hold your horses, Mr. Curtis. Any fool can see that the south side is the much better route!" returned the Forest Service foreman.

"Why, you crazy government pencil pusher! The damned road is already more than halfway around the north side, and we've been going that way for more than 10 years!" shouted Mr. Curtis back.

"I don't care if it's 100 feet from being done, the road we are building is going on the South Side of this mountain, not the North!"

And so, just short of a "fist fight," the trail was built around the south side of Bauerman Ridge. If you want to get to the Tungsten Mine today, from the east, you go around the south side of Bauerman Ridge on that government trail. It was never a road, and a wagon could never use it. But it is interesting that the government got interested in the mine in those early years.

There is a camp around Rock Mountain called "Wagon Track Camp." It was called that by the sheepherders, the Smiths, because of the deep ruts left in the ground by the wagons coming and going to the Tungsten Mine. Somewhere around this camp, called Fire Place Camp today, there can still be seen an old sled made of very old logs and, too, a leveled bench with four squared logs where a tent was set. Was it this far that the wagons came in the summer of 1916? The wagons did not get all the way into the mine in 1916, with the exception of the dangerous ride over Bauerman Ridge. Also, could the miners of 1916 really have gotten as much mining and milling done that they would have gotten out six train shipments of ore in one year, as it is reported (The cars were not full railroad cars.),then leave a tailing pile that would fill one more car? All things considered, especially with the high price the Germans were willing to pay for a bag of tungsten, could anyone sit on a new mill and tungsten ore worth $24,000 a ton?

Harry Sherling mentioned a rumor that went around that the tungsten was taken to the east coast and smuggled onto Germany submarines waiting off the Coast. This proved in every way true through research done at the University of Washington. The sources confirmed what Harry had said, the ore was indeed "smuggled out of the U.S. on ships bound for Germany." Herb goes on with his story, speaking about the mine going into receivership:

"...They came in the next year and talked about another option as Mr. McDaniels had passed away. (Bill passed away August 10, 1916) We went to Mr. Loudon and gave our consent, but I spoke up and said, As the price of tungsten had fallen and wages were increasing, they had better think it over."

The company wanted to take another option on Herb's, George Loudon's and now, Loy McDaniel's property; the year would have

The Great Era of the Tungsten Mine

been 1917. Here are some more big questions that cannot be answered fully: Why did Herb seem to have talked his partners, and possibly the mining company, out of leasing the mine? And why did our boys not take the lease? Or did they? It was probably worth all of $30,000.00 to the three claimholders. Debatable also is the question: "When did the mine actually shut down?"

Culver and Broughton, the 1942 engineers who studied the mine 22 years later, reported that the Tungsten Mine ran until 1920. Don Zellweger did a thorough thesis on the Tungsten Mine in 1938, just 18 years later. After reading numerous reports, including those from the U.S. Bureau of Mines, and also talking to local citizens who worked at the mine, he speaks of the Tungsten Mine as "shut(ting) down in 1920, after the price of tungsten fell to little or nothing." Then there was a verbal report from a man claiming "he knew for certain the mine ran in 1920."

Herb would seem to lead us to believe that the mine never really ran after the flume froze up in 1916. What happened for the next 4 years? The Germans were whipped by October of 1918 but were never really stopped or crushed as a functioning nation. However, the astronomical prices they paid for the "Black Gold" before October 1918 ended. The United States had learned how to work tungsten. The price probably stayed above the $12.00 a pound mark through 1919 and then plummeted in 1920. But this is merely speculation. Whatever happened, happened suddenly, for Herb and the boys left the loaded "Yukon sleds" right on the trail of the South Fork of the Ashnola River that last winter of the great era of the Tungsten Mine!

[1]Note: A note found on Baron von Alvensleben says: "..after some development work, the mine then known as 'The Tungsten Mine', was leased to a German financed company under the direction of Baron vol Alvensleben, well known to this day (1952) as a fine mining engineer and operator, the Baron was forced to leave the country just prior to the entrance of the United States in World War I. He later returned to Seattle, where he maintained his home. He is now actively engaged in mining enterprises in British Columbia at the age of 75."

CHAPTER 10

Wild Times

IF YOU WERE A HORSEMAN, and had a string of horses back in 1916, and you contracted to be a packer with the "Tungsten Mines Company," then you had to have, not just horses, but "pack horses." Now basically, a pack horse is its own breed, a selected horse for a selected purpose. And, this being the case, if you were going to take up the occupation and skills of getting supplies to and from the mine, you had better have many pack horses. Interestingly enough, a pack horse is not really bred to be a pack horse. He's just gifted with the ability to carry 150 to 200 pounds on his back. Size doesn't mean all that much, but it helps. A horse just plainly must have "poorer" breeding in him and be rejected as a good riding horse before he becomes a good pack horse. Next comes many miles of trail-training with a pack on his back, and then — maybe — you have a "pack horse."

In 1916, in the area of Loomis and Keremeos, the demand for good pack horses was hard to satisfy. And it happened that Harry Tweddle, of Keremeos, British Columbia had lots of land, cattle and horses. The horses he had fit the right category of breeding to make good pack horses, but, most of them ran wild on the mountain ranges and unused

TALES OF THE TUNGSTEN MINE

Indian land. They were not yet true pack horses. Billy Cohens was hired to teach them packing skills that would get the 150 to 200 pounds of goods into where he wanted them. Now Billy was just 16 years of age in 1916. He was short, wiry, and tough for his age. Harry Tweddle turned the horses over to the kid, paid him $35 a month, and pointed him up the rugged mountains to the Tungsten Mine. Billy was on the trail four days out of seven. The rest of the time he was butchering beef at the forks of the Ashnola, rounding up cattle, busting horses, or just working to put it all together.

Now the way they trained a pack horse back in those days was to put 150 pounds on his back, a halter on his head, and lead him down the trail. Preferably, he should have been "broke" first, for best results. However, with the heavy demand for pack horses, there was little time to properly work up a good horse. Many a pack horse got an early start behind Billy's lead saddle horse, and it was all too often that the young man spent his time picking up gear off the ground that had been bucked off a new, green pack horse. There were two wild times, though, that Billy found hard to forget. They happened in the year he packed for Mr. Tweddle and the Tungsten Mines Company.

Billy had packed-up horses all morning, weighing boxes of supplies, tightening up saddle cinches and cussing his uncooperative horses. After an hour or two, he was finally on the trail and sat in his saddle with a string of eight pack horses lined out behind him, tied, one to the other and stepping-out for the Tungsten Mine 25 miles away. The horses carried black dry powder (The miners called it gun powder.) on their backs in four-gallon wood barrels. Three of the horses carried three kegs of the substance under each pack tarp. To the young cowboy as he crossed the rocky, wide, fast-running Ashnola River, this was just another trip. The cold, snow-fed waters ran into his boots as he spurred and cussed his horses across the rocky river at its wide point. Things went well for the first hour or so, and Bill was just starting to relax as

Wild Times

he stuck a "roll-your-own" into his mouth and pulled a match out of his shirt pocket. His head was down in the smoke of his small fire when "all hell broke loose behind him!" His saddle horse shot forward like a scared jackrabbit shot from a spring! Eight horses stampeded behind him, beside him, around him, and even ahead of him. Billy quickly forgot about his cigarette because nine barrels of gun powder and eight lead ropes tangled around his legs, his saddle, his neck, and under his horse's tail. Nine scared horses ran, bucked and stampeded up the trail. It was a long half mile before the packer finally was able to cut himself loose from his wild string of running horses. "It sure was relieving," because nine barrels of gun powder were being systematically dumped along the trail in a rather exciting manner.

"Never did figure out what set the string off," said Billy. "But you can be dang sure I didn't go running after them, once I got loose from those stampeding horses." All it would have taken would have been the right combination of one steel horseshoe on one hard granite rock making one little spark in the middle of one broken barrel of black powder to get ONE BIG BOOM!

After a while, when nothing happened, Billy figured it might be safe to go on up the trail and see where his string of pack horses went. Two hours later, after a lot of rope-pulling, Billy sat on his horse with another cigarette in his mouth. His head bent over the bowl of his hand as he sheltered another lighted match. Behind him, eight bouncing pack horses followed. They were short just one keg of the black powder.

Harry Tweddle had some good horses, and he had some bad horses. He had some horses that were neither good or bad, and it was this kind of horse that made the trip interesting for Billy. "We'll make a pack horse out of this guy yet," said Harry, as he helped Billy load and pack the horses that day.

"I don't care for that roan horse one bit, Boss!" Billy lamented. "The son-of-a-gun either bucks, or damn near bucks every time I drag him up that trail. He screws up every time! Look at those beady eyes watching you, Boss. He's no good — except for making trouble!"

"Ya! You may be right, but he's worth a fifty-dollar bill if we can get that stubborn streak out of him. He's got real good lines; he's out of one of my better mares. I'll tell you what I'll do. I'll load him down so heavy this trip, he'll be thinking more about keeping his feet under him than bucking. Hell, we'll make it so damned heavy he won't be able to buck!"

So, Harry, Billy's boss, started loading the beady-eyed horse down. Billy watched and shook his head in disagreement. There must have been 100 pounds on each side of the roan when Harry yelled for help.

"Give me a hand with this blacksmith's forge," the Boss called out.

The forge weighed all of 200 pounds, Billy figured, as he and Harry pushed the forge to the top of the horse. The red roan grunted and groaned as Billy quickly grabbed the pack tarp and cinch and covered it all with a fast diamond hitch.

"Keep 'em moving Billy, and he'll be alright," were Harry's last words.

"The cayuse did real good with the 400 pounds he had on his back for the first few miles," Billy recalled. "Then the son-of-a-gun stopped dead in his tracks as the rest of the horses piled up around him. I jerked his head. The horse bellered and put down his head, then let her fly, bucking for the sky!"

The forge slapped around on the horse's back for a while, then slapped around under its belly for a while more. The red roan stomped over it, kicking it as hard as he could in the process, and kept bucking. Of course, once the pack "turned turtle" on Billy, and its load laid there in a hundred pieces, the crazy $50.00 Tweddle horse was getting out of the situation as fast as it knew how! It broke loose from the other pack horses and made a last run in the general direction of the Tungsten Mine, still miles up the trail. The forge, the canned goods and supplies stretched for miles all over the mountain trail.

Wild Times

"Never did find the saddle." said Billy. "Hell, the horse is up there, too, running the mountains still, I suppose! Never did find him, and never did look."

And There Was Death

Horses weren't the only things lost in the great push of 1915 to 1916. The "Devil's land" took three lives in holding off its hopeful conquerors. One was a miner in the spring of 1916. He was crushed to death in a cave-in at one of the main diggings. His name was Vic. They packed him out on a horse and buried him in one of the unmarked graves in the Loomis cemetery, so one story goes. More on this later.

The other man was blown up very badly, when a box of blasting caps exploded in his face. It was a sad and bloody scene, not easy for a man to look at. Everybody knew he wouldn't live, and probably shouldn't. The miners patched him up as best they knew how, but his only hope, if there was one, was the doctor 40 miles away. But how were they to get him out? No wagon could get in or out safely or easily. And even if it could, it would be way too slow and way too late. The poor miner needed help quickly and the sooner the better! So, they wrapped the man in a blanket, then canvas, and laid the bleeding patient out on one of the Yukon sleds. But no snow was on the ground this time. With the tore-up man roped to the sled, a good rider jumped upon a strong, fast horse, and took a few turns on the horn of the saddle with his lariat. The other end was tied to the Yukon sled. Another man grabbed the handles of the sled, jumped on the runners, and the race for life began! The sparks jumped and flew from the smoking, dusty runners, as the sled skipped across the trail of rocks. The horse at a lope became lathered in sweat. It ran when it could, over, around, and through the boulders, stumps and trees. It was a sad, sickening ride. The sled was in the air as much as it was on the ground. It was talked about for years by the men who saw the skipping, flying, bouncing, sparking sled cutting for town. The fast-blowing, lathered horse pulled to a stop at thee Big Horn Camp, 32 miles from town. The rider did some fast talking, and in no time, a fresh horse was secured. The wild ride was repeated again and then again at each camp along the trail. A change of horses and maybe a change of riders. A wagon was eventually found, and the miner was hauled in the wagon to the Loomis doctor - DEAD!

The third man to die on the big push between 1915 and 1920 was a man working on the road going through Sunny Pass. It is believed to have been summertime, and he just fell over dead. It happened in one of the most beautiful places in the world where 21 different kinds of wildflowers have been counted. On this colorful break in the mountains, with the lovely, grass-covered Horseshoe Basin looking over it all, it was surmised that the road worker died of a heart attack. He was also taken to the Loomis cemetery and laid to rest beside the others.

American Ingenuity

Now Abby Jorgenson was one of those gifted mechanics that could do anything. He set up most all the machinery at the mine and made it run in record time. There was nothing, it seemed, that this talented man couldn't do. The Tungsten Mine owed much to this handy little guy. He was praised by Herb Curtis, Bill McDaniel and all others who watched him work. One of his most talked-about feats was his repair of the compressor when it broke down. This machine kept the miners digging and the mine running on compressed air, but the darn thing blew a piston one day, and the mining had to stop. A downed compressor meant that it was back to hand-drilling — or stop completely. Either way, it was going to be time-consuming, and with ore selling at $24,000 per ton, time was one thing they didn't have. It would take weeks to get in a new part, and the result was that ore production was going to drop to the speed of Darwin's evolution.

Wild Times

"I think I can fix that compressor good enough to get us by... that until a new one gets in here," Abby said to the boss Harold Savage.

"Go at it!" Savage encouraged.

Abby pulled down the new compressor and unhooked the bad piston. He picked up a hand saw and walked out into the woods. Later that day he was back in camp with a knotty *burl* from an old lodge-pole pine tree. He went down to the blacksmith shop and slowed down the forge to the right heat, covered the forge, made it into an oven and stuck in his wood burl. It baked in the low heat for some time, and at the right time, he pulled the black piece of wood from the oven. Turning the hard, charred piece of wood somehow, he came up with a shape that matched the round piston. He then drilled the darn thing, in a most perfect manner, hooked up the pushrod, slapped the whole machine back together again and fired up the compressor. Surprising everyone but Abby, the compressor worked. It worked for weeks, allowing the miner s to go about their mad quest for the black tungsten ore. As the story goes, the compressor ran all summer, until the winter closed the mine down and the compressor was shut off. It was a case of American ingenuity.

I Won't Go Down Without a Fight

Now Harold Savage was one of the most liked and appreciated foremen at the mine. He was hired by the Tungsten Mine Company that originated from the West Coast. It was not clear exactly where he came from. Possibly, he came from Centrailia, Chehalis, Bellingham, Bucatta, or Tenino, all coal mining towns at the time. But he just might have come from the Couer D' Elenes, being brought in by Paulson. He made the big push work and had tungsten ore for the company before most men would have had their desks set up. He took over the mine, probably in May of 1916, but didn't really stay that long in those fast-moving times. He was replaced when Granby Mines of Phoenix British Columbiia selected good old "Eisman" as superintendent. Eisman stayed until the heavy snows of the 1916-1917 winter threatened to lock him in for the season. But it was Harold Savage who was most liked and talked about. He had the superintendent's office and his home built above the main cookhouse. Today we call it the "upper cabin." He put some extra work into this place, He had the walls wood planked, made sure light came in by having three opening windows on three sides with screens, dug an outhouse close by, put in a kitchen counter with cabinets, had a good heating stove set up, painted the ceiling white, rolled out a carpet on the floor and then brought in his not-so-unattractive wife. She rode in on Billy McDaniel's best horse, Wild Fire. Both she and Harold fell in love with Wild Fire and soon bought the horse for the tidy sum of $150.00.

Harold was a terrific man. Though with that said, not all agreed; his wife didn't really think so. You see, Harold had suffered a terrible accident, undoubtedly from a past mining accident and had some serious burns on his body. They could easily have come from an acid spill or an out-of-control fire. At any rate, he had a severely deformed hand and part of his face did not look too good. Well, with one pretty wife, and sixty-five single men around, trouble and a wreck looking to happen — and it did. Savage just could not keep his eyes on the business of the mine and his wife at the same time. She soon became interested in counting the flowers with one of the sixty-five. Harold, not being completely dumb in this case, soon caught his wife in the arms of another man, who just happened to be tied into the mine municipality too tightly to be fired — Frank Curtis.

Harry Sherling, a young man of 16, had his bunk below Savage's cabin. He remembers the bitter fighting that took place between Harold and his wife. "At least he looks like a man!" came the cutting words from the unfaithful wife!

"I'll kill you and him both if I ever see you two together again!" Harold roared, out of control.

Wild Times

Harry was the one who was sad to hear them fight. Because sound travels so well in the mountains, it didn't take long for these words to get around the camp to the "lover-boy," and he, not wanting to have his days ended before their time, strapped to his hip his six-shooting revolver. Seeing this, and taken aback, Harold Savage, too, began to think he would not go down without a good fight, if he went down at all, and a steel equalizer was soon seen tied onto his leg in the same manner. The mine took on the atmosphere of Deadwood City and smoking Tombstone Arizona, with men packing six-shooters on their hips, taking the long way around each other, and making threats when they met — all from a high, lofty little "town," 7,000 feet in the air and 40 miles from any true law and order. Happily, they all survived, but it was a tense time for a while, and by September-something, Harold Savage, his wife, and Wild-Fire were on their way to their real home in some far-away city.

Sixteen-Year-Old Harry Sherling

Harry Sherling was hanging around the pool hall in Loomis, killing time, and waiting for the new irrigation flume project to start up again, said to happen in early July that year of 1916. A sawmill owner by the name of Tilman was playing cards with Paul Loudon in the pool hall, waiting for things to break, also. Tilman was going to get the lumber bid, that seemed sure, but as of yet, there was no final word on the job. Since the only reason Harry was in Loomis, was to get a job on the flume project because he was anxious and broke, he tried to speed up the job.

"You going to need any help at the mill when the flume starts up again, Sir?" asked Harry.

"Don't think so, Son," came Tilman's reply as he hardly looked at the young sixteen-year-old standing before him.

Harry just stood there and watched the cards fall around the table. "Going to get hot today, isn't it, Mr. Tilman?" Harry said in a sheepish way, smiling as Tilman took a quick look over.

"You bet, kid."

"Had the mill long, Sir?" Harry asked.

"Hey, kid!" came a strong, fast voice from the man beside Tilman. "Go see if Hall needs any help with his packing contract to the Tungsten Mine. He just pulled out of town, headed up the Toats Coulee. If you hurry, you can catch em." The man speaking in no low tone was Paul Loudon.

"You bet, Sir1" Harry yelled. Darn rights. Thanks!" Harry peeled for the door and started at an Indian trot for the Toats Coulee River.

Six miles later he was coughing in the dust of Joe Hall's wagons. Joe was driving his team of big Percherons in one wagon and Ed Renne was in the other. They both had their wives with them. The girls were mounted on saddle horses and rode along beside the rolling wagons. Harry jogged along beside them, smiling and waving to the teamsters as they rolled up to the big bank at the fork on the river.

"Ya, we can use you on the road crew we're putting around Bauerman," Joe said.

Harry smiled and said, "That's great, I'm really glad to hear that! I need a job real bad."

He was looking over at the heavy-set Mrs. Hall with a big grin on his face when he saw two golden eyes pop out from under the flap on Rosie's saddlebag. The head of a big yellow, brown and white tomcat stared into Harry's eyes.

"Whoa-Ho! There's a cat in your saddlebag!" Harry shouted as he walked over and gave the big tom a pat on the head.

"Couldn't go anywhere without him," Rosie said, as her horse stopped, and she stroked the nose of her cat.

Wild Times

Harry watched in amazement as the little wagon train, pulled by its big Percherons, pulled up the long grade at the forks of the Toats Coulee. By afternoon, the train had made its way up the steep mountain to the Duncan James cabin-site and after a short rest and meal. The tired Harry hoped this was the place where they would camp, but Joe moved his teams on out. At the end of a hard day's climb of seven more miles, Joe Hall called it quits, high up on the mountain at the Wagon Camp, which is known as "Iron-Gate" today. With horses tied, fed and brushed, Harry could finally stop walking and running. Rosie turned her cat loose. He padded over to Harry and brushed up to his leg. That night he heard all about the explosion of work at the new mine. It was late when Harry finally found a bunk in the big tent where he could sleep. He had run and walked all day long, for close to 20 miles.

The next day he followed the horses around and over the mountains to a place they called "Tungsten Camp," where some supplies were dropped off, and the wagon trains spent another night, higher up yet.

Joe was up early and had a horse saddled and on the trail for the Tungsten Mine with his teamster, Ed Renne, while young Harry stayed behind with the girls. Fifteen miles later, at the mine, Joe heard that the company had decided to put the road coming from Loomis on hold; they would cut a new road down the south fork of the Ashnola River, north into Canada, canceling Joe Hall's road job coming in from the east.

Harry told how Joe hadn't forgot him, the big, husky, young (and persistent) boy who ran up the trail beside his wagons; "Go on in, though, son. Harold Savage said he would find you a job," said Joe when he got back to their camp on the outskirts of Horseshoe Basin.

Harry never lifted his head for the next five months he was at the Tungsten Mine. He worked ten hours a day, seven days a week, for five long months. His first job was assigned by Savage and was out in the spruce forest with the loggers. The job was called "bucking-up" the logs. The job went like this: because it was a small operation, there were only about five loggers needed to keep up with the demand from the sawmill. Two men pulled on the crosscut saw that fell the large spruce and pine trees, and two men with axes, cut off the branches, and then snipping the ends of the log. Snipping was chopping an angle, or beveling the cut end of the log, rounding its end to keep it from plowing into the earth and rocks. The log needed this rounded nose to bounce up and over uneven rocks and boulders, while being skidded into the mill. Each of the 12- to 16-foot logs had to be rolled and snipped on the end so that the skidder man could slip them into the mill with his team of logging horses.

Harry and another fellow were working on the same log with their axes. Harry was really making the chips fly with his axe, trying to impress his older partner. In his chopping zeal, he didn't give any thought to the fact that axe heads, on occasions, can come off the ends of their handles. And this one did! It flew for the bald head of his partner, knocking off his hat as it flew past. A string of cuss words that would have embarrassed a sailor erupted from his partner.

"HELL'S FIRE and @,%,#,~ Damned kid!" the man shouted. "A bullet never moved that fast! Turn the HELL around and chop the other way when you chop around me from now on!"

Harry slunk over to another log and stayed on a different log.

Frank Schull was the man's name who contracted to work his team of horses skidding in the timber to the sawmill, and soon had Harry driving and working his team of well-trained logging horses while Frank dozed under a nice tree.

"Never used a finer team of horses in my life," Harry said, and he was qualified to know. "They knew more about skidding in a log than I did. They would turn on a dime with a 'Gee' or a 'Haw,' and I never had to touch the reins. Because of the steep and rocky terrain, we could not work them side by side, so we had to run them in tandem, one in front of the other, but oh they were a sweet team of horses to work." Harry remembers in fondness.

Frank Schull, the skidder, soon decided to quit his tough job of teaching Harry how to skid logs from under a shady tree, and by and by, being lonely for real civilization in the valley below, he worked up a deal where he sold the beautiful team of jogging horses to the mine company, recommending the young man Harry, for the job of skidder-man.

"It was the best job I had up there, and I should have been happy with it," said Harry, years later. "But I wanted to make that extra fifty-cents a day the other miners made in the underground workings. I kept after Eisman, who was running the miners at the time, to put me in with the miners underground, that at the first opportunity of an opening- but he wouldn't do it!"

With his feelings hurt, Harry finally complained to Harold Savage of his being passed over for the coveted mining jobs, and Savage, looking the boy over, must have seen a future career miner, for he got the young man in the black hole. Eisman was now the one not happy, so with vengeance in his eyes, real vengeance, that Harry could see and feel, he loaded the young man down with work.

"If he wants to be a miner, okay! I'll make him a miner!" Eisman plotted.

Poor Harry worked his guts out under that mountain of granite — mucking, dragging high grade ore out from the 4-foot stope, lining this out, doing this and doing that. Eisman found enough work, Harry knew, to keep three men working hard. How Harry soon longed for the open blue sky, the sunny days, and the singing birds, the days he had lost with his fine team of horses.

After 6 weeks in the black hole, the youngest man at the Tungsten Mine had enough! And finally, after some more complaining, he got out into the open air and daylight again, this time on the road crew with Herb Curtis. They were working the new way in and out down the

South Fork of the Ashnola River to the north. It was about this time that Harold Savage was let go, and Eisman made over-all superintendent. It was all Harry could do not go away with Savage too. If he had not been working with Herb Curtis, who was overseeing the northern road job, a man Harry enjoyed, he might have quit.

It was on one of those sunny days, while working on the road, just a few miles down the way from Mail Box Camp, now called Scheelite Pass, that Frank Arnold came walking up to the crew with a paper note from Eisman at the mine. The message was to the effect that Herb was to send someone right out, and to catch up with the last packers heading out to Loomis to get a message into town. One of the crew men would have to run after the last packer.

"Who wants to run this message out to the packers?" Herb asked his crew.

All the men looked at one another with dumb expressions on their faces; no one being willing to take the assignment.

"Harry does!" one of the men finally said.

"No.....ah...ah..no.."

"You're the youngest, Harry!" said one of his crew members.

"Shoot! Okay, I'll do it."

"Good!" said Herb. "You should find them along the trail somewhere. Give them the note, and they'll take it on to town."

Well now it wasn't as if Harry had lived in those mountains all his life. He had been over the trail one time, and that coming in with Joe Hall in July, weeks before, and he had just been too excited to have looked it over very well at all. No matter, the packers were just up the trail a little way, and he wouldn't be gone for long.

Four hours later, the young man was still looking for the packers and hadn't seen a soul. He was just now getting even with the big mountain they called "Windy," and his light was beginning to fade out. Hours later still, Harry was in the dark and lost! It was black as coal out there under those big spruce trees. He had lost the trail and was wandering around in one big, black maze. He figured he had no real choice but to just keep walking, on and on, over the mountains and hoping his sense of direction was at least close. Miles more were covered, and more hours went by.

"I finally came into a big open mountain side, lit up by the moon light, and it looked kind of familiar. I thought I had seen it from Duncan James' coming in." So Harry headed downhill and soon ran into a fence. "Boy it felt good to hit that fence," he recalled years later. It was 2:30 A.M. when the young man finally saw the light from Duncan's cabin window. It was a hungry lad who stumbled through the door to Duncan's surprise. Harry had walked 15 miles that day and 15 miles that night, and that after building road that morning. A nice 30-mile walk for the young man.

Duncan cooked the famished sixteen-year-old a fine meal on the spot, and life looked a whole lot better for the leg-weary messenger. The lights went out again on him, but this time he was sleeping in the corner of James's cabin.

By the first of December 1916, all but a small handful of men had gone back to town. Harry was one of the last to go. Frank Arnold didn't count. Word had come in to stop the road crew and close it down for the winter. Now finally after five months, it was time for Harry to go home. The date was December 6, 1916. Herb was staying in, but Harry and two others opted to go out down their new road that followed the south fork of the Ashnola River, 25 miles north to Keremeos, British Columbia.

It had been a nice fall and early winter with only a little snow on the ground. That sweet, intelligent and eager to please team of logging horses Harry used were still at the mine. They would never come out. It is not an easy story to tell: the sixteen year old, who took greater interest in the horses than most, wanted the horses to get out of the mountains before they couldn't get out, so he led the horses down the trail a mile or so to Sheelite Pass, and turned the horses loose with a wave and a shout toward Loomis.

"GET OUT OF HERE, GIRLS!" he shouted and waved.

The horses spooked and galloped on up the trail and out of sight as he had hoped. Satisfied, and being eager to get home himself, Harry took off with the other two men down the South Fork of the Ashnola on their new road, which was a shorter route north to the valley below. But the horses did not run down the trail as far as planned. They soon turned back for their summer home at the mine, instead of going on to Loomis as Harry had counted on. They were smart, but not smart enough to know they had to leave their home with its "brought-in" oats and hay. Most everyone was gone or apparently not planning to leave for town and the late, heavy snows of winter soon came. The sweet team of skid horses never left the Tungsten Mine! Out of hay, and in 4 feet of snow, Frank Arnold, it is said, had little choice but to make marten meat out of the best team of horses in the country!

The three men made quick time down their new road and the next day, 20 miles later, came to the plains of the Similkmeen River where they broke into the wide valley and were hot-footing-it to the town of Keremeos, British Columbia when a huge herd of horses came pounding down on them. A young Indian lad was at the reins of a green, high-stepping bronc, and just as the big herd of horses got to them, the Indian horse, being reined-in, went wild and bucked until it threw its rider. A young John Terbasket went high into the air, but the force of gravity was too strong, and he soon bounced off the frozen ground. He groveled and groped to the pain of a swelling, bent and broken leg. His riding companions were watching the scene and trying to hold the 100 head of wild Indian horses in a group at the same time, with much difficulty. One of the riders broke away and rode over to the miners,

Wild Times

who were standing over the broken-legged Indian with wide eyes and frightened faces, not knowing what to do.

After one good look, the rider spoke in panic, "Would one of you men ride into Keremeos and tell Harry Tweddle to come out here quick and pick up John with his car. We can't leave these horses, and John's hurt bad! I guess the only horse that can be rode is that high-stepping bronc John was on. The rest are wilder than him by a long shot!"

"Hell, I don't know how to ride!" said one of the miners.

"If I could ride, I'd be on a horse now!" said the other miner as he looked at Harry.

"Harry, you're going to have to ride in and get help. You're the youngest one here. Here, I'll get the horse for ya!" The tungsten miner walked over to the standing bronc and brought it back to Harry.

"Stuck again!" young Sherling thought as he slowly took the reins that were hanging in front of his face. "You hold this ##@@XXZZ of a horse until I can get on him," he instructed his helpers.

Harry no sooner hit the back of the horse than the high stepper, jumping and side-stepping, took off running like a bolt of lightning shot from heaven! Trees, rocks, fences, brush, and river rushed by. It was like a fast-running movie as the wild Indian horse shot over the ground like an arrow, as fast as it could move its legs. Poor Harry had forgotten how to ride, too. His hat went flying to the wind as he hung on to the saddle horn with both hands for his dear life!

"We must have run flat-out for 7 or 8 miles," said Harry Sherling years later. "The dirty horse was safer, I figured, at a dead run, than when I tried to rein the bucking guy in. He'd start crow-hopping every time I did!"

The wild, run-away horse finally wore himself out by the time he reached the town of Keremeos, and the young Harry was never so glad to jump off a horse in all his life. He led the horse the last mile into town and into the blacksmith shop where Mr. Tweddle had his new, 1916

TALES OF THE TUNGSTEN MINE

Cadillac that got a little dusty that day bringing in the broken-legged John Terbasket.

"The check's no good, Son! The Tungsten Mine checks are bouncing like rubber," the man in Keremeos said.

Harry could not believe what he heard! He was sick now, if he hadn't been when he stepped off the wild horse. He opened up his wallet and counted the five checks he had accumulated all summer. It represented five months of hard labor, and now... they weren't any good? He counted them again. It came to the same: $450.00. If he could just, just find someone to cash them.

"Damned! Five bad checks! It can't be! How could they do this to me? No....No!!"

After giving it some quick thoughts, Harry figured he might have one more chance. He caught a ride to the U.S. Border, then walked a few more miles to Nighthawk. From there he had to run in his Indian trot the last 9 miles into Loomis. But once in town, he ran into the first place of business he came to, the pool-hall,. The place where this crazy mining job had started. Quickly through the doors he ran, hoping to hear some better news.

"Are the Tungsten Mine checks any good, Mr. pool-hall man? Can I cash them here in Loomis?"

"Oh, ya, good as gold," the man said. Harry lifted his eyes to the heavens and then sped on for the bank. There was a big grin on his face as he walked through the doors of the Loomis "Lending Institution." Suddenly, he stopped dead cold in his tracks. A sickening feeling came over him again and almost stopped his heart — as he slapped his pocket.

Again, he felt and searched his empty pockets. His wallet was gone! Harry did his fastest double take ever. There is just no way to explain the way he felt. Once more he broke into his Indian trot down the main street of Looms, into and out of the pool-hall, and on down the road back to Keremeos he went. His hopes were slim to none, he knew, as his

Wild Times

eyes strained and scanned every inch of the road that he had just traveled. About a mile from town he ran into a couple, a man and his wife.

"Excuse me Sir... you didn't see... or I mean, find my wallet on the road, did you?"

"Why no... we didn't, Son, but we sure weren't looking, either."

"Thanks," Harry said and was off again.

Scanning the road like a hawk, and after another half mile, Harry was a wreck. He wandered and staggered out of breath, from roadside to roadside, back trailing himself in a daze. Then he almost stumbled on his face. He put on the brakes. As if by a miracle, there in the middle of the road that he and the couple had walked over, maybe an hour before, lay his wallet and the $450.00 in checks. From malediction to happy elation, the young Harry whistled a happy tune back to the bank, his two hands tightly clenching his lovely wallet.

CHAPTER 11

Down with the Germans — Down Went the Tungsten

These tales are based on newspaper accounts and reports by Bob Curtis, Harry Sherling, Art Gjerde, George Honey and Bruce McPherson Jr.'s, along with courthouse records.

ON APRIL 6, 1918, WITH 10 feet of snow yet on the ground, the Tungsten Mine might or might not have been producing ore. On the same day, a German U-boat sank a U.S. ship, and though a great war had been fought in Europe since 1914, this action was the straw that broke the backs of the U.S. Peace Doves. The United States of America entered into the "Great World War." This was the timber that ultimately broke the backs of the German warriors.

By September of 1918, the German empire had fallen, and by October, the war was over - and so were the glory days of the Tungsten Mine. The big tungsten blow-out that sparked it all was gone. The vein had narrowed, and only a few hot spots were hit now and again, though there was consistent ore to be found. It was rumored that the ore mill never had been set up right, and many thought a lot of the ore went right over the side to pile on the ground. According to Herb Curtis, early pure high-grade wolframite, that came right from the rich blowout, made up the bulk of the ore shipments during that First World War period. How much went through the ore mill is anyone's guess, but there were thirty tons of tailings lying on the ground. But, the world had changed quickly and dramatically. The German tungsten buyers were gone and so was their big money. Britain, in their expanded empire, had always controlled the best mines of tungsten and their rich mines eventually satisfied the U.S. and world markets. The war also forced the rest of the world to learn the science of smelting the in-fusible heavy stone with the electric arc furnace, or by even simpler smelting methods.

By 1919, with the high prices quickly deteriorating, the far-away mine with its narrowing veins was no longer attractive to big mining companies. In addition, the machinery and supplies had a lien and judgment against them. The lien holders had a problem though. How do you get back hundreds of tons of supplies off a distant 8,000-foot mountain, forty wilderness miles away with no road to it? Under normal conditions, all improvements and the permanent milling equipment would go with the mine to whoever held the claims. But Herb, Loy, and the Loudons had to wait and see what the lienholders were going to do. The boys and the lien-holders didn't have too long to wait. Herb writes:

"... in a couple of years, it was put up for a tax sale. William Ford (Ferris Ford's dad) and I bought it and packed some of the better things out. After paying off the packing expenses, the watchman, Frank Arnold, was hollering for money, so I gave him what I had."

The state tax man had not been paid in 4 years on the personal property bought by the Tungsten Mines Company in 1915. The date of the sale would have been early 1921or so, and the packing out of the equipment was in the summer of 1921. Herb and Bill Ford now owned the mining and the milling machinery. Jimmy Dexter and a man named O'Teal were hired to pack out the more valuable things. There was a lot

Down with the Germans — Down Went the Tungsten

of good stuff that came out from the mine in that process, but it paled in comparison to what was left there to stay. The sale (which could have been another reason why the mine suddenly closed) included mostly things that could be easily packed out on a horse: 200 pounds worth per horse. Articles such as drills, hoses, pumps, some of the dynamite and fuses, parts of the electrical workings and motors came out. One compressor was torn down and packed out. But generally, if it entailed much work and was heavy, it was left on the mountain. Herb Curtis and Bill Ford bid just enough to get the mining goods, which covered barely, they said, Jimmy Dexter's and O'Teal's packing charges.

But what about the watchman? Poor Frank Arnold didn't want to be forgotten, entirely. Not when it came to money! He thought he should get his watchman's wages regardless of all the left-over free food that he ate, the free rent that he received, and the firewood already cut for him. But maybe they had a deal? However, it worked, Frank wanted his money, and Herb made it right. They were his claims, and Frank had helped, He had, in the very least, watched over the mine as a good watchman should.

At the time, to Frank, the Tungsten Mine was like a small heavenly gift. Here he was, finally alone, with a good roof over his head in a vast mountain wilderness where few men wandered. This place was even deeper into the woods than he had been before, and he was surrounded by its beauty and its isolation. There were cabins for shelter and goods of every description left by the miners, goods that only Frank Arnold was there to use. He didn't lack a thing. He held down the little city high, waiting for the miners to return and do it all again.

Frank set up housekeeping in the best cabin up there, Savage's superintendent's cabin. He had running water, wood-planked walls with a white-painted ceiling and screened windows. It was the warmest cabin up there with an efficient, pot-belly stove. Frank didn't even have to cut firewood for years. The little sawmill worked so well with its neat cutoff saw that the miners found it much easier to just lop-off bolts of wood with the quick swinging sawblade, rather than use the devil's whipsaw. There were cords and cords of neatly stacked firewood piled up for but the lone mountain man to burn. He had the mine virtually to himself for close to 10 years with just a trickle of interference in the summer months.

Given the swings life can take, things did not always go that perfectly for Frank there on that lonely mountain. Frank and the Tungsten Mine had a bad experience sometime in these early years of the 1920's. The problem again stemmed from his love for the liquid spirits, alcohol, a hammer he was always hitting himself with. After a few months of being alone had rolled past, and prohibition had come into effect back in 1916 for Washington State, Frank Arnold had put together another "real good still." With the government's bad view of alcohol, a still was a necessity for the "mayor" and "city council" of the little mining town that had no people in it. So out in the Baldwin cabin, the very first cabin to be built at the mine, Frank again set up his moonshine-making machine. How long it ran well is hard to say, and just when it started not running well is also hard to say, but in one of those early years, Herb Curtis related, in not so happy of a tone, Frank Arnold's moonshine-still blew up! With horrific effect! The explosion started a fire that raged out of control and burned down the first cabin, which had been built in 1905. Just what went wrong in Mr. Baldwin's cabin is open for some good guesses, but when a contained still runs out of water and builds up steam, dangerous things happen. Whatever Frank's condition was at the time, the still blew up like a World War I bomb and set the cabin and the woods aflame.

What started out as a good idea on Frank's part, almost ended the story of the Tungsten Mine as we know it today. Frank could probably do little to slow the wild burn, and it must have been the dampness that really arrested the jumping flames from burning it all down. The fire circled the mine and burned not only the Baldwin cabin, but the

Down with the Germans — Down Went the Tungsten

horse barn, Joe Bazonie's cabin, Mike's cabin, two of the bunk houses and perhaps one or two other outbuildings. The watchman learned a hard, heart wrenching lesson, and it seemed it was the last still he ever built, but this didn't help Herb Curtis' disposition any. In 1929, another devastating fire put an end to much of the mine as it was known in 1916. The 1929 fire was a very damaging fire, and more will be told of its destruction in the story to come.

With tungsten prices low, down to the $1.00 to $2.00 per pound bracket again, the high country mine sat in pristine limbo, preserved by its long snowy winters and far-away location. Herb Curtis, with the help of Frank, continued his assessment work through 1921. After that, the Tungsten Mine sat open to claim-staking by anyone who wanted it. For 9 years more, it went unclaimed.

The men who filed on the tungsten claims next were none other than the one keeping an eye on it, Frank Arnold himself along with Clyde L. Andrews, a long-time mountain explorer, and Frank E. Maron, his new trapping partner. The three of them claimed the mine. Clyde took the Sunshine, Hyland, and Morning claims, the choicest property. With an interest in those three, Frank's claims appear to be over across the valley to the south on Apex Mountain, and Maron claimed an interest in them all. It's not clear just where each of the individual claims were situated, but what is known is that all the claims were relocations. The three men, by September 5, 1930, had staked eight claims on Wolframite and over on Apex Mountain across the valley. Frank Arnold's claims across the valley were some that Herb Curtis and Johnny Bell had filed on and fussed with in the early twenties, where small out-croppings of quartz-tungsten were found on the east side.

A search of the courthouse records is confusing. It is not clear who had what, with what interest, and under what claim names. Numerous claims were filed by different people at and on the Tungsten Mine in the early thirties. Also coming on the scene in 1930, was Ferris. R. Ford,

Bill Ford's son. Ferris Ford had been around Loomis apparently all his life and had worked with Frank Arnold in 1923 and 1924 for the Coast and Geodetic Survey. He was a bit of a packer in those years, supplying a number of high mountain Forest Service look-outs. In later years he worked as a road locator for the Forest Service and on the side dealt in real estate deals. The Tungsten Mine was one of those real estate deals.

So, with the ink just dried on the claim notices filed by the three, Ferris Ford, now a mining promoter, cooked up a transaction with the three mountain men. It was on September 20, 1930, that both Clyde Andrews and Frank Arnold sold their claims (or a share of the claims) to Ferris. In August 1932 (before Frank Maron went to the hospital at Medical Lake), Ferris Ford had Maron quitclaim his one-quarter interest in the Tungsten Mines over to him. So, by 1932, Ferris held control over the Sunshine, Highland, Morning, Ajax, Hercules, Wolframite, New Lake, and Climax claims. The fine details of this transaction are shrouded in smoke. It is believed that Clyde Andrews ended up, after 4 years of waiting, with Ferris finally deeding over a piece of property to him. Frank Arnold was supposed to have gotten $500 from Ford, but the story goes that he, too, had his problems getting this money. A great depression had hit, hit like a sledgehammer!

In reality, from all appearances, Ferris Ford never paid any hard, real money to any of his "Grantors," but instead, worked out deals with them in goods or services. In Frank Arnold's case, not being a full and legal citizen and with his home now controlled by his "business partner," it is surmised that he had little choice but to go along with Ferris. Ferris did help him out, though, whenever he could. He was said to have grub-staked him with food, welcomed him to his home, and being a packer with horses, saw to it that Frank and his supplies were packed into the mine through those years of the 1930's until Frank disappeared in 1934 or 1935. Stories are told of Ferris taking him to Spokane to sell his furs at better prices or running him to Oroville or Omak to get supplies and see old friends. Ferris was to Frank a friend and a partner in the Tungsten Mine. Arnold, on his end of the partnership, would, in turn, do Ferris's assessment work, about $100.00 worth of labor per year, as required by law, which could entail a lot of work. He was also the watchman at the mine and kept the claims from thieves and claim jumpers. It seemed like a good working relationship and lasted until Frank dropped from sight.

Frank Arnold's Mining Claim Notice

In 1930, the price of tungsten started to come up again, and with the renewed activity at the mine, Herb Curtis was just a little mad that he had been cut out of the last deal by his friends. To him, Frank Arnold, Clyde Andrews, Maron and Ferris Ford had just plain "jumped" his claims and left him on the other side of the fence. So at the beginning of 1931, things were all shook-up; the country was in a hell-of-a-depression, Herb Curtis was mad at Frank Arnold, Frank Arnold was mad at Ferris Ford over not getting his $500.00, Frank Maron was mad at Frank Arnold for some reason (probably relating to the poor trapping, or relating to their mining claim), and Frank Arnold was mad at Maron for taking off with some, if not all of his groceries. Ferris Ford, not to be left out, was said to be mad at somebody for not being able to come up with the promised money on the mining deal. The Great Depression made things more than tight; they were terrible. But, the price of tungsten was up, and the price of furs were holding their own. They would all get by for a while. Happily, before too much time ran off the clock, Arnold, Maron, Ferris, and Herb Curtis had ironed out most of their problems.

Regressing back to the 29th of September 1930, just 24 days after Frank Arnold had filed his claims, Ferris had a hot deal going with a man named Hugh M. Lawrence. "Hughy" Lawrence was going to buy the Tungsten Mines. Hughy Lawrence, the baseball player, the butcher, and the notary public in Tonasket, Washington, was the one who had notarized Clyde Andrew's, Maron's and Frank Arnold's mining claims just a few weeks before in August and again in September. Hughy now decided he wanted the Tungsten Mine! And wrote up the following agreement:

212913
Hugh M. Lawrence to Ferris R. Ford et ux

AGREEMENT
THIS AGREEMENT, made and entered into this 29th day of September,1930, by and between Hugh M. Lawrence of Tonasket, Washington, hereinafter called the First Party and Ferris R. Ford and Ruth E. Ford, his wife, hereinafter called the Second Parties,
WITHNESSETH:
WHEREAS, the Second Parties are the owners and in control of certain mining property and claims located in Okanogan County, State of Washington and described as follows, to-wit:
"Sunshine, Highland, Morning, Ajax, Hercules, Wolframite, New Lake, and Climax claims, all being re-locations in sections 12 and 13, Twp. 40 North, Range 22, E.W. M., at a point about 42 miles from Loomis, Washington and about 6 miles north of Rummel Peak, I. B. Survey."
AND WHEREAS, the Second Parties are desirous of granting to the First party an option for the purchase of said mining property and claims and of selling them to the First Party, and the First party is desirous of having said option and sufficient time wherein to make an examination of the properties and certain tests of the ore thereon.
NOW THEREFORE, in consideration of the premises and of the sum of one dollar and other valuable considerations paid to the second parties by the First Party, receipt of which is hereby acknowledged, the parties hereto agree as follows:

Down with the Germans — Down Went the Tungsten

FIRST, the Second Parties hereby grant to the First Party an option to purchase the above described property for the total sum of $5000.00 upon the following terms and conditions, to-wit:
(a) The First Party shall have ten (10) months from the date of this agreement to get and engineer on the ground and make his tests of the ore, and on or before the expiration of said ten (10) months he shall notify the Second Parties in writing whether or not he will purchase the property.
(b) (Etc. on, Etc. on.)

This deal appears not to have gone through completely, for one reason or another, but Hughy and Ferris Ford would not part company for the next 7 years.

Bruce McPherson

Bruce McPherson was an Oroville miner, and a true miner he was. He kept himself busy working on his Epsom-salt mines west of Oroville and his claims on Mt. Hull, east of Oroville. It was here that he was working when he heard the story about the rich tungsten diggings high up to the west. It was the fall of 1935 when a man named Roy Rolyer, but perhaps it was Edward Eisman, filed a claim on Wolframite Mountain . This was surely the same Eisman that had been the evil, tyrant foreman to Harry Sherling in 1916. Well, whichever way it went, Eisman talked about the rich ore in the tailing pile that lay up there waiting for someone to haul it down and sell it. He knew it was high grade ore because the miners of 1915-1920 couldn't get the mill to run efficiently, and most of the white sheelite went right over the sides of the mill and into the tailing pile with all that white quartz that held it.

"Shoot-Fire! There's tons and tons of high-grade tungsten ore laying up there on the ground. I know it. I worked on that mill."

And it was like water to a fish when the words fell on the ears of Bruce McPherson; and ultimately, on the ears of a big French-Canadian named Harold V. Dardier (Dar-dee-a'), Bruce's soon-to-be partner. Tons of concentrate, rich in tungsten lay on the ground waiting for someone to scoop it up and sell it. Bruce and Harold saw lots of big dollars signs before their eyes. No right-minded miner could pass up a deal like that! The only thing that could be easier was inheriting money.

Bruce made a quick trip into the mine from the Loomis side to investigate the story. It was late fall 1935 when he left. The ore was there, alright, a good thirty tons, he figured, laying right on the ground all crushed and easy to handle. It looked darn good. He gathered up a sack full of the concentrate and headed back home, just beating the first snows of winter. The ore must have given a good assay that winter because Bruce and Harold put together the next big deal with Hughy Lawrence and Ferris Ford. They made arrangements to start mining the next spring, 1936. Also, while at the mine, Bruce did not see the caretaker, Frank Arnold, and assumed the worst. The Tungsten Mine was mysteriously quiet and lonely, for its one last citizen was not to be found. But the tungsten ore was there, and that is all that counted at the time. Bruce McPherson and Harold V. Dardier would just do a little mining.

CHAPTER 12

High Prices, High Country and Fine Furs

These tales are based on many trapping stories from Lefty's accounts, Al Smith, Clyde Paul (who told many of those related to Lester "Shorty" Fairbrother), Bob Curtis, Jim McDaniel, Oren Dodd, Lester Lucas and a few other old timers.

IT IS SAID BY THOSE who should know that there is a little furry critter that has one of the finest, most desirable of furs to put around a person's neck. However, this little critter is a scavenger, and one of the most vicious killers that haunts the forest. He can decipher which way a rabbit is going, and when on a trail of blood, will always go in the direction the blood is going. Never will he go the way it came. He will do this without hesitation or back trailing. The blood-thirsty critter will blindly try to walk through a hundred steel traps for just one bite of fresh meat. This beautifully furred, 10-pound, chocolate-colored animal is called a "sable" in Russia and a "marten" in North America. The Tungsten Mine and surrounding high country is prime marten ground. And interesting, too, comes the fact that this mountain area had not only an unusual outcropping of tungsten ore, but also an unusual crop of marten. The martens were unusual because of their beautiful copper-colored bellies. A fur buyer's eyes would light up when he ran his fingers through the luxurious copper-toned fur. This fur was most desirable and rare, worth at least an additional $10.00 a pelt to the trapper that had one. The high mountains around the tungsten deposit had them in numbers.

Now if rare and unusual things happen in numbers, then the Tungsten Mine had yet one more diamond in its pocket. For in this beautiful high mountain forest ran a big, lean, pin-eared cat. The cat was rare because with few exceptions, the big luxurious cat was found only in the U.S. along a narrow strip of land comprising the land called "Pasayten," the land of the lynx. The lynx cat, like the marten, thrived in this high, dry, rabbit and squirrel infested forest.

With the coming of the 1920's came prohibition, peace and plenty. It was the dawning of a new age: "The Roaring Twenties!" People had money, cars, radio, the Charleston, boot-leg whiskey, and fur coats. Lots of fur coats. Dollar for fur dollar, prices had never been better. Furs brought, in some cases, about the same money as they do today, 70 years later. One good tom cat would fetch you at least $80.00 to $90.00. This was twice what some laborers would make in a month. Frank Arnold was always good for thirty lynx cats a season. That is, in the early days, before the big forest fire. But as good as he was at catching lynx cats, Frank was called a "marten trapper," and it was marten that he caught in even greater numbers. Marten in the 1920's would get you $20.00 to $35.00, hands down, for every pelt, and up to $125.00 to a dealer on the right years. The country Frank trapped seemed to run thick with the little scavengers. A hundred marten a season was not an exceptionally good year for the Englishman, but it was more than likely an over-all average. Frank, in the 1920's, was a marten-catching son-of-a-gun.

High Prices, High Country and Fine Furs

Frank must have loved the high country he snowshoed over. He thrived on the land, and it treated him well. It seemed to fit his life like a glove. It also made him some very good money. Trapping, as the prices show, was no poor man's game. A clever, hard-working trapper could, in five months, make more, twice as much at least, than what a union laborer could make in a year. When the day came that Frank couldn't trap, his leather poke bulging with green backs would see him through.

From Frank's earliest years, it was said of him that he was a "humane" trapper. He would cover his line regularly and tried to avoid the steel trap, though he used it often enough out of necessity on many of his game animals. (None of Frank's steel traps were ever found, though they would have numbered into the hundreds.) Frank championed the use of the dead-fall trap. Clyde Paul found some of Frank's old dead-fall traps in the 1950's when he scouted trail for the Forest Service on Cathedral and Tungsten Creek. (This is the same Clyde Paul who in The Story Begins tells of the wild-eyed mountain man who cashes a $350.00 check from Ben Prince at Len Easle's Tavern in Oroville.) Lester and George Lucas, later on in the same decade, found what looked like dead-fall traps on Horseshoe Mountain. This skilled man of the woods had at least two variations of the dead-fall trap, one used a heavy log, perhaps 7 feet long and 3 or 4 inches in diameter. The trap would be tripped by a trigger mechanism when the animal moved the bait, triggering the log to fall on the animal. The log was held up and tripped by the old Indian, Boy Scout, figure four, stick release setup. The whole wooden mechanism was called a "dead-fall." The other variation of this trap used a 2-inch pole with a heavy rock tied on the end that fell. It was a deadly mechanism that would kill the animal instantly with a crashing blow to the head. The cold steel trap would merely catch a leg of its victim, and the animal was sometimes found alive, a few days later, when the trapper tromped up on his snowshoes. The animal was supposed to have broken a leg in the steel trap, and consequently, froze to death because of the shock. If not, the trapper had to perform the "coup-de-grace" on the unlucky varmint. (This is the reason why the steel leg traps are now outlawed in more than one state.)

At other times, on certain fur bearers, Frank would use a store-bought trap that worked on the same principle as a mouse trap, called a "jump trap." Clyde Paul again found a few of these out on Frank's old line. Frank had one more known method of catching a marten. That was by using a home-made "knot-hole" trap. It worked like the old medieval mouse traps — the mouse could stick its head in the small hole, but it couldn't pull it out. In the case of a marten, if a marten stuck its head in the small hole, a small needle or nail would run through its neck. It was a simple homemade trap that worked extremely well and was used by many a marten trapper. Simply grab a wood hand-drill, put a 2-inch auger-bit in it, walk up to a dead pine tree, drill a 2-inch hole 5 inches deep, place your bait in the hole, hammer a 16-penny nail in at an angle, and wait for a marten to come along and stick his head in the hole.

Not to be forgotten was Frank's use of the snare. One time, he was found meticulously unwinding the steel wire window screens found on a window at the Tungsten Mine, braiding the wire into a snare to be used as a trap-set for some kind of bigger animal.

Frank had one more money-maker that took great skill and time to out-smart. Frank went after the bear. Now when you caught Mr. Big Bear you really had something because not only was he big and strong, but he was worth $100.00 to the Fish and Game department, a considerable sum in the early twenties. The $100.00 bounty was on his head, and the hide made extra money. Frank was known not only to use large steel bear traps, which were about 3 feet long and weighed maybe 50 pounds or more, but also to build home-made log cages to trap the bruin. The bear would walk into a 6-by-6-foot log cage and spring the locking door on himself. Imagine the adrenaline rush that would follow walking up to a wild, enraged bear, caught in a steel leg trap, or pacing

High Prices, High Country and Fine Furs

back and forth in a "hopefully secure" log cage. Frank caught bears and caught them often. Two old log bear cages and two large rusty steel bear traps of his were found years later, as mute testimony to the challenging duels Frank fought with these wild animals.

The aforementioned animals were Frank's three main money makers, but he sure wouldn't pass up a coyote for $10.00 to $50.00, the bounty alone was $5.00; a rare otter for $100.00; or a rarer-still fisher for perhaps $60.00. Mink and beaver brought a good $45.00; fox and bobcat were worth perhaps $20.00 or $25.00; and the little white, quick moving weasel, who couldn't resist your bait, brought $1.00. Once in a great while, a lone mountain lion would cross in front of the sights of Frank's rifle, and he would have a hide that was worth another $40.00 in bounty money.

There was one more animal that was fortunately "few and far between" and still up there today in those high-country mountains of Washington State. It is the crafty wolverine. They were smart, hard to catch, dangerous, and costly to the trapper. The stealthy wolverine would gamely run your trap-line ahead of you somehow avoiding all steel traps and enjoying the easy meals you conveniently provided for him. If you didn't devise a way to stop him, he would keep your traps clean all year long because he knew you were feeding him. You had to kill him. The wolverine was, if you asked the English trapper, an animal fearless of even man!

Arnold had an experience with this wanton scavenger one night as he laid over in one of his winter line-cabins. His gun, not really being needed with 70 pounds of iron traps on his back, was left behind at another lay-out, but he thought of its importance as he heard a heavy beast jump onto the roof of the little 6-by-8-foot log cabin. It was late at night. He had been asleep a number of hours when the unwanted creature started rumbling around on the sod roof above, looking and working with its claws for a place to crawl through and join the sleeping trapper inside.

What could it be? Frank wondered, as he heard the pieces of loose dirt and wood that made up the roof fall on his blankets. The cold winter night was pitch dark. Frank jumped up to find the matches and candle he had last placed on a small shelf. The light flared in the small enclosure as the man's eyes met a muzzle full of snarling teeth and sharp claws that could only belong to one beast — the wolverine! An ax was outside in the dark. Little good it would do now as the agile scavenger clawed again at the roof. The blood-hungry devil was mad for the smells of the freshly killed marten and Canadian lynx that lay in the corner of the cabin. Frank waved the candle in front of the animal, but it scared little. Picking up a willow stretcher he used on his furs, he poked at the intruder, with no success. This vicious animal was not at all willing to leave those freshly killed furs because it was on the smell of blood. Realizing this, that desire, an idea came to the old trapper. Maybe he didn't want this unwanted night visitor to leave after all. He scurried around the small enclosure, opening jars, and gathering up the materials at hand.

"Okay you hungry, blood-thirsty varmint. If you want some supper, I'll feed you!"

He stepped out of his fortress long enough to chuck a ball of poisoned meat onto the roof of the little log structure. It was meat from a lynx cat, some fat pre-prepared, and enough strychnine to kill a half-dozen wolverines. It was now just a matter of time. Arnold threw two more balls of the flavorful cocktail out to his hungry guest. Frank laid back down on his pine pole bunk, stuck his cold feet back under the blankets, and waited. In thirty minutes, all was quiet, and he knew that $25.00 in fur lay outside in the deep powdered snow.

High Prices, High Country and Fine Furs

There Was No Better Trapper

By today's standards, Frank Arnold would probably be the best trapper in the whole country. In the 1920's and 1930's, when fur prices were at their prime and tens of thousands of trappers were in every corner of the vast forest land of the United States and Canada, Frank, even then, would have been a very good trapper. He was above average and one of the best. He must have started trapping in Eastern Canada, and then wandered into Montana and the Flathead River country. From there he must have gone to Idaho, where he no doubt continued to trap. From Idaho he went to Spokane, and there found work for a fur buyer. He eventually, ended up in the Pasayten Wilderness, where he trapped for furs for 25 long years.

As said before, there were a few things that set this city-hatted Englishman apart from the others besides his hat, clothes and accent. One was his wide use of the dead-fall method that he perfected. Although it took a little more time to put together, once made, it would last for years. It was a deathtrap that did not smell of man.

The skinning, fleshing and stretching of the hide was every bit as important as the hide itself, and a poorly prepared hide would sharply reduce the price of a good fur. Frank always had a razor-sharp knife and was known to be very meticulous in his care of the furs. He made a three-legged stool for skinning that was at the mine for years and years, and just drifted away in the last year or so. Nobody realized Frank had made it, or it would not have been there as long as it was. It was very well-crafted and made with a curved, comfortable seat.

Another thing that set him apart was the fact that he lived all year round in the forest home of the animals he trapped. He was not just a winter visitor as all other trappers were, and because of this, he knew the forest for miles in all directions. They said he knew the Pasayten better than any ten men at the time. Not only trapping and hunting the animals but photographing them in all seasons of the year. Yes, this man was also an artist in photography. His whole life was spent observing animals and their environment. Whereas most trappers trapped as a side-line in winter, Arnold was there all of 20 years, making a detailed study of the life around him. Wisely, he never "trapped an area out," but prudently harvested the fur animals as a farmer would his stock, knowing well how many animals could be taken from a given area and what was to be left. He knew who was trapping what mountains and valleys and where there was open ground that could be used as a new line on a given year. Considering the broad area he was known to trap, and the large number of fur animals he caught, he must have just put on his snowshoes and headed out, making broad circles of perhaps 40 miles or more, with distance and shelter being of little concern, and time being of no importance at all. The mountain man had nothing to stop him but the space between him and the next man's trap-line. He could sleep all night in a snowbank and think nothing about it. He could snowshoe up and down steep mountains all day and that with a 70- or 80-pound pack of traps on his back, and then get up and do it again the next day. He traveled so many thousands of miles on a set of snowshoes with their extra 4 pounds of weigh on each foot (not counting the snow-balls that always rode the top) that like the "old bull-legged cowboy," he walked with a snowshoe-gait, legs a bit straddled, all his life. Few today could walk in his footsteps and fewer still would want to.

But even with all this, it was his gifted ability with his guns that moved him steps further away from his peers. The gun was a lightning bolt in his hand. One quick aim was all he needed. Add this up, and you have a man who was second-to-none when it comes time to sell his furs. If a cougar is within sight, Frank adds $40 to his payroll. If a bear steps out in front of his rifle, he adds $100 to the "puke." If it's only a coyote, he has a fast ten bucks. Frank was an unbelievable shot, and this shooting ability could give the trapper another twenty or thirty percent cash at the end of the year.

High Prices, High Country and Fine Furs

An example of this was when Clyde Andrews saw "seven grizzly bears" in one group. They were grizzlies alright, but this old mountain man had second thoughts about shooting at even one them all by himself. Still, he knew seven grizzlies were worth seven hundred dollars in bounty money if he could. Clyde thought this was a good reason to run to town. Clyde came running into town as fast as he could go to find Frank Zackerman, the young sheepherder who already had a reputation as a good shot. Clyde knew, too, that he had the courage to look a grizzly bear in the eye and pull the trigger. However, Frank Zackerman was tied up at the time and couldn't go out right away, and it was never known whether Clyde even got one of the bears. Not too many people would want to pull down on seven grizzlies alone. A marksman like Frank Arnold, though, might have tried it. He did on several occasions shoot the dangerous grizzlies; one time he shot a mother grizzly and her cub right below the Tungsten Mine. The cub's hide was given to Jack Dolan, a good drinking buddy, who had a store on the west side of the Okanogan River near Ellisforde.

When Frank Zackerman met Frank Arnold on the trail in the Horseshoe Basin in 1927, he happened to find out a number of interesting things about the aging caretaker, one being, Frank's good health. And with that, his strength — few men could walk 50 miles a day over those steep mountains, thought Zackerman, let alone one with gray hair. However, Frank Arnold in conversation told Frank Zackerman two other things of note, things that shed some light on the secret life of the old trapper: one was the fact that Frank had a bad year trapping. He said that he made only $2,500.00 trapping that last winter.

Only made $2,500.00? Zackerman must have thought.

Frank Zackerman was herding sheep at the time for $25.00 a month. If he worked all year at that wage, it amounted to only $300.00. To Frank Zackerman, $2,500.00 sounded like all the money in the world, but Frank Arnold said he had a bad year. *What would Frank Arnold have made in a good year* he wondered.

Arnold then told Frank Zackerman about the reason for the poor year. A wolverine that he couldn't catch had beaten him to a lot of his furs. Yes indeed, the cityhatted Englishman made a lot of money trapping, and it made the freezing cold months alone in the wild woods worth all the hardship and suffering the man took.

If $2,500 was a bad year, what would a good year have been?

My guess would be close to $4,000.00 a season, though the price of furs, unlike today, had held a steady with reliable price since long before the turn of the century. And even though the rich beaver era had ended about 1840, and the riches made in buffalo hides in 1880, furs in general were always a good source of income for the hearty mountain man. The thing with selling furs was that you could get a different price at a different place on a different year. If you shipped your furs to a dealer in St. Louis, Missouri, or even New York City, you could get $100.00 for every one of your martens. If you sold them to a local fur buyer, you might cut that into half or even a quarter. A prime coyote could be worth close to $50.00, maybe more in the 1920's, but a lot of coyotes sold for fifty cents.

Frank Arnold once told Frank Maron he could average thirty lynx a year before the big fire of 1929. Lynx would average probably $50.00 to $60.00 a cat in the Okanogan, so if you had thirty, you had a good $1,500.00 in lynx cats alone. But it was said that Frank excelled in marten. Shorty Fairbrother said that he went after lynx cats and Arnold concentrated more on marten. Shorty was said to have averaged a hundred marten on some of his better trapping years. "Lefty" and "Iron" were getting 45 to 50 marten after the fire in the early forties. Jim Dodd did well on marten, but Frank did better than them all. There were years before the fire when Frank must have gotten close to 200 marten a year. A hundred marten would have been a slow year for Frank, and a hundred

High Prices, High Country and Fine Furs

marten were worth every penny of $2,000.00. Frank must have made up to ten times the average yearly wage for a working man in the six months he trapped those high mountains. And this isn't counting the bears he killed. Six might be a good conservative guess, which meant he had $600.00 in bounty money. And then, not to be forgotten, there were the other fur-bearing animals that ended up on the fur stretcher; beaver, otter and such. To be sure, Frank was a top trapper and made well over $3,500.00 a year, for years, spent almost none of it.

There was another important piece to Frank Arnold's puzzling life that Frank Zackerman found out while he had him stopped on that trail, that day, for some badly needed company, and that was what Frank Arnold did with his furs. For years and years, he would come down into Loomis twice a year with a big load of furs on his back, once in early winter and then when winter was over, probably the first of April. On that spring trip, he would all but by-pass Loomis (after a few days of visiting), and catch a ride down to Oroville, to the Oroville fur-buyer where he made his deal on the wooden counter of Ben Prince's General Store. Ben Prince and his two brothers were fur buyers and loved to see the nice, prime, high-mountain pelts lying on their shiny counter. They were the best buyers in the area, and you could trade your furs for supplies and keep an open account at their store. It was a good arrangement and lasted until about 1930 when Ferris Ford started taking Frank to Spokane to sell his furs for a much higher price. Perhaps Frank at one time even worked for the Spokane buyer years before.

So it was that the Tungsten Mine fur trapper was thought to sell all his furs when he came out, both in mid-December and then, again, the next spring in April. But Frank was a wise old coot, and he had learned long ago not to show all his cards, even to the point where some of the people around Loomis got to thinking old Frank had to be on the lazy side. After all, he came to Loomis those two times every year with all his furs on his back and he just never, never showed any signs of prosperity.

He owned no car, land or property, no horse, no dog, no good clothes, and sported no woman. When Jimmy Dexter, Fred Owens, or Al Smith packed him in, come fall, one pack horse was enough to bring in Frank's total supplies for the entire year. Frank Arnold was to most just a poor old trapper "who had seen better days," they said. "A destitute trapper," Dick Loudon called him. Just a man who lived a "hopeless life," he said. A "recluse," who did some interesting things.

Shorty Fairbrother also knew that Frank Arnold was a very good trapper though it is doubtful Frank ever disclosed his financial status to Shorty. Both Shorty and Frank worked diligently at their trapping business. They didn't spend all winter socializing around the cabin stove, as some might have supposed, but took their winter's occupation very seriously and made it pay big dividends. There almost seems to have been a silent competition between these two men who cut the snow side by side for miles. If Frank was a "heck-of-a-woodsman," Shorty was never going to admit it. For he, too, could give-it and take-it from this hard land as well as any man. And, so the two kept a mute work ethic, with their shoulders to the wheel, nose to the grinding stone, and snowshoes moving. The season lasted five months, November through March, five-and-a-half months at the very most. And Frank E. Maron, remembering that he trapped as a partner with Arnold after the great fire had killed all things living. Then after 2 years, he left without saying good-bye. Maron also by his very silence gave a testimony to Frank's skillful ability.

In addition to telling Frank Zackerman about making $2,500.00 in a bad year, he also told Frank Zackerman another important piece of information. It had to do with what Frank Arnold did with his furs. He he sold them in Canada. Frank Arnold told Frank Zackerman that he went into Canada to sell his furs. Now this was new information. Frank Arnold lived just one and a half miles from the border, 30 miles from Keremeos, British Columbia, and maybe 50 miles from the copper

High Prices, High Country and Fine Furs

town of Princeton, British Columbia. And, sure he trapped Canadian soil. Now, it looked like the wily old trapper split up his furs and take a good part of them into Canada, probably Princeton, to sell. Frank Arnold had the best of both worlds: he was a Canadian (at least at some point in his life}, he lived on the border, and he went both ways when it came time to do business.

I must have talked to close to twenty or so people from the Keremeos area trying to run down anyone who might have known the trapper. I found two. Both have since passed on. One was an old Indian by the name of Jimmy Steves of Headley, British Columbia. Jimmy, at the time of the interview (1988), was 104 years old. In his early years, he had lived on a ranch on Wolf Creek, southeast of Princeton, British Columbia. The picture of Frank Arnold was shown to the old man, and he was asked if he remembered an old trapper who looked like him a longtime ago. Jimmy made a long hard study of the man in the wool button pants with the city hat on his head.

"He used to come through my place on Wolf Creek." Jimmy said. Jimmy Steves remembered Frank walking through his ranch on his way to Princeton. Jimmy indicated Frank would stop once in a while on his way through.

The other person who remembered Frank Arnold was none other than "Gent" Cawsten, from Cawsten, British Columbia, 3 or 4 miles south of Keremeos, Canada. The town was named after his family. Gent also remembered Frank Arnold, though he said he rarely, if ever, came to Keremeos or Cawsten. But Gent knew him and told of a trip into the Tungsten Mine to see Frnak. Gent and Hans Richter, a local rancher, rode their horses up the south fork of the Ashnola River, up the old 1916 mining road to see Frank. Gent was very impressed by Frank's photography and his ability to get close-ups of the big mountain sheep that ran the high mountain range. Gent remembered the lone mountain man well.

So Frank Arnold was part of the early history of the Canadian Ashnola. And if Frank sold a lot of his furs in Canada, it was only fair, because that's where most, if not all of them came from. How far into Canada Frank trapped can only be guessed at today, but there is no doubt that Frank Arnold trapped deep into the Canadian territory. At the time, in those years, there were few trappers, if any, using the upper Ashnola River lands, but you can bet your boots that Frank got at least a third of his furs, if not half his bounty from the rich fur lands north of the border. The hardy winter wanderer could run mile after mile of winter trap-line and never cross another man's snowshoe track.

The Fire Changed It All
1929 is a year that is branded into the scarred land we call Pasayten like a calf thrown into the branding fire. Sixty years after the biggest burn in modern times, the cruel evidence of that inferno is still seen in abundance. Ten thousand loggers couldn't have stripped the land as quickly as the 1929 fire. The land before the holocaust was a trapper's paradise, rich with every game animal a trapper needed, but not so after 1929. The paradise came to a sudden end, and in doing so, forced its trappers to trap other regions outside the big burn or find another occupation. Frank told Herb Curtis that the timbered islands the fire missed were good trapping that winter of 1929-1930, but the following years were "no good." Frank had stripped those islands of land of their furs.

After the fire, "Shorty" Fairbrother gave back to Frank his old trapping area. It was thoroughly burned over. The trapping area included the Windy Mountain and the southern Horseshoe Basin over to Snowshoe Mountain, which Johnny Bell trapped. But it wasn't much of a gift that Shorty gave back. Shorty then went west to Island Mountain and along the east fork of the Pasayten River where the fire only touched. However, he came back 5 years later, after Frank disappeared, and trapped his

High Prices, High Country and Fine Furs

last year, 1935 to 1936, on Windy Mountain with Bill Higgenbotham. Bill Higgenbotham was my old school bus driver. He had also been a horseman who went into the Tungsten Mine many times for many years. Shorty also took over some of Jim Dodd's ground on Sheep Mountain because 1928 was Jim's last year in the high country. Jim Dodd died in 1930, an old man, having entered the high Pasayten well before 1914. "Lefty" and "Iron" also moved into some of Jim Dodd's ground. They trapped Lake Creek, the headwaters of the Ashnola, Andrews Creek, and the Chewack River to the Thirty Mile Ranger Station. But that, too, was poor trapping after the fire.

Frank now had to trap his old "pre" World War I trapping grounds. Miles and miles of trap-line now had to be covered by Frank to get the same results. Though Frank was being edged out to the north by Canadian trappers, he still worked where he could. Where his line really stretched out was to the south, southeast and west. Frank trapped, not only the North Fork of the Toats Coulee River, but also the Middle Fork and South Forks. Frank "just happened" to find himself in the "Conconully Game Reserve" where no man had trapped in years, and the last man who had was more than likely Frank himself in 1912-1914.

Shorty Fairbrother told an interesting story about when he did trap in the reserve one year against regulations in retaliation for the Game Department messing him up on some bounty permits needed for coyote pelts he had gathered in to rebate. They didn't honor their permits, and Shorty couldn't cash in his hard-earned pelts. Frank knew this country and probably worked it wherever he wanted: Thunder Mountain, Skull and Crossbones, Douglas Mountain, Twenty Mile Meadows, and on down to Beaver Meadows.

It must have been in the winter of 1933 to 1934 that Frank pushed his line to the very Pacific crest of the Cascades. He told Farris Ford that he trapped that far west; into the Chuchuwanteen river drainage, which takes in Frosty Creek and the Dead Lake area up to Mounument 83 on the border.

Frank Maron Enters the Story

One day in the late fall, just after the 1929 fire was put out, Pete brought a young man into the Tungsten Mine to meet Frank Arnold. Pete came riding in on a sorrel horse, and the new man rode a white. They packed Pete's mule. The new man had black hair, dark eyes, and was small in stature. He was a nervous and fidgety man, his name — Frank E. Maron.

Maron, as previously mentioned had come from Kettle Falls to work on the big fire that year, securing a job fighting the fire with Pete. And seeing times were hard and Frank Arnold was getting older, Pete apparently thought the two might get along. And, Maron needing a home and with no job, might be able to stay at the Tungsten Mine with Frank. The Great Depression was gripping the country and few men could find work, anywhere. Frank Arnold was about 60 years old at the time, and Maron couldn't have been much over 20 or 25 years old. It had been 20 years since Frank Arnold had taken a trapping partner way across the valley, east, 80 miles to the little town of Chesaw; and, why Frank would take in a partner at all after all those years is a good question. It probably had more to do with Frank's age and eyes, than Maron's need for a place to stay. Nevertheless, for whatever the reason, a lot of what we know about Arnold is because of this one man's association with the old Englishman. The two trapped for two seasons together, and it was not the best time to jump into trapping. All of Frank's old-line camps were burnt out, and the fire called for some new ground to be sought. It is said the two trapped one year from a cabin off Windy Mountain. We can assume that first year that they worked the border of the burn and the timbered islands it had missed. Yet if 1929-1930 wasn't "real bad,"

High Prices, High Country and Fine Furs

1930-1931 was. That was also Frank Maron's last year with Frank Arnold; he left that summer of 1931, working his way into the mental institute.

Frank Arnold and Frank Maron had a bit of a hard departure after their 2 years of trapping together. An old newspaper had this to say when a summer visitor went by to see Arnold:

"Frank was hopping mad. Some young guy (Frank Maron) he had taken in, had gone off with a whole load of groceries, and Frank was down to potatoes and salt... Frank said the catch of furs last winter (1930-1931) was poor. The Indians were trapping in the north."

"Indians trapping in the north" could only mean one place: Canada. The Englishman's northern trapping country was now being taken over. What the fire didn't take, the Canadian Indians and Maron did. Frank Arnold's world was changing and changing fast.

By winter of 1934, Frank's last year alive, his trap-line ran from the Chuchuwanteen River, far to the west, to Snowshoe Mountain in the east, and from places north into Canada, and south to Twenty Mile Meadows. Because Frank snowshoed into the Beaver Meadow C.C.C. camp one winter day in 1934, he probably ran a line down there, too. Beaver Meadow is a cool 50 miles or more from the Tungsten Mine, as is the Chuchuwanteen River.

Frank Arnold started trapping the Pasayten Wilderness border lands when he was over 40 years old, and he trapped it for close to 25 years. Folks now know that he was the best trapper that High Country ever knew, though few, if any, knew it at the time. Frank had the land at its best and loved it. He was a strong but gentle man, solitary to be sure, who made the years in the lonely mountains work. It was because of this beautiful, yet tempestuous place he chose to live, because of his great and many skills, because of his uniqueness, the man came to be a wonder in his own day, and a legend in ours. Paying the ultimate price for such an honor, he was swallowed up, in the end, by the land he loved. It was while on his trap-line in an area he had covered so many times in the past that the 65-year-old mountain man was cheated out of his life. Cheated by this land of seeming sugar and salt. The only man in the vast land's history who could truly call the Pasayten "home!"

In the twenty-some years that Frank trapped the wild wilderness, he left a legacy of forgotten cabins and lay-outs waiting to be stumbled upon by future wanderers. Most of his really good ones were destroyed by the big fire of 1929, and today, little is left of those that escaped, or were later rebuilt, for on every one of them there is a fallen, deteriorated roof, or a collapsed wall brought down by the ravages of time. Of Frank's many cabins scattered along his miles of trap-lines, at least 10 have been found. They were all small and measured only about 8 by 6 feet or so, with one or two being slightly larger. The one exception to this quaintness was his cabin in long-Swamp, which measured about 10 by 12 feet. The lay-out on Douglas Mountain, which could have been his permanent home before the first war, was nothing more than logs piled against a rock wall, making a "lean-to." Over at the camp where he was found hanging, his winter quarters were simply a small lean-to just 3 feet high by 7 feet long, open on the high side, and covered over with canvas.

Frank Arnold built a number of cabins that got no farther than just four sides, but never did he seem to get a roof over them. Putting on a leak-proof and dry roof in those days was not an exact science, or altogether an easy chore, with dirt being the main component. For Frank, there was so much canvas left over when the Tungsten Mine shut down, that he found it easier to just cover his cabins with this leftover material. Remember that all the goods brought into the mine that winter in 1916 were first wrapped in canvas tarps and covered with big canvas tents. Also, there were a number of cabins that were already built when Frank came on the scene.

There was one cabin he took over at Pocket Lake on the Chewack River. There was another standing above Canadian Camp, called also Tungsten Camp, just west of Rock Mountain. It was said that another one along the border not far away was built by a Canadian, though I don't go along with this, for the cabin isn't that old, and is just too difficult to get at from the north. Besides, it sits on the U.S. side. Some say that Frank never built one total cabin in all his years in the wilderness, but this is not true. Frank did build this one along the border and put a good concave log roof on it. He built a least three more with good hand-hewn, concave log roofs. They all looked about the same, just 8 feet by 6 feet lodge-pole cabins. Again, each of these cabins had labor-intensive hewn and "cupped" log roofs, and to make them complete, each had a cheap five-gallon oil-can stove, with cutouts for the stove-pipe and home-made sheet-iron doors. Frank actually made a number of nice, neat cabins. Some of these are found on Windy Creek, Basin Creek, Horseshoe Creek, Long Swamp, Rock, Haig, and Good-enough Mountain. And the rock solid proof that Frank built this last one on Good-enough Mountain is not because of it being in his trapping area, or being of the right age, or displaying his "cupped" log roof and small size, but because of the half bottle of good "whiskey" they found in the cabin un-drunk, 15 years later. Father and son, Irving and Lester Lucas, found the bottle when they stumbled on the cabin by chance in the 1950's while out hunting the same lynx cat Frank was after sixteen winters before.

Frank did an interesting bit of construction here at this mountain spot off Good-enough Mountain. The cabin sits above a cliff over-looking the north. So, on this cliff, looking toward the mountains and the north land, Frank nailed some logs together and built a "deck," of all things. About 8 feet by 10 feet, the deck hung out over the cliff's edge, projecting out, giving an unhampered view over a majestic mountain scene looking north. No doubt its only need was to have a scenic overview as he ate his meals — and they said Frank had no class.

Back over in the Horseshoe Basin, on the far west side where both Shorty's and Frank's trapping lines came together, the men shared a cabin, each one trying not to be there when the other was using it. The exception was on Christmas Day when the two would have an annual celebration together in the small cabin. It is said they had a big turkey dinner together every year, for years. The turkey was always one that Frank had brought in after selling a few furs in the town of Oroville. It was a good time for both of them, and Shorty would talk about the fine visits with Frank many years after he, too, gave up the hunt and Frank had disappeared.

He told of a time one Christmas that Frank brought up the subject of a "bob-tailed" marten he had caught that winter. Now martens are not bob-tailed, and Frank was wondering and surmising how this old marten had lost its luxurious tail. "What do you think a bob-tailed marten is worth, Lester? You know the tail is about half the fur on a marten, and this guy is a good copper-bellied one. I bet you, they won't give me ten dollars for this guy without a tail." Shorty sat there with an interested grin as Frank bewailed his loss of a prime fur with half its fur gone.

When Frank got through lamenting the shortfall of catching a marten without a tail, Shorty asked, "where did you catch that funny thing at, anyway?" After Frank told him, Shorty got up and walked over to a box on the shelf of the small cabin. Opening the box, Shorty pulled out a fluffy, furry marten tail. Holding it up, he said; "I caught this tail in my trap not 1 mile from where you caught that big bobtailed one." The two trappers got a good laugh over both of them coming up with part of the same marten in their traps. Shorty gave Frank the tail, which brought the price of the "bob-tailed Marten" up a great deal. The two later split what Frank received for the fur.

The difference between Shorty (Lester) Fairbrother's cabins, who used his only in the winter, and Arnold's, who might use his at any time of the year, was that Shorty always put his cabins into the ground about a foot or more, while Frank rarely, if ever did this. Building a cabin down in the dirt has the effect of keeping the cabin damp in the summers and therefore keeping the pine rats and mice out. Lester hated rats! Frank, on the other hand, kept his rodent population down by using all the dozens and dozens of rat and mouse traps left to him from the early days by Herb Curtis of the Tungsten Mine.

It is always a thrill to come upon an old trapper's cabin, especially one of Frank Arnold's. That said, the chances may not be that small for those who wonder off the main byways because the better part of a 1000 square miles of trapping area took a lot of "lay-outs."

CHAPTER 13

Fire and Destruction

"On account of the rugged character of the country in which they are burning, several fires have grown to rather dangerous size."
　　　　　　　　　　　　　　Oroville Newspaper: August 9, 1929

"A. Judd who came out early in the week, states there are fires throughout the mountains in the Chewack River and Cathedral districts."
　　　　　　　　　　　　　　Oroville Newspaper: August 11, 1929

"It sent up in flames millions and millions, and still millions, of board feet of timber. It was a powerful burn that will scar the land for decades."
　　　　　　　　　　　　　　Harold MacWilliams

"He would throw buckets of water on his shack until he collapsed gasping, then dipped into the earth with his hands for a breath of oxygen, then get to his feet again to throw on more water."
　　　　　　　　　　　　　　Ann Briley, a noted author

THE 1929 FIRE HAS BEEN called by many names throughout the years; Dollar Watch Fire, Pasayten River Fire, Ashnola Fire, Horseshoe

Basin Fire, Windy Mountain, and the one I and George Honey will use: The Rummel Lake Fire. However, whatever name you put on it, you wish to explain it: the Rummel Lake Fire of 1929 was the worst fire the Pasayten has ever seen in modern times. It turned a beautiful, pristine wilderness into a pile of black ashes and cinder 3 feet high. It made a sea of crisscrossed logs called "Jim-Jacks" that blanketed the burned-out area like a shambled rug. Three hundred years or more of growth in the older trees was all but destroyed. Some areas today still look like an atomic bomb went off 60 years later. It was a wicked fire that killed animals by the thousands.

George Honey and his brother, Leonard, Joe Kelsey, the Hill brothers, Francis Lufkin, Charley C. Johnson, the Mackey boys from Okanogan, and more than a dozen men marched from Thirty Mile Ranger Station high on the Chewack River under the command of Chuck Kakendal, the Forest Service fire boss. The cross-cut saws bounced on their shoulders, and their backpacks bulged with food and supplies for the task that lay before them. It was early August 1929, and it was swelteringly hot as the young men hiked up the Chewack River for the troublesome fire that burned up at Rummel Lake. At the end of a long 17-mile hike, saws bit into trees and sweat rolled from the young men's chests as they battled the smoking flames that jumped and popped not too far away. The fire had been caught in a good spot, a place where it all came together in this semi-open area of scattered trees. It was relatively flat country, well-watered and much of it covered with green, lush grass. The wind had died, and by the fifth day of slaving by the young, strong men, the fire was well under control and all but contained. Victory was in their hands like a gold victory cup, and every man on the job felt good about the battle he had helped win.

"We got it in the bag, Boss!" shouted young George Honey to Kakendal who was also standing around being proud of himself, over the nice, circling fire line he had engineered. A fire "stop" to be sure.

Fire and Destruction

George and Joe Kelsey had been pulling on the same saw, like John Henry and the jackhammer. For 5 days and 6 nights the men had fought a winning battle, and as the day drew to night, the boys knew they had it well under control and were thinking about a short week of mopping up, and then the walk back out, and home. The three men walked over to their very last tree, a big 3-foot spruce, 100 feet high — the last tree that stood between them and a perfect circling line of open space. All the felled trees were laying the right way. All the downed logs and brush had been removed on a 25-foot strip. It had taken 15 men 5 days working 20 hours a day to capture the great fire.

"Chuck... hey, Chuck. Joe and I will knock that last tree down there, buck this small log over there up, and this fire will be all but history. Sound good, Mr. Kakendal?" George Honey asked.

"Few more days of mop up and if that blankety-blank wind just stays down, this fire will be out. Hell! It's just grass smoking now. You boys have done a right smart job working these last few days. I'm getting tired of eatin' Mike's salted biscuits and need to get off that rock I've been sleeping on," Chuck answered.

George and Joe could relate to that matter.

"Shoot, George. You and Joe stand back," said this Forest Service man, "Let me backfire this son-of-a-gun tree and save you boys some work. It was time to quit three hours ago, and no use sawing on that tree for another hour when we can "burn" it down! Besides, you boys have sweated enough over that shark-tooth devil you got there in your hands. Stand back! Here goes what we Forest Service call a "CONTROLLED BACK BURN."

Chuck Kakendal lit a match, reached out and touched it to the black Spanish moss hanging on the big, old Spruce tree. The fire ignited and seemed to run up the tree like magic — and— the tree EXPLODED like a large gasoline torch in front of them! The fire fighters jumped back as the heat and sparks poured out on them. The cinders rose in a big mushroom ball for hundreds of feet up and drifted north with the light breeze into the kindle dry forest not far away. The three men stood there dumbfounded, struck by the way the tree had exploded, transfixed at the dancing flame and hypnotic waves of fire and blue smoke that were sucked into the late evening sky, mesmerized, in a stupor of fatigue caused by the many long hours of work. Minutes went by as they stood there in a trance, of wondering at the huge flame before them.

Chuck snapped out of the trance first and got a grip on the new situation he had created. The reality of it seemed to hit them all, one after the other; Chuck had created a flaming monster! They hoped against hope that what they saw before them would not materialize into what seemed to be happening — a devastating firebomb had been let down on the earth by the awesome power of wood and flame. It took only a few minutes for this "controlled-back-burn," to "back-fire!" It turned the entire northern mountain into a new catastrophe. Chuck began to cuss and shout then scream for all he was worth. George, Joe, Frank, Leonard Honey, Francis Lufkin, Charley Johnson, the Mackey boys, and soon the whole crew of fifteen ran around like chickens with their heads cut off trying to control Chuck's "controlled burn." It seemed like there were now thousands of little smoking cinders falling everywhere starting little smoking fires everywhere. The thousand little fires were blanketing the ground and fighting to kill and destroy everything in their reach. The day went from the joy of victory to devilish defeat. The young men beat the ground with their shovels, stomped the ground with their boots, flung their shirts at spot fires and turned over dirt again and again. All were futile acts. It was a loss! For they soon found that they were now the losers, not only in this battle to save the forest, but even to their very lives! In their zeal to regain the day, they had failed to see the waves of fire surrounding them like a net. The strings of their trap were being drawn up with a deadly, subtle force.

Fire and Destruction

At the very last minute, Chuck came to his senses and realized the grave danger surrounding them. He yelled at his faithful young men to make a run for their lives and follow him.

"QUICK! HURRY BOYS! MAKE A RUN FOR IT! UP THE MOUNTAIN!" came Kakendal's almost too-late command.

Shovels dropped as the shout went around. With smoke-filled lungs; black-singed clothes, hair and skin; and scalded hot feet, his men ran after Chuck, hoping that he could now lead them to safety somewhere. Waves of fire licked at their heels, and smoking firebrands slashed their faces as they dodged through doorways of flaming trees and walls of exploding fire, leaping like jack rabbits over smoking logs. Up, up the mountain, they fled in the now dark forest; and somehow, through strength of youth and fate, they found the only — the only — safe place on the whole mountain. They made it to an open and bare rock ridge that was free of timber. Here, far up the mountain, they collapsed in utter exhaustion. The great yellow fire raged at the forest all around them. But safe on their rock fortress that night, the men sat trapped, surrounded by their new master, death, that had almost snatched them up that day. The powerful, sweeping scourge slowly moved on north before their eyes: Cathedral Mountain, Apex Mountain and Saddle Peak, all went up in huge flames of fire. It was a sinister, beautiful fire display that ran all night before the handful of dejected and exhausted men. They had lost a war and battle that had been an assured victory. With just one last tree, the land called PASAYTEN, Devils Land, was now a blackened ruination for the next 50 years.

The Next Day

Emmet Smith, the sheepherder, coming up from Loomis, had the job of riding as fire messenger for Frank Burge, the District Ranger, for P. T. Harris, the Fire Superintendent, and now also for Chuck Kakendal, the fire boss at Rummel Lake. Emmet Smith was riding in one big

50-mile circle. He had started in Long Swamp with the fire fighters there after riding his horse up from way down the valley where his sheep were held up and pastured, unable to advance up the mountain. Emmet moved from Long Swamp, where one fire was only a few miles away on Windy Mountain, down the steep mountain into the Chewack River drainage, a fall-off of 1,500 feet, cutting down on the treacherous Chewack sheep and cattle trail. At the bottom, against the river, in the smoke-filled valley, he followed the trail up the river to the sheep bridge at the mouth of Horseshoe Creek. Crossing the river there, he pushed on past the trail going north to the Tungsten Mine at Tungsten Creek, riding on up the river, carrying his message from P. T. Harris, the Fire Superintendent. The message was an important one for Chuck Kakendal who was supposedly holding out at Rummel Lake. But three hours later, after riding through a smoldering forest, and arriving at what must be Rummel Lake, Emmett could see that things were out of control there, and nether Chuck nor his crew were anywhere to be found. The only thing that was clear was that the hope that Chuck would be able to stop the fire at Rummel Lake hadn't happened. The consequences now were too massive to think about, for now there was no chance of the fire being stopped anywhere, by anyone, not even the Canadians, who now were the recipients of Washington's smoking gift.

Finding the forest ablaze and no one at Rummel Lake, Emmet could not wait around for things to materialize. Not wanting to turn around and re-face the fire behind him, the fire that he had just barely edged through, and thinking there might be a good chance of beating the fire to the mine, where hopefully Chuck and his crew now must be, Emmet thought that once he rode over Cathedral Mountain, he could pick up the high-running Boundary Trail and ride back east to familiar grounds, there to meet up again with P. T. Harris and his crew at Long Swamp. He knew that by circling around Cathedral Mountain, he could report on

Fire and Destruction

the exact status of the fire from that far northern boundary trail, where hopefully the fire had found a place to burn itself out.

Spurring his jaded horse for the Tungsten Mine by way of Cathedral Mountain, he rode at the very foot of the awesome Cathedral Peak that was totally hidden from his sight by a fog of smoke. Barely able to even find the trail, he sensed his way through country he had never been through before. Breaking over the 7,500-foot-high Cathedral Pass, he found the descending trail that snaked down from the pass in flames. Stopped by the fire before him, Emmet had only two choices. One was to turn around and go back to face the backfire at Rummel Lake. The other was to make his own trail around the burning valley below him. Cutting high up on the mountainside where the smoke and fire pushed him into the rocks, his horse scrambled desperately to keep on its footing with torn-up hooves and no metal horseshoes. Over the rocks and around huge boulders he negotiated, keeping himself and his horse just barely above the timberline and out of the flames' reach. Slowly he rounded the valley rim, just a little speck in the vast basin of smoke. Making the east side of the basin at last, he found the trail again and scampered up onto the flat ground of Apex Pass. But there, he could see that the next basin to come, Tungsten Creek, was marked for destruction too. The yellow flaming dragon had crossed Apex Mountain also. The Tungsten Mine sat doomed!

The cabins were barely visible just feet away in the heavy blue smoke that burned Emmet's eyes and filled his lungs. He had almost ridden by them because of the poor visibility. He had never been this far west and now there was little to see past 20 feet in the thick fog of smoke.

"CHUCK.! CHUCK! Are you there? FRANK! FRANK! Frank, where are YOU?" shouted Emmet, hoping for an answer from some form of life. But he heard no answer as he waited beside his horse. Emmet had been leading his gimping horse for the last 3 miles. "

TALES OF THE TUNGSTEN MINE

This mine is as good as ashes, Emmet thought as he pushed on. *Now it was all but impossible even with a crew of a thousand men to get in here in time to save this northern forest or to save Canada. It was all lost!*

The fire was close, and his first responsibility was to get the latest fire report back to Super Harris. Word had to get out back to him about the fire jumping the line at Rummel Lake. Emmet yanked on the reins of his sore-footed horse that did not want to move. His faithful horse had never gotten the iron shoes for his feet he so badly needed, and this rocky trip had torn them up. Now after 30 miles of rocky riding, it couldn't move. He pulled with both hands, trying to inch the animal forward because there was just no way he could stop now. To stop here would mean death! He had no choice. He had to escape this place with his message for the fire fighters back to the east. Their fire might be under control, but he had to tell them that another wildfire was coming their way.

Where Frank Arnold was when Emmet came by could only be guessed, but you can bet he wasn't far away. The "mayor" of the Tungsten Mine had been watching the fire with deep concern. No other person had more to lose than he with the coming of the unstoppable fire beast that blackened the sky with smoke, ash and cinders 6 miles up. It did not look good. It looked impossible!

Frank had been over at Rummel Lake watching the Winthrop fire crew battle the flames and felt they had succeeded that day as he walked back over to the Tungsten Mine. But his heart sank that night when the heavy smoke, cinders and flames lit up the sky and poured over the southern peaks, 6 miles away, telling him a sad story. He knew he would very soon have his own battle with the wild burning flames that moved steadily, foot by foot, toward him. The flames moved from south to the north and from the east to the west. He knew as the flames crossed over the mountain early the next morning that he needed one thing and one thing badly — WATER! Now water is the one thing that the Tungsten Mine does not have in great quantities; at least, it is not running by the

Fire and Destruction

cabin doorsteps. It was said that before the fire reached the doors of the mine that Frank had rigged up some sort of water system, with even a pump, to get water onto the tinder-dry, wooden cabins.

So it was, as it turned out, through the engineering of a water system that the 60-year-old man fought like a crazed "fire chief" to save his beloved home from the flaming yellow fire that roared all around him. The fire came from every direction. The hot gasses, ashes and flames threw themselves at the cabins and millworks that stood in their way. Like a lone soldier fighting under the blazing fire, making a last stand, alone on a hilltop, Frank Arnold himself saved the Tungsten Mine from total destruction. It was far from a complete victory. It was at best a standoff, for from then on, the Tungsten Mine would be only a small remnant of its former glory.

It was in the month of September, about the 10th, that Frank walked through the black desolation. The forest was nothing but utter destruction and burnt waste. Down to the town of Loom, he came with the news of the big fire that had burnt a good part of his Pasayten Wilderness.

"Fire in Stumps and Logs Will Burn until Snow Puts Them Out"

Frank Arnold walked into Loomis Tuesday from the Cathedral Peak District, about forty or more miles west of town. He states the forest fires, which raged in that district during the past month, almost burned the buildings where he has his headquarters. He put out the spot fires and worked night and day for seven days, doing without much sleep or food in the time. He said branches of the Ashnola Creek fires and Rummel fires advanced from five different angles. According to Mr. Arnold, who has lived in that country for about 15 years trapping each winter, the contour of the country looked different, and it is hard to know where one is since it has burned over. He also said the ashes are almost waist deep in places."

Loomis News: September 13, 1929

If Frank was guilty of almost burning down the Tungsten Mine in the early 1920's, he made up for it in 1929. The cabins survived only because of his 7 days of constant battling the deadly flames. And deadly they were, for another account of his experience chills us more…

"He would throw buckets of water on his shack until he collapsed gasping, then dipped into the earth with his hands for a breath of oxygen, then get to his feet again to throw on more water," writes Ann Briley, a noted author.

It was almost at the cost of his own life that Frank fought to save that vestige of man. He did not run! Indeed, he was on the verge of death by fire through the whole ordeal. Today, it's ironic that the Forest Service, in their zeal, harbors the thought of burning these cabins down. Indeed, they have burned down many, many historical cabins.

The 1929 fire did take its toll, though on the Tungsten Mine. It burnt the ore mill, the sawmill and the boilers. It is said that the boilers exploded like a big bomb, "BOOM!" during the fire and blew up the mills. Frank was just able to save the big cookhouse built out of sawed lumber and the log cabin attached to it. He also saved his cabin, the one built for Harold Savage and his wife, the superintendent's lodging. And, he somehow managed to save the one remaining bunkhouse below the main cabin along with its outhouse. Everything else went up in smoke. In actuality, this wasn't that much, with the exception of the mills because the earlier fire, caused by his liquor still exploding, had already erased a good number of structures.

You might as well say that the 1929 fire burned the whole of the Pasayten Wilderness as we know it today, for there wasn't much it missed. It missed only parts of the far west side, that area west of the Pasayten River and some of the southern drainages. The snows of winter are what finally put it out after three months of burning. Sadly, George Honey almost had the western fire out at Rummel Lake, but Chuck's "backfire"

Fire and Destruction

really backfired with sad consequences. The fire not only burned the Pasayten, but then went on north into Canada and burnt most of the Canadian Ashnola as well. It burned basically from the Pasayten River east to the lower Toats Coulee, and from the southern boundary area of the Pasayten Wilderness to the northern Ashnola, 20 miles or so into Canada. The big 1929 fire must have destroyed close to 600,000 acres of land. It was a terrific fire, throwing ash into the sky miles high, and after more than 60 years, the land is finally starting to give us a glimpse of its former beauty.

CHAPTER 14

30 Tons in 1936

The story of the road job was told by George Honey. The story of the packing out of all the ore and mining was shared by George Honey, George Miller, Harold MacWilliams, Foss Creveling, Bob Erwin, Bob Curtis, Hank Dammann, Jr. and Bruce McPherson, Jr.

IT WAS EARLY MAY 1936. The steel tracks rolled, and the smoke belched from the little tractor. The cat-skidder, the driver, was being jarred around like a bronc rider as he rammed and pulled on the levers that controlled the up and down movement of the cable blade. A big boulder rolled over the bank and down into the Chewack River. A green stump and a whole lot of dirt tumbled down behind it. The crawler moved back again as the man at the throttle turned the machine back up the river, walking it through melting snow drifts and brush, pushing more rocks and logs out of the would-be road. The man driving the tractor, Johnny Jorganson, was following the Chewack River.

"Mac," Bruce McPherson, was two hundred yards in front of the tractor with "H.V.", Harold V. Dardier, a big French-Canadian who weighed 255 pounds. They were cutting down the trees that lined the trail, widening the trail of trees and logs for the coming little crawler. It was back-breaking work with the ax and cross-cut saw. The two cutters walked by anything that looked like the tractor could handle. The C.C.C. had built the first half mile of road past Thirty Mile Ranger Station the year before but had dropped the project after the first mile. Mac and Dardier slowly cut their way up along the high mountain river from where the C.C.C. had quit, some 30 miles from the town of Winthrop. McPherson and Dardier were headed for the 8,000-foot Wolframite Mountain.

That winter McPherson, Dardier and Hughy Lawrence had reached an agreement with Ferris Ford, now the sole mining claim holder of the Tungsten Mine, as to what they were going to do to get all the tungsten ore that was just lying on the ground waiting for someone to pick it up and sell it. It was the ore that had gone through the mill between 1916 and 1920. It was surmised that the sheelite had not been captured by the milling and had gone over into the tailing pile. The big Canadian, Dardier, must have had a little money to put into the operation, because Mac did not. It was Mac who earlier had made a lease option to buy the mine from Ferris Ford. The option gave Hughy Lawrence and the old mountain man, Clyde Andrews each a one-quarter interest. He still having his name on the claims, which apparently, he had never sold to the wheeler-dealer, Ferris Ford, in 1930.

But this was May 1936, and Arthur Lund, a Tonasket banker, had underwritten a certain amount of the present venture for Mac and Dardier. The two miners were very enthused about the whole deal and were more than a little interested in getting the ore out very quickly. A war was again building in Europe and the price of tungsten was up. The world powers again needed 60% tungsten ore for their iron works. This mining venture though, compared to the last one 20 years before, would be easy, all that the two miners needed was a road into the mine and things would be set. The old ore dump, waste rock from the first

30 Tons in 1936

war, was just lying there, tons of it, so all they had to do was scoop it up and send it out to a buyer. It would be an easy job once they got this new road busted through because now there were modern machines to move rocks instead of hand shovels. Johnny Jorganson was running one of those machines. Johnny also had a trailer with a 4-yard dump box that hooked onto the back of the tractor to bring out the ore. Everything could be run by one man, but he needed this road.

"About a week, total, maybe two. I figure." said Mac to Dardier as they pumped on the saw to put down yet another tree.

"I think that might be a little short." answered Dardier, as he pulled back and forth on his saw. "We're on our third day and only on our second mile!"

"It's just right up here on this river a few miles." said Mac as he laid the saw into another tree. "We'll be there in 6, maybe 10 days at most; just keep pulling on your saw and we'll get in there!" he encouraged Dardier.

The tractor's tracks smoked and sparked on the hard granite ledges, slipped and spun again in the late spring snow as it crawled over the trail making slow progress for the ore on Wolframite Mountain. Mac came up to the driver waving his arms to stop.

"You're going to have to pick up the pace if we're ever going to get back there this century, Johnny! Keep as close to us as you can," came the commanding voice from Mac.

"Do you want a road, or do you just want me to drop this machine from an airplane into this mine?" Johnny countered.

"I know... I know John, but don't do any more than one lick for now, ok?"

"Ok, you're the boss, Mac! How much farther is it into this mine anyway?"

Seven days later, on the Chewack River, Dardier had great doubts about his partner's reckoning ability.

"Are you sure we're even on the right damned river, Mac? There's three rivers that come together right in here, and which one are we going to take?" Dardier bellered over the burning campfire that evening, as the three men camped for the night. It really wasn't all Mac's fault. Dardier had looked at the map, too, and Ferris Ford had indicated that this was the best and shortest way in.

"I know it's the right damned river, H.V., and you do, too, but neither one of us has been over this route before, because I came in the other way from Loomis last fall. Ferris said this was the best way in and out for the road, and down to the railroad. I can't say for sure where this other creek here came from. The main trail crosses the creek here on this bridge, but this one creek goes due north and so does that one up there a mile. I guess I had better hike on up that trail at its mouth and find out exactly where it does go. The mine can't be that far up. You boys work up to this creek tomorrow, and I'll walk up the trail going up that distant creek and see how far we've got to go. There's not much snow left here, and probably not much up on the mountain, either."

The next day, Mac was off for the lost Tungsten Mine from the forks of the Chewack River and the creek called Horseshoe. Johnny walked the tractor on up to the fork and turned off the motor to wait further instructions. Dardier found some soft grass and stretched out for a long siesta in the spring sun. They were less than 7 miles from where they had started, camped at the sheep-bridge and the nice, open, grassy glade that made it an ideal camp to wait for Mac's report.

The sun had long since passed over the mountains when Dardier opened up a can of beans that was to be their dinner and poured it into the pot.

"Must be further up than he thought," Johnny said as Dardier disgustedly ate his dinner, wondering where Mac had gone. It was a cold May night with ice along the creek edge. Mac, high up on the mountain, lay curled up in some old blankets that he chanced upon in the upper cabin at the Tungsten Mine, many miles away. It had been a long, long walk uphill. There were 7 miles of too much snow between and Horseshoe Creek where his partners were camped, waiting. Mac's clothes were all wet because of it, and he had come unprepared to spend the night.

"It's just not supposed to be that many miles more into the mine, and damned it's high up here on this mountain!"

How had he misjudged the distance so badly, he wondered, as he rolled around in his new-found bunk. *I'm sure glad all this stuff is here*, Mac thought. *Must be some of old Frank Arnold's things, but I'm glad these blankets are here tonight, for it's not summer on this mountain yet.*

Mac knew now that it would take all summer to get that new road blasted up this last 7 miles to the ore. So far, they had not had to blast a single rock, but from the mouth of Tungsten Creek, there would be many miles of blasting, and with that, dozens and dozens of steep switch-backs to cut in the mountain if any ore was going to get in and out by tractor and trailer. Ferris Ford had not mentioned that part. Besides, there was still 2 feet of snow up here and a mess of fallen logs under that snow all the way up! Mac was whipped! He could see plainly that a new road was now out of the question. It would be drilling and blasting and cutting all summer long just to get that tractor close to the ore pile.

"I can see 2 years of work here before there is even one paycheck coming back to us," Mac said aloud. He turned over on an empty stomach that hadn't seen food since Horseshoe Creek, but sleep wouldn't come that night as he turned and thought the new situation over in his mind.

At 10:00 the next morning, Mac stepped back into the boys' camp on the mouth of Horseshoe Creek.

"Where in the heck you been, Mac? You got lost, didn't you? We were just getting ready to go back to Winthrop for some help. Where you been these three days? Did you find the mine?"

"Boys! The road job is over with! DONE! We're going to head back to town. Johnny, turn that tractor around."

Mac, of course, had never been to the mine from the Winthrop side and in looking over the map of the country, he had mistaken Windy Creek for Horseshoe Creek. Windy Creek came down to the Chewack River just down from the Thirty Mile Ranger Station. Mac had cut off 8 miles to the mine by this mistake, both creeks coming in from the northeast and looking about the same on a map.

George Miller's Pack-String

Back in the town of Winthrop, the first place Bruce and Dardier went was to George Miller's packing service. Would George Miller be willing to put together a pack-string for them right away? Bruce and Harold explained to George what they were going to do, sack up the old tailings from the mine, have George pack the sacks of ore off the mountain and down to the Ranger Station, and then they would ship them by dump-truck from Thirty Mile to the railroad siding at Pateros, down on the Columbia River 75 miles away. George's job would be to pack the ore out from the mine the 14 miles to the Forest Service Station. Now seeing George was out of work, and so were some of the best hands around, he took the contract offered by Dardier for .80 cents a day per horse, and $90.00 dollars a month for himself and each one of his helpers. In a few short days from the handshake, George Miller was on the trail for the Canadian Border. Over the next four months he would hire George Honey, Foss Crevelin, Harold MacWilliams and Charley Smith to ride and pack for him.

The first sacks of ore came out on the 15th of May 1936, which is amazingly early, and to be sure, they were working in snow. Bruce and Harold had a crew of five men hired to sack up the ore tailings that lay around the old burned-out mill. The men with the shovels and sacks were Bob O'Neil, Henry (Hank) Dammann, Lyle Bott, Dale Bott, and the camp cook, Charley Hartz. Mac's son, Bruce "Jr." McPherson and young Hank Dammann, "Jr.", would come up after school was out, as well as Bob Irwin, a school-mate of Bruce "Jr." to put in their fair share of time with the tools of the trade.

McPherson and Dardier had originally planned to use the tractor-crawler to run up and down the mountain and bring the ore out in the small trailer, but of course that idea was dropped after Mac's long, steep and rocky walk into the mine. Johnny Jorgenson stayed with his dump truck at Thirty Mile, possibly cooking and tending camp for the packers there. Or he just came up once a week to drive the truck to Pateros, dumping the ore in an open train car at the siding. To be sure, it was a long haul those 75 miles of rough, dirt road all the way only to turn around and drive back up. On the weekends, too, the packers and miners could catch a ride with Johnny on the truck to Winthrop.

George Miller put at least 24 horses on the trail to pack out the 60-pound ore bags, one on each side of a horse. Two or three strings of pack horses would pull out of the mine with each string amounting to twelve head at the start but leveling off to about six horses as the weeks went by. The bags were to be ready and waiting for the packers every other day, but as the summer rolled on, it turned out that the burden of keeping up was on the miners and not on the packers as first thought. Bruce "Jr." remembers throwing "not-so-good-of-rock" into the ore bags just to have a load ready for the packing, but Harold MacWilliams did his fair share of toting 60-pound bags. MacWilliams remembers putting boards under the bags to keep them from rubbing sores on the horses' sides, just one of the many tricks he learned over a long career as a horse packer.

The packing job went like this: on riding in, George Miller and a packer stayed overnight in the bunkhouse at the mine. Then in the morning, after catching and saddling their horses, they packed up the ore on his six to twenty-four head of horses and reined the pack-string down the mountain. Five or six hours later, at the dump truck, they would dump their ore in the truck. By then, the day was pretty much done. They unsaddled the horses, fed and grained the stock, made camp and dinner, then called it a day. The next day was spent wrangling horses for the return ride back up the mountain, packing in like in the old days, food supplies and such for the miners on the return trip.

Sixteen-Year-Old School Boy

Bob Irwin of Oroville was a boy of sixteen when he stepped on the big Washington Motor Coach bus at Oroville. By noon, Bob found himself at his destination in Pateros, Washington. It was Friday, and the ore truck from the Tungsten Mine was due that evening to dump its load of ore into the railroad car at the siding. Bob looked over the train yard that day waiting for the big truck to come rambling down the Methow River; and sure enough, along about evening, into the siding drove Johnny Jorganson. Bob threw his bedroll into the truck and soon after the truck dumped the ore, the two headed back for the Ranger Station, some 75 miles back up the river. It was dark when the dusty truck braked to a stop. "You may have to wait here till Monday, Bob," said Johnny. "I don't know for sure if they'll be packing ore this weekend or not."

Johnny was right. Bob waited three nights and two days for George Miller to return and pack him into the mine.

"Hell, kid, we don't even have a saddle horse for you to ride, let alone a saddle."

Now no self-respecting cowboy puts a young man on some gentle old pack mare. Nope, a strong young lad gets a horse with some "*spunk*!" Pack saddle and no bridle does not make a difference. George found the right horse, padded up the packsaddle with some ore sacks, and Bob jumped up on the green horse like he was a cat, and away they went. Things went along fine for the first few miles, Bob thought. He was getting adjusted to his new horse and saddle with no stirrups, thinking how nice it would all be if he could just find a spot to sit on that didn't hurt so much.

They made their usual stop for lunch at the edge of Horseshoe Creek and were just getting the horses moving out again when Bob's horse decided to do some "sightseeing" in the trees. The green packhorse threw down his head and made strange 'crow-hopping' moves toward the woods to the first good tree that had a nice limb that fit just right under Bob's chin. The jumping horse scraped the young sixteen-year-old off the packsaddle like a bug scraped from a window. It took Bob a little time to get up off the ground, clean the bark and blood off his chin, chase down his independent-minded horse, and find a suitable club! Bob figured the packhorse deserved one more chance before he used violence. George wasn't saying too much about how to handle his green horse. So, the agile young Bob jumped back in his saddle with a cat-like move and pulled his favorite horse back in line behind the others. But the independent-minded horse had gotten a taste of freedom and came to his last chance. Again, down went its head for a second time as it took off jumping for the trees. His chance for willing obedience ended with the second crow-hop. Bob was ready this time. He pulled back on the makeshift reins as hard as he could pull, and when the horse's head came up, down came the 2½ inch club! The horse stopped, shook its head, stretched out its neck, and stepped back in line with its buddies. The young Oroville boy had a good horse after that. He had a horse with some spunk!

Mac, H.V. Dardier, Packhorse Nicely Loaded, and Foss Creveling the Packer

Bob Irwin of Oroville had ridden in that early July to visit his school buddy, Bruce McPherson, Jr., also of Oroville. Both were 16 years old, and both loved to fish and hunt whenever they could make it happen. The two kids weren't disappointed when they, along with young Hank Dammann, took a packhorse over to Cathedral Lake, hoping to find some big cutthroat trout swimming around. They found more 16 to 20-inch fish in that lake than they could keep, and they sure tasted good when Charley Hartz cooked them up for dinner.

It was a neat trip and outing that summer, even though Bob had to work right along with the rest of them. They stayed with young Hank Dammann down below the main cookhouse in the one last remaining 1916 bunkhouse. By the end of July, the team of miners had all the old tailings from the First World War cleaned up and down to Pateros. At the time, the train car still wasn't full, so Dardier and Mac went to work in the old tunnel. In the 350-foot diggings below the cabins they dug out some tungsten ore. They put the three boys to work chipping away the white quartz from granite country rock and then sacking it up. They thought it was boring work when they could be fishing over at Cathedral Lake.

Later, after Bob Irwin went back home, young Bruce found himself down in the black hole with his dad double-jacking the small vein in the tight quarters. Both Mac and H. V. were good miners and knew what to do underground. The only trouble was, they lacked the machinery to do it half-way right. It was slow work, this hand drilling on the narrow vein, and they knew that if the vein went down any farther, they were in trouble because if the vein went down, it would soon fill with water and the digging and drilling would have to stop. There were no pumps to keep it dry.

Well, the vein was dipping down and was just off the floor when Mac and his son finished up the last drill hole. A big "BOOM" shook the cabins and a cloud of dust belched from the earth at the mine entrance. In time, Mac and Bruce went back into the hole to investigate the new blast. "Come on son, you get to muck this one out, " Mac said. Bruce picked up his shovel and walked with his dad back into the tunnel. Bruce started mucking as his dad picked through the rock. "Boy, Bruce, look at this!" There before the two miners' eyes was a large rock of black Wolframite. They had hit a pocket of pure tungsten ore, 73% wolframite. The only bad part about it was, the vein was headed down; one more blast and the diggings filled with water and they were out of luck. But it was sure moving while it lasted, black, heavy and pure wolframite; the stuff that had made Herb Curtis rich.

In 1936, the mine shafts were still open and easily entered to work. Frank Arnold had done a lot of work on the mines through those years to keep the shafts open. Retimbering for one, making it easy and safe for the 1936 miners to take off where Frank and Herb Curtis and the early miners had stopped 16 years before. Hour after hour, Bruce stood in the damp cold cave turning the cold steel drill by hand as his dad struck the end of the steel over and over again with a 6-pound sledge. Henry Dammann, Sr. was topside and was a kind of "roustabout," doing things like helping H. V. sharpen the dull drill-steels at the forge and sacking the new ore, cutting firewood, etc. The Bott boys and Bob O'Neil were also laborers of this sort. Bob was said to be handy at fixing things and could do about any job. It can be surmised that both H. V. and Mac led the mining operations in the shafts because they still needed ore to fill that ore-car. Charley Hartz was the cook and kept everybody well fed. Charley was long at cooking but short on hearing — the man was stone deaf. It affected the miners only one time. One day when everyone was either down in the main tunnel working, or back in town. The men in the tunnel were busy mining away, when the rock and gravel began to fall not far from the miners. It was a cave-in! The miners watched their backlight slowly disappear before them in a cloud of dust. In a few minutes, the tunnel was closed tight. The fear of all miners gripped them as the dust from the cave-in choked the men's breath out of them.

"Well, Heck. Charley sure-as-shooten' isn't going to hear that cave-in, or us hollering down here! It sure won't do any good to shout!" Bob O'Neil said. "I guess we are going to have to dig ourselves out of this one, because Charley won't miss us till dinnertime."

Mac grabbed a shovel and started throwing dirt, and if they hadn't all been so scared, with their hearts in their mouths, it might have been a bit funny, knowing that Charley couldn't hear a rock drop beside him. Not that hollering from down in a cave would have done any good anyway but knowing that one man was always on the surface had pacified them over the days. They dug like their lives depended on it for a few minutes when a shot of light bolted through the rubble. The cave in wasn't as bad as their imagination had made it, for what had caved in was an air shaft, and not much dirt had dropped in. But it was enough that they always had someone aboveground with Charley from then on.

Time went by, and it was the end of August. The train load of ore was on its way back east to a refinery, and the miners were out of the high country. The mine was left to the solitude of the mountains. Mac and his son made one last trip into the mine later in October to bring out a couple hundred pounds of supplies that had been left behind. Young Bruce would go back in again, but he wasn't young anymore when he did. It was 30 years before Bruce set foot on the far away mountain one more time. This trip was to see if there were any of those 20-inch trout left in Cathedral Lake. And, as it turned out, both Bruce, Jr. and Hank Dammann, Jr. ended up owning the Tungsten Mine in the 1960's, hoping also that some mining deal would materialize, but none did.

As for George Honey, he cussed the miserable rocky trail George Miller had carved out less than 10 years before up Tungsten Creek. It was a wicked trail as it left the mine, dumping them out 7 miles down at the mouth of Tungsten Creek. Any way you diced it, it was a mean, steep trail, with poor and steep switchbacks, cliffs at their feet and lots of boulders until you reached the Chewack River, 7 miles down the mountainside. Ferris Ford worked on district Ranger P. T. Harris every time he would see him, trying to convince him to put in a new trail up Tungsten Creek, and he finally succeeded. By the first of September 1936, the trail crew, consisting of Lefty and Pete were working on this new trail following Horseshoe Creek up to the Tungsten. The new trail passed within a few good stone throws from where an old trapper was found hung by his neck by Forest Service Trail Crews on September 12, 1936. Today, we ride that same "new trail" built by those 1936 Forest Service men.

The miners of 1936 worked on nothing more than "a-wing-and-a-prayer," a "shoestring budget," and "pure optimism." They were counting on the rich tailings left by Herb Curtis to pay for the cost of the whole mining venture and even show a good profit. It never happened. Mac had talked to the old mill man who had worked for Herb Curtis those years of 1916 to 1920. He had been thoroughly convinced that most of the small, in-grained ore, Sheelite and small grains of Wolframite, had simply gone over the sides of his mill. He wasn't all wrong. He had just overestimated its worth. The 1936 train car load of ore was shipped to New Jersey, but it was weeks before it was run. Art Lund, the Tonasket banker who had underwritten some of the cost, said years later to Bob Curtis that the tungsten in the shipment had just barely covered the cost of the rail freight trip back to New Jersey.

Most, if not all of the 1936 crew of miners never got their last pay checks. But looking at it from a positive point of view, they did receive some money for their work, and keeping in mind the fact that the whole of the country was still in the depth of its worst depression ever, perhaps it was worth the chance taken by Mac and H. V. Dardier that the tailings would pay. After all, the boys were fed well, and if they hadn't found work that summer up at the mine, they probably wouldn't have found work at all, anywhere! Besides, what better place could they have spent the summer? Getting 30 tons in 1936.

TALES OF THE TUNGSTEN MINE

CHAPTER 15

Lost Stories of Frank Arnold

FRANK HAS BEEN CALLED A big man, a good 6 feet tall. He has also been called by others a small man, perhaps under 5 feet, 3 inches. Still others have said he was of average build and height, say 5 feet 8 inches. The men interviewed who remembered Frank as being in the 6-foot range were kids at the time (7 to 12 years of age), with the exception of Harry Sherling, who said Frank stood around 6 feet tall. In another account, Harry described him at 5 foot 8 inches. Harry was sixteen when he met the Englishman and spent all summer of 1916 with him. It's interesting to perceive that the older the witnesses were, the shorter and smaller Frank seemed to get.

A picture of Frank and Jimmy Dexter next to a horse gives a good indication of the Englishman's size. The little cowboy, Jimmy Dexter, it is agreed, was a small man, somewhere around 5 feet 2 inches or so. As can be seen from this picture, Frank wasn't much of a bigger man than Jimmy Dexter. It must have been his countenance, his long arms, big hands, heavier hips that led one to believe he was somewhat larger. At age forty, he was probably an inch or so taller than Jimmy. Add to this his energy, his good health, his big caulked boots with triconys (a metal cleat), his over-sized wool pants and shirt and some good bear stories, and his relatively average stature got a boost.

When George Honey saw the Englishman in Okanogan one day in the fall of 1934, stepping out of Jim Lee's barber shop, Frank was 64 years of age and decked out in his best.

"He came in there with a new pair of boots all ironed up and caulked with triconys. He had his pack setting there. He said he was headed back to the Tungsten Mine. I had a few words with him is all, and so did Jim Lee. Frank had a rough beard, but with no real mustache (which helps confirm his last picture at Beaver Meadows that shows him with none), and he yet had his teeth. He was kind of thin, but he was wiry and looked kind of tough, strong, you know. He stood about 5 feet 8 or 9 inches and weighed about 135 or 140 pounds." This was the last time George would ever see him.

Frank was known for a mustache, which came and went in later years. It was often shaped in a good long handlebar style. He wore a small-brimmed felt "city" hat, and often was seen in bib overalls. If not bibs, he was wearing his loose-fitting wool button pants that could stand up in a corner. He wore strictly wool Mackinaw heavy shirts, and, as tough as he was in cold weather, he was rarely seen in a coat. This was his uniform, and he did not vary. Nobody remembers seeing him in anything else. He seemed to prefer the heavy leather, caulked boots which worked well for scrambling over all the downed timber that blanketed the land in later years. A size 10 rubber slip-on shoe (not a boot) was found in one of his trapper cabin. It was more of a pullover shoe, so it seems to indicate a smaller shoe size. Interestingly, those new boots that George Honey saw him in were never found.

If the story so far has told about Frank Arnold, it has not done it to total satisfaction. Sixty years ago would have been a much better time to describe him because way too many who had firsthand information are now gone. Yet, at the last hour we grab a glimpse of this unusual stranger that chose to live, not in civilization, but in the wilds of the Cascade Mountains.

"He was not the average sort of human being! Though we did not recognize it at the time." said Lloyd Ford, who knew Frank when he was growing up in Loomis. From his earliest memory Lloyd and his brothers would anxiously wait for the return of the old mountain man who lived in the woods like a "wild animal," so they thought.

"He would come out about the first of April with his load of furs like clock-work, year after year."

The boys' mother, Mrs. Ruth Ford, would tell the three boys when to go out and start looking for Mr. Arnold. So out in the road the boys would go and play. Sure enough, within the day, or maybe the next, down the road would come the Mayor of the Tungsten Mine, always with a sack of candy in his pocket for the boys, and a load of furs on his back. Of course, their sister would run, screaming at the top of her lungs, to her mother, shouting that the dirty old trapper, Frank Arnold, was headed for their home. Frank was always welcome at the Ford house, though Mrs. Ford made sure the Victorian furniture was covered and the first place Mr. Arnold went was to the wash tub for a bath. And a long bath it was, too. Frank would sit for hours, it seemed, in the hot tub washing weeks of dirt from his leathered body. Frank was then given a clean suit of clothes and soon sat down to one of the best meals served in the country. Mrs. Ford and her hired kitchen help, Mrs. Landergreen, really knew how to put together a dinner, and to the hollow-legged mountain man, everything was delicious and meant to be eaten in great quantities. For Frank had not tasted such a meal as the Fords put on since the last year when he sat at the same table. What a grand change from the trapper's bland, monotonous diet of venison, lynx cat, bannock and oats. He just could not seem to get enough of the ten-course meal that they sat before him. And, the desserts — oh, the desserts that were cooked in Ruth Ford's kitchen! Frank would eat, eat and eat some more. His eating ability was remembered and talked about in amazement for years after. He could eat great quantities of everything over and over again until he absolutely could not eat another bite. Of course, after he left the table, he couldn't do anything else, either. He would go outside and lay down on the lawn and moan and groan for hours trying to recuperate. This was Frank's annual spring feast and his first stop in Loomis.

Mrs. Ruth Ford was in every way a very kind and special person. She abounded in many fine deeds. She was especially good to Frank when he came to town, and her brother, Dick Loudon, said this about her and the Ford family in his family book:

"During her lifetime she was kind and charitable to all. Some of her charitable works far exceeded that of any person I have ever known. On four different occasions, while she and Ferris lived in Loomis, they provided food and shelter for several aged and homeless men who had seen better days... These were Harry Forde (a distant cousin); George Bowers (who lived up on Chopaka Mt., and was a long-time mountain man, and trapper), John O'Herin, Billy Smith, and Frank Arnold, (a destitute trapper whom they grub-staked many times). By a strange coincidence, three of these men committed suicide to end their hopeless lives."

Frank Arnold hung around the Ferris Ford place for days and helped with the chores where he could, such as putting up hay that seemed always to come up when he was there, mending fences, or helping to train a small colt that needed work. When eventually Frank would talk about leaving, the boys would beg him not to go, but to stay just a few more days. The young kids were fascinated by the man with his strange and different ways of doing things. Rituals like filling his cup of coffee with all sugar except for a small portion for the hot, black liquid over the top really impressed the kids. He did this for the first few days he was there. He slowly tapered off on the sugar as time went along. He ate sugar by the pound and was caught by his little followers more than once in the kitchen taking a handful of pure, white lard, then dipping his paw like a bear in the sugar bowl, eating the lard and sugar straight. It amazed, befuddled and tickled the little boys to no end as the sheepish trapper looked their way and gave them a wink.

At times Frank would not talk for long periods, but when he did, he kept the family enthralled in his accented English as he told tales of trapping a big bear, facing down a crazed cat, or killing or photographing some wild animal at close quarters. He was an educated man, they all said, highly intelligent in his conversations, which were more often than not, way over the young boys' heads. As one person said, "He was a nature student and very well informed on astronomy and kindred subjects."

Lloyd Ford, one of Frank's young admirers of the Ford home, remembered Frank as being on the serious side and rarely smiling, though another friend of the Ford home, Al Smith, remembered Frank as a good natured man, kind and pleasant to be around. He considered Frank a good friend even though Frank was a much older man.

Before returning to the mountains after a few weeks, Frank would make a trip to Oroville, Tonasket, Omak, or Okanogan to do some shopping, get a haircut, and visit friends. He would then walk back to Loomis where he would pick up his mail, which one man remembered as being "quite a few books." There also had to have been magazines, radio parts, chemicals, and other odd purchases. He would then head for the mountains to spend the hot months of summer, coming back out one or two more times before the heavy snows of winter locked up the land.

Of course, the Ford house was not Frank's only stop when he came to the lowlands. At the Herb Curtis home in Loomis he always brought a young boy a homemade toy, a carved wood toy of some description, such as a well-made stick-gun or a bow and arrows. In one of those years, the gift amounted to an elaborately carved sailing vessel, a windjammer; a piece of art that took weeks to carve. It was so splendidly made that it impressed a passer-by as the young Bob Curtis showed it off later. The man was so taken by the carving he enticed the wonder ship from the little boy with a big pack of firecrackers. "An even trade," Bob thought at the time — but later in life, never forgave himself for making such a dumb transaction.

"When I was about 10 years old, he taught me how to make figure-four traps and snares. All I ever caught in my snare was the neighbor's tom cat." laughed Bob.

His family also happily fed and bedded the old trapper who would show up at their front door. Of course, again, he would eat way too much, and pain would overtake him so that he would just have to go out and lay down on the lawn moaning and groaning. Their special bed for the lone mountain man was an outside bunk on the porch where on the coldest of fall nights, Frank would contentedly sleep.

"He was a real close friend of my father's. I was just a kid and he was my idol," said Bob Curtis. "He used to tell us stories about the mountains. He was a real educated man and polite. He always wore (bib) overalls and plaid shirts." Bob shook his head, "Walk! You'd never seen anyone walk like him. He could really cover the ground."

Frank had lots of friends in Loomis, one was Jay Hill's family, whose dad owned the general a store in Loomis. The Hill family would also feed and enjoy the interesting mountain man. He would bring them many a fine picture he had taken of some wild animal or far-away mountain. With the pictures came stories about an adventure, or some educated subject to keep the family entertained. He often stayed all night, and Mrs. Hill would do his wash and mend his clothes. Yes, the Hill family were good friends of the watchman and caretaker of the Tungsten Mine.

The rest of Loomis, too, helped and respected the curious Englishman. Grace Eastman thought nothing of running the old man into Oroville to see the dentist. And when he did not come out that last year in 1935, everybody talked of his vanishing and wondered what could have happened to him. His disappearance made the local newspapers as a notice. Indeed, Frank Arnold was a curiosity, a friend, a mystery, an adventurer, an idol, a citizen of Loomis, and was missed when he never returned.

He Drank His Share

In the early years, it would be fair to call Frank an alcoholic. It was what had brought him to the Okanogan in the first place. But the Englishman was smart enough to know he had a problem and kept his drinking mostly to himself, away from the taverns and the probable trouble he would find there. He fought his alcohol addiction all his life. He loved the stuff and would never pass up a drink. Between staying in the woods and prohibition, Frank kept his problem almost under control.

Mickey Kinchelo and Herb Curtis seemed to look upon Frank as an alcoholic. They witness ed times when he was found in the woods crawling and rolling and rumbling around in the bushes by Duncan James' cabin, and was almost mistaken for a bear growling in the bushes. He was "drunker than a boiled owl," they said. Then there was another time Mickey remembered seeing him behind the Loomis store, also "three sheets to the wind and loaded to the gills." Here he spent the whole night talking to himself. However, in the later years, he was not really known as a drunk. Al Smith never saw Frank drunk in all the years he knew him, and neither did Lloyd Ford. Leonard Honey worked with him at the Ross Woodard cattle ranch in about 1928 putting up hay. Of course, prohibition was still on, but any good drinker could get his alcohol. Leonard worked with Frank for a number of weeks and had this to say about the hay maker, "He was a gentle man and a nice man, friendly enough, but kept to himself... I never saw him drink."

Frank, though, could put it down. The following story starts in the early thirties when a dude ranch was running in the Sinlehekin Valley, up from Loomis. Al Smith was their packer, and when it came time to make an excursion into the mountains, their destination was the intriguing Tungsten Mine. The "dudes" were city boys about 16 years of age. Their well-to-do parents were sending them over to the Okanogan every year for some practical experience in the great outdoors.

Al Smith, who wasn't much older than the dudes, got them into the mine with only saddle sores. The first day was uneventful as boys settled down to their new environment. The first night the young boys threw their bed rolls out on the floor of the log bunkhouse and started playing around, having a good time. Mr. Arnold stuck his head in the cabin with a warning message, "You boys had better put a ground cover under your bedrolls or sleep up on some bunk, because there are some awful big porcupines under that floor, and they come out at night! They'll stick you full of needles if you're not careful. I'd put down a ground cloth on the floor if I were you!" The boys' eyes lit up as they glared back at the watchman.

"Really, Frank? Okay!" was the patronizing remark. Frank turned and walked up to his cabin. "Was that old guy lying' to us, Al?" asked a young Phil Van-Pool. "Next thing you know he'll be telling us there's a grizzly bear in the frying pan!" said the young boy in disbelief.

The boys gave Frank Arnold's warning little attention. When the lights finally went out, they pulled the blankets around their necks. So, the exhausted young men never heard the night stalkers rustling around under their heads, beneath the floorboards. But what a surprise met their eyes as they went to roll up their bed rolls the next day off the floor.

"What in the heck are these things stuck in my bed roll, Al? They look like a bunch of white needles of some kind!" Phil Van-Pool said as he looked at the neat row of porcupine quills running the full length of his sleeping bag. The floor planks were just a little too wide, and Mr. Porcupine had left his mark.

It was the fourth of July, and the city dudes were ready to celebrate. They had come prepared for the occasion! The boys, being boys, had managed to smuggle three gallons of

pure alcohol from their dad's medical infirmary. They had taken great care to get the jugs up to the mine without breaking even one jug, and now was as good as time as any to see if it worked. The pure alcohol worked alright, It kicked like a mule! And, "MAN was that liquid "HOT!" The three gallons of alcohol was going to last them for three months the way it burned from head to foot — burning all the way down and for a long time after it hit the bottom. The three boys could only gingerly sip the strong, 100% firewater as they laughingly passed the jug around. Suddenly they got the bright idea of inviting Mr. Arnold down for a drink. "We'll see if he likes this stuff!" they laughed.

"Hey Frank! Hey Frank! We're doing a little celebrating down here, this is the fourth of July, ya' know! Come on down and have a drink! We brought a little alcohol with us."

That was all Frank needed to hear.

"Sure, I'll take a drink!" came the quick reply from the watchman, as he stuck his head out the door of his cabin. Frank walked down to the party as the young boys filled up a quart fruit jar to over half-full and tried to keep a straight face as they handed the pure, 100% clear, alcohol over to their new friend. Frank took a look at the solution he held in his hand, smelled it, held it up to the light, swirled the clear firewater, stepped back, said "Cheers, boys," and pointed the bottom of the jar toward the big blue sky. The boys watched in utter amazement as the undiluted alcohol disappeared in a matter of seconds. Their mouths hung open and eyes bugged out as Frank went "FFHoo!! That was good stuff! Thanks." He handed the empty jar back and coolly walked back to his cabin without a waiver. The city boys, with mouths hung wide open shook their heads in disbelief as the iron-gutted Frank disappeared behind the walls of his upper cabin. Few men they knew could copy that and stay on their feet. "I'm glad we brought three gallons, Skip," said Phil. "We'll need it if Frank comes back down here."

It was the long years of prohibition from 1916 to 1933 that did the most to slow down Frank's drinking. Though living as he did with his back door opening into Canada, this probably wasn't much of a deterrent. His ability to blow up his stills didn't hurt, either. After the one still blew-up in about 1921 and almost burned down the whole of the Tungsten Mine, Frank apparently wised up and quit building them. By 1930, Frank had pretty much lost his reputation as an alcoholic, though he was still no doubt, "a good drinker."

The Shooter That Never Missed

This whiskey drinker of the mountains did have a reputation, though, and the one most talked about was his marksmanship. A day or two after Al Smith had his upper-class Seattle boys up at the mine, the dudes brought out their shooting-irons. "Slam! Blam, bang, bang!" The boys were having a fun time plunking away at some cans they had set up down over the hill, 50 feet or so away. "Hey! Yah' think old Frank can hit those cans down there?"

"Hey, Frank! Frank! Get down here and see if you can hit these cans! Come on down, Frank, let's see if that long-barreled .22 of yours can do more than look pretty."

The old trapper stirred and walked down to join in the sport with the city dudes. "Alright, Frank, we know you're probably better than us, but let's see how many of those cans down there you can hit in a row."

Now it just so happened that the Tungsten Mine was being overrun by chipmunks. Their grandsons and granddaughters are still overrunning the place today, and down over the hill from where Frank stood, just beyond the tin cans, a little furry chipmunk was scurrying like lighting over the rocks and boulders. "Watch that squirrel down there," Frank said and took quick aim. The gun went "BLAM!" The little rodent flew in the air and came down dead.

"Whoa - Ho!" said one of the boys. Another critter darted out over the ground like a low-flying arrow. Again the .22 popped and the chipmunk rolled into a ball and stopped.

"I better quit. Those little guys are my friends," said Frank as he turned and walked up the hill to his cabin with his supernatural gun in his hand. The city boys stood in silence and amazement as the old trooper turned his back on them once more.

"How'd he do that, Al?"

Omar Smith also had a chance to witness Frank Arnold at play with his gun. Omar was herding sheep in the Horseshoe Basin when Frank came along and stopped for a friendly meal and some conversation. Somebody put up some cans and started target-practicing. Frank soon had his gun out, the long barreled .22 revolver, and showed the boys how to hit a can.

"He just never missed," said Omar.

One day in Loomis, a shooter came to town, a real marksman. He came to put on a show, and these were the days when a show in town was not to be missed. All the men and half the women in Loomis came out to see a marksman by the name of Peterson. He came to show-off his abilities with the gun. Frank had stayed over a week to see the show, and there was no doubt about it; Peterson could shoot! He knocked over all the wood blocks he had on his shooting gallery, and rarely missed his mark. After giving a good show he decided to make things interesting.

"Ladies and Gentlemen, I always like to give a local citizen a chance to show off their marksmanship. Would any of you men or girls like to give it a go? — remember Annie Oakley now. Ha! Ha! Step right up, anyone, and have a crack at shooting a few birds?" A silence fell over the crowd. The men started looking at one another to see which one of them would be the one embarrassed by this fine marksman, Peterson.

"Frank, you can shoot!" said a Loomisite to Frank Arnold.

"Hey, ya! Frank Arnold can shoot real good." said another.

"Give it a try, Frank, I hear tell you can shoot better than anyone in Loomis. You can't do any worse than us, that's for sure. Go to it, Frank!" came the encouraging words from the town folks.

Frank Arnold stepped forward and introduced himself to the marksman named Peterson. "Well, you're welcome to use my gun or your own, Mr. Arnold; whatever you wish."

"As you can see Mr. Peterson, I left my gun at home, but from the way that thing of your shoots, I you'd say there's nothing wrong with it. Where do you aim on the open sites at?" asked Frank.

"It's set for 60 feet top to top. Go at it when you're ready," said Peterson.

All eyes were on the trapper in his wool button pants with mackinaw shirt and city hat. He eyed the 3-inch little shooting ducks that sat in a row 60 feet in front of him.

"Show 'em what you can do, Frank," came a holler from the crowd!

Frank slowly turned on his heels as his eyes penetrated into the sky. When he stopped, he was facing the crowd, but his eyes were searching out past them all. Not a sound could be heard as Frank brought up the gun in the wrong direction!

"What the hell you going to shoot, Mr.?" Peterson remarked.

Frank didn't say a thing for a few seconds as all heads turned to a point across the street.

"Just watch those sparrows over on that building, on the roof line," came Frank's answer.

"Sparrows? Roofline?" A shot went off from the gun in Frank's hand. A puff of feathers filled the air 130 feet away. Again, the gun sounded, and again a puff of feathers filled the air.

"Ahhss!" and "Ouuss!" came from the crowd. "Wow. What a shot!" Three or four birds flew away. The gun went "Blam!" and a sparrow fell from the sky.

"I hope you're not going to be in Republic next week, Mr. Arnold," Peterson said as Frank turned over his gun. Frank was not only an amazingly good shot, he amazingly quick.

At one of Frank's lost trapper's cabins, this writer was amazed to find dozens of the tin cans laying out from the cabin — hundreds of them — each and every one having a small bullet-hole through it.

Wizard on the Mountain

Some around Loomis looked upon Frank Arnold as a "remittance man" from England. A remittance man was a rich man's son who did not really belong at his home for one reason or another. He was, therefore, sent away, usually far away, with his father sending him some money for support. England was indeed famous for sending away their remittance men, and this Englishman may have had a rich father, but it is doubtful he obtained any money by mail from his family, at least in the late years in the Okanogan.

It is unclear if Frank really needed more money than he made trapping or whether he just worked for others at different times for the change of pace and companionship. When he came to the Tungsten Mine in 1915 from Windy Mountain, Frank carried all he needed on his back, along with most of his possessions. His earliest job before or just at the time he came to the Pasayten, was said to be at the apple box mill in Oroville. One of the years in the late 1920's found him at work at the Ross Woodard ranch putting up hay, but if he worked just one summer, or a number, it is not known.

There is also quite a story of Frank and Ferris Ford working as packers for the Coast and Geodetic Survey in 1923-1924. (Dick Loudon also worked on the crew.) At the time, radio electronics were just being discovered, and right away Frank started working with wires and understanding the principles of such things. The surveyors used an instrument called the "theodolight" to measure the elevation of mountains. The light had to be set up and used at night from the tops of mountain peaks. In this basic way, by the use of the "theodolight" and a mountain-climbing expedition, all the mountains in the northwest, and for that matter, the world, were measured. Frank and Ferris would pack a horse as far as they could get it up the mountain side, and then from there they would pack the theodolight and other instruments the surveyor needed the rest of the way on their backs. An interesting thing happened, though, as rodents chewed up the wiring in the theodolight one night, fouling it up bad. The engineers were sure the instrument, with its bare wires black from shortcuts, was of no use and in need of a hefty repair job that could only be done in the far away country of Germany. This is where the lights were made. But the Englishman asked to look at the light, and with nothing to lose, the engineers handed Frank the broken spotlight. How long it took and where Frank gathered up the replacement parts is not known, but much to the surveyors' relief, Frank soon had the light back together and working as good as new. From that day on he was considered a "whiz" with the light and given exclusive care of the instrument. For 2 years or more, the surveyors covered the whole of the Pasayten Wilderness measuring and calculating the heights of its rugged mountains.

On another year, Clarence Landergreen, "the cave-man of Loomis" as he was called around the boxing ring, and a friend of the electronic whiz, worked on a trail across the Cascades to the Skagit River. Frank was part of their crew. Their employer was the Forest Service. Frank was said to have hired out to the Forest Service more than once through the years; at times as a cook, it seems, and it was probably Ferris Ford that put him to work with his crew.

Lost Stories of Frank Arnold

Though Frank worked out several summers, he truly loved to roam the high country on prospecting jaunts, taking photographs of the wild animals that shared his mountain space. He seemed to have lost his camera when he landed in Molson in about 1910. But by 1916, he had found it again. The earliest-known picture, presumed to be his, was that taken of Albert and Minnie Lynch of Oroville, in 1917, at the Tungsten Mine. He soon went into developing his own photographs in the small 15-by-15-foot cabin. It became a menagerie of equipment, chemicals, developing pans, enlargers, and cameras. His talent as a photographer could have and should have carved his name in stone, if only his pictures would have survived in number. He might have worked with photography long before he came to the Pasayten, for the picture of him with the moose harnessed to the wagon was taken from an old newspaper. He had told a number of people over the years that he sold a lot of his animal pictures to noted magazines, like Field and Stream, trapping journals, and such. His fine pictures were known to include his trapping of animals, wild moose, big-horned sheep, and bear. Many of his photographs got worldwide circulation, but few locals knew anything of it.

If someone new and different, like the Lynchs, Frank E Maron or Mary Roberts Rinehart of Cosmopolitan Magazine came riding into the Tungsten Mine, Frank would quickly get out his camera and take a few pictures for the new tourist. He would then hurry up to his cabin and develop the scene for the explorers, hoping to make a buck or two on the sale of a beautiful picture that no normal person could resist.

Over the years, Frank took lots of beautiful and lovely panoramic pictures, developing and enlarging them to unbelievable poster sizes in his little studio. In the era of only black and white photographs, many times he would color in different areas of the picture to make a lovely tinted or colored photo. Colored film had not yet come about. After many hours of tedious work, Frank would tote his masterpiece down to town and happily give it away to some friend. Perhaps his greatest picture, other than the team of moose pulling the wagon, was the picture of the big blast of hot gasses and flame that erupted from the 1929 forest fire over the top of Apex Mountain. It was an amazing picture that hung over his bed for years in his cabin. The photo strangely disappeared right after his death. Here is how one viewer described it: "In the midst of the inferno he managed to snap a picture of the huge tongue of flame which spread from one peak to another before setting the Tungsten afire. This he himself tinted and set up in his room." It was an awesome picture to behold, and it would be nice to know who has it or where it went. It is said the Loomis School had dozens of Frank's old pictures that were given to them by him over the years. How he got those amazing close ups without zoom lenses amazes one today. He had not one or two close ups of wild animals, but dozens of photos of various kinds of big game. Frank Arnold had to have been one of the premier photographers of wildlife of his time, an artist with few peers. Sadly, though perhaps to his liking, Frank went mostly unrecognized by all but a few of the local citizens, and it is regrettable, too, that so few of his great pictures are known to have survived to present. A selection of Frank's remaining photos appears in Appendix II.

Not to go without mention is this man's remarkable ability with radios and his achievements with electronics. Most living at the time didn't hear their first radio until the late twenties or early thirties. Not Frank. He was building the things as early as the mid-twenties, learning how to put together an early "Cat Whisker" radio and progressing on to become a self-taught engineer in the new field. "He made his own radio and battery charger up there," Jim McDaniel said. "My dad (Loy) said his radio covered about 3 feet, but it played real nice."

It was said by Al Smith, Shorty Fairbrother, and hinted at by others; "that everything Frank Arnold did, he did it well and to perfection," from his trapping to his photography, to his radios, his card games, and his raising of moose. Frank worked at them all scientifically, methodically and intelligently. He had mechanical gadgets up there in his little mine cabin that nobody could figure out. He was a forgotten wizard on a far-away mountain that seemed to be way ahead of his time. He had short wave, long wave, and any wave radios. He had batteries, generators, parts and more parts. There were wires and strange things strung all over the place. He had funny machines, smelly chemicals, tools and trays crammed into the 15 foot by 15 foot space that was workshop, studio, chemistry lab, skinning room, kitchen, living room and bedroom. He seemed to belong, not to the Tungsten Mine, but somewhere else, misplaced by a system of selection that didn't always work. At any rate, it made things interesting at the place, and there was usually a tune playing on Frank's radio when some tired cowboy rode in on a sweating horse.

When the young 16-year-old, Bruce McPherson, Jr., dragged out the last of Frank Arnold's paraphernalia from the upper cabin that early summer in 1936 after school was out to make a place for the miners to stay. Frank Arnold's replaced worldly possessions lay in a heap off to the side of the lower bunkhouse. There was a book or two, a few bottles of chemicals, clothes, old blankets, a number of pictures, quite a few radio parts, photo-paper, aluminum sheets, batteries, and a few things that no one recognized. At the time. In one case, Bruce, Jr. described one contraption like this: "It was a round affair made of metal, somewhat like a wheel with spokes and slots." It looked maybe like a miniature Ferris-wheel where pictures could be placed around about, and maybe there was even one or two in this machine. The contraption seemed to spin on a stand, and possibly could have been driven by a small motor." After years of thinking about it, Bruce, Jr., said, "I really believe Frank was experimenting with "T.V." Now Bruce had good reason to believe and know what he had seen when he dragged out Frank's stuff that last time because Bruce McPherson, Jr. would grow up to be an electronic genius in his own right! He did not follow in his dad's footsteps as a miner, disappearing into an unnamed hole in the ground, but became the brains behind a company called "Radar Electric!" He was indeed qualified to know that Frank Arnold was playing and working with early television in 1933-1934.

Another contraption the radio man engineered was a copper or aluminum foot. George Honey said aluminum. Ted Boland said copper. He had the foot cut out of a sheet of heavy copper and made into an outline of his foot. This solid piece of metal had wires running from it and over to an electric magneto taken from an automobile. The wires led to a battery. It was a most interesting and puzzling setup that lay before George Honey and Ted Boland that day.

"It's got to be for shock treatments, Ted. Look how the wires run over to the battery, and here's the switch by the chair!"

"Ya'!" said Ted. "Old Frank sat there in his chair, put his bare foot down on that big copper outline of toes and sole and hit the switch! That juice from the magneto had to have made his hair stand up on end and his eyes light up. I'll bet you he and that chair went 3 feet in the air!" Ted laughed.

"It sure would work great for waking yourself up in the morning. What do you think he used it for?" returned George.

Frank kept a well-stocked library at the mine, but few people could pull a book off the bookshelf and understand what he was reading. He read things like science journals, radio books, "Ell of the Odyssey," and material that was heavier and deeper than the norm. All his books came through the mail and were carried on his back up to the mine. His library was also never found after his death, like all his other things, it just strangely disappeared off the mountain, like magic, before Emmet Smith looked over the mine that spring day of 1935.

What Did the Mountain Man Eat?

Of all of Frank's unique abilities, the one that caused the most questions in town was what he ate all winter. Everyone in Loomis who had ever heard of Frank's measly provisions was at a quandary as to how he could stay alive for 5 or 6 months with such incredibly short rations. Just one loaded pack horse, with mostly sugar loaded on its back, it seemed, was all Frank wanted for months of winter isolation. How did he survive, and what else did he eat all those months alone in the mountains?

It is true that Mrs. Ford and Mrs. Curtis would swear to the fact that Frank had eaten enough at their house to last him all winter, but still, only one pack horse, lightly loaded? Shoot, today a packer figures one packhorse a week per person. What did Frank live on all winter? The truth is, Frank actually lived off the land as few men ever did, knew how to or cared to. He was the last of a dying breed of men — the true mountain man. The man was good for at least six to ten deer a year. He must have shot or trapped, six bear a year. And, the old trapper loved to eat all the lynx cat he could catch. "Marten wasn't worth a damned!" he used to say. Yes, Frank ate a lot of the game that came up in his trapline or ran across the sights of his gun. He carried two guns with him in his later years. If he needed a deer, he would pull out his 12-inch barrel, seven shot, .22 revolver. He never missed when he pulled the trigger. The .22 was good for rabbit, porcupines, coyotes, ptarmigan, small deer and cats. His other gun was a sawed-off .410 shotgun. It, too, was good for grouse, ptarmigan, and any hapless rabbit on the run. In his later years he started to have eye problems and needed the 410 shotgun Omar Smith remembered seeing. He also harbored a .303 Savage rifle and a 30-30 Winchester. These would have been good for deer, bear, moose, sheep, goats and a rare caribou. Frank was said to have shot two caribou over the years, one on Bauerman Ridge and the other on Windy Mountain. In fact, there was said to be a small herd of caribou living on Bauerman Ridge at the turn of the century. Caribou were rare, but also seen to the west of the Pasayten River.

Back in 1916, when the Tungsten Mine was running, the Welsh miners ran out of tea. But Frank didn't, because he had a whole forest full of the stuff. Because of their moaning, out he went into the sticks to pacify them, and finding what he wanted, he soon had the miners happily drinking "Indian tea," also known as "Labrador tea." It was made from the leaves of a bushy plant standing some 3 feet high, and almost always green. He must have known what kinds of plants to eat to keep healthy, for every person, with the exception of "Lefty," said that Frank Arnold "was in the picture of health." The 65-year-old man was strong, robust, and very active up until his dying day, even though his diet seemed to be mostly wild meat.

On Frank's last trip into the mine that fall in 1934, he and his packer, Al Smith, ran into some deer about a mile from the mine. "Go on in with the horses. I want to get me some dinner. I'll be along shortly. I'm out of meat at the mine." Frank took off stalking the herd of deer and the packer went on into the mine.

"I never even had the horses all unpacked when Frank appeared at the mine with this long yearling deer over his back." He was about 65 years-old at the time and had walked most the way into the mine already, and a good half mile up the steep mountain below the mine with this 100-pound deer on his back. It was the finest eating one in the herd. "He had it skinned, gutted and in the frying pan by the time I was done unpacking. And he didn't have just a small piece of meat, he cooked up a whole hindquarter, and though he offered me a meal, I passed on the invitation, it being so fresh of a kill. Frank then ate the whole cut himself!"

Though it was anticipated that Frank would come out to Loomis in mid-winter on his annual treks, it was not known that Frank went into Canada, probably toward the end of the trapping season. He probably went north about the first of March each year to sell some of his furs in Canada, and then, no doubt, buy some fresh supplies. Frank, in doing so, renewed his supplies about every three months, or perhaps two. Frank's diet was known to include potatoes, oats, flour, and lots of canned goods such as milk and fruit.

Frank's Personality

The Pasayten mountain man never missed a thing in the woods. To him it was like his own big back yard. And, Shorty Fairbrother reiterated this by telling of the time he went in one summer to check and work on his trap-line, which he would have done every so many years. He came to his traps that were on a well-used trail, probably on the Chewack River, and decided to pull the ones that might be seen or found. After pulling a trap or two, Shorty saw a nice fish jump in the creek and decided it would taste awful good in the frying pan. He pulled a fly and some line from his hat and found a nice tree to cut down for a pole. Every time the little fly hit the water, up came a nice shiny trout. Soon Shorty had more fish than he could eat at one setting, so following his trap-line he headed towards one of his cabins, pulling one or two more traps as he went. An hour or so later, Shorty walked up to his cabin, and who should be dancing back and forth at the door — Frank Arnold.

"Shorty!" Frank shouted. "Someone's stealing your traps and is just ahead of us. If we hurry, we can catch them. They're stealing your traps! I saw their tracks and have been following them to here. They stopped and did some fishing down the river then headed up this way!" spoke Frank in a rush.

In the first place, Shorty was surprised to even see Frank at his cabin door but had a grin on his face by the time Frank had quickly ran the facts by him. "Okay! Okay, Frank! Good. But let's fry up these fish here in my pack first, for some dinner, and then we'll think about getten-em'," as he walked on up to his cabin door. The Englishman hadn't realized Shorty was even in the High Country. It was summer, and Shorty wasn't supposed to be up there yet. Frank had seen some footprints and had followed them to the tree where the traps had been pulled, and he had noticed the fresh sap running from the bark. Then he had seen where the thief had done some fishing with the new cut tree, and then had headed on up Shorty's trap-line for his cabin, pulling Shorty's traps as he went. The mountain man was bound to catch the trap-steeling thieves at Shorty's cabin, and in doing so, he somehow ran past Shorty in the woods and beat even Shorty to his cabin door.

Frank must have loved to walk, but he wasn't much for horses. He was in such good shape that he could cover miles in a day, and if given a choice to ride a horse or walk, he chose to walk. When Al Smith packed him in, those last few years, he always brought Frank a horse to ride if he wanted it. Frank usually rode some and walked some. Leonard Honey remembered Frank getting on a horse at the Ross Woodard cattle ranch, but riding a horse just wasn't Frank's long suit. Interesting, one of his better portraits shows a man believed to be Frank on a stylish English horse, taken perhaps in England or Canada.

On the political side, Frank was against the encroachment of civilization and spoke about it more than once. He didn't feel the need for the Forest Service and was against their intrusion on his domain. At one time, Ferris Ford suggested he apply for Social Security. It sounded like a good idea to Frank, seeing he was getting older, but after pursuing it up to the paperwork, he dropped it. Sometime in here he also applied for citizenship, but backed out on it, too. Frank almost surely was a Canadian citizen.

This man was also a real loner, and from all indications he liked it that way. While alone he was his own best friend and he certainly was the best "one-man conversationalist in the world." He could tell himself stories that would last for long periods of time. He was way past the point of just talking to himself. The old man had been a loner for so many years he couldn't help himself. He talked to himself and then answered himself and then talked on again. Harry Scherling said,

"When he told a story to himself, he didn't like to be stopped or talked to until he was done."

"I have been alone for so long I can't help it." Frank told Al Smith. It seems funny to talk about today, but just try to spend even a week alone. Talking to yourself was part of life for a solitary mountain man and few were the men who could live in this total isolation and not become just a little "tweaked" from their years of solitude.

It was interesting, too, the way Frank dealt with people over the years. It certainly seems that Frank enjoyed having someone show up at the mine once in a while, but as George Miller said, "He would talk your leg off for the first few hours you were there, but after he had talked to you for a while and said his piece, you got the feeling he wanted you to leave." He did ask Leland Thrasher and Hecktor Smith to leave. The two young boys were about 16 years old at the time. For a number of years in the late 1920's, they would load up a pack horse and lead it into the mountains for a couple of weeks of fishing and camping. When at the Tungsten Mine, they visited with Mr. Arnold and always stayed for a few days in one of the cabins. On one trip, Frank came out about the third day and said, "Boys! I'm talked out, and I wish you would leave today."

"Ok, Mr. Arnold!" said Leland. "We were thinking about heading back anyway." They didn't take offense, but left Frank the last of their provisions and walked back the 60 miles to Oroville.

Emmet Smith tells of him and another rider who were riding up on the old-boy's lay-out in Long Swamp one summer day when a "crash-boom-bang!" started coming from his little cabin, and not just once. Frank for some reason was beating pots and pans together. "He set-up a racket that would scare away even the devil," said Emmet. And the two men rode on by without stopping, wondering what his problem was.

An Oroville schoolteacher, who had packed in during the 1930's, later recounted his trip to his class, stating, "One got the feeling that Frank Arnold wanted one to move on." But if Frank wanted to be left alone, at least by strangers, he wasn't really unkind. The funny thing was, he truly seemed to enjoy having some company show up once in a while. An old newspaper had this to say about the tungsten miner:

"(He) ...was always at home to the wayfarer; his kerosene light a welcome sign to the person tired and cold and hungry who topped the rise above the cluster of abandoned buildings."

So, he could be gracious, and to those who met the man on the trail, he was always friendly and pleasant, though Frank Zeckerman said that he almost had to grab him by the leg to get him to stop and talk. Zeckerman, a sheep herder, was in bad need of some conversation too. At other times, such as when Frank ran into Emmet Smith and his helper in the Horseshoe Basin, he would stop and spend a couple of days with them at their camp. And when in town, Frank would look up all his old friends and spend hours talking to them before heading back into the lonely mountains.

But when Frank wanted to be left alone, he wanted to be left alone! The story is told that people would come into the mine and step into Frank's cabin and find the fire roaring away. Maybe the coffee pot was perking, the radio was playing, but Frank was gone. Thinking he would be right back, the visitor would wait, wait, wait, and then wait some more, until they got an uncomfortable feeling, and left. Frank just wouldn't come back until all was clear.

If Frank had friends up and down the valley, over in the Methow and into Canada. If he was seen at times in Tonasket, Omak, Okanogan, Keremeos, and Princeton, he was not seen one cold late winter in Loomis. Seeing he always came out on a supply run in early winter before Christmas, but not this winter, the folks in town, including Jack Richman, Bill Ford, and Fred Hill, got to missing old Frank. Jay Hill remembers the story well. It was late in the winter and Arnold just hadn't come out like he always did. *What had happened to Frank?* Everyone wondered. It could only be one thing, they figured — Frank was hurt and couldn't get out.

Now the townsfolk in Loomis could have sent into the mountains any other person in the whole country except Johnny Bell. To send Johnny in to check on the old trapper was a mistake. Any other person would have been alright, but not Johnny Bell. The trouble between John and Frank dated back a long time, all the way back to 1916 at the tungsten mine. It was not necessarily a two-sided problem. Johnny wasn't mad at Frank, and heck, most of the town in Loomis was half mad at Johnny, half of the time. Dick Loudon called John a "taciturn" and "ugly-tempered" person, "given to long periods of silence." He could be cantankerous and borrow things and not bring them back, liked whiskey. And, he tried to push some people around. But, even at that, he was still part of Loomis and had lived there all his life. He really wasn't that bad all the time. Young Jay Hill thought a lot of Johnny, and Johnny had lined Jay's pockets with candy more than once.

Johnny was also a trapper, hard as flint. He trapped the lower Toats Coulee, Chopaka and Snowshoe mountains next to Frank's lines. To the Loomisites, he was the one tough enough to snowshoe back the 40 miles and check on Frank. He was certainly no stranger to the high country. The part-Indian trapper had spent a good part of his early life in those mountains, hunting, looking for lost Indian gold, and helping Herb Curtis at the mine. He had been there on the original tungsten discovery in 1903-1904 and had dug tungsten for the Germans in 1915-1916. It had been while working at the mine that summer in 1916 that he had his "set-to" with Frank Arnold. Just what it was over is lost today, but it was big enough for Johnny to get fired over and sent home, and big enough that Frank never forgot the ordeal. But to Johnny, it was just water off a duck's back, and he had nothing against Frank. So, when the towns people of Loomis asked him to go back and check on their friend. He said he would do it. He had to go part way there anyway, to check his own traps, and after all, he, too, was a trapper and understood the dangers that might befall a lone mountain man, isolated in the far back country. Sure, he would snowshoe on back and take a look.

It was probably in late February, maybe 1933. The snow was deep and crusted low on the Toats Coulee as Johnny pushed up the mountain, past Duncan James' cabin he "mooshed." Seventeen miles he traveled uphill out of Loomis and when night fell, he was at Iron Gate. It was a cold night for sure, but Johnny could handle it, and he was up and, on the trail, again before daylight hit the snow. It was a gray, cloudy day as John snowshoed up and over Sunny Pass. He had the grade now, and it was just a matter of moving his sinewy legs across the tops of the snow-white mountains for the next 15 miles. He knew all too well it would be a race against darkness before he got there, but no matter what the weather, he could make it with a hard push. He had been there too many times before and couldn't get lost. Altogether, he had to cover 22 miles.

It was a black night without a star, moon, or a light in the sky to give even a shadow of light. He followed snowshoe tracks in the barely visible snow up to Frank's upper cabin door. A bit of windblown snow blew off the roof of the cabin and down Johnny's neck. He unlaced his snowshoes and hollered, "Frank! You in there?" He knew Frank was there because of all the tracks around the cabin and the warm glow of light that came from the window and under the door. "FRANK!" Johnny yelled. This was all Johnny got out as the door swung open. There stood Frank Arnold in all his glory — gray, rough beard; blue, piercing eyes; wearing old, oily, weather-beaten wool pants that covered his wool, long handle long-johns.

"What in the hell do YOU want!?" Frank asked in a surprised, unfriendly voice that grew with anger.

Johnny Bell must have been the last one in the world Frank wanted to cast his eyes upon that cold winter night in February. Johnny Bell would never be welcome in Frank Arnold's house. No! Johnny was not coming into his cabin. Frank had not forgotten a thing. The half-breed Indian learned that one fact, real fast, that cold dark night at the Tungsten Mine.

"I came up to see how you're doing, Frank. The townspeople are beginning to wonder about you!" Johnny replied as he edged closer to the warmth of the hot air that came rushing out of the cabin door.

Frank hardly heard what John had said. "Well, you just better get the hell out of here!" Frank said in a very matter-of-fact way.

"Get out of here? HELL! I just snowshoed 40 miles to check on you for Hill, Bill Ford, Richman, and the rest of them. Damned. Let me in to warm up!"

"Let you in, be damned! If you don't get off my porch, I'll blow you off with lead!" Frank was now backing away and trying to close the door Johnny had his foot in.

"Why you son-of_XXZZ@#**xX." The door slammed closed!

Johnny stepped back and shook his fist at the door, then back into his snowshoes he went. That night under a lone spruce tree, where Johnny slept, the temperature was twice as cold as the previous one, even though the temperature around the Tungsten Mine was a bit warmer.

After a very hard, two winter days and two cold nights, again under a spruce tree, Johnny made the 30 miles to the Duncan James cabin and at last a stove and a warm night's sleep.

At the Loomis café, he let everyone know he would never go back to check on Frank Arnold again. "I don't give a damned if he never comes out of those mountains! You Got That! He's there alright, but he can freeze and go to hell for all I care or burn up there with every frozen bone in his body broke! Or, he can rot up there forever! I'll never go back up and look for the XX@#* Englishman again! No, never! Got That? So, don't EVER even think about asking me to look for that Damned Englishman again. Roll that in your damned pipes and smoke it.."

TALES OF THE TUNGSTEN MINE

Jack Richman, Fred Hill and the others rocked back in their chairs and could only shake their heads. "Well at least he's okay," said one to the others. But Johnny had prophesied wrong. He would go back into the high country and look again for the missing Englishman — to rectify, one more time, a long past error. For there would again come another winter when the lone trapper didn't come out.

Nothing Stays the Same for Long

Things begin to change it seemed at the Tungsten Mine after the big forest fire of 1929. With the higher demand for tungsten in the '30's, Ferris Ford worked much too hard for Frank's liking to make a deal of some kind on the mine. Mining men were riding in right under Frank's nose, and he couldn't have liked it. He didn't relish the thought of losing his home or the possessions that were left at the mine when he had claimed it. There had been lots of items packed out for the tax sale in 1921, but what was left was "his!" His by right of "adverse possession" if nothing else. They were not going to get all the tools and assortment of items he had collected, used, saved from the weather, fires and people for 15 years. In fact, if he had just been a citizen of the country, he could have had a legal mining claim to it all and to heck with the rest, but as it was, he was really just playing games in a land where he had no true legal rights. Frank could see the handwriting on the wall. Those new miners may get the tungsten, but not the mining supplies! So it was in the summer of 1934, Frank came to the Ford ranch to borrow a good old white pack mare that Ferris Ford possessed, the pack mare that he and Frank had used many times throughout the years. She was altogether reliable. *This was really out of character for Frank*, Ferris thought. *He never messed with horses.*

But it was no big deal. His partner needed a horse and Ferris obliged by letting him use the gentle old mare. But Frank had the pack mare for way too long. When he finally brought it back later that summer, he gave no good reason for needing it at all, and Ferris was just a little curious.

It was the summer of 1939, 3 years after Frank Arnold had been found hanging, and 5 years after Frank had disappeared, that Loy McDaniel and Mickey Kinchelo were doing some hard riding in the back country not far from the Tungsten. It is said they were hunting deer, though they may have been hunting for just what they found. For it had always been rumored after Frank died, that he must have left a lost cabin somewhere that nobody had yet found, a hidden cabin that would account for all his lost personal items. Whatever the cowboys were doing in the depths of the black woods, they came upon some small pieces of old cloth and some bent-over brush making a faint trail.

"That's a snowshoe trail, Mickey." Loy said, as he followed the bent-over brush and the faint hint of a trail on his horse.

"I think you're right Loy, but it's too late and too dark now to follow it out; let's head back to the mine and find out where that cloth came from tomorrow," returned Mickey, looking at the old trail disappear in the darkness. The next day the cowboys beat through a swamp, some bog, and a lot of spruce forest before they ran headlong into Frank's "lost cabin." What a sight greeted their eyes.

Frank had used the old white mare to chuck away hundreds and hundreds of pounds of goods and old mining supplies from the Tungsten Mine. The boys had hit a small gold mine. The boys were fascinated and amazed at their discovery of this wood structure full of goods of every description. The small 10-by-10-foot cabin was so full of stuff they couldn't move through it; only the bunk was empty. Outside they stumbled all over things, and it took the two men all day long just to paw through the many treasures Frank had hidden away. Such a hardware store did not belong lost in the high mountains.

It was just a few days later that Jay Hill, riding for Loy, and Mickey Kinchelo headed back into the lost stash from the Duncan James cabin on Toats Coulee with six packhorses. They were destined to bring out not a little of the goods Mickey and Loy had found. Putting the miles behind them as they rounded Haig Mountain, one of Loy's pack horses stumbled off the trail and ran a wooded stick into its jugular vein. Thing's suddenly turned ugly as the horse stood there with blood pumping out of its jugular like water from a spigot. "Hell, Jay! Look at this horse bleed! It's a bad cut, and I can't stop it! Damned! It looks like I'm going to have to shoot it! He's hurt bad and look, he's laying down in all that blood!" Mickey pulled out his pistol.

"I'd lay down, too, if I was bleeding like that," Jay answered as he watched the dying horse go to its knees. "There's sure no way we can stop a horse from bleeding like that. But Wait Mickey!" he hollered as Mickey took aim with his pistol. "Don't shoot him yet." Jay said, "You never know. Let's leave him here and go on to the mine and if he's dead when we come back out, then, we lost one horse. If he's hurting and not dead, we'll put a bullet in him then. Let's just leave him and see what happens. After all, he is Loy's horse!" reminded Jay.

"Ok with me, but that guy won't be alive when we come back," said Mickey as he slipped his gun back in its holster, grabbed the horn on his saddle, and swung back into the saddle-seat. Miles later, at the mine, the packers found they weren't alone. That year, 1939, a man by the name of Don Zellweger with his wife and a friend were there, and they were miners.

The next day found Jay Hill and Mickey at the lost cabin and at the big stash deep in the woods. They were again like kids turned loose in a candy store as they loaded up tools, lanterns, bear traps, mouse traps, copper wire, pots, buckets, bells, a government Coast and Geodetic compass, knives and a hundred other goodies hidden by the old trapper that summer in 1934. Five pack horses loaded with booty pulled out from the hidden cache and headed back for the Duncan James cabin. As they came around Haig Mountain, the cowboys' thoughts turned back to Loy McDaniel's bleeding horse that was probably dead on the trail ahead of them. All of a sudden, they heard a loud nicker and up a-running came Loy's horse, the one they had left for dead. "The guy acted like he had never been hurt and wondering why he had been left behind," Jay said. The cowboys felt good about it all. It made a fine trip out of a unique experience into the deep, forgotten woods for the lost spoils of Frank Arnold.

Moose: Who Can Raise Moose to Pull a Wagon?

The mystery of Frank's past is like a big puzzle with the pieces being old photographs, old papers and old memories. Herb Curtis, Pete, Frank Maron and Harold MacWilliams knew the old trapper was from, or had been in Canada. George Miller said he had worked as an engineer in a mine in Idaho. Shorty Fairbrother knew he was from back East, but "Pete," uncannily, and alone, knew he was from New Brunswick, Canada and passed this secret information along to just one other person, George Honey. This known secret of Pete's was the key to unlocking Frank's past.

A picture of a harnessed team of moose was developed from a negative found in Frank Arnold's cabin in a cigar box and this story from the Wenatchee Daily World was told by F. D. Duffy to the Wenatchee Daily World in 1959:

"*F. D. Duffy Saw Moose Picture Back in 1889*"

"*A Wenatchee man believes he knows the story behind the harnessed-up team of moose published in the Daily World last week. The picture, developed from a negative found in a miner's cabin above Winthrop about 20 years ago, (1936), was taken of a newspaper picture published in Fredericton, New Brunswick, Canada, 70 years ago, F. D. Duffy of Walnut St., said today.* "I saw it in the paper when I was a kid there." *he said. Duffy is 82 now. According to Duffy, the farmer who domesticated the moose also was shown in one picture riding down the ice in a sleigh pulled by the "wild" animals.* "There were lots of moose in that country then." *he said.* "Caribou *too." He recalls horses shying wildly whenever they'd meet the moose team coming down the road."*

Mr. Duffy at this date is long gone. He spoke the same words about the local horses "shying wildly" as Frank Arnold had used when he told Harold MacWilliams in 1930 that he had raised moose in Canada. Frank spoke of the horses "going wild" and "putting on a real show" when they met his team of moose. Frank could have photographed the picture from the paper, the Fredericton Daily Gleaner, the town's only real paper, which goes back to November 1889. Or he may have even screened the picture for the paper, being a photographer. At any-rate, if one ever wondered what Frank Arnold looked like when he was 16 or 17 years old, the picture of the young man on the sled being pulled by the young moose should give you a good idea. The unscreened picture of the lad and his calf moose by the barn was found in the collection of a Mr. H. F. G. Woodbridge. In the "Mr. H. F. G. Woodbridge Collection" found in the Provincial Archives, there were three pictures of this young moose and two pictures of the driver. The team picture found in Frank Arnold's cigar box was not in the collection.

Not much was known about the pictures found at the Canadian Provincial Archives. The pictures were donated in July of 1967, and whoever donated them had this to say: "Thought to be the moose domesticated by Clarence Vance, manager of Gutta-Moose Lodge around 1925." Mr. Wenford Camerad (sp) at the Provincial Archives thought that the 1925 date was much too late because Mr. H. F. G. Woodbridge had died around the turn of the century. He believed the pictures were probably older than the turn of the century, which would make them the right age to be our man Frank Arnold, for we figured Frank was born about 1870. If 17 (or 19) years are added to the age of the young man in the picture, then 1889 would mark the picture date, as Mr. Duffy remembered.

I feel strongly that these three pictures are photographs of the same moose Frank Arnold raised as a farmer and are also of the same moose F.D. Duffy speaks about in 1959. The man at the reins in all three pictures is no doubt our lone trapper, Frank Arnold. He must have rescued them, raised them and trained them. He kept at least one picture of his unusual team as long as he lived. He still held the negatives 50 years later.

The lad sitting on the little sled with the reins in his hands certainly doesn't look like the hardened military man that Frank Maron, Shorty Fairbrothers and I envisioned. Instead he looks like a farm boy that found two moose calves and made pets out of them. Here the young Frank is working with his calf, teaching it to pull him around on the sled. Looks like fun! The young moose is a female and is less than a year-and-a-half old. If Mr. Duffy has his year's right, which he seems pretty sure of, then the young man in the picture holding the reins is the right age to be our Frank Arnold. Frank was born around 1870. Mr. Duffy says the man that raised the moose was a farmer. Frank Arnold strangely wore bib-overalls like all farmers have done since the first bibs were made for them. (Have you ever seen any old-timers other than a farmer in bibs?) The man in the team picture and wagon is wearing bibs.

After a close look at all three pictures, they have a surprising number of similarities. For one thing they are all scratched. Another is the fact that there is what looks like water bubbles on the two main pictures, and a bubble is on the ear of the older moose team pulling the wagon. In addition, the hill on the skyline is of the same grade and looks like it was taken just at the other end of the far pasture. A convincing detail is the bridle used on the moose. Though the moose in each picture are of different ages and sizes, obviously being a year or so apart, the bridle is the same. Anyone who has ever rigged up a bridle for a different kind of animal knows that the chances of two people coming up with the same style and type of bit, head-rigging and reins hook-up are somewhat remote. Because the team moose picture is known around the world, but unknown in its origin and history, it is highly controversial and curious. Some said it was a fake, but no longer. To me these similarities all indicate that the man, the moose, the pictures and the place are all from the same source — Fredericton, New Brunswick. Though the pieces of the puzzle were found thousands of miles apart, and years and years removed from each other. The man we know as Frank Arnold and maybe the man they knew as Clarence Vance were one and the same.

It is probable that Frank or someone else may have shot the mother moose, not knowing she had two small calves at her side. And not being able to leave them (and this is all speculation), he managed to get a rope around the little guys and drag them home because they would be as good as dead if left in the woods. At home, Frank "raised them like oxen." This is how Frank put it whenhe told Harold MacWilliams about raising the moose that day on the trail off the Pasayten River. It was in "Canada," he told Mac. "They worked real good pulling the wagon down the road, but if you wanted to see a show, wait until my team of moose ran into a team of horses! The horses just went crazy!" Just what F.D. Duffy said in 1959. The Pasayten River is where even today there is a good number of moose to be found, as there were back then also. It is likely that as the conversation turned to moose, Frank spoke of raising the moose like "oxen," so he must have "cut" the bull and fed them like cattle around the barn seen in the picture.

Harold never forgot the story and didn't realize there was a photograph until years later when he saw the moose/wagon picture in the Wenatchee Daily World, 20 years or more after he had talked to the mountain man. He knew then that this "wonderful man" had not told him just a story.

Again, the picture of the moose team was found by George Honey while riding for George Miller in that year, 1936. It was in negative form and was in a cigar-box with a number of other pictures; some of them on old tin backings, showing them to be old. The pictures were one of the few glimpses into Frank's hidden past and inspire a lot of speculation. One of the pictures was of an oriental lady in a room weaving on what looked like a reed mat. (Had Frank been to the Far East?) Others were of a bear paw, a big bull moose with no background and a man taken to be Frank Arnold with a mosquito net over his hat. There was also one of Clarence Landergreen at one of Frank's trapping lay-outs. These photographs were the ones that were remembered. Interestingly, years later, in 1952, when Rolan Darling was working up at the mine as cook, one of the workers found the same moose picture in a size of about 4-by-5 inches. It was found in the big lower cabin in a crack on the floor, back by where the old bathtub use to set.

The importance of moose being domesticated by Frank can hardly be appreciated enough, for rarely has this been done in the past, or since. "The Alaska" magazine for December 1990, had Frank Arnold's famous picture of the moose team and wagon, and covered the subject of moose being domesticated. The article mentioned a part of F. D. Duffy's piece in the Wenatchee Daily World, and went on to declare what was known about moose being domesticated - quoting it said; "...Moose were used as beasts of burden in Dawson in the late 1800's. In the late 1700's, villains in northern Russia saddled up moose to use on crime sprees because they could outrun police riding horses..." And the magazine went on to relate what biologist, Dave Kellyhouse, said, "Moose don't lend themselves to it. Basically they are solitary animals. The only time they get together is during the fall rutting season. The Soviets tried for three decades to raise moose for meat and milk. Then they threw up their hands and closed down their experiment stations. The main problem is that moose are not selectively bred for disposition (like cows) for thousands of years, and you can still get kicked by a cow that doesn't want to be milked," said Dave Kellyhouse. "A moose is basically a 1,000-pound animal with an attitude."

An attitude Frank Arnold seemed able to overcome. Truly this "Canadian" was a unique man. The photographs are indeed rare, and are at the time of this writing, the only recorded photographs of domesticated wild moose in use. The picture of Frank with his team of moose pulling the wagon has often been called a fake. Now we have three "fakes" of Frank's moose.

CHAPTER 16

Frank's Lost Gold Mine

"**LIKE ALL GOOD MOUNTAIN MAN** stories, Frank's just wouldn't be good without rumors of a lost gold mine," said one interviewer. "There's no gold in that country," he reasoned. "But it is a good story." The report of a gold mine hidden away in the depths of a wilderness, lost to all but one lone mountain man, would spark a person's interest.

A statement like this, "that there is no gold in that country," begs the question, what country are we going to talk about? Frank's country took in hundreds of thousands of acres and miles. How far out does a person have to go from the Tungsten Mine before colors of gold show up? It is true that the very first assays done by J. E. Beaton proved to Herb Curtis and Bill Johnson that there was no gold in that quartz rock they laid before him. But there wasn't supposed to be any tungsten in it, either. For that matter, there was not supposed to be any quartz rock up there in that granite rock cap either, but there it was. Like tungsten, gold is where you find it, and Frank Arnold was a traveling fool, a person who was known to range near and far throughout the 22 years he called the Pasyaten home. A person does not have to go farther than the first page of history in the land to find out that gold was found in quite an abundance in the early years. Gold founded the towns of Loomis, Oroville, Twisp, Winthrop, Barron, Chancellor, Conconully and crossing the border, Hedley. Gold, silver and copper founded these towns.

The first white men to enter the high mountains were prospectors. These men "hit'er" big on a creek called Slate, just quarter mile from the present Pasayten border. The first man's name was Rowley. He had walked down from Canada, probably following the Skagit River in about 1870 something; 2,500 men followed this prospector and rushed to the diggings on Slate Creek. There were camps all up and down the river. The first boom lasted somewhere around 12 years, which was quite good for a small gold rush. They fanned out in all directions looking for the best diggings and found themselves working the Ruby, Slate and Pasayten River and Canyon Creeks.

In 1891, Alex Barron started it all over again by taking out 82 ounces of placer gold in 82 hours from the same Slate Creek. Barron was one of those lucky miners that found gold wherever he fumed. On the North American Mine, Barron hit a glory hole that made him $20,000 richer. And with such strikes, placer miners became hard-rock miners, and some found many favorable hard-rock mines in this southwest corner. The early day placer miners were said to have taken out at least $300,000 in gold dust and nuggets, and the hard-rock miners did even better.

But it was the poor man's gold that was found in the placer deposits of the stream bed. All it took was a gold pan, shovel, sluice-box, and a lot of hard work. If you had been working with the crew of miners in 1936 at the Tungsten Mine, you could have asked Henry Dammann, who was working there that year, how placer mining was done. Henry made a good strike on Slate Creek around the turn of the century. It seems Henry panned some gold off a bench above the creek and, "low-and-behold," it had gold in it! He reasoned that if it showed up in the pan, it should show up in a sluice-box. So, he went to work bringing in water and soon had gold behind the riffles. The little bench paid off quite well for Mr. Dammann. It is said he cleared a cool $6,000.00 off the bench when gold was no more than $20.00 dollars an ounce.

Though Slate Creek and Ruby were the most productive in the area, they were far from the only gold producers. A good number of the creeks in the western half of the Pasayten would provide the pan with some color. With this in mind, we turn back to the lone mountain man with the pack on his back. It started with horse-packer Harold MacWilliams (Mac).

Mac first went packing in the Pasayten in the early 1930's. He packed for the Forest Service and he packed for the Game Department. He lifted pack boxes for George Miller and did the same for paying hunters and for himself. He had three chance meetings on the trail with Frank Arnold. One was on the Pasayten River. One was at or around Hidden Lakes. The other was perhaps at Black Lake.

"Quite a prospector he was. A wonderful man," were the words Mac used to describe the fast-walking Englishman. But Mac had one particular conversation with Frank that would shed some light on the gold story: "It was down on the Pasayten River that I ran into Frank," and although Mac couldn't remember all the things they talked about, one of the things he did remember was that Frank was out on a prospecting tour. Frank said he was looking for... "THIS!" Frank held out his hand and in it was a small bottle about half full of gold. On picking it up and looking at it very carefully, Mac could see that there were two or three pieces with some size to them. It wasn't much, but he could see it was all gold. They had some conversation about this and that, and then they both went their separate ways. Was Frank looking for gold, or had he already found it?

There is the story, one of many, of a lost hunter in the Sheep Mountain country who supposedly found a "picture rock" full of gold, but he could never relocate where he found it at — a sad, old story. Perhaps Frank's gold came from that area.

Frank E. Maron, who stayed with Frank for two winters, came to believe that Frank had some gold or could get some gold. It is uncertain whether he saw it or whether Frank told him about it. However he learned about it, whatever the quantity, Maron believed Frank had the yellow stuff. Maron didn't know where the gold came from, but that didn't stop him from going back into the woods years later and looking for it. In the early fifties, Loy McDaniel brought Maron up to Loomis from Walla Walla for a visit. Once in the Okanogan again, Frank Maron, Jim and Loy McDaniel took a trip up the Toats Coulee River to pan one of the creeks off the drainage. Maron was in a wheelchair by this time, so young Jim did the shovel work, throwing the sand into a sluice-box Jim had made for the venture. Maron looked on with eager expectation as the sand and water rolled through the gold box. At clean-up time, Jim and Maron found a lot of black sand, and Maron was quite tickled, it was said, but it was far from the color of gold.

In the pictures that were found in Frank's old cabin up on the shelf, in the old cigar-box, there was one believed to be of Frank panning for gold on some lost creek. George Honey always figured Frank had been to Alaska years before, and that was not out of the realm of possibility because he was at the right age and the time was right. But if he had, he never mentioned it. However, if he had been up north mucking for gold, he might have kept some nuggets and showed them off at different times. Most all prospectors have some gold just to look at once in a while to keep them fired-up.

Still, there is one more story about Frank's gold that seems to be quite strong. Two vials of gold that were found. They were said to be in old Alka-Seltzer bottles. They showed up in one of his cabins after he was found dead. They were found, as one person said, "at the Tungsten Mine," or as another person said, "in one of his line cabins." It seems that after Frank disappeared, and when people were looking for him, someone found over his bunk, on the logs that made up the wall, two

Frank's Lost Gold Mine

Alka-Seltzer bottles of placer gold. Of course, no one has admitted to finding the bottles, or to having them, but the story had feet, and persists yet today.

There are several questions to be asked. If Frank had some gold, did he ever sell any? If he did sell it, where did he sell it at? What did he do with the money? And more important than that and highly pertinent to the whole case, if it was known to some people around Loomis and Winthrop that Frank had a gold mine, could this have been a motive for murder? Could a murder be committed in the heart of the Great Depression of the 1930's when few men could even make a dollar for gold? Did some of Frank's acquaintances know more than we do today about a lost gold mine? I believe so because Art Mitchall, the Deputy Sheriff who went in that dark night to find Frank, said in the Omak Chronicle: "His notebook bearing the date, several circles, and the inscription "T-l," "S-C," which officers believe may be either the arrangement of his traps or the location of a mine." It seems that the three men who buried the hanging "prospector," Frank E. Maron, Art Mitchall and Pete talked about the possibility of him having a mine. The land was big, the man was strong, and the time was long. To be sure, Frank Arnold could have had a pay streak hidden away in the vast land we call the Pasayten.

CHAPTER 17

Don Zellweger on the Hatfield Claim & Foss's Missed $100,000

IN DECEMBER, ON THE 3RD, of 1937, John Hatfield of Wenatchee bought the Tungsten Mine group of claims from Ferris Ford. The claim names being the Wista, Grace, Wolframite, New Lake, Climex, Sunshine, Highland, Morning, Hercules and Ajex. The price Mr. Hatfield paid to Mr. Ford is not known. And, how Ferris Ford was able sell the mine to three different people at about the same time is also yet to be figured out. Two months before the sale, on September 21, 1937, Ferris sold and deeded over the claims listed above to Harold V. Dardier (the H. V. Dardier of the 1936 activity), deeded the claims over in Wenatchee. The claim was filed, though, in the Okanogan County courthouse on October 11, 1937, at the request of a Richard E. Johnson. And if this was not confusing enough, at almost the same time on the 4th of October, Ferris sold all the claims again to Hughy M. Lawrence in Okanogan, but the date it was recorded at the courthouse was December 6, 1937, at the request of John Hatfield. Strange dealing to say the least because it was on the 3rd of December 1937 that John Hatfield bought the claims flat out and supposedly incumbent free from Ferris Ford while Old Clyde Andrews, the long-time mountain man of the Pasayten, was still a player almost up until this date, and held a one-quarter interest in the Tungsten Mine, but he died sometime in 1937 of a heart attack. So, in the end, John Hatfield ended up with the famous high country mine.

While up at the cabins, John had some ore sacked and taken to the University of Washington for their help and analysis to determine the best method to processes the ore. There a young college student, who was majoring as a mining engineer, became interested in the black ore and the mine. His name was Don Zellweger and he would get a good dose of the Tungsten Mine Fever before it was all over. He worked parts of two summers on Woframite Mountain and not for big wages. He wrote his college thesis on the magical mine, and the opening words were:

"I was employed by Mr. John Hatfield of Wenatchee, Washington, owner of the Hatfield tungsten mine, beginning August 1, 1938, to examine the property, then dormant, and to do the necessary mill-testing prior to reopening. During the week of August 14 to August 20, 1938, he did field work on the property, collecting specimens of ore and country rock in addition he obtained 250 pounds of ore representative of the mill feed. Upon these specimens, the ore sample, and the other material collected, this thesis is based."

Mr. Hatfield was certainly interested in reopening the mine and Don's report was encouraging and progressive. The thesis covered the mine's early history to the geology of the land and proposed mining methods in 50 pages. It is one of the most thorough of all reports put together.

Don Zellweger worked with great interest on John Hatfield's 250 pounds of ore at the university that winter of 1938-1939, coming

Don Zellweger on the Hatfield Claim & Foss's Missed $100,000

up with the best milling methods that engineers of the northwest could develop. Using the college's equipment, he studied the ore and the options available to concentrate such quartz rock to the needed 60%, which was still the minimum industry standard percentage for a marketable product. He also kept in mind the location and the mining procedure that a far-removed mine like this one would have to have. On their first experiment in the classroom with the tungsten ore, as the quartz rock ran through the noisy crusher on the table, a "violet dust" rose from the machine and escaped the dust filters, covering the whole room in a cloud of colored dust. The strange, un-containable violet dust blew and moved like magic at will. It got into everything and seemed to walk as they walked in little clouds around their feet. And trying to sweep it up was a joke, an exercise in fumbling futility. The dust was Wolframite, so brittle, so tiny and charged that they could not contain it or even collect it.

"The convincing fact of the entire run," Don said, "is that practically all the tungsten is liberated at 20 mesh, (not that small – 20 holes per inch), and with good screening and careful tabling a high recover is possible." Don and his teachers did eventually come up with the best procedure to get Mr. Hatfield the 60% tungsten ore. Tungsten was not difficult to work with. Don suggested that 10-to-15-ton-a-day mill, carefully managed, should turn Mr. Hatfield a good profit. In scope, the mill was really close to what the 1916 miners had. The next year, when school was out in 1939, Don Zellweger was an engineer with a degree in mining in his hands, and by the time the summer sun came, he was back on Wolframite Mountain, picking up rocks and ready to put all those years of schooling to work.

He had come-up with a loose deal with John Hatfield to work the mine. John would cover the basic expenses of the project. George Miller's packing charges, food, tools, mining machinery, supplies, and basic wages. But understanding that the wages weren't high, the return and incentive would be what Don could pull out of the white quartz in tungsten ore. With the help of Don's wife and a good friend from high school, plus one city slicker from back east, Zellweger proceeded to rebuild a tungsten processing plant. Most of it lay in pieces amongst charred and burnt timbers that had seen better days. The 1929 fire had turned the 1916 mill into a junk pile, almost. The 8-inch jaw crusher still turned, and there was no way you could destroy the 2-ton roller crusher that had come over Bauerman Ridge in the hands of Joe Hall and Harry Sherling. It took a lot of work and good engineering, but before too many weeks went by, Don and his skeleton crew of two men had a new ore mill working.

George Miller, the packer, managed to pack in a "Model-A car motor" on his horse to power the moving parts, and before the summer was over, the new mill was crushing the white and black tungsten ore. It was quite an achievement for the three young men and one lady, and if you look at the old mill today, 50 years later, all it looks like it needs is gas for the old Model-A motor, someone to give it a kick, throw in some ore, and stand back and watch it work. It was a fine little mill that the three men built that summer. A job to be proud of.

The hammer beat steady as Don turned the cold steel drill in one hand and swung the 4- pound sledgehammer in the other. It was slow work and they sure needed a running compressor to keep this job from being an archaic operation, but the vital parts were somewhere out there in the mail, and this was just the first year of setting things up. There would be another. So, the men hand-drilled and blasted, hand-drilled and blasted, hand sorting the quartz-wolframite ore as they mucked out the rubble of rock. But this vein was not being cooperative, and at each blast it pinched down smaller until finally it no longer made sense to work it.

Don was certain the ore body was a continuous blanket that stretched clear across the valley and over to the claims on Apex Mountain, where

Don Zellweger on the Hatfield Claim & Foss's Missed $100,000

quartz outcroppings also could be found: outcroppings Johnny Bell had found years before and Frank Arnold had claimed in 1930, and with Bob Curtis in 1950. The college engineer must have spent hours and days and weeks trying to trace out the 3 miles of vein, but with little, to no, success. It wasn't there! After much looking and kicking over rocks, he decided that the quartz vein just wasn't continuous, and this was a bit of a letdown, for it meant that the ore body was limited to just what was below the cabins and just a reasonable extension there from. It had taken all summer and most of fall to set up the mill and explore the quartz veins out from the mine. The season was winding down when Don finally gave up on trying to follow the teasing ghost veins and started busting rock on the veins that had made Herb Curtis wealthy. And while deep in the mine in a stope, off the main tunnel, Don found a pile of old ore boxes used by the early miners of World War I. They were a little smaller than apple boxes, and many of them still held ore. The last hand-picked quartz of 1918-1920 never made it out. Don never found any old machinery back in the adits, such as a diesel motor or air compressor that were rumored to have been stashed in the mine shafts. There was a compressor on the mine site that Don needed to get running for the air drills, and he had torn it down to fix it up. He was in the process of rebuilding it, and the parts were there, and brand new, but unfortunately, he never got it back together — winter had arrived.

The weather was cold, and the first snow had already fallen; it was time to go home. *There would be another year*, Don thought. He and his new wife went home feeling good about the little mill that shook, rattled, and rolled so well. Some of the quartz rock he knew could have used a bit finer grinding to be perfect, to make the twenty mesh needed, still, the mill made him about 300 pounds of concentrate in the short time it ran. Considering all the work that was done in one summer and fall, with only three men and one cook, it amazes one to think about it, and leaves you asking how they did it. For the three did basically what it took sixty men to do in 1916. But it was the vein that worried Don. It just didn't trace out much past the general area around the cabins, and a good part of that had been worked.

Then there was one more bad deal that played even a larger role in what was going to happen to John Hatfield's claims. The government, it seemed, was playing yo-yo with the price of tungsten. It fell in 1939 and 1940. These were war years! When it was setting on a low price, the government put a fix on it. It would go no higher. Germany was not going to get this tungsten. It was discouraging to the claim holder, and Don knew it would be tough to make a profit at the fixed price, so John Hatfield reluctantly put the Tungsten Mine on the back burner, once again.

There was a big mining company that was interested in the diggings about this time, it was said, but they were too far away from Hatfield on the purchasing price. Don Zellweger did the assessment work for John through the year of 1944, though he said he never got back after 1939. John did the assessment work for one more year, 1945, and then dropped the claims. Hatfield's last year with the tungsten mine was 1945.

Certainly, Don Zellweger did an excellent job. He went up there to mine and find a way to extract the ore in the best way practical. He did this well, even though he never really had all the equipment he needed: a good compressor, air drills, finer ore crushing, and the 99 other items needed to make it work perfectly. His time ran out, the price of ore strangely fell, and the veins, though rich in tungsten, were marginal to mine at the government price. (Some of the veins in the mine Don found ran 10% tungsten ore.) It is my opinion that both his written and physical work is by far the best done on the mine from a practical aspect. And there is no doubt that Don found tungsten. It was laying all over the college work-room floor from representative quartz rock, and a big company in Arizona bought his 300 pounds of concentrate.

Don Zellweger on the Hatfield Claim & Foss's Missed $100,000

Don got to know George Miller in those years, for he kept him busy packing in needed mining supplies and the food for his crew. George, often staying over in the cabins, told him the historical stories as they passed the time around the dimly lighted miner's cabin: stories about the old caretaker Frank Arnold, AND How he, George Miller himself had found him dead? He had found Frank on Horseshoe Creek hanging from a rope. Don got a pretty good feeling for how the lone mountain man lived while he himself stayed at the mine. He also found an old box of Frank's film in the attic, but the film slipped away somewhere.

The mill stands as a silent witness to Don's work 50+ years ago. As charm — rough or not is appreciated — Don Zellweger enjoyed his two summers in the Pasayten and never forgot the experience. John Hatfield passed away in the late 1950's and his feelings were said to be a bit on the bitter side when talking about the mine, for he never was he able to bring his challenging mine into production.

Foss's Quick Interest

John Hatfield's last year holding the mine was 1945, and his interest ended that year. Others, though, sat in the wings waiting, such as the packer Foss Creveling and the packer George Miller, both of the Methow Valley. Foss latched onto the mine sometime around 1947, just after the Second World War ended, and George Miller, aced out on the best claims, filed a claim, maybe two, down on the creek for whatever reason (based largely on hope). It was at this time, too, that a mining promoter showed up in Foss' back yard in Winthrop — literally! Now a mining promoter — one and all — wants just one thing, marketable mining property. And, Foss now had one. So the Winthrop bunch, Foss, his sons Dwade and Bill, with George Miller went back to the rich diggings on Wolframite Mountain to promote his interests, and, of course, the mining promoter, Charley Dent, who just happened to be staying in his travel-trailer in Foss' backyard went along. For two weeks they explored the grounds, digging and picking at rocks, and throwing some into sacks. During this time, young Dwade Creveling couldn't help but pick up all the beautiful quartz/wolframite crystals he found in such abundance in the adits, shot full of black tungsten and white sheelite. He sacked up a couple hundred pounds of these specimens too, if nothing else, to build a rock fireplace down at the house. The sacks of pretty rocks did get packed out to his Winthrop home, but never got mortared into that crystal hearth.

While he was up at the mine, Foss' wife, down in the valley, received a jolting phone call from the big city of Spokane, coincidentally from another mining promoter named Amesworth, asking; "Would Foss be willing to sell his interest in the Tungsten for a $100,000?" Shocked, after picking the phone up off the floor, she said, "More than likely!" Well, by the time Foss got off the mountain and home, two weeks later, the $100,000 offer had disappeared into the past as did Foss' interest in his mining claims a year or two later.

CHAPTER 18

In All Fairness, Was It Really Suicide?

This local newspaper article that was presented in an earlier chapter, though only a short note to its readers, is ever so important to this story. It was on the front page of the Omak newspaper for September 15, 1936, not even of "passing interest" at the time. This find, hidden away and fully forgotten about, with the exception of Frank Zacherman, the old Horseshoe Basin sheepherder who worked for Emmet Smith in the 1920's, remembered reading the account in the "Omak/Okanogan" paper as he told, 50 years before. I stumbled upon the article by sheer chance during the third or fourth year into my research of this story while scanning old newspaper microfilms. Its importance and information were "jolting." For there it was in print! All the Loomis stories were true down to the "swinging-body" and "rattling-bones!" It put to rest, as if in stone, the old controversies as to just when Frank Arnold went missing, and when he was found "officially" by the Deputy Sheriff. It was in every way the "Rosetta Stone" of this investigation.

"SWINGING BODY CLEARS MYSTERY OF MISSING MAN"

Frank Arnold, 65-Year-Old Trapper Dropped from Sight A Year and A Half Ago Date

January 1935

Notebook Found in Suicide's Pocket Indicates Time He Hanged Self

Discovery of a year-and-a-half-old suicide was reported to the county Sheriff's office after forestry trail crews found the body of Frank Arnold, a 65-year-old trapper in the upper Methow district hanging from a limb of a tree at an unfrequented spot near the Canadian border last Saturday.

Arnold had been missing for more than a year and a half, but residents believed that he was out tending to his trap-lines which were far removed from civilization. The old trapper had been in the country for over 30 years.

Nearby was found an iron kettle on which he had stood before he apparently kicked it out from under himself, springing his own deathtrap. He is believed to have been dead since January 1935 from an inscription in his notebook bearing the date, several circles, and the inscription "Tl" "SC," which officers believe may be his traps or the location of a mine.

Omak newspaper for September 15, 1936

DID IT CLEAR THE MYSTERY?

It would indeed be nice if the swinging body' did clear the mystery of Frank Arnold's death. But the question remains; was it suicide? True, a number of local people interested in the disappearance of Frank Arnold, if given the task of writing this story, would have felt strongly that finding the swinging body of Arnold should indeed be the last word on the subject, the closing tale of "old" Frank Arnold. Certainly, Deputy Art Mitchell felt that the obvious conclusion was that the old trapper's death was a suicide, mystery solved! The Sheriff's office, driving this idea home, mentioned it in the short article two times. Indeed, it could be said that about 40% of the people who knew something about Frank

In All Fairness, Was It Really Suicide?

Arnold, and had time to think about it, felt that suicide was pretty much a cut-and-dried conclusion.

"Hey! Frank lived a dangerous life up there in the wilds by himself, and the mountains are a very dangerous place; we all know that. After being so lucky for so long, something was bound to happen in the way of an accident. He was an old man, ya know! And besides, an old man like that, what did he have to live for?" some said. Or they would reason; "Come on, now, this is America, there is no other answer, for who would have possibly done such a dastardly deed, such as, kill a gentle, old, destitute trapper?"

Indeed, I would have liked nothing better than to have dropped and ended the story at Frank's *"Suicide Death."* This would be the easy way to conclude it, the way that so many others have done. I could have just let it go, just dropped his unnatural and strange hanging under that fir tree up there. The newspaper account says it all — understand: Frank E. Maron, Art Mitchell and Pete cleared the case. So, one could turn his back on this death and walk away feeling this strange happening was resolved, wrapped tight, and put away in a nice neat box. Yes, it ended with the authority's written word in the newspaper and everybody involved living happily ever after. But to end the story here, would have in no way cleared the case or the mystery. For instead of a nice, neat, pretty package presented in a tree, it would leave Frank's death looking to me like something wrapped in a wrinkled mess, in a wet paper bag with holes throughout, a bag that cannot even hold itself together.

What Does It Tell Us?

What is known about this strange death up there in the Pasayten Wilderness? The newspaper article telling of Frank's death reinforced some already-gathered facts: one being, "the swinging body." Maron told the truth! The body was blowing in the wind, with the "rattles" excluded. With that statement in the paper, Pete and Maron's story of going in at night and being spooked, jives. A second fact found in the clipping was that Frank was 65 years old when he died. This we had also determined to be true or close from bits and pieces gathered together. Pete and Maron must have had good reason to believe and tell Art Mitchell that Frank was that age at his disappearance, putting the birth of the trapper right at 1870. This we figured because Herb Curtis could only get Frank to say; "he was a few years older than him." Herb was born in 1872. Pete somehow got much more information out of Frank. Frank's exact age was not common knowledge. To be sure, he wanted that part of his life to remain unknown.

Now 65 can be mighty old or not that old at all, depending on who you ask. But whichever way it is cut, Frank was past his prime and he was certainly getting old. Iron, who knew him in the 1930's and trapped beside him for 4 years, used to refer to Frank as "Old Man Arnold" in the years following his death. And the picture of Frank at the C.C.C. camp in 1934, at his tent door, does show an aged Frank that doesn't need a second look to comprehend. Now if Frank was getting old, there is the question about his health. For if Frank was in poor physical condition, it would be a lot easier to believe that he was indeed willing to "cash-in-the-chips" and head over the "great divide;" that is, if he had gotten into a bind that winter he could not get out of.

So, what do we know? When George Honey saw Frank Arnold in the fall of 1934 at Jim Lee's barber shop in Okanogan, how did he look? These were the closing days of his life, and Frank was probably dead within four months of Jim's haircut. Frank looked darn good to George's eyes. He had on new clothes, a good haircut, spiced up with after-shave, nice new shiny boots and a big pack on his back. And he didn't "grunt" and "groan" when he picked it up. George said he looked strong. "He looked kind of tough," were his words. "Tough," as in well-conditioned and able to hold his own against anyone. It is important that he did not "groan" when he grabbed his backpack. Arnold was also "a-foot."

In All Fairness, Was It Really Suicide?

He was getting ready to hike back to Loomis, a cool 45 miles away, and a total of 85 miles from the Tungsten Mine. A person would be hard pressed to say the man was not in good health if he was preparing for an 85-mile walk.

Once back in Loomis, there is no doubt that young Al Smith was the last one to pack Frank and his supplies into the mine that fall in 1934. Al packed him in not too many days after leaving the city of Okanogan. Al spoke of Frank as taking in the normal amount of food, and Al even helped him stock his line cabin caches with that food. Al Smith and he stocked each of his main trap-line camps with food. Al rode a horse up the mountain from Loomis, again, 40 miles into the mountains, while Frank followed along behind. (There might have been a horse along for him to ride, but most of the time he didn't use it.) When the two were a 'half mile or so from the mine, a herd of deer ran across the trail in front of them. Frank was out of camp meat at the time, so he shot a small deer out of the herd and packed it in the rest of the way on his back. That would not be an easy task for a young man to accomplish, much less a man of this woodsman's age. Remember that this was after pulling the 6,000 feet in elevation from Loomis to the Tungsten, though it is likely they stayed at the Dunkin James cabin the first night up from Loomis. He then proceeded to eat darn near the better part of the deer as Al watched in amazement. (Again, Frank was known for his ability to put food away like a cunning wolverine.) So up to this time, early fall, September or early October of 1934, the mountain man, by all appearances was still strong, hungry, healthy and happy.

In the winter of 1934, Frank took a 40- to 50-mile trip on snowshoes south over to Beaver Meadows, to the C.C.C. camp running that winter. The records for the C.C.C. camp could not be found and were presumably and sadly destroyed. But this story tells us that before he met Mr. Grim Reaper, Frank embarked upon another 40- to 50-mile trek, this time on snowshoes. Keep in mind that traveling on snowshoes is at least twice, or even three times as tiring as walking on solid ground. If the traveling Englishman was considered old at 65, he was certainly the toughest 65-year-old man in the country. He still had phenomenal strength and endurance, and could walk not one, but hundreds of winter miles in the last years of his life.

There is one report, though, that in all fairness should be mentioned, and that's Lefty's statement as told over the phone to me. His story had changed though by the time I personally interviewed him a few months later. Lefty, told me the first time, over the phone, that he had seen Frank that winter of 1934/1935 alive out on his trap-line, but not in good condition. Lefty said, "He looked awful rough." This encounter would have made Lefty the last person to have seen Frank Arnold alive, out on his trap-line. This was an important statement and factors in greatly as the story unfolds. But I was not the only person that Lefty made this remark to. He also told Bob Curtis the same thing, that he had seen Frank alive on his trap-line the very winter he went missing and he was in "poor shape." Twice he stated that he had seen Frank his last winter alive. Lefty and Iron, being trapping partners that winter, said they had run into Frank alive, out on his trap-line. The meeting was presumably on the Chewack River where the two trap-lines came together, perhaps somewhere between the Thirty Mile Ranger Station and the Chewack Driveway Trail, a 3-mile stretch. Lefty and Iron would have no business trapping above this trail, nor would Frank have any trapping business south, below that drive-way trail. So, if they met, as Lefty said, it would have been for some other reason, and at some other place higher up the river. Where could that have been? Horseshoe Creek? This story of Lefty meeting Frank on the trail made the rounds for years, especially in the Winthrop, Loomis area. But, for some dark reason, years later, in a face-to-face meeting with me, Lefty denied he had ever seen Frank. "In his whole LIFE!" Which we know to be a false statement and a strange statement to make under normal circumstances.

In All Fairness, Was It Really Suicide?

Frank Had Some Problems

Still, with all that said, things were not all good with Frank Arnold. If the truth beknown, the facts do show that Frank was not in absolutely perfect health or body condition. At 65 years of age, the aging Englishman might have had as many as five suspected health problems which are worth considering:

Problem #1: Frank Arnold could have had a slight heart disability. This is just a guess, and a doctor could answer better than this writer. However, it is known that Frank took an ever-so-small amount of strychnine. He would gingerly put a small amount on the end of his long narrow knife blade and put the tip of the blade under his tongue. Now strychnine is known to be a strong

stimulant (as well as a deadly poison), and sometimes was used for heart problems. But it also could be the reason he could hike 50 miles in a day. For it also gives a person one "hell-of-a-kick!" It should still be considered that Frank had used this stuff for many years, at least 15 or 20 years, before his death.

Problem #2: Frank's teeth. After Al Smith took Frank in that fall of 1934, the old man came back out a few weeks later and stayed at the Herb Curtis home. He was having teeth problems and needed to get to the dentist badly. Grace Eastman (sister of Micky Kinchelo) gave him a helping hand and took him to the Oroville dentist. Given Frank's great addiction to sugar, his bad teeth isn't surprising. The 65-year old mountain man apparently did not have a tooth in his head worth saving because when he walked out of the dentist office there wasn't a tooth left. Whether this was a problem or a solution to a problem, is open to speculation, but it factors in, in a big way, to his mystery death.

Problem #3: Frank's winter drunk at Long Swamp with the hunters in 1915 had left him with a damaged foot. He had passed out in the creek and frozen his foot. Once a limb is frostbitten, it is forever a problem to the person when they go outside in the cold. Understand that Frank must have had a very badly frozen foot because it needed a doctor's treatment that winter in 1915, and he was still favoring it the next summer in July. Harry Sherling remembered him still hopping around on one foot over eight months after the injury. Evidence of how much his foot bothered him was the magneto shock-treatments he administered to himself in later years. George Honey and Ted Bolen found the contraption after his death. Frank would apply a stimulating electrical jolt to his foot with the copper foot/car magneto setup. On the other hand, it must have healed well enough, for the trapper walked tens of thousands of miles on his bad foot over the next 20 years.

Problem #4: The broken leg story and theory has surrounded Frank's death like a halo ever since he was found. This is a popular story, but one without any real roots that I can find. Pete or Art Mitchell could have told the story about finding Frank hanging in the tree with one leg laying on the ground under the body. Someone might have guessed this was an explanation for his supposed suicide hanging. To be sure, a leg bone was found on the ground in a rubber boot below the body. That is a fact. Also there was a crutch found by Loy McDaniel, Mickey Kinchelo and Jay Hill over at Frank's lost cabin by the Tungsten, 8 or 9 miles away, the cabin where all his supplies were squirreled away. But that crutch was laying some 9 miles from where Frank was found dead. So, it was probably just a leftover from his days of paying the price for getting drunk and passing out with his foot in an ice-cold creek all night. The broken-leg theory is open to a whole lot of pure speculation and uncertainty. But when the grave site on Horseshoe Creek was exhumed, one of the rubber boots and a leg bone appeared to have been thrown in the grave after the body was laid out. The body was laid out horizontally, and the leg bone and boot were on top of the other bones, and out of place. Yet nobody but Pete and Maron would have known about this out-of-place leg bone. The idea that the bone may have been broken before he died instead of dropping off after death due to the bodies long

In All Fairness, Was It Really Suicide?

exposure has created the "broken-leg-story" that is one explanation of Frank Arnold's fate that cold winter day. The story goes like this:

"It was while on his trap-line one cold winter day that Frank somehow stumbled in his snowshoes and fell, breaking his leg along with a snowshoe. It was mid-winter and the poor trapper was in the greatest of pain and misery. He couldn't move but inches, and stuck where he was at. Soon, he was out of food. Days had gone by and the pain was constant, he was slowly starving to death. Frank knew, and knew well, like a broken-legged animal in one of his own traps that death was not far away. He was 40 miles from the nearest person and he could count on no one coming up this mountain trail until spring — he knew he would never make it. The only light at the end of this dark tunnel was to try to get down the long Chewack River with its easy grade to the town of Winthrop or to find help from another trapper somewhere along the way. Frank just could not make it! The old man was weak and out of food, without hope. His life would never be the same again, now with the bad leg. Life had been hard anyway, with little joy, and now with this bad stroke of luck, life was no good at all. He only managed to make his camp at the mouth of Horseshoe Creek before pain and starvation overtook him. The old trapper took a rope from his well-laid camp and threw the rope over a limb (or as George Honey said, "it was tied around the tree," and he should know, because he cut it out of the tree). Frank then set-up a five gallon bucket, stacked on a block of wood for more height, worked his way up on the bucket, put the rope over his head, said a prayer, and kicked off."

And so is told the basic "Frank Arnold broken leg suicide story." It has as many variations as there are storytellers. The broken leg story is just that — a story — because nobody was there to see it. For argument sake, and because this idea is so popular, certainly Art Mitchell reasoned Frank had hung himself that winter, there are some begging questions a person might ask if wishing to reason along this line:

(A) First, there were no snowshoes found at the site, something he would have had to have had if it was winter. Remembering that Frank's last picture at the C.C.C. camp in Beaver Meadows shows a good foot or two of snow on the ground.

(B) Frank was wearing rubber boots at the hanging sight and in the grave. But as fact, no trapper runs his lines in open rubber boots with two or 3 feet of snow on the ground. A trapper needs to keep his feet warm at all cost, especially Frank with his one bad foot. Heavy boot-packs are what Frank would have worn in wintertime. Yet such boots were not found.

(C) To be sure, the suicide was supposed to have happened in January given what was written in the notebook found on the body. Yet the evidence ascertains a "no-snow" hanging for the body. For the feet of the hanging man were only a foot or two off the ground. If Frank had hung himself in mid-winter, then his feet should have been 4, 5 or 6 feet off the ground. For he would supposedly have jumped from a bank 2 or 3 feet higher than the level ground. Add to the bank height (plus the snow), another 2 feet for the bucket and block of wood and it is only logical that his feet should have been 5 to 6 feet off the ground.

(D) Does it really sound reasonable to believe that Frank, or anyone, could have balanced on a 3-foot bank, climbed onto a pot and block of wood stacked on top of one another in 2 or 3 or 4 feet of snow while weak from starvation and suffering a painful and badly broken legt? That did not happen my opinion.

(E) If Frank was in so much pain, and wanted to kill himself, why didn't he just shoot himself? He probably had two guns with him, one for sure, for he said he always carried the .22 long barrel revolver. There is hardly any doubt Frank had a gun. It can also be a for-sure assumption that Frank had some deadly strychnine in his pack, and this stuff provides a quick death.

In All Fairness, Was It Really Suicide?

(F) Also, do not think for a minute that Frank was inept. He could have made a splint, then a crutch and hobbled on out the 7 or 8 miles to the Thirty Mile house and Ranger Station, where there would have been some food and help. Lefty and Iron's trap-line came right to there, though they were working on a C.C.C. job for at least part of that winter in Beaver Meadows. If he was at the Tungsten Mine, as has been suggested, why did he not stay there, or go back there on his splint and crutch? Grant it, a crutch would be next to impossible to use in 2 to 4 feet of snow. Still, there was always the possibility of someone coming up to the mine that winter. Jim Thornton did one winter. Charley Johnson and Frances Lufken, two neighboring trappers, were said to have gone in to see Frank in the winter a time or two. Not to be forgotten, either, was the fact that Shorty Fairbrother might have come back through from the east to the Chewack Drive-way Trail. This point was on Shorty's old line off Windy Mountain. Frank could have waited for him at the Drive-way Trail, 3 miles south from Horseshoe Creek.

(G) If he broke his leg at, or around the mine, why did not Frank take the shortest route out through Canada? He could have gone down the old mining road built in 1916. There was also help not more than 20 miles to the north, and probably a lot closer than that. He knew that the Canadian Indians were trapping north of him, so the South Fork of the Ashnola would have had trappers on it. This road going north was every bit as good as the trail going out Tungsten Creek and down to the Chewack River, even better and shorter.

(H) It must be remembered, also, that Frank stocked his line camps with food in the fall by building high caches in the trees and supplying them with venison and staples. Could you get at them with a bad leg?

There are still more questions and speculations to ponder than these, but in the over-all truth of the matter, there is no evidence that Frank even had a broken leg. The bones today are so deteriorated. The coveralls were full of "dry bones that rattled," making it easy for a lower leg bone to have slipped through the tied-off cuff and fallen out from the pants, pulled by the weight of the boot. For Art Mitchell, though a suicide, it seems the "broken leg" idea wasn't a known death cause, or he would have mentioned it to the newspaper man.

Problem #5: Putting all of this to the side and getting back to the previous list of Frank's known health problems, the one that was truly life-threatening to the old trapper, was snow blindness. Snow blindness is the bane of all winter wilderness travelers. It burns the eyes like fire. Frank needed to avoided at all cost! It silently snuck in like a ghost from too much glare off the white crystalline snow. The dreaded blindness that blackened the trappers' world would drag him to the grave more stealthily than a stalking panther. It would overtake him at the worst possible times, and conversely, the most beautiful. For it was while he was out on his line on those lovely sunny days, when he knew that he had the greatest occupation in God's creation, that the killing blindness was apt to strike. Snow blindness could get you even on overcast days. When it struck Frank in his later years, it caused a blindness that would not go away. For days Frank would stumble around with burning eyes, lost in the vast cold land he could not see. He ran into trees like a sick, mad man, banging his face and body on limbs, poking his already blinded eyes on sticks and branches as he groped for fuzzy outlines. The trees had always been his friends, but now it must have seemed that they were trying to kill him. With outstretched hands, Frank would try to feel his way back to his last held trapper's cabin, being solely at the mercy of the wild land he lived in. He was as vulnerable as a baby left to the wolves. If he was lucky, the painful blindness would catch him near one of his cabins, one that was stocked with winter provisions where he could lay on his bunk in some safety. If not, for days the blind trapper would have to lay out under a tree, in the elements, waiting for the blindness to pass with the hand of death holding out its bony fingers.

Frank had snow blindness at least twice, and it had almost killed him both times. Each ordeal left his eyesight a little poorer. On Frank's last

In All Fairness, Was It Really Suicide?

pack-trip into the Tungsten, that September, or early October with Al Smith, he told the young Al the danger that he faced from the dreaded blindness and wanted Al to know that if he went blind again, he didn't think he could come out of it. Snow blindness surely played a part in Frank's decision to make this his last winter in the mountains.

Al remembers Frank taking a pair of glasses and holding them over a smoking fire to smoke up the lenses, making himself a pair of make-shift sunglasses, dark glasses that would protect his tender eyes. Interestingly, there was a pair of plastic, old-style tortoise-shell sunglasses found in the grave of the old trapper, suggesting by their presence, that it wasn't snow blindness that brought down the great trapper that winter on Horseshoe Creek, for he had his eye protection with him.

Shorty Fairbrother made the statement, "No trapper wants to die and be left on the ground, for the martens will eat on you all winter and clean you to the bone." The account of finding the body given by both Maron and Pete told that the gloves and boots were either sewn on, wired on, tied on with string, or a combination of all three. If a man with snow blindness was going to kill himself, why not blindly find that rope, bucket, and block of wood in 3 feet of snow, and just hang yourself from that limb there, 7 or 8 feet up the tree? But, first, cover your head with your stocking hat, which you never wore in life, tie it in the back so tight that it will be there when your veins and muscles decompose completely, leaving only bone. Then, put on your gloves and tie wire and with that sew them to the coveralls. Of course, make the stitches fast and tight so that your flesh will have long turned to dust, but the gloves survive and will remain wired, tied and sewn. Then lash and wire on your rubber boots, the boots that you would not have worn in winter, and tie them tightly to your legs so they also will stay on long after your legs have deteriorated. And, oh yes, not to be forgotten, be sure to wear the kind of coveralls you never wore while living, the kind that cover all your upper body so your bones will never fall out to the beloved earth. Do all of this, of course, while you are blind and cannot see a thing. How much sense does all of that make?

Shorty was also the first one to say, "Frank Arnold would never have hung himself like that; he was too practical." Herb Curtis once asked Frank about this very subject. Herb asked, "Frank, why don't you come out and live in town? What are you going to do if you ever hurt yourself up there? What if you break a leg?

"That's why I always carry my gun with me, Herb. If I ever get into a jam that I can't get out of, I have always got my gun in the pack," answered Frank.

Frank knew things were changing, and his mountain world was getting smaller as every mile of road cut deeper into the Pasayten. Government men, miners, and others were seen all too often. It wasn't the same anymore, and Frank was giving some serious thought to giving it all up, quitting the woods to beat his destiny with the "grim-reaper." He was thinking about quitting the woods and moving to town. Bob Curtis remembered him saying something to that effect one of the last fall day he saw him. The changes in his mountains could only get worse, not better, Frank had said. The trapping had been ruined by the big fire. His northern grounds were being taken over by Native Americans. His eyes were quitting him. The Tungsten Mine was going to be sold. His teeth were bad and now out of his mouth. Frank had lost his youth, and snow blindness was trying to blind and kill him. His young trapping partner had robbed him and left him. Winters were indeed getting dangerous for all the above reasons. The possibility of a Social Security check being available made town not look too bad anymore. But the mountain man wearing bib-overalls and a city hat who watched over the Tungsten Mine never got a chance to give it a try.

CHAPTER 19

The Boom of 1951

"The advent of the Korean War, plus the entrance of Red China in the conflict in the fall of 1950, (Red China produced 35% of the worlds tungsten) effectively shut off our major sources of tungsten. A serious shortage, dangerous to our national security, immediately developed and prices skyrocketed until held by the establishment of price ceilings."

"Under the direction of Stanley Cook, Foreman, the underground workings have been rehabilitated, and adits-tunnels retimbered. The Boundary Mine is now in a position to produce tungsten ore from the underground exposures."
So reads the August 1952, Border Lord mining prospectus.

THE BIG QUARTER HORSE BUCKED among the cold snowbanks. His head was jerked by his rider around the deepest drifts as he floundered and fought for his footing. Snow, dirt and mud flew in the air as his shod hooves slipped, caught up in the white drifts and earth. The horse stopped, lungs heaving, trying to rest its belly on the deep snowbanks it was fighting to drive through and jump over. Bob Curtis, knowing what he had to do, spurred his stalled horse hard in the flanks as he yelled and cussed the powerful animal over the last of the snowfield and finally up to the front door of the Duncan James cabin on the Toats Coulee River.

Loy McDaniel, who had been following Bob, swung off his horse too, and walked over to the cold log cabin and flipped the door latch. "We darn near didn't make it, Loy!" Bob said as he slid from his wet, sweating animal, beating the snow off his pants. "We're doing good to make it this far anyway; couldn't go a half mile further," he said as he turned to untie his snowshoes from the back of his saddle. It was the first of March 1951. The two riders were Loomis-ites and their destination wasn't the Duncan James cabin; it was the Tungsten Mine! The government had lifted the lid, so to speak, on tungsten ore, and the price had jumped. There was a new war now to fight, this time in Korea. The government found itself short of 60% tungsten ore, and Bob Curtis and Loy McDaniel knew where there was an unclaimed, abandon tungsten mine.

Bob and Loy had taken their horses further in than the snow should have allowed. Strapped on their backs, behind the saddles, were snowshoes. They didn't stay at the cabin that day, for the high price of tungsten kept running through their heads, and the mine was open now for staking. They had seen no new tracks ahead of them. Still, they were edgy, and had no desire to linger or waste time laying around the Duncan's cabin, losing one more day. They had 30 miles to cover in wet snow on snowshoes, all of it was uphill, so the sooner they started, the closer to their destination they would get. Putting out some grain for their horses and strapping on their snowshoes, the two Loomis-ites set out. What they lacked in sleeping gear, food and warm clothes, they could make up for with enthusiasm. A good fire and a handful of claim notices was all they needed. The Tungsten Mine would be theirs in a hard day's climb, maybe two.

The Boom of 1951

And so, after 30 miles of freezing sweat, and three bitterly cold nights out in wet snowbanks, on top of 8,000-foot mountains, the two would-be miners straggled into the cabins on the south side of Wolframite Mountain, a mile and a half from the Canadian border. Nearly frozen and with wobbly legs, they had made the grade to the mine by shear guts, youth and determination.

"There's the cabins, Bob!" Loy managed to shout as they struggled through the last of the snow that held them off from the mine. Although exhausted, they both had half-hearted grins of success on their faces as they made their snowshoes move just a few more times up to the big, snow-covered cabin that rose before them. The trip had been a fight against 40 miles of winter mountains, chilling cold, and poor provisions. But they were tough, young, and the hardships they endured were the same endured by the men who had come before them. The reward of the quest was all but in their hands.

"Who in the hell made these snowshoe tracks around here, Bob?" Loy asked.

"I'll be damned if I know! But I sure don't like it!" answered Bob.

The boys opened the door to the cabin and walked inside. It was obvious to both that somebody had been into the mine not long before them. Loy made a fire as Bob scratched around hoping that what his eyes and nose were telling him was wrong, but the signs were plain. It wasn't a good feeling that welled up inside the two men. The fire Loy made jumped to life as Bob called him over to investigate a small note left on the wood table. The note told a disappointing story — the two Loomisites were LATE — one Doc. Dewey, one C. C. Sherman, one W.R. Fowler, and one Herman Gallagher had just claimed the Tungsten Mine *the day before*! Or, perhaps one or two of them had come up and staked it for the four. They had come in from the Methow side, up the Chewack River, to put in the first mining claims that boom year of

1951. The Omak group had filed three claims around the cabins; they called them the "Boundary Group."

Bob and Loy were as frustrated as wet cats that had just lost their tails. The cold, miserable trip had just about been for nothing. But the two miners weren't completely beaten. They went below the mine and put up a claim stake or two, then they went over to Apex Mountain and staked some more ground above Tungsten Lake. The claims were called the "Whistlers" and the "Mary Group." The men put three names on the claim notices: Bob Curtis, Loy McDaniel and Paul Loudon — all sons of the 1908 Tungsten claimers. Somewhat sadly, the three sons had to take second best this time around.

By the summer of 1952, the whole mountain around the mine had been staked, placer claims were filed on the creek, and would-be miners were coming and going like army troops. Men like Foss Creveling and George Miller had filed claims down on the creek (again). A gal by the name of Shirley Calaleri had filed on or took over some of the Border Lord Group. Things looked good, the price of tungsten was high again, and the government was encouraging tungsten production. All during that summer and into the next, Bob, Loy and Paul Loudon would ride back to their claims on Wolframite and Apex Mountains sack-up ore and ship it out to any and all mining companies, trying to land the big one. They sent ore to Butte, Montana; Couer D'Alene, Idaho; to Arizona; and to any company they thought might want a good tungsten mine.

And the engineers came. All that summer and for the next two they took mining engineers into their claims. It got to the point where it seemed like the Loomis boys were running a regular guide service into those beautiful high mountains (and they were). They would come in on the mountain horses, furnished by the boys, spend a few days at the cabins looking things over, and then ride back out. In and out they'd go all summer long. They'd talk nice, but that was it. The ink pen and cash never came out of any pockets, except Bob's, Loy's and Paul's.

The Boom of 1951

"The engineers were having a great time," said Bob, "tickled to death to make a trip into the mountains at our expense. Ya', we were running a regular guide service into the Tungsten Mine for their fun and our expense."

Finally, a mining engineer gave Bob some friendly advice. "You had better stay home and raise apples, because the out-croppings of ore just weren't that strong, and no company was going to put money into those small veins." Young Bob took his advice and never again went after the black ore his dad had found in 1903-1904.

Omak Miners

Doc. Deway, C. C. Sherman, W.R. Fowler and Herman Gallagher were not sitting around on $6.00 a pound tungsten, either. By 1952, the claim-holders had worked up a deal and formed a new mining company called the "Border Lord Mining Company," "a group of people interested in developing tungsten and strategic metals, mainly in the Okanogan of Washington State," said the organizers that were now mostly from the Seattle area.

The new Seattle company hired Stan Cook from Loomis to get things going and make a showing at the mine. One of the first things Stan did was hire a tractor-cat out of Malott to start a road from the existing Toats Coulee Road, starting at the beginning of what is now "Iron-Gate Road," and up and over to the mine. The new road was probably better than 25 mountain miles. But, whoa! Tractors were no longer allowed to just put down a blade and go to work. Wanting this new road was the start of a lot of haggling with the Forest Service. Times had changed. The land now had a new planned status called a "Primitive Area," and the Forest Service was dragging its feet over permitting a road to go in. But the U.S. needed tungsten, and the tungsten ore they wanted was back in the mountains 25 miles from the closest road. So, the new road finally got started "after darn near an 'Act-of-Congress,'" said the claim holders, which was not too far from the truth.

The road story gets a bit fuzzy and contradictory as to who did what, and how far Ralph Miller got in with his new tractor-cat from Malott. Apparently, he only made it some 12 miles in, up to SunnyPass that summer of 1952 before the winter snows put a stop to the work. This would mean he got to what is now Iron-Gate Road, 4 or 5 miles long and ending at the "Iron-Gate." Then, he plowed up 7 more miles to Sunny-Pass. The next year, June at the earliest, Ralph plowed in past the Horseshoe Basin before problems arose; he "shut'er-down" and went home. Sometime thereafter, Border Lord hired Duke Reinhart with his International tractor to take off where Ralph Miller had quit. Bub O'neal and his brother, Leo, were said to have driven the tractor, probably to the foot of Wolframite Mountain, where Duke also ran into problems. He never made it to the mine but stopped some miles short of Border Lord's hopes. The company, going through two focal cat owners, now turned to a man in Oroville to finish the task, George DeMerchant, whose big D-7 cat, the largest ever made, pushed in the last miles of road to the Tungsten Mine. This was most likely in 1954. While there at the doors of the mine, while the skidder was rolling rocks around at the mine, just feet from the lower cabin, the boulder that Bob Curtis remembered that had the elevation chiseled into it by a 1916 miner, was rolled over and covered. It read, "Elev. 7,000 ft."

Stan Cook may have been foreman, but Rolan Darling and his wife, Doris, from Riverside, Washington, would make it a special place. Doris Darling was hired to be chief cook and bottle-washer. Rolan would be top hand to Stanley. Stanley, needing a good cook and a steady hand, had asked them to come in for the summer. Thinking it might be downright fun and exciting, off they went.

It was the first of June. Paul Loudon met the Darlings at Four Point Camp with his string of horses. He packed them up, put them on horses, and away they went into the wilds of Washington State for 3-and-a-half months. After two days of riding, working on saddle sores, they stood at the doors of the famous mine to join a small crew of young boys there. There were three to be exact plus a roust-about by the name of Bob Lovagan, a miner by trade, and ready to dig. It took them a couple of days to get organized, but soon under the instructions of Stan Cook, Rolan Darling and Bob Lovagan rolled up their sleeves and went to work. But what were they supposed to do? Get everything running for the production of tungsten. Stan was waiting for equipment and orders to drill and blast. Don Zellweger's 12-year-old ore mill need to be up and running again, and the new road need to be completed. But the orders, equipment and money hadn't arrived. So, in the meantime, he put the men to work on a very important job — They started dismantling the rare old pipe boiler. Maybe they needed the pipe for something, or maybe they just needed something to do. At any rate, Rolan put in a lot of time uncoupling right and left-handed fittings that were rusted-on to old pipe.

After a week or so of unscrewing pipe, Stan put them down in the old mine, below the cabins, and there they worked in the second to the deepest adit, to the west of the main diggings and above the ore mill (west of the road). They spent a lot of time re-timbering. He said the vein of quartz was about 10 or 12 inches wide, but a drill steel never touched it, for as it turned out, no ore was mined in the 1950's or ever again.

Lost in the Mine

One time, Rolan and Stan, on the "spur of the moment," decided to take a trek back into the main tunnel above the mill, just to see what was there, look at the veins, and see how far back into the mountain it went. So with a quickly grabbed flashlight, back they went, further and further they crept into the earthy world of stone and darkness, following a beam of light that led them on. Then, at the most inopportune time their light went out suddenly, and along with the light, their courage! They realized they were in a "real-good" fix!

"Boy was it frightening, trying to scratch our way back out of that black hole; we seemed to back-track for miles," said Rolan. "It was the blackest of black in that hole. You couldn't even see your hand in front of your face. We were totally blind, and there is a lot of hole under there to feel your way out of."

The two moved slowly together, stumbling over each other, through the water and mud back out, bumping their heads on mining timbers, hitting their knees on rocks and bouncing off the cold, wet walls as they inched their way back, just hoping they were headed out the same way they had come in, and not following some side adit. In the grips of the mind-warping jail they found themselves locked in, it seemed at one point that they couldn't go anyway or in any direction without falling over large, mud covered rocks, or hitting flint hard, jagged stone walls. Blackness and rocks had them trapped!

"There just has to be a way out of here," Stan said to the partner that he couldn't see, though only 2 feet away.

"Think, Stan! We were foolish enough to get in here, now we have got to be smart enough to figure out where we went wrong." At the same time he said it, Rolan remembered a narrow edge past a cave-in he and Stan had negotiated coming in and hardly noticed. Paul Loudon, who had packed the miners in that year, after hearing of their blind walk out of the tunnel, claimed the cave-in had happened a few years earlier when the earth had fallen out from under two horses and their riders who had ridden over the tunnel. It had to be this one that was confusing them. The two miners climbed over and around the large fallen rocks, finally squeezing into what they hoped was the main adit. With only the touch of their hands to guide them, and in a time lapse where minutes were hours, and hours were days, they finally saw the light at the end of the tunnel - daylight! They at last stood in the beautiful beams of sun, glad to be alive and safe.

The Boys at Camp-Tungsten

The three young boys at the mine, mentioned earlier, were school kids from Seattle, and out for the summer, out to experience the events of "Camp-Tungsten." Their parents were said to be the company stockholders. That being the case, Stan had to give them a job of some kind, he gave them the job of keeping the firewood cut for the three big wood cook stoves. Along with these three boys, there was a helping hand of sorts, really no more of a visitor, a man who showed up out of the blue forest. He soon attained the name of "Private Charley," for he had an opinion on about everything being done up there. He was actually a cowboy who was supposed to be up there riding herd on Mr. Lesamiz' cattle, but the cooking was just so much better over at the Tungsten Camp than at his camp, and the conversation with the cows was not all that interesting either.

Then, there was the time Charley's horses got loose and were roaming the high country free and happy. And about this time, too, Stan decided they needed a box of dynamite that Paul Loudon had given them over on Apex Mountain. This was past Tungsten Lake and over at the "Mary Group" of claims that Bob Curtis and he had used. Bob Lovegan and Rolan set out to retrieve the box of explosives, and as they were high stepping it around the lake, they ran into Private Charley's lost horses. They went on up and got the box of dynamite, but on the way down, Rolan got the bright idea of loading the high explosives on the back of Charley's horse, instead of using his own back. Rolan snatched up one of Charley's horses and commenced to lash down the dynamite on old Betsy's back. She stood right there and let him tie it all down. Things went all right as Bob and Rolan walked and talked down the trail for home. All right that is until Rolan and the old pack horse came to a muddy creek they had to cross.

"Well, that old horse acted like it had never seen a creek before in its life," Rolan said. "It jumped back... it ran back and forth... it bucked... and the box of "DYNAMITE" started bouncing all over! After the next jump, it was under the horse's belly and bouncing like it was alive!"

All this time Rolan was having "*flashes*" in his head of a scene where the whole half of the mountain was blown into space. And being paranoid of dynamite anyway, Rolan proceeded to jump on the horse's head and grab anything that he could find to slow down Private Charley's wild, bucking horse. The trick worked when he grabbed the ears and gave a pull. The horse stopped and stood there with his ears pinned down, thankfully dead in her tracks. Bob Lovegan made quick work unloading the box of explosives from under the horse's belly, and then he decided he'd pack the box of explosives in on his own back!

Border Lord also hired a carpenter to come up and do some work. His name was Jim White. He was there trying to do his job by "ramrodding" the kids around and putting boards together. By this time, in the 1950's, the big sawed-lumber building that ran off the west end of the main log cookhouse, and the building that held the 20-foot stove that was so famous in those years, had fallen in and was all but gone. The miners there now needed more room, for there were eight of them; nine if you counted Private Charley. So, Jim White proceeded to take on the construction of what can now be called, "Rambo's bedroom," where a young man named Rambo would set up in a king-sized bed. He was a Californian from the city. He was given the name "Rambo" by his Methow packer, the long-termed Claud Miller, because of his camouflaged suit of clothes, arsenal, and mindset. Rambo was a young man who not long ago, (early 1990's) added one more short story to the Tungsten Mine. Rambo was a nice, but troubled young man who tried to be nothing more than a latter-day Frank Arnold. Buying a horse

The Boom of 1951

up there that year off some late fall hunters who came by, he somehow hoped that the 7 months of winter wouldn't come as he whiled away the time. He moved down to Oroville with his horse that fall. There he got himself shot down, killed on the streets of Oroville in a fluky one-sided gun fight with his gun that was not functioning. But it was his fault, and you play with fire, you often get burned. Before he was killed, this young man built a large bed in Jim White's new bedroom, bed that took up half the room.

Back to 1953: Jim had the young schoolboys cutting lodge-pole pine logs, packing them to the project and then helping him put them on top of one another. He was building a bunkhouse onto the west end of the main cookhouse. Jim, in doing so, somehow lost complete control over his crew. The young boys started to outsmart poor Jim, and they proceeded to "tom-foolery" him to the brink of despair. This battle of the minds, which Jim was losing, went on for a good two or three weeks as the west bedroom took shape. Finally, with great frustration and befuddlement, Jim managed to get the three-sided addition built on to the main cookhouse, but by the time it was finished Jim was fit to be tied! "They had him so damned mad he'd have bitten himself!" Rolan remembered years later. He could not or did not even want to wait for Paul Loudon to come in with his horses to pack him out. No, he just rolled up his bedroll and pointed his feet down the trail toward Loomis, many miles away, leaving his three antagonists and the west addition to the cookhouse as his lasting mark on history. It was the last major construction project to completed at the Tungsten Mine.

It Came in by Air

The low hum of the small plane could be heard in the far distance. "Here comes our bacon!" Rolan said to Doris as the plane closed in on the mine. Millard Fowler was at the controls of the little Piper Cub. The modern age had indeed caught up to the ole' Tungsten Mine. It was a tight fit for the pilot to keep the little plane off the rocks of the mountain that shot up beside the cabins as he buzzed down on the mine. Herman Gallagher's timing was perfect when he kicked out the groceries from the little low-flying Piper. The groceries came down by parachute and were supposed to miss the rocks when they lit on the ground. There wasn't much open, rock-free space to shoot at. But more times than not, not an egg got broken out of the 30 dozen that came floating down by every 3 weeks. The plane drop was a neat way to go, and it saved the long ride in with pack horses over a rough, steep trail of close to 20 miles.

In 1953, the next year, the Piper Cub was still flying in a few mining supplies. It was early one morning when the drone of the little motor was heard over the roof of the log cabins on the south side of Wolframite Mountain. After a buzz, with the plane just a few inches off the roof, and nobody stepping out of the cabins to wave a "hello." Millard Fowler told Herman Gallager that they had better drop the drill steels right by the door so the miners would be sure to see and find the dropped package. Coming in closer, Millard flew like an ace World War I fighter pilot, zeroing in on the cabin door as Herman stood ready to push the 70 pounds of steel out the open door of the plane. The plane buzzed in skipping over the trees not 20 feet above the cabin roof. Millard Fowler held the Piper on a tight course. "Here goes," Herman shouted as he pushed the 70 pounds out the plane door. As the iron cleared the flying supply plane, a sleepy miner in his long-johns stepped out of the main cookhouse door. KERR-TUUDDW! The sack of steel dropped 2 inches from the miner's toes. The miner stood frozen like a block of ice, sweat beading up on his forehead, and his eyes popped out, glued to the dust cloud that rose at his feet. Just 6 inches north would have been enough to send this miner to the "promise-land." And Herman's shaking head hung out the open door of the plane for the longest time as the piper flew on out of sight.

The Boom of 1951

Rolan and Doris Darling went out on the 20th something of September 1952. The next year, in 1953, Stan Cook got the road well along and did some work on the old ore mill. He was the one who put in the Humphrey Spiral Concentrator to better concentrate the tungsten ore. This was again the result of experiments taking place at the School of Mineral Engineering at the University of Washington. It was found that simple gravity concentrating was all that was needed to bring this ore up to a marketable grade of 60% tungsten acid.

The U. S. government wanted tungsten so badly in those years that they set up the Defense Minerals Exploration Administration. This department sent in a field engineer to examine the deposit of ore. The ore was there all right, looked good to him (contrary to the Forest Service geologist 35 years later). It passed the government test, which meant financial aid could be attained, exactly what the mining company was hoping for. So Border Lord Mining Company, with its ten main officials, mostly in Seattle, and the four Boundry Group claimholders applied for the "seventy-five percent exploration loan" and "matching funds." The money grant appeared to have been "ok'd," — mining could start — but the fourteen or so important players couldn't agree on who was going to hold, count and distribute the money as needed. The grant never got into anyone's hands because they argued and played around too long trying to decide. And so, again, development of a working mine was thwarted.

Once the road in was finished, a host of people could now bounce their way into the mine by motor vehicle. Jack Jett, a noted newspaper reporter out of Wenatchee, went in with State Representative Web Hollauer, a stockholder. Jack Jett ended up with a number of rare pictures that came from Frank Arnold's stuff. Frank with his team of moose got wide circulation through the pages of the Wenatchee Daily World at this time in the 1950's, thanks to Jack.

TALES OF THE TUNGSTEN MINE

Jim White's daughter came in for a look at the famous mine where her dad had worked a year or two before, and she fell in love with the last old, sawed-wood, 1916 bunkhouse that stood below the main cook house. According to Bob Curtis, she turned around and brought in a new "Dodge Power-Wagon" and commenced to tear down the wood planked building with the intention of hauling the pine-weathered boards over to Seattle to panel her bedroom or "some damn-thing."

It took her two or three trips bouncing over the long miles of boulder-strewn road and "Bang!" On her last trip out, the new "Power Wagon" gave up the ghost somewhere around Horseshoe Basin. It was a long walk out to Loomis, and being thereafter mad as a mother tiger, with much growling and snarling, she secured another truck from somewhere and got the last of her boards over to Seattle. But she was so mad at her stuck-truck that there was no way she was going to go back to get that broken-down Dodge Power-Wagon that had "powered-out" on her. So, there it sat. It just sat there for many months, perhaps a year or so, before the bank (or someone) came up and managed to find the broken-down truck, fix it, and drive it out of the mountains.

One of Fowlers' old Model-A ton-and-a-half trucks is still up there, too, half-way between Horseshoe Basin and the Tungsten Mine. And like the Power-Wagon, it just never made it out, or in, stuck halfway between, waiting for somebody to fix it up, load it with ore, and head down the mountain to town. The road into the mine was never much of a road to start with, and it for sure was never maintained. Today, it would call for a lot of tree-cutting, as well as log and ditch-jumping, for a person to get through it. But from an airplane, that old road can still be seen snaking its way amongst the trees for miles, headed to that distant mine.

Border Lord was never able to bring the high mountain mine into production for whatever reason. By 1955, the price and demand for tungsten was back down to pre-1950's levels. By July 1960, when I first

The Boom of 1951

rode into the mine, I was 10 years old and bitten by a strange bug. The mine was quiet and lonely. The large tailing pile represented a lot work. I looked up the steep mountain side at the old mill with the 1950's Humphrey Spiral Concentrator and the old, 1916, standing-rock, pipe-boiler on right, somehow intrigued. The mine sat in a state of limbo looking out at the beautiful mountain called Apex, looking and waiting, waiting as if for somebody else, like an old city-hatted watchman should come walking up its wood planked steps.

CHAPTER 20

A Mouth Full of Teeth

TO HIS DYING DAY, FRANK Maron never believed that the man he found hanging in the tree was Frank Arnold. When he told the story in later years, he would get all up-tight and start shaking, remembering the scene he saw years before on that dark creek bank called Horseshoe. The hanging man of bones in that tree was *not* Frank Arnold! He was sure of this.

Frank Maron, by trapping two winters with the old Englishman, had come to know Arnold more than most. He was familiar with the things that he did, the things that he used, and the places he went. For at least the better part of 2 years Maron lived with Frank. He was a lot younger, and Arnold got just a little mad at the young man for taking off with some of his paid for and packed-in food supply. But Maron wasn't thinking right in those years, and the isolation with the old man hadn't helped his mind any. What Maron really thought of Frank, and why he took off with some of his food, has never come out. He must have had some respect for the man, for he never said anything malicious about Arnold. He did not seem to hold anything against him.

TALES OF THE TUNGSTEN MINE

As Bob Curtis told it, Pete thought Frank Maron could find the lost Englishman so Pete drove clear to Medical Lake, a town by Spokane, in his new 1935 Red Dodge just to bring Frank Maron home. Maron was, by this time, back together mentally it seems. He found Frank Arnold hanging in a tree, yet Jim McDaniel said that Maron found work there at the Grand Coulee Dam and while working there, hurt his back so badly that it put him in a wheelchair. Maron, we know was in Loomis from 1929 to 1931, his last year with Arnold, and he must have stayed in Loomis until 1934 when Frank had all his teeth pulled. After that year he had to have gone into the mental hospital. So, he must have hurt himself at the Grand Coulee Dam after 1936, with the injury putting him in a wheelchair. It was in late 1936 that this strange man found another strange man hanging in a tree and he was not in a wheelchair at that time. Against the strong current of opinion held by most, Frank Maron never believed it was Frank Arnold hanging in that tree.

Al Smith, as we know, packed Frank Arnold into the cabins that fall of 1934, using Pete's horses. He never dreamed it would be Frank's last winter alive, for to be sure, Frank was still healthy and strong. Al knows absolutely that he was the last person to pack Frank in. Al was going to go back early the next spring to see Frank. Frank had asked him to come in around the end of May that next year — i.e., the 28th of May 1935 to be exact. But when the time came in the month of May for him to think about getting things ready to go back, Pete told him that Frank was gone. "He wasn't around — in fact — he was GONE!" Pete said. Frank Arnold wasn't at the Tungsten Mine anymore. Pete said that some "Snowshoers had snow-shoed back to the mine that winter, and that Frank had strangely disappeared." Pete never said who the "snowshoers" were. We can surmise that they came from over the mountains in the Methow Valley because they weren't local Oroville or Loomis trappers.

Al was absolutely sure that he was the last one to pack Frank into the mine with his normal amount of food. But what Al Smith did not

A Mouth Full of Teeth

know was that a few weeks later that fall, Frank had come back down to Loomis to get his teeth worked on. This is a very important clue to grasp, and these are the facts to back this up:

Proof #1: Frank Maron knew that Frank Arnold had gotten all his teeth pulled. It is most likely that he saw Arnold in Loomis that late fall of 1934 with no teeth, as Arnold hung around town recuperating, but it is possible Frank Maron heard it from someone else.

Proof #2: Pete's son remembers Frank without teeth, saying, "I don't think Frank had a tooth in his head!" Pete's son also had seen him that fall before Frank headed back into the mountains because Frank did hang around Loomis for about a week while he healed up.

Proof #3: Bob Curtis also remembers Frank coming to Loomis late that fall. Bob said, "Then in the fall, he came back out with some badly-infected teeth." Bob then told of Grace Eastman taking him to Oroville and the dentist. After getting his teeth pulled, he came back to the Curtis home and slept on his bunk out on the porch. "When it was colder than 'billy-hell out," as Bob put it, making it around the end of October before the first winter snows, Frank Arnold headed back into the cold mountains. "I really don't remember seeing Frank after that," said Bob.

His Last Days in Loomis

After Frank had gotten his teeth pulled and was ready to head home, he went to the Loomis Store, Jack Richman's, where he charged two quarts of beer, a tin or two of tobacco and two boxes of .22 shells. The bill is still owed, and the account still open. Frank never got back to pay it. From that point, the city-hatted Englishman went and looked up his old friend, Clarence Landergreen, who also spent time at the Ford place, and was probably there when Frank called. Clarence had also worked a summer job with Frank, cutting out the trail over to the Skagit River a few years back, and might also have been with Frank and Ferris Ford

TALES OF THE TUNGSTEN MINE

on his mapping with the Coast & Geodetic Survey job in 1924. At any rate, Clarence was a friend of Arnold's. After they had consumed the two quarts of beer, they pulled out for the High Country in Clarence's Model-A Ford. Their destination was Long Swamp, 25 mountain miles away, and a 4,500-foot climb.

Clarence and Frank stopped and made one more pickup at Jack Richman's store on their way out of town, picking up a little more "suds," which amounted to a case of beer (24 bottles), and two more boxes of groceries for Frank. Clarence started working the Model-A up the long, twisting grade for the next 25 miles to the end of the road at Long Swamp, elevation 5,500 feet, marking his way up the mountain with empty beer bottles. This is how the story got started that Frank did not have much food with him that last winter he went missing. Clarence said that Frank had only two boxes of groceries when he dropped him off at Long Swamp. However, this is contrary to what Frank actually had in food, for instead of being low on groceries, the two boxes that he brought up with Clarence were in fact two extra boxes of groceries. So that instead of being short on groceries, he was long on groceries by his standards.

They made Long Swamp in good order; and once there, they sat in the car at the end of the road, so the story goes, and "got gloriously drunk!" And when the beer was gone, the old trapper walked, just a little tipsy, into the trees and disappeared into the back woods forever.

Turning his Ford around, down the steep mountain the Model-A plunged. This old car, with its steel-shafted, mechanical-run, "Rocky-mountain-type" braking system, just one step above a wooden drag-stick, had a mind of its own as the blue smoke rolled-out from the smoking-hot brake-shoes. The mountain road was bad, and still is! It was hellaciously steep, like a carnival ride, it wound, turned and corkscrewed down and down. The dirt-and-gravel Toats Coulee Road was long, and it is said, unsurprisingly, that Clarence "lost-it" on one of its many tight turns.

A Mouth Full of Teeth

The Model-A rolled over on its side, inches from a plunge into the valley abyss, and there it rocked precariously on its running board. This was "No Problem" for the big 6-foot Clarence, the pugilist who had fought even George Honey for a minor profit in the boxing ring. "The Caveman from Loomis," as he was called in the fighting circle, a man with quite a reputation as a prize-fighter for his wild "hay-makers," fought his car back on the road. The 200-pound Indian prize fighter, with a lot of grunts, pushing with logs and wedging with rocks, managed to get the Ford pulled and flipped back on the road right-side-up, and somewhat more soberly, down to Loomis in slightly less than one piece. "He was all tore up and looked like he had been in a fight with a Grizzly Bear," said Bob when he stepped out of the bent-up auto in Loomis. Mission accomplished. But, Frank Arnold was never seen alive again!

No. Not quite. It is true that this was the last time he was seen by a Loomis-ite, but there were things going on that Loomis didn't really know about, or factor-in. For 50 miles away, as the crow flies, the Methow Valley side of the mountains had a job going on that winter, and according to George Honey and Harold "Mac" MacWilliams, the C.C.C. was building a right-of-way road through to Beaver Meadows.

The right-of-way they were building ran from Winthrop, up over the mountains, through Beaver Meadows and on toward the small town of Conconully. There was a cabin at the meadows, and the crew of out-of-work men would build another. It was here that the C.C.C. would put in a good winter camp by adding a few tents and another log cabin. Some of the names of the men on the crew were Clent Hanks, mentioned before as an East Pasayten River trapper, and probably his partner, Romie Johnson; Charley Burgett; Al Anderson; Lefty; Iron and Pete; Harold MacWilliams; George Miller; George Honey and the cook; and maybe Frank Arnold. At least he was there for a while. Somebody had to have told him about this work program. It might, and probably was, someone in Loomis that late fall while he was recuperating from the trip to the dentist. Pete, being a Loomis-ite and a Forest Service employee, was there at Beaver Meadows also. So, it can be assumed that Frank knew of the C.C.C. project from Pete. It is conceivable and probable that he ran a trap-line that far and stopped in for a few days of conversation and a hot meal. Whatever the reason that brought him to Beaver Meadows, Frank Arnold was there and got his picture taken, probably by Iron. This is a very important picture. It proves that Frank Arnold did not have teeth!

I saw these pictures of Frank. Iron had a number of old photographs that were taken with Frank Arnold's camera, pictures from around the Tungsten Mine. The question becomes, "When did he obtain them?" And though the pictures taken at the C.C.C. camp that winter in 1934 were not taken by Frank's camera, still, two of these were of Frank Arnold himself.

I was in Winthrop interviewing Lefty, George Honey, George Miller and one or two others about this story, and was told that Dalia Northcot might have some information and photos about Iron and Lefty in their trapping days. Now Dalia lived very close to Lefty, within easy viewing distance, and after interviewing Lefty, I stopped by Dalia's and looked through her old pictures that she so generously shared, pictures she had held for 25 years after Iron's death. Lefty saw that I had stopped in at Dalia's, and she later told me he had stopped in after I had left. But while I was in her home going through her old pictures, I came upon the two pictures of an "*old man*" that looked like it could be Frank Arnold in a city-hat in a mid-winter scene. So, I borrowed a number of pictures from her, taking one of the two thought to be Frank Arnold, hoping that once the small picture was blown up, it could be confirmed as Frank. Al Smith did confirm the picture was of Frank. Returning a few weeks later to Dalia's home for the other picture, the very one that showed clearly that Frank had no teeth, I found that Lefty had been there shortly after the first visit and taken the picture showing clearly Frank with no teeth.

A Mouth Full of Teeth

Dalia said that Lefty had been there and taken some pictures with him when he left. Frank's picture with no-teeth was gone from its envelope where the writer had left it in the shoebox. Only Lefty had been there going through those pictures. I had held it in his hands, a clear picture of Frank with no teeth!

In the interview with Lefty, I expected to get many good stories about Frank and the Tungsten Mine, but despite the fact that Lefty was in good health and of sound mind, instead of historical stories, I got little to nothing at all. And this, indeed, was strange because on a phone interview a few months before, Lefty had said very clearly that he and Iron had seen Frank Arnold on the trail that last winter and that he had looked "awful rough." Touching on some of Lefty's involvement with Frank, to which more will be said later, Lefty and Iron had trapped beside Frank for some 6 years. That last winter, Lefty, Iron and Pete had been there on the C.C.C. job when Frank showed up. Lefty had actually told others in the area that he had found Frank Arnold "hung" in the tree on Horseshoe Creek while he worked on the new trail that went right past Frank's camp on the other side of the creek from the new trail. Hank Dammann also testified to that story. Lefty had spoken of going in to see Frank more than once, as George Honey and Bob Curtis had said. Lefty did tell me that he and Iron had snowshoed into Cathedral Lake one winter, but even though so close, they didn't make it over to the mine, 4 miles away. By his words now, they hadn't been there *EVER!* Yet Iron had left messages twice on the log walls of the cabins, signing his name on both.

Now think about it; if three men work together for 10 years — Lefty, Iron and Pete — spending days and nights together in the same tent out in the woods for weeks at a time, year after year, a person would think that such three men would tell stories and adventures closely related. But not in this case, nothing could be further from the truth.

The reason Frank Maron knew the man he had found hanging from the tree on Horseshoe Creek was not Frank Arnold was because the man in the tree HAD TEETH! Maron was confused until his dying day about the man that was supposed to be Frank Arnold — yet wasn't. On the other hand, there was absolutely no doubt in Pete's mind that the man in the tree had to be Frank Arnold. And if it wasn't, there was a good reason to Pete why it *"had to be him."* Understand that Maron wasn't mentally or physically strong, whereas Pete was. Pete was not a man to cross. He was of large stature and had a strong personality. Maron was a mouse next to him. When Maron first found "the man" hanging in the tree, and he pulled up the stocking cap with the stick, and a mustache fell out, the hanging man had a mouth full of teeth, good teeth, lots of teeth. When the body was exhumed many years later, these teeth were absolutely confirmed; the skull of the man in the shallow grave had ten teeth, and all in the front of the mouth. So, Mr. Maron indeed knew what he had seen, and had a right, not only to be confused, but half crazy. Maron, more than anyone else, in fact, was the only one to realize and reach conclusions beyond the obvious.

But if it was not Frank Arnold who was found hanging in the tree, then whose body was it? And just what, then, happened to the real Frank Arnold after he left the C.C.C. camp that snowy winter in 1934/1935? Frank Maron, anyway, he highly suspected that Frank Arnold had left the country for good, walking out on his own two feet from the Okanogan, probably north into Canada, leaving forever. Maron figured that Frank Arnold had to have had a *"run-in,"* a *"serious confrontation,"* a life and death confrontation with this man in-the-tree because the man in the tree was not the old trapper, Frank Arnold. This he was sure of. In Maron's mind there had been a fight of "Titans" up there in those forbidden mountains, and Frank Arnold had come out the victor. The loser in this fight was hanging in the tree. Old man Arnold had just made a diversion, a confusing paradox there on Horseshoe Creek to cover his tracks. His

A Mouth Full of Teeth

cabin had none of his things in it, and all of what he had heard that fall from Pete and others stacked up to this one and only conclusion. It was the only reasonable explanation. And Frank E. Maron was pretty darn sure that Frank Arnold was still alive somewhere. And, if Frank Maron had demanded that the truth be found. If he had insisted that the man in the tree was not Frank Arnold, then his old trapping partner would be sought out, and if not found, looked upon as a murdering fugitive. In Maron's mind, the man in the tree — whoever he was — must have deserved his fate by Frank's quick hands. And Frank deserved his freedom! This is the story he told Loy and Jim McDaniel in later years.

CHAPTER 21

The Rogue Trapper and The Wandering Prospector

The Rogue Trapper escapade is as ingrained and interwoven into the story of Frank Arnold's death as the sand that rolls on the creek-bed of Horseshoe Creek. It is part of the legend and the drama that has kept this man's life alive and in the minds of so many. This man's doings were written on the mountains, in the valleys, on the shores of lakes, on the log walls of cabins and in town newspapers. To know and understand the death of Frank Arnold, one must perceive the mysteries of the "Rogue Trapper." There are two basic divisions to this story and after many hours of interviewing, the stories trace back to two people: Lefty and Iron on the Methow side of the mountains, and three people on the Loomis side: Mickey Kinchelo, Ross Woodard and Pete.

OUT OF THE PEOPLE WHO were approached and interviewed, out of the ones who were there in the 1930's, or were close to people who were there, perhaps 60% of the old timers felt that Frank Arnold "was done in," "killed" by a murderer. They were convinced that there was some sort of "foul-play" up there in those mountains. The few people who had known Frank Arnold well, such as Shorty Fairbrother, Frank Maron, or even Pete, figured that Frank, if he had to kill himself, just wouldn't have done it like that. Though there were some exceptions. Even Pete expressed doubt in the suicide reasoning. His son had this to say about his father's feelings: "I always got the feeling my dad felt there was more to it than that." Indeed, there was a lot more to it than that, and one of the "more to it(s)," was the story of the "Rogue Trapper!"

This story starts once again at the Duncan James cabin on the Toats Coulee River 11 miles out of Loomis. It was Ross Woodard, a well-known cattleman, and Mickey Kinchelo, an early cowboy and packer, who first got involved with this stranger. Bud Shaffer was his name and he started his brief appearance in the Okanogan by appearing at the Elgin dairy that summer along the Similkameen River, not far from the small towns of Nighthawk and Loomis. He seems to have just drifted in during the hard years, looking for work, and finding some at the dairy. It must have been summer of 1934, though nobody really remembers for sure. But apparently, later that year, whichever year it was, Bud Shaffer moved around in the Toats Coulee country and must have been seen by Ross Woodard and his cowboys who drove cattle up and down the long creek drainage. He was presumed to have been a trapper in the short year or two he was around, and said to have had a cabin on the Middle Fork of the Toats Coulee, though the cabin has never been identified, or found, and no one really knew for sure if he trapped or not. But the fact that he was up there is an indication he could have, at the least, had ideas about trapping, for even though one couldn't find a job in the 1930's, if one could find a marten, it was worth a month's wages. But Shaffer did not get to trap long, and he did not stay long, either because the man ran into a problem, and the problem was Ross Woodard. The name "Ross Woodard" was a big name in the cattle industry around Loomis in that era. Today he has a road named after him and his old ranch is still a working cattle ranch.

The Rogue Trapper and The Wandering Prospector

Ross was using the Duncan James cabin at the time. He had some gear and supplies stored there. One day the cabin was entered, for it was probably not locked, and a good number of things were taken: "blankets, food, an alarm clock, etc." said Mickey Kinchelo. Somebody fingered Bud Shaffer as the culprit, so the cowboys, Ross and Mickey Kinchelo, rode up the river-drainage to find the "thieven" culprit. When the boys managed to find and catch up to Mr. Shaffer after some tough riding and looking, they didn't find the merchandise. When questioned, Bud denied taking anything. That didn't stop them from making it plain to the man, in the way that only cowboys could do, "that he had better remember where he got the extra free merchandise at," and he "had better remember real good and fast how to put it back."

Emmet Smith, the sheepherder, being interested in such matters, also heard the story about this man from Ross Woodard himself. Emmet said that Ross and Mickey followed him up the Toats Coulee to about where the Middle Fork bridge is, and there had some strong words for Mr. Shaffer. Ross told Emmet that he had taken some food from the James cabin. And, wouldn't you know it, "lo-and-be-hold," whatever it was Bud Shaffer had taken, the cowboys were glad to see it back a few days later. "Rattlen" Bud's cage had made an impression on the man, but it had also marked him, and in not a good way.

The year he had all his troubles and supposedly trapped the Middle Fork, Schaffer apparently got all the way up to Horseshoe Basin country, through Long Swamp, because Emmet Smith remembers seeing his name written on a sign post in the Basin where he ran his sheep every summer. And Bob Curtis, too, saw his name on the signpost at Long Swamp, 10 miles from where Emmet read his name in the Basin. Bud Shaffer was leaving his proud name, his "mark," in more ways than one. This was as wild as the Loomis story of the Rogue-trapper got. And it was all that could be gleaned about the man who started out as a humble cow-milker from Nighthawk. But not so further west. As it turned out, the Methow Valley had its own problems with this troublemaker.

Pete, being from Loomis, but moving away in 1935, was working for the most part in the Methow Valley at Winthrop, and in working there became good friends with Lefty and Iron. From that point, the three worked together year after year with the Forest Service and the C.C.C. as said before. For Lefty and Iron, the years after the 1929 fire, which had stripped and burned them of any furs for a good long time, this government relief work of development projects during the Great Depression was a saving grace, as it was for many, many other men. Pete, Lefty and Iron worked side by side in those "Dirty Thirties." Pete surely heard the story about this thief, Bud Shaffer, and when Lefty and Iron told of their encounter with this man that winter in the high mountains, out on their trap-lines, it made everything come together. They were convinced that Bud Shaffer had a run-in with, not only them, but apparently with Frank Arnold.

To reiterate and put forth again some historical facts that need to be understood: Lefty and Iron were the closest of friends from 1929 until about 1966 or so, give-or-take, when Iron passed away. The two men were inseparable, living side-by-side for some 30 years. "Want-a-be" trappers they were those winter months after the 1929 fire, and when summer came around, they worked all through the high mountains for the Forest Service, putting in new trails, building shelters and look-out stations, working on fire suppression and logging activities. Iron, as his history tells us, had moved to Winthrop in 1928, teaming up with Lefty the next year and working with him up until the winter of 1934/1935 when Iron came up with enough money to buy a restaurant in town. Iron ran the eatery until 1939. Then, he went back again to the white snow and black steel traps where he and Lefty again tried to catch the beautiful marten and agile lynx cat. Ten years after the fire, furs had made a small comeback. But, Iron didn't trap long, only until 1942 or

The Rogue Trapper and The Wandering Prospector

1943 when the hard winters forced him to leave. From there, he ran trail crews for the Forest Service, bought a logging truck, and speculated in real estate. (My father actually bought a city lot from Iron in the 1960's.)

It was on one of these trail crews of Iron's that a young man, Clyde Paul, from Oroville heard an intriguing story about a rogue-trapper who had a "run-in" with an old trapper. It was out in the wild Pasayten Wilderness one summer night that Iron spun his gripping story around the campfire. At the end of a long day's trail work, his crew of young men, some fresh out of high school, sat around the fire listening to a gripping story. The story he heard that night would stay with him as long as he lived. For his trail boss, Iron, was a man who had known an old trapper who stayed for years at a far-away mine, and this fact was of more than passing interest to the young Clyde Paul.

Hearing this credulous story with the greatest of interest, and with a mind like a steel trap, he memorized the words that fell from the lips of his trail boss, like a sponge taking in water. This young man, for good reason, had more than a casual interest in what Iron had to say about this rogue man running the wilds of the Pasayten and also about the mountain trapper from the Tungsten Mine. Clyde Paul had gazed at a family picture in his living-room ever since he could first remember. The picture that the family so cherished had been taken by this very same mountain man and photographer who had lived at the famous mine, the old trapper named Frank Arnold. The picture showed Paul's grandfather and grandmother at the mine in 1917. But that was not the only reason for his total attention that night, for he had traveled to the Tungsten Mine himself at the early age of ten. His family had put him on a horse and traveled to the distant mine for the sheer adventure of the trip. The date was 1936 and he remembered that Frank Arnold was strangely missing at that time, and nobody knew why. He had disappeared just a year or so before, and the talk was that perhaps he would even show up again when they were at the mine that summer.

Around the campfire Paul and his companions sat, cross-legged, with yellow glowing faces and white eyes as the dancing campfire shed its glowing light on their tired faces. The Chewack River talked too, its water splashed its story as the boys lay on its bank and beneath its trees, but they heard not a word of it as Iron spoke about the gripping event of a crazed trapper who had "killed" Frank Arnold.

The Killing of Frank Arnold?

> *The story is as Clyde basically told it, but he indicated as he told the story that he had heard the story from two different sources: the one from Iron of course on the Chewack River, and the other from a friend of his whom I call "Joe." The trapper who was sitting on a barstool right next to Bud Shaffer. This account was also heard by Bob Curtis. It has been told and retold around more than one dark campfire since the first one on the Chewack River back in 1953, just below "Bud Shaffer's sled!"*

"It was about 1953 that Iron told us about the renegade, because we camped right below his old sled," said Clyde. The Forest Service trail crew was camped right beside an "old sled" on the Chewack River trail. Just 4 miles north, up the river from this sled, was the mouth of Horseshoe Creek where Frank Arnold was found hung that not-too-long-ago day in 1936. And, 3 miles south from where that old sled sat on the Chewack trail was the Thirty Mile Ranger Station and the end of the road from Winthrop.

The campfire sparked and popped as its smoke rose high and drifted north, north through the trees and up the river toward an unmarked grave. A grave of bones that lay on the banks of a creek called Horseshoe. I asked Clyde if Iron had ever seen the man.

"Iron never mentioned seeing him, but went on to say they (he and Lefty) didn't know if he was a Canadian or where he had drifted in from," said Clyde Paul.

The Rogue Trapper and The Wandering Prospector

"We figured that sled there was left by that renegade trapper. We (again speaking of Lefty, too) found it here the next spring and that was the first time we had ever seen it," said Iron to the boys.

The old sled lay just down the river, maybe fifty or hundred yards from where the Long Swamp and Chewack Drive-way trail meets the Chewack River trail at an elevation of about 4,000 feet. The sheep trail that was used for cattle too was one of the longest, steepest, "bad-est" trails to be found in the eastern mountains. It was carved down a rock face that ran for miles and was hardly fit for the sure-footed sheep that first found it. It was a stock-killer trail to the later cattlemen who had to use it to move their herds from the grassy green pastures of Long Swamp to further green pastures far to the west, miles back into the lush grasses of the high country. But it was the only way that could be found down off the steep mountain. The sled Iron talked about lay by the river trail for years.

"That killer," Iron went on, "must have run out of snow and left his sled right here, or else he just didn't want to pull it up this steep mountain to Long Swamp. We figure he was the one who killed Arnold. He was a stranger to this country. We had never heard of him before and figured he was just traveling through. But we are sure he was the same man who came into Oroville to the Len Easle Tavern that noisy Saturday night. The music was playing non-stop in the smoke-filled tavern. In 1935, Oroville was every bit the rip-roaring border town that called miner, lumberjack, apple-knocker, and saw-miller, cowboy and a lot of Indians to its fun-loving night-life. Yes, it was Saturday night at Len Easle Tavern.

The tavern sat right below Ben Prince's grocery store on Main Street Oroville. Everyone in town knew Ben Prince, including the bartender pulling on the beer tap that Saturday night. The dark, smoke-filled tavern didn't help the looks of the unshaven, wild-eyed mountain man who sat himself down at the bar and asked for a beer.

This wild-eyed man seemed to stand all by himself in this noisy tavern with too many people in it. He was cold when everybody else was warm and having a good time. He was different; that is all there was to it. Even the bartender sensed it, but he could not stop to give him any more than a second look, and a beer, and another. The big man must have sat there for close to an hour, and seemed to drink beer as fast as the bartender could keep his mug filled. It was the heavy wool clothes and the wild looks around the room that made the man next to him take note. Joe Baker, a trapper himself sat next to the wild man. But what really caught the attention of both Joe and the bartender was that on the man's last beer, instead of a greenback coming out of the man's pocket, there was a check written out to 'Bud Shaffer.' The check was from Ben Prince for $350.00. The bartender had never in his life seen this man before. He stood there in a quandary of befuddlement trying to figure out what he should do with the man's $350.00 check that lay in his hands. It was a lot of money! He turned it over, looked, turned it over again and looked at the big 'Ben Prince Groceries' in bold lettering across the front and knew that the check was probably good.

"Are you Bud Shaffer?" he asked in the strongest tone he could muster.

"Ya Damned rights I am!" the man roared. "Ben Prince wrote me that check just an hour ago when I sold him my ##**@@ FURS!"

Now that was something that made sense, Joe thought, as he sat there listening in. The bartender walked over to the cash register machine and popped open the till — "Ding." It made sense to him, too! It was Ben's signature and it had to be good as the groceries upstairs.

Mr. Shaffer picked up his change, three hundred forty-nine dollars and so many cents. He turned and was gone before Joe could take another look. But the image of this big, cold man stayed in Joe's mind for years. It was two days later that the story got back to him about the trapper with the Ben Prince check — the man was wanted by the LAW!

The Rogue Trapper and The Wandering Prospector

The man hadn't totally lied; he had sold some furs to Ben Prince, and beautiful furs they were, too, worth much more than the $350.00 Ben had given him. There were at least fifteen prime marten furs, some of which were copper-bellied, and these only came from the high mountains west of Oroville, common around one place, the Tungsten Mine. There were also six big lynx cats in prime condition that also only came from the west. The furs were worth twice what Ben had given him, to be sure. Ben knew these furs were not this man's. They could only be from one place and one man, Frank Arnold!

"Ben had been looking at Frank's furs for better than 20 years and knew with certainty that these could only be Frank Arnold's. Frank hadn't been to the store that winter to trade in his hides for some of Ben and Louie's (Ben's brother) merchandise, which was unusual in itself. So, he wondered, as he smoked his big cigar, why this rough-looking man had martens that were copper-bellied. Frank had trapping methods no one else used. Some people would call it more humane, but to Frank it was just the best way to trap. Frank used a 'dead-fall' to kill his marten, and not the steel traps often used by others. Because there was no leg damage, his furs were worth a bit more. Add to this the extremely fine cleaning, stretching and fleshing of the animal, and it all added up to one man, Frank. Frank's skills as a trapper showed in his furs.

So, this man might as well have written Frank's name on each one of those furs that Saturday, because Ben had this stranger pegged. He not only looked and acted strange and nervous, especially when he noticed Ben looking intensely at the fine cleaning and skinning work done on the hides. And for some reason, he just grunted and didn't argue when the storekeeper talked of the low fur prices and the difficulty he was having moving marten hides. But he did speak up when Ben started to write out the check that March day.

"Don't you have any real money?" the man blustered.

"I don't keep cash like that around!" was Ben's answer to the rough and uneasy trapper. "And say, what's your name, Mr.?"

And so, the transaction was made. Both Bud Shaffer and Ben Prince had few options. Shaffer was as nervous as a cat in a dog kennel, and Ben had the end of his cigar worked over more than usual. If the transaction had been made with Frank Arnold, he would have gotten top cash and hoofed it home to the mine with a good $600 or $700 in his pocket, but not to this man. A check for $350 was it. Now a check from Prince's was as good as cash in Oroville, but Ben was hoping Shaffer would heed his advice when he said "The bank will cash that Monday for you, Mr. Shaffer," for Ben wanted to talk to the town police as soon as he could get over to the station. Ben didn't know Frank Arnold was missing at that time, but he was still 99% sure those hides had come from the man of the Tungsten Mine. This man had taken an awfully low price for top quality furs and Ben smelled a rat.

However, a businessman cannot always lock-up early and run to the police station on a hunch, no matter how sure he was. It was a good few hours before the fur-buyer would lock the door, close the ledger and swing by the police station on his way home. It was later that night before the town lawman got the message, and too late to catch Bud Shaffer!

Someone saw the rough stranger leaving town and heading east. So, the county sheriff, Boyd Hildebrand, from Okanogan was called in. The sheriff took out after the man with his coon and cat dogs, somewhere east of Oroville, as the story goes, and they trailed him 30 or 40 miles past Oroville to the little towns of Molson and then Chesaw, Washington, losing him near the Ferry County line when the snow gave out. He was said to have been seen in Republic, Washington, but only for a short time. From there, he disappeared into the expanse of society.

But Bud Shaffer ran out of luck and money over in the state of Idaho, and he could even at this writing be rotting away in the state prison. Bud Shaffer, according to Iron, was caught and put in prison for killing some

The Rogue Trapper and The Wandering Prospector

poor, lonesome trapper in Idaho for his marten hides. That happened 80 years ago last February. Quite a story for a cow-milker from the old town of Nighthawk."

Of the five men who told firsthand accounts of Bud Shaffer, only Lefty is still alive at this writing (1988). Lefty told a completely different story from that of Iron's, but it still put the guilty finger on Bud Shaffer. This is Lefty's story as he told it to me in an interview:

It was in the middle of trapping season that Bud Shaffer caught Lefty and Iron hard at work on their winter's task of laying in the furs. The two trappers had taken over Jim Dodd's territory on Lake Creek 4 years before and suddenly, this year, a wandering trapper came busting into Lefty's trapping grounds without warning. If Lefty had run into the snowshoe tracks down off Black Lake, coming up from down in the valley, off the Chewack River, it would have been no big thing. In fact, he might have expected a hot cup of coffee when he got to his small log tepee of a camp on Fox Creek. But never in his days had a person "busted" into his trap-line like that! It wasn't "out-of-the-blue," it was "out-of-the-WHITE!" Off a steep cliff-faced mountain, far too steep and rocky for any kind of a trail.

"I was somewhat shaken!" was Lefty's cool way of saying it. It is a rare thing indeed to run into a set of snowshoe tracks out in the middle of God's Great Wilderness off a cliff like the one above Lake Creek. You can imagine the feelings that go along with the surprise. "He had on a set of Bear-Paw snowshoes, and he hit the trail through brush and bushes down off of Black Lake Ridge about one-half mile down from our lay-out." And, so it was with apprehension that Lefty moved on through the snow toward his lay-out, following these strange new "bear-paw" snowshoe tracks. He said it was "kind of spooky!" Lefty made it to his lean-to-tepee in good order and must have been surprised to find Shaffer's tracks going on past their simple camp. He passed it up! "He went past our lay-out and on up Fox Creek Trail," Lefty said, not touching it. He was following Iron's snowshoe tracks now.

It was getting to be the close of day as Iron shuffled down the steep Fox Creek Trail with a marten in his hands. He did not know it, but he was on a collision course with a thief and killer!

"Iron didn't have too much to say about him, other than his name was Shaffer and he was headed on toward Hidden Lakes," Lefty said. "They talked a little bit. I don't remember Iron saying much about him." So, when asked about Bud Shaffer's size, Lefty said that Iron said, "he was average size." Iron wasn't too impressed it seemed, by this stranger on small bear-paw snowshoes. Later, he said that he himself had never even seen the man, spinning a totally different account than Lefty's.

Bud Shaffer Raising Hell

But the escapades of Bud were far from over. Headed west now, up the snowy, steep, 3-mile Fox Creek climb, Bud Shaffer went on through a maze of mountains, up-over 7,000-foot mountain passes, edged along snow covered rock cliffs and down into hidden valleys to the head waters of the Pasayten River. Finding the Hidden Lakes after 25 miles of wandering, he somehow managed to find Romie Johnson and Clent Hank's nice cabin on Ptarmigan Creek empty. With Romie and Clent gone, resting their trap-line that year, and working instead on the C.C.C. trail in Beaver Meadows, there were no snowshoe tracks to follow through the maze of mountain valleys to their cabin. Bud Shaffer, despite that, nevertheless found the cabin hidden away far back into the Pasayten. His uncanny luck and abilities were holding.

"Romie said someone had hit their cabin," Lefty went on to say. "Yet the rogue trapper didn't lay over long it appears in the nice cabin there on Ptarmigan Creek. He was driven to move on out of Ramie's and Clent Hank's trapping area. He did not go empty handed!

The Rogue Trapper and The Wandering Prospector

"He took Romie's and Clent's traps, two, three or maybe four bags of traps, each weighing about 75 pounds per bag," said Lefty.

From here on, Bud's travels, and travel he did, get a bit confusing, if you are not confused already. The traps of Romie's and Clent's were found by Lefty and Iron the next summer "on the sled at the Thirty Mile Ranger Station, nice and neatly placed *in the garage*," Lefty told me. Romie and Clent identified them as being their traps. "Someone had stolen them and they figured it was this Shaffer," said Lefty. He also said that when he and Iron came in the next year, the winter of 1935-1936, Bud Shaffer had come back through their camp and used their tepee-lean-to while they were gone, messing with it in some way Lefty could not make clear as he was questioned. "And the dirty bugger, Shaffer," Lefty said, "…came back over Diamond Point Ridge and broke into the mountain-top lookout station there, too, vandalizing it all up like a ragging bear!"

Bud Shaffer was on one hell of a rampage, killing, stealing and now vandalizing high mountain top lookouts with no shame, boldly writing his name on signposts just to let everybody know he had been there. And, he wasn't done yet. The out-of-control thief hit the Dollar Watch Lookout Station too, vandalizing it as he had done the other. Both lookout were lonely and isolated, setting way up on top 8,000-foot mountains in 6 feet of snow. And, he didn't leave without leaving his signature mark in writing.

Lefty and Foss Creveling remembered Bud Shaffer's name written on the distant Peepsite Lake signpost. Peepsite Lake is indeed a hard place to find and get to by anyone, then or today. It sets way up and back on a lone, high steep mountain, at better than 8,000 feet, far off the main trails by many twisted miles. Yes, to be sure, Bud was making a name for himself. He was a traveling wild man who covered better than 100 steep, snow-covered mountain miles in 3, 4, 5 and 6 feet of powdered snow, and all that on little "ole" Bear-Paw snowshoes, which sink down into the snow 2 feet with each step. Lefty and Iron, Romie and Clent had cleared out of the area while working for the CCC, leaving the Pasayten wide open for plundering.

When I asked Lefty, why he felt Bud Shaffer would have "done-in" our man, Frank Arnold, Lefty said, "The only thing I could figure was to get Frank's furs." He talked about the sled on the Chewack (for him, the sled was in the Thirty Mile Station garage), and the traps belonging to Romie and Clent's, three sacks weighing 75 pounds each, that he found there at the garage door of the Thirty Mile Ranger Station. Lefty at first thought the rogue trapper had packed the traps (total weight 225 pounds) the long 40 miles from Hidden Lakes to the Tungsten Mine, pillaging in the process, and there built the sled. But as the conversation went back and forth in a somewhat analytical conversation, we both concluded that rogue trapper must have built the sled in one of two places because Bud didn't have a sled when he passed by Lefty and Iron on Lake Creek. So he either built the sled at Romie and Clent 's cabin or packed the 225 pounds of traps and whatever else he stole to the Tungsten Mine, and there built the sled, as Lefty believed was the more likely.

It was at the mine, Lefty said, that Bud stole Frank's furs and traps. True it was that Frank Arnold's traps and last year's furs were never found. So at this point of his inexhaustible travels, after attaining Frank's goods, Bud was pulling out of the Tungsten with a sled loaded with over 450 pounds of traps, plus anything else he wanted, emptying Romie and Clent's cabin, two lookouts, Lefty and Iron's camp, and now Frank Arnold's cabin. Remember that all of Frank's possessions were gone when Emmet Smith, the sheepherder, walked in. Not to be forgotten in all of this is Bud Shaffer's own gear. He must have carried it on his back. So, putting it all together, at this point, Bud Shaffer had enough traps and supplies to run a trap-line from Washington State to the State of Alaska.

Interestingly, George Honey, in 1936, while packing out tungsten ore for George Miller, studied the sled at the foot of the Chewack

The Rogue Trapper and The Wandering Prospector

Drive-way trail (for despite Lefty's tales, that is where it was in truth), and found that the belting used to pull it with was of the same type as the belting found at the Tungsten Mine. It was a heavy, gear-pulling type of belting, making it an almost absolute that the sled did indeed come from or through the Tungsten Mine, or at the very least, the belt used to pull the sled came from there. The belt or sled, or both, had been there.

In discussing what Lefty thought happened in this plundering trip, he figured it went like this, "After packing his stolen 225 pounds of traps over to the Tungsten Mine on small Bear-Paw snowshoes," which seemed totally possible and probable to him, "Shaffer left the mine, and then went down the snow-covered trail, south to Horseshoe Creek, 6 or 7 miles away. There he killed and hung Frank, or contributed to it by stealing Frank's food, and therefore Frank had to kill himself rather than starve to death or walk out. Then Shaffer went on down the Chewack River and out of the woods all-together, leaving the country, and going out the 30 miles down-river to Winthrop, on past the Thirty Mile Ranger Station. That's where we found the traps and the sled at the garage door of the Station." He didn't pin-point the likely time that Bud had come back down Lake Creek from Diamond Point Lookout and once again "hit his and Iron's tepee camp," as he said. He did not speculate on how Bud's trek up and back to the DollarWatch lookout factored in either. Like a spinning tornado, it all happened in one winter, the winter of 1934/1935. After a look at the map of the central Pasayten, it becomes clear that Bud Shaffer on his little Bear-Paw snowshoes zig-zagged, back-tracked; snowshoed up dozens of steep, vertical mountains; knew where all the cabins, fire look-outs and lay-outs were; and had unbelievable strength and stamina to haul all his hundreds of pounds stolen loot all around the Pasayten, adding more and more as he went. In steel traps alone, he probably had 450 pounds and that would not be an exaggeration according to Lefty's story.

Again, during this interview, Lefty denied ever seeing Frank Arnold in his life, though, over the phone, when I first talked to him, he said he had seen Frank Arnold that last year, and he had also met Bud Shaffer on the trail by Black Lake. Lefty was just a bit confused, it seems, and adding to this memory loss, he was completely dumb and ignorant of Pete's version of finding Arnold hung. That is, of Pete, Art Mitchell, the Deputy Sheriff, and Frank Maron finding the hanging body in a tree, no small event to forget. This was indeed strange, because again, Pete and Lefty worked together for at least 3 years after Maron had found Frank, as backed up by the newspaper report of the find.

When asked what he remembered about Frank Arnold, Lefty said, "I know very little about him because I was just a kid then working for the Forest Service. I didn't know of him... or about him... It is pretty faint now... I did know that he was a photographer... We (Iron and he) went by there one time..." We found some camera fittings and stuff like that... old film... things like that." This had to have been between the winter of 1934/1935 and early spring of 1936, for that's when Frank's worldly possessions were gone during those dates. Lefty went on, "We had heard that he was a photographer... We didn't really know what he was doing back there... Whether he was 'boot-legin, taking pictures or whether he was working in the mine... or just what. But at one time, later in the years, that was after he had died, or got hung, or whatever... George Honey and I went back into one of his cabins, over in the Cathedrals...." Lefty went on to tell a detailed account of what Frank's cabin looked like at the Cathedrals and where it was. He had to have been there, but not with George Honey. because George, being very sharp, knew what he had and had not done. He said he had never been back there. George did trap with Lefty though, for a year or two, but was clear that he and Lefty had never trapped that far back. So though Lefty was back there, it wasn't with George Honey.

The Rogue Trapper and The Wandering Prospector

Lefty went on to say something of great importance: "We actually built the trail (the new Horseshoe Creek trail, built in September 1936) practically on top of him... We made a switchback there... toward Tungsten Creek." Lefty proved by that statement that he knew exactly where Frank Arnold was hung and buried — close to the "switchback!" He and Pete (Iron had just bought his Winthrop Restaurant) were working together on the new trail that fall, just on the other side of Horseshoe Creek from where Frank Arnold was found that September Saturday. Just coincidence? Note what deputy Art Mitchell said, "Swinging body found by forestry trail crews." "Crews," as in more than one.

I went ahead and related Pete's story, which Lefty strangely had never heard before, and then he went on to say, "I was in town when the report came out that he had been found. A prospector had been up prospecting on Horseshoe Creek and had found him hanging in the tree, or what was left of him. I don't remember who he was." (Now Lefty's mind seems to be clearing up and conforming to Pete's account.)

"That was probably that Maron!" I said.

"No! No, this was a prospector. He was up there prowling around, prospecting on Horseshoe Creek and found him hanging there," said Lefty. Ok, who was I to argue with him? It wasn't Maron; Lefty knew that for a fact! And yet another twist to his story and the stories of Frank Arnold. Now, there was a "Wandering Prospector" story to fit in somehow, and it came from the lips of a man who was right there on Horseshoe Creek at the very time (within a day or two) that Frank was found hung.

Lefty volunteered no added information about Frank Arnold, and he seemed at a complete loss in describing anything about this man, which would be understandable if it were true that he "didn't know of him" or "about him," as he said. He did say that he thought he died about 1938, and his mind was very good on all other subjects. So is told Lefty's story about Bud Shaffer, the renegade, rogue trapper of the Pasayten Wilderness. But Lefty's last story, one more, is yet to be told.

CHAPTER 22

How George Miller and Pete Found Frank Arnold

FOR YEARS ON END IT was a blind guess as to what year it was that Frank Arnold went missing, and just as blind a guess as to when he was found. It was never clear. Absolutely no records could be found on the man, though there were some good guesses based on some known fact that seemed to be all that we had to help satisfy our curiosity. But when it came time to prove when he was found, the dates that were thrown around were "way-off." That is, if you call 2 or 3 years "way-off," and if you call spring "way-off' from fall. All the local people had to go on was what Pete had said and what a handful of old timers could remember. Lefty was little to no help a tall with all kinds of conflicting stories. The man seemed to be at a far greater loss than any of his peers, yet he was a main player. "Talking through his-hat" as he did when I interviewed him was not how he talked to the local town folks down through all those years about his dealings with Frank Arnold, Bud Shaffer, and his depression-era existence with Iron.

Pete was funny about talking about the deaths of anyone, let alone Frank Arnold. But his sons had heard the story of Frank Arnold's life and death because their father had told it to others in their presence. They could back up a lot of what Pete told Bob Curtis, George Miller and George Honey. Bob was greatly interested in what happened to his old "hero." Those who heard the story as Pete related it, felt it was in the month of June, on like the 21st of 1938, that he, Maron and Art Mitchell came on the hanging body. A few guessed Frank was found in the spring of 1937, while others were convinced it was the spring of 1935. We had all deciphered one thing for sure; it wasn't 1936, because that was when the miners were hauling ore out and Frank was gone by then. But he perhaps was not found yet. All we were sure of was that Frank was found in the spring of the year. (This may prove to be the only real thing we got right, as George Miller will tell.) If Pete said it was in the spring of the year that he, Art and Maron found Frank, then he should know. But there was more support to the spring finding than Pete's story. And the clues to this date came from the Tungsten Mine itself.

The clues for dating this mystery death came from the names and notes which have sat for years, carved in the log walls of the cabins by travelers who made it into the mine those hard, uphill 20 miles: hikers, horseman, hunters and forest personnel. The inner and written voice speaking that said, "I, too, accomplished the quest to this amazing place — don't forget me!" But it was the carved and penciled messages that told a story that gave the clues, the names written on the cabin walls that predate the foot warriors of the seventies and eighties. Going back even earlier and further than the writings of the high hunters of the fifties. It is those notes that were written on the log walls by the earliest visitors: trappers, forest personal, and the men that knew Frank Arnold. Writings of the 1930's and 1940's — these would help sort things out. Herein were the witnessing dates, the only written word as to just when Frank Arnold was found. The message was on the south wall of the big lower cabin, in the room that held the bathtub, not far from the main door. It a message left years ago in the targeted era. The

How George Miller and Pete Found Frank Arnold

message seemed to have answered the question as to when Frank Arnold was found, and when he disappeared, or at least the time he came up missing. But instead of clearing up that important date, it only made it muddier. The cabin wall messages in two writings said:

"Arnold
Found on Horseshoe
Near Mouth Hung By Neck
June 16, 1935
Iron"

"Snow Level With Roof of This Cabin
Temperature 6 Degrees Above 0
No Sign of Arnold
Pulling Out Tomorrow
James A. Thornton
January 18, 1931"

"JUNE 16, 1935 and JANUARY 18, 1931?" Did these men know what they were talking about? Nobody who I talked to today seems to have even heard of a James A. Thornton. I speculate that James Thornton must have been a resident of one of the two valleys below and from the wording of his note, it seems he knew Frank. It is my guess he was just out on a winter outing, cutting through 4 to 6 feet of snow for 80 miles of sport. They question is "Was Frank really missing in 1931?" If these two old notes left on the log wall were not confusing enough, there was one more message that only made it worse. The message seems to be lost today, but was read by Bob Curtis, and was supposed to be under the window on the south wall of the big cabin, about where the sink sets today. It said something to the effect that Frank Arnold was hung on Horseshoe Creek. That he went missing in 1935 and being found in

1937. This note was signed by "Iron." The man was making it confusing. But take note: Iron, by his own hand, had been to the Tungsten Mine more than once, yet supposedly not his twin partner Lefty!

For 55 years these were the only known written accounts of Frank's death. Nothing could be found at the county police office, other than a small card that Bob Curtis found in the 1950's that said, "Frank Arnold," with nothing else written on it; Otherwise, it was all but a blank card. Of course, in later years, nobody in the area could remember when the 1936 era mining took place, either, or the mining in 1939 under Hatfield for that matter, so that wasn't much help. The few people left who did know when they mined, 1936 and 1938-1939, knew that the old trapper couldn't have been found in 1935, as Iron wrote on the cabin wall, and it wasn't 1936, either, for Frank was still missing that summer and un-accounted for. So, the confusion went on, year after year, with no hope of getting the dates, time, or seasons straightened out.

The stage for Pete's story of Maron finding Arnold, as he had told Bob Curtis, was backed up by Frank Maron. For in the twenty-some years Maron lived past 1936, he told the story of finding Frank to his friend Loy McDaniel and his son Jim. This story was solid! And further backed-up by the memory of Pete's sons, who remembered Frank Maron and Art Mitchell at their house, both before and after the event. The three men who found Arnold sat and talked about the mysterious event around the kitchen table when they came back that Sunday, and it was quite a story for three young boys to hear. Pete's story is sound, for deputy Art Mitchell became Sheriff in 1938, and was around a long time. He had told the story to his deputy Jim Vandiver, and the Vandivers were friends to the writer's family.

Frank was Found by Four Different Men?

If the stone-cold facts weren't so serious, it could be surmised that this story is rolling out to be "just one big fabricated myth," for to be sure, it

How George Miller and Pete Found Frank Arnold

borders on something read in "Ripley's Believe-it-or-Not." Strangely and perplexingly, there are still two other stories of who found Frank Arnold. Two of the stories and people who found Frank have already been told; that is, Frank Maron's account, and then Lefty's "wandering-prospector" story, not Frank Maron, but a prospector who stumbled onto the hanging Frank. These two conflicting reports you have read. Now I state as fact, that interesting as it is, out of the twisted, convoluted facts that come floating to the top of the "crock-pot," three of the four stories are also to be believed (in the main). And, I would declare them true (sort-of). All three stories came from the Methow Valley, and not one of the three main accounts was a secret.

The third account of finding Frank (not already related), was told to me over the phone by Lefty somewhat early in the work on this book. According to Lefty, Frank was found in 1936, at about the same time that Frank Maron walked up on the hanging body of the man we call "Frank Arnold." It was in the fall, the first of September, and Lefty and Pete were together on the same Forest Service crew putting in the new trail to the Tungsten Mine from the mouth of Horseshoe Creek. Frank Burge, the Forest Service Superintendent had finally been talked into putting in this new trail. They dropped the trail George Miller had carved out 10 years before, almost straight up Tungsten Creek. Now instead, the new trail would follow Horseshoe Creek for its first quarter-mile of easier going, and then zigzag west up the mountain to eventually tie into George Miller's old trail 2 miles or so up the mountain.

Pete and Lefty begin their work at the end of August and probably finished their 2 miles of trail by the middle of October. After riding that same trail a hundred times, as steep as it is, a few more switchbacks wouldn't have hurt anything. Nevertheless, this second attempt at a trail to the Tungsten was certainly a needed improvement, but for George Honey and George Miller, who had packed out the "30 tons" of ore that summer, it was two months too late.

TALES OF THE TUNGSTEN MINE

The story Lefty told Foss Creveling of the Methow Valley was somewhat more complete. Like George Honey, Foss packed for George Miller that summer of 1936, bringing ore out, just weeks before Frank was found. And it was Foss who shared this story with me. Lefty told Foss this story:

"I was working on the trail going up the mountain from the mouth of Horseshoe Creek, when I decided to go down to the creek and get a drink of water. I cut down over the hill (about thirty or 40 feet), to Horseshoe Creek and bent down to take a drink of water. When I satisfied my thirst and stooding up, there on the bank, I took a look around. What a shock hit me when I saw before me the body of a hanging man. He was across the creek from where I stood! It was Frank Arnold!"

End of story. And just what did Lefty do after that cadaver find? NOTHING! Lefty's story ends right there! "I found Frank, and then a space-ship landed, and all becomes void." Lefty gave no further details. We are left with a cliff-hanger because Lefty never said what he did after his find.

Lefty also told this story to about finding Frank Arnold to Hank Dammann, a citizen of Winthrop. Hank Dammann told me the exact same story that Foss recounted. So Lefty told at least two of his friends that he found the old trapper — not Maron — not a prospector passing through., and not Pete. With that said, when I, first talked to Lefty face to face about he himself finding Arnold, as he had told me over the phone, he adamantly denied saying such a thing to anyone. Also in this faceto-face interview, he denied EVER SEEING FRANK IN HIS LIFE! So when I told Hank Dammann about Lefty's complete denial when talking to Hank about his experiences in the mountains, Hank did not believe it, or could not believe it because Lefty had told him, and so many others, that he, Lefty, had found Frank Arnold hanging. So, Hank, right there on the spot, called Lefty up on the phone and asked him, as I sat there listening in. Which way would the compass

How George Miller and Pete Found Frank Arnold

needle point? After Hank had hung-up the phone, he shook his head in disbelief. He had to agree that Lefty did, in fact, deny ever finding Mr. Frank Arnold hung. He had changed his story, both to me and to his close friend Hank Dammann. For again, as Hank had remembered the story:

"Lefty was working on the trail at the mouth of Horseshoe Creek, and on a switch-back, turned and saw Frank Arnold hanging in the tree."

George Honey was an over-flowing cup of information on all points, and remembered Pete and Lefty building this new trail going up from the mouth of Horseshoe Creek — and for good reason — he had learned to hate that steep, rocky trail George Miller had cut out 10 years before. And, though it could be said that Frank Arnold's camp "was just across the creek from the first switch-back that turns away from Horseshoe Creek," the real fact of the matter (and this is a big problem with Lefty's story) is that Frank's camp cannot be seen from any side of the creek anywhere near that first switchback. Frank's hanging site is *up the Creek more than 200 Yards,* with 200 trees of one sort or another blocking the view looking up the creek from that point. So, it was really impossible for Lefty, or anyone else, to see Frank or his camp from the west side of Horseshoe Creek where the trail switches back. Either standing down on the edge of the creek, as Lefty said, or up on the trail itself, as Lefty also said, you just cannot see the hanging tree from that far down the creek. So, for Lefty to have seen and found Frank while working on that trail, he would have had to cross the creek, which means getting wet to your knees, because Horseshoe Creek is wide and deep enough to get wet while crossing. Then, once across, he would have had to walk up the creek 200 yards to find Frank. To make the statement by Lefty even more untrue is the fact that the tree Frank was actually hung on, stood about 20 feet back from the creek. Frank had purposely gone up the creek from the bridge about a quarter-of-a-mile to hide his camp. If Lefty did find Frank hanging, he walked up the dry east side of Horseshoe Creek to do so.

Now facts being facts, there is a whole lot more to this account than meets the ears and eyes, for there are dots to connect, and words to put between the lines. Although Lefty later disavowed ever telling either one of his two versions, even to his life-long buddies in Winthrop, Pandora's Box had been opened. Lefty had told one too many stories, to one too many people. So, taking Lefty at his first words; it was not Frank Maron who actually found Frank Arnold, it was Lefty himself. And, if Lefty found him, Pete sure as the devil found him, too. Ask yourself, if you found a body hanging from a tree, what would you do thereafter? Just keep it to yourself and walk away? With Frank Arnold, missing for 2 years, and now you finally found him in a tree.

With this "cat-out-of-the-bag," the story takes a 180° turn. There arises all kinds of unanswered questions. Seeing that it is entirely possible that Lefty did find Frank first (with Pete), then it changes the whole scenario. Was Maron just a "patsy?" And if a patsy; why?

If we go back again to Art Mitchell's statements to the Omak/Okanogan newspaper, where he definitely stated that it was *"Forestry Trail Crews"* who found Frank Arnold, Lefty's account of finding the hanging body suddenly becomes much more solid.

The Fourth Finder: George Miller

If the reader has not by now thrown up his hands in confused befuddlement, which I suspect Lefty, Pete and Iron would certainly like your state of mind to be, then you might for sure throw up your hands after reading the following account given by George Miller. In actual fact and understanding about what was going on up there in the mountains, there really haven't been too many untrue events per-se. They have been misplaced in time, yes; changed around, to be sure; and tweaked and twisted, absolutely. But the stories nevertheless have stayed within the

How George Miller and Pete Found Frank Arnold

"property-lines" of events because these were the stories handed to me after I had completed a couple of years or so of research. I was handed scrambled eggs to weigh out and conflicting accounts to figure out. It was this way from the start. I remember the feeling in the beginning, before asking the first question, the strange reality that a long time ago a photographing trapper from the Tungsten Mine had been found "hung" in a tree on Horseshoe Creek. That was all. That one fact was all there was. The mystery of a trapper hanging from a unique spot sprouted this hunt for more information. Everything found out thereafter was thrilling news and added to that mysterious event as a bonus.

Still, the seriousness of it was always there: a man was found hung and probably strangled to death That is serious! And there can only be two ways in which that hanging could have happened: either number 1: The man was "murdered," or number 2: He "hung himself." There are no other options. The difference between the two possibilities is that "murder" has powerful ramifications and brings forth feelings that demand justice, where as "suicide" has acceptable consequences, and brings forth the feelings of sympathy. So, it is with these philosophical thoughts in mind that we move to George Miller's very enigmatic, but credulous story.

The aged George Miller, who has ridden those trails up the Chewack River to the mine one more time than I, had an account that completely threw me a curve, a real surprise. The account was altogether believable. George was 85 when I interviewed him, and he didn't have old age dementia, just the opposite, he had a good memory. George, as the history has been told, was an early packer into the Pasayten, slinging pack boxes around up there as early as the mid-1920's. Interestingly, too, in all those years he never remembered Frank Arnold coming into the town of Winthrop. George's wife, Clara Northcott Miller, who sat at his side the night I interviewed George, also was there in the very early years of the 1920's. She had known George since she was 4 years old.

TALES OF THE TUNGSTEN MINE

As a teenager in 1924, Clara started working at the hotel in Winthrop and stayed there, For 40 years, she bussed tables and wrote up orders at the town restaurant. Nobody came into town for more than a day that she did not know about. She knew every trapper, mountain man, Forest Service person, cowboy and logger who set foot in Winthrop. She is a gem and one of the last of a generation. Interestingly enough, although Clara had heard of Frank Arnold, like George said, never in those 40 years of waiting tables and watching the men and women walk by on the streets of Winthrop, did she ever see or even hear of the mayor of the Tungsten Mine coming to town. Even to me this seems odd on Frank's part. Winthrop was just not that much further away than the town of Loomis. The only answer seems to be, contrary to Loomis and Oroville, he just never cultivated any close friends down the Chewack that he felt a need to go see, or perhaps he had a "gut feeling" of trouble associated with the town.

Being a packer during the 1920's and 1930's, George knew Frank Arnold and the mine well. George said it was spring, probably June 16, 1935, and Frank Arnold hadn't come out of the mountains that winter to Loomis. He hadn't come out that spring, either. Pete knew this, for he hadn't let his young packer go back into the mine that late May, on the 28th to be exact, to see Frank. Frank had asked the young lad to come in to see him on that very day, but Pete would not let him go in with the horses because there was no use to do so. Frank was not there. Frank was gone. "So, don't bother!" In the early days of May, you can't get into the Tungsten at its 7,000-foot elevation without bucking miles of packed snow 2 feet deep. Before the first week in June, a horse cannot get through the heavy snow. I have tried it more than once. I made it into the mine over much snow on a horse on the fifth of June and felt lucky to have accomplished it. Then once at the mine, I couldn't go a mile in either direction from there. The Tungsten Mine is on the south side of Wolframite Mountain, the sunny side, which makes that side of

How George Miller and Pete Found Frank Arnold

the mountain open first in the spring. So Frank, by asking his young friend to come in on the 28th of May, was cutting it close. He would almost surely have had to walk in the last 3 or 4 miles in snow. With that said and all that explained, just how in the world did Pete know Frank was gone "for sure" in the month of May of that year 1935?

With that question hanging, Pete, privy to Frank's disappearance, for some reason, a month later in June, talked George Miller into taking a trip with him in to check out Frank and the mine. The reason for needing the trip, Pete told George, was that he wanted to do his yearly assessment work up there. But as the facts roll out, it is much more likely that Pete just wanted to go in and check on Arnold. George Miller (and all the world), at this point, had no reason to believe Frank was not still among the living. Though George, in our interview, did quickly bring up the fact that Lefty and Iron had run into a "rogue-trapper" that winter up on their trap-lines. The "mad trapper" was thought to be generally "raising-hell" over Frank's way. So, with George saying that, it can be assumed that the two rode in that spring to see if Frank was okay. The horses moved on up the Chewack River that day, again, probably June 16, 1935.

"Where did you find Frank Arnold at, George?" was the question Emmet Smith, the sheepherder asked George Miller years afterwards, in the 1940's or 1950's. For George, too, had a first-hand, very reverent story of finding the lost trapper, and the sheepherder, Emmet, had heard of it. Emmet explained it like this: "During the big fire in 1929, George Miller was packing for the Forest Service and riding up the Chewack River with a string of horses and had stopped at the mouth of Horseshoe Creek." Emmet, who was also working on the big fire, as the story tells, came walking also into the forks of Horseshoe Creek and the Chewack River at the same time from the north; leading a gimping, bloody-footed horse that had traveled far more miles than it should have without shoes. The last horseshoe was laying on the ground, many miles back. The two young men stopped and compared notes. It was the first time they had ever met, and the two had lots to talk about as the '29 fire burned all around them. Emmet told him about the fire jumping the fire-line at Rummel Lake, about his not being able to find the fire-fighting crew, and now, how "darn-it," things were a "hell of a mess" if they hadn't been before. George had to take his pack-string in anyway, to Rummel Lake, if for no other reason than to find the lost fire fighters. But before the two went their separate ways, George put Emmet in the saddle again, coming up with some farrier equipment and some horseshoes. With a mouth full of nails, the Winthrop packer went to work on Emmet's horse there at the little meadow along the river. George became Emmet's ticket to a ride home. Emmet's feet were as sore as his horse's, and he had miles yet to travel. So, the creek was aptly named "Horseshoes" Creek.

"Remember, on Horseshoe Creek, where I shod your horse, there on the trail in 1929, during the big fire, Emmet? That is where I found Frank Arnold hung at," said the packer to the sheepherder.

You see, George had always said he had found Frank Arnold. He made no real secret about it, but he told only a few people. He told Don Zellweger in 1938-1939, who was mining up there. He told Emmet Smith. He told his wife and his son, Claude, He told me, so he must have told others. It is just that he did not tell everybody all the time, and he sure did not make a show about finding Frank. (For Frank's sake, he should have.)

Nevertheless, the facts being as they are, he did find Arnold and had a right to tell someone. There was a reason why he didn't tell everyone, and the reason was Pete. Pete had his reasons why he wanted George to "keep a lid on it." You don't find somebody shot dead, then don't go tell the authorities unless someone else is going to handle it, and that someone else would be "Pete" of course. George knew that Pete was really busy working on a deal to sell the Tungsten Mine. The sale date was 1935. George, being a good friend; and Pete, had helped George

How George Miller and Pete Found Frank Arnold

find work more than once and George was a good friend so if his friend wanted him to "keep the lid on it" for a while, there was a good reason for doing so. Besides, to George's way of thinking, Lefty and Iron knew who had killed Frank. They even knew the guy's name: Bud Shaffer.

So just what transpired on that spring day of June 1935, along the Chewack River? Here is what George Miller told me:

"We didn't pack the ore out until the next year." George remembered the thirty tons in 1936 that he contracted to haul for Mac McPherson and Harold Dardier. "Pete and I were riding into the Tungsten Mine to do assessment work and rode over into Frank Arnold's camp on Horseshoe Creek (which Pete had no problem finding). Frank was laying there, but he was dead!"

"Who was with you when you found Frank Arnold?" I asked.

"Pete," said the old packer.

"Was there a man by the name of Frank Maron with you?" I asked.

"No! Just Pete and I," said George.

"Was the Deputy Sheriff there?"

"No! Just me and Pete," George said again.

Clara, his wife, cut in, "George has always said that he and Pete had found and buried Frank Arnold up in the mountains with no undertaker present." Clara just didn't feel right about it.

For me, this was hard to grasp at the time. It was a new spin of what had happened to Frank, so I may not have asked all the questions that should have been asked, but I did get the surprising basics.

"Who found Frank Arnold, you or Pete? Who found him first?"

"I think I found him first," was the reply.

"What time of year was it when you rode into Frank's old camp?" I asked.

"I think it was early spring," he answered.

"What did Frank look like when you found him, George? Was he in good shape? Was he hung-up off the ground?" I wanted to get the death stories tied together. But what a surprise answer I got.

"Frank looked in pretty good shape. He was laying on the ground with a bullet hole in his head. He was shot in the head. We figured he shot himself. He was on the ground. Bud Shaffer had stolen his groceries and left Frank to starve to death!"

"Frank never made it that winter, but shot himself rather than starve to death, or Bud Shaffer shot him," so reasoned the old packer about his and Pete's find. Lefty and Iron backed it all up and said the same thing. There was just no doubt in his mind that this Bud Shaffer had killed or contributed to the death of Frank by stealing his groceries. Over and over again, George emphasized and incriminated Bud Shaffer's actions in dealing Frank Arnold a death blow. Bud Shaffer killed Frank Arnold in one way or another; to this there was no doubt.

"What do you see in your mind's eye about the scene, George?" asked Clara, for this was now new information to her, too.

"I see Frank dead, laying on the ground, shot. We buried him right on the creek 'cause that was the only place we could find that was soft enough to dig a hole," said George.

"George has always said that he buried Frank Arnold on Horseshoe Creek, always! He and Pete," said Clara Miller.

"Frank was in pretty good shape when we put him in a canvas tarp and buried him. I can't remember if he had his teeth, but it seems he had his mustache," he answered to the next question.

This is the story of George Miller finding Frank Arnold as told to me that night in their Winthrop home. George didn't really try to hide the fact that he and Pete had found Frank; however, he did change the story this last time told. What was there to hide anymore? As Clara said, he had always, expect this time said that he and Pete had found Frank "hung in a tree" not laying on the ground in "good shape" with

How George Miller and Pete Found Frank Arnold

a "bullet hole in his head." All George had ever said was simply that he and Pete had found Frank "hung" on Horseshoe Creek and had buried him there with no details.

Why did George change his story this time? Was it finally time that the real truth had to be known and not the story Pete wanted the world to have? Or is it really a truth that Frank was hanging, both in the spring of 1935 (despite George's story), and then the body was allowed to hang there for a full 15 months more... that is, until Pete got around to bringing Maron and the sheriff, Art Mitchell, in to investigate? Or as George said, was it in truth that he and Pete found Frank that spring with a "bullet hole in his head" burying him in the sands of Horseshoe Creek? If this is the one true story, then did Pete dig him up and re-hang him for the sheriff to see? The reader is left to decide.

With all these questions to answer, and probably a few more, we move on to other details that could make George look a little bad if taken out of his and Pete's perspective. Why did George not go straight to the police with the death? A lingering question. George never did tell his good friend, George Honey this story. Yet George Honey worked side-by-side with George Miller the next year, through all of 1936, riding right by Frank's grave. Then Honey worked most all of 1937 with George Miller over on a packing job on the West Coast, packing horses on another government job. When the job was done, later that year in 1937, George Miller, George Honey and Pete all together made a trip back into the high mine in late 1937. Frank had now been found. Pete stopped and guided them back to the camp, to the spot where "He, Frank Maron and Art Mitchell had found poor Frank hung the year before." George Honey, on his horse, reached up and cut the last of the rope off from around the hanging tree, and George Miller didn't say a thing to counter Pete's story.

Of course, Honey knew that he and George Miller were not even in the area that September of 1936 when Frank had been found "officially."

TALES OF THE TUNGSTEN MINE

As soon as the tungsten ore had been packed out that year, a job that ended in August, the two packers headed for work over on the coast and were gone from the region until the next early fall, 1937. Of course by that time Pete and the newspapers had told everybody, including Honey, that "he, Frank Maron and Art Mitchell had found poor Frank hung, which in turn, would make any involvement of George Miller out of place and unaccountable and uncomfortable. George Miller *couldn't* say a thing and *didn't*! At least for a while… But that doesn't mean his story is not true.

By 1940, Pete had moved out of the state with his family, and George Miller was working for the most part out of the area, too. So, who could straighten things out? Who knew both accounts? Who wanted to? Friends and families were involved! Frank Arnold, on the other hand, was just an old, lone trapper who was found dead, however you wanted to believe it. It is just that if Frank was dead and buried, he wasn't, by far, forgotten! His legend would not die that easily, even 84 years later. The high mountain mine and he himself were "institutes" to great to be forgotten or bypassed like a fading shadow.

Adding It Up

I would say that George Miller tried to do the right thing, in Pete's own way. Pete, to be remembered, as I have tried to emphasize, was not a man to be crossed, and nobody did; he could darn-near kill you with his look alone. He was strong, very strong both in physical strength and countenance. Did I already say that he was a big man? To many people he was certainly reputable: he had money, a good job, a good car, a good family; he was often easy-going, with many relatives in the area — an all-around good citizen. Forget the fact that in the years of the 1920's and early 1930's he was a "bootlegging son-of-a-gun." That didn't count. Half the upper valley was also involved one-way or another in that money-making trade. Canada had lots of booze to sell in those

How George Miller and Pete Found Frank Arnold

days — and the border — what border? Winthrop, too, was about as far-and-away from law-and-order as a civilized town could get. Law? What was that in the towns of Loomis and Winthrop? Winthrop was the end of the road, to be sure, and almost lost itself — 65 miles from the sheriff's office. It was all but a "wide-open town" for decades. Loomis, even closer to the border, was almost as remote, and just as drunk.

But most important to George was that Pete was a friend who could help George get work. George had a family to feed. Remember, it was the heart of the Great Depression. Why argue with Pete about how to handle poor Frank's body? Pete, to be sure, was not only a friend of George Miller, but of Frank Arnold also. He would take responsibility and had everybody's best interest in mind. Besides, again, Pete also knew who did it — Bud Shaffer! Lefty and Iron made "no-bones" about their own run-in with this renegade up there on their trapping grounds; a half-crazy, mad trapper who was all over that country that winter.

Pete, of course, had a lot to lose if word got out that Frank Arnold of the Tungsten Mine was found dead with a bullet hole in his head. Who would have done it? If Bud Shaffer couldn't be found, which it now seemed likely, then things would look bad for even Pete, and now even George.

So, Pete told the young George a good story. "Hell, yes, let's first find Shaffer, and if not, well, darn, let a sleeping bull-dog lie. We know that Shaffer guy did it. He came over from Loomis and took all of Frank's food, so the poor old man had to shoot himself to keep from starving to death. Remember what Lefty and Iron said — he tore up all those trappers' layouts on Robinson Creek. Damned that Shaffer; now he's got us messed up in it. What if they finger *me* or *you*, George? Let me check into it and see if I can run down this Bud Shaffer over in Loomis or Nighthawk. I'll tell the Sheriff where he's at, and we can get this thing figured out. Let's just keep this under our caps until I find Shaffer and then get by the Sheriff's Office in Okanogan; for it's in his jurisdiction."

George worked the following summer for the miners of 1936, then went west, and worked for another year. And when he came back in late 1937 and talked with Pete, Pete told him Bud Shaffer had never been found, but Frank Arnold had been by the Sheriff, if only the Deputy Sheriff. It was even in the same camp where Pete and George had first found him. The law had gone in and made it legal, and the only difference was, "You had better tell them you found him hung, George, cause that way it makes it a lot easier to explain. They have never caught up with that Bud Shaffer yet!" And, so it was, Pete got his way as always, and was out of the state a few years later. It is doubtful George ever even heard the details of how Frank was covered-up. His clothes tied on and such — that was the Loomis story — and it didn't matter. George knew what really happened. It sure never screwed up any mining deals for the two, and Pete and George seemed to have come out of an ugly mess okay.

I believe George Miller's last story to be true and the date on the Tungsten Mine wall- right on:

ARNOLD
FOUND ON HORSESHOES NEAR MOUTH
*** JUNE 16, 1935 ***
'IRON'

CHAPTER 23

Foul Play on Horseshoe Creek

The story and the facts are truthful as told. The speculation, bottom-line and presumed innocent, is yours to decide, but the deceiving lies, the convoluted cover-up stories, and the cold, hard facts, can only lead me, the writer, to thinking about Pete, Lefty and Iron! And this also I do believe... that there is a man alive today (1992) who knows exactly what happened to Frank Arnold 60 years ago up there on that far away Pasayten Creek.

THE DEATH OF FRANK ARNOLD is bizarre to say the least, and a close look at the facts , is our only chance of finding an answer to what really happened up there on that dark creek bank some 60 years ago?

We know what Pete told us about finding the strange hanging body. We know what Art Mitchell said in the paper. We know what Frank E. Maron saw, said, and did after he was picked up at Medical Lake. Lefty was still alive in 1985 when I interviewed him, and he was there. George Miller is still alive and knew them all. Iron and "Old Man Arnold" trapped beside each other for 6 years. These six men are the six sides to the coffin of Frank Arnold, and from their lips come the hard facts and questions that crisscross around the death of the man they thought of as *not your average sort of human being*.

May we never become dull in our thinking because of time has passed or because of the host of information that was part of Frank's history. There was a terrible, sad death that took place up there in those beautiful high mountains that cold winter day in 1934 or 1935, and nobody was there to champion the life of this lone, wandering, fur trapper, bear trapper, mountain man, photographer, moose tamer, dog musher, astronomer, prospector, miner, cook, card sharp, chess champ, toy maker, wood carver, electronic and radio whiz, chemist, marksman, Englishman, Irishman, Canadian, Montanan, Idahoan, Washingtonian, and Tungsten Miner — except Pete!

It was close to the mouth of Horseshoe Creek that Frank Arnold chose to build a replacement camp for the cabin that burned down a mile away on Tungsten Creek. This new camp was not much of a camp by anybody's standards. Only a lean-to and a table gave any signs of permanence to the camp. The lean-to was small, 3 or 4 feet high, by 7 or 8 feet long, and covered with canvas, probably the same canvas George Miller and Pete used to wrap Frank in for burial. Besides the table, there was just a small natural bench of land at the side of a steep, deep canyon wall. Still, the simple camp, had a considerable number of things laying around. Most all of them have been carted off over the years as souvenirs by high mountain horsemen who found the old line-camp. Frank may have had ideas about building a more permanent cabin there, for hanging in a tree was one or two cross-cut saws, and one or two axes. Besides these a small prospector's pick, eating utensils, pots and pans, one large five gallon strainer pot with holes in the bottom, a copper tea pot, trapping gear, and bedding were found and taken. Only the taker will know the whole inventory of things.

Foul Play on Horseshoe Creek

The Dutchman and the Baseball Player

Coincidentally, as fate would have it, that very winter of 1936, just after Frank Arnold was found, two trappers and one loaded, old, bay, pack mare worked their way up the Toats Coulee River. They were two days out of Loomis. They were coming from Oroville and Tonasket and they'd make it down to the Chewack River by night, so they figured.

Had they known what trail to take when they came to a cross trail, they would have made the river as planned, but as it was, they took the long way around and a terrible winter storm got them first. Up on a high mountain, called simply "Corral Butte," they got very lucky that cold night because there on the high mountain, at the very top, they found a badly needed refuge, the Forest Service Look-out Station. Outside, a bitter blizzard raged and roared as the thermometer plummeted to below zero. Their pack horse stood outside in the dark night shaking, rump turned to the 50-mile-per-hour north wind, ice building up on its back, tail blowing horizontal. One of the winter travelers jumped through the door opening in a wild gust of snow and wind, into the little, one room, wood-planked, summer lodging. The door almost came off its hinges as it flew against the wall with a bang. Blankets, clothes and other loose items flew around the room in the whirlwind of snow. The blast of wind held the door open as the little man fought to close it. His partner ran over to help, and he fumbled to latch the door. He said in his broken English, after the door was closed, and he was now fumbling to take off his gloves, "Were going to have to geet that puoor hworse inn-here. Inn soome shellter from dhat' DDWAMN' Windd, or he'll be a boock' of ice inn dthe morning."

"In here? The horse in here? Hells bells," his partner shouted as he stood curled around the little pot-belly stove, that was way too short on heat. "Dutch, look! (Dutch was a German immigrant.) There ain't no-way we can bring that horse in here. There's barely enough room for us! The old mare would tear the place up, step on us all night, and go crazy in the process! This place will be match-sticks by morning if we bring that animal in here…and Dutch, listen to me, if that horse takes a @#*, it'll get all over us, and our supplies! There's just not enough room, Dutch. Hell! This shack is only 12 feet square! Shoot," he said slowing down a little, "she won't walk through that narrow door anyway."

"Dhat' puoor' ddwamn' hworse' dhas' got-to commes' inns' here! I'll's feeaks' her-ups so she damwn wells can't takess a @#!*!!!" said the little German/Dutchman, knowing his horse would be dead in the morning if he didn't bring her inside the warming fire lookout.

So later that night, after a hard won can of beans, the boys laid out their bed-rolls on one side of the little Look-out Station, and Dutch brought in the poor freezing old mare. She darn near knocked him down trying to get in through the narrow door first. There she stood, without moving, all night. The Dutchman knew his partner had a point about the possible "@#*," so he grabbed the long tail and pulled it between her legs and roped it up tight to her belly. As long as she couldn't lift her tail, the two trappers were safe.

The two trappers were Dutch Wasifurth (sp), and Carl Gibbons. Dutch was a German trapper, who as a very young boy, had managed to stay alive in Germany, in those hard years after the First World War as a trapper. Carl was a baseball player and a local apple-tree pruner who, ironically, had spent the previous winter in sunny Yuma, Arizona under the hot desert sun, snagging flyballs and hitting baseballs, trying to make the pro's at spring training camp. Dutch knew he could do better at trapping animals than at pruning apple trees, and if there was something better than pruning apple trees, Carl Gibbons was all for it. Even if it meant a darn cold winter in the high mountains.

Dutch had talked to Charley Hartz that fall, who had been the cook at the Tungsten Mine that summer for Harold Dardier, Mac McPherson and the 1936 crew of miners. Charley talked to Dutch about the disappearance of Frank Arnold and of him leaving his prime trapping

Foul Play on Horseshoe Creek

ground open. It was a sweet song to Dutch's ears; and before long, Dutch and Carl were ready to go and soon miles deep in the primitive mountains of Washington State. It was a wild trapping trip that winter, full of funny times, hard times, and dangerous times, keeping alive on venison and mare's meat.

Finally, after a day, the storm blew itself out. Down the steep mountain they snowshoed onto the Chewack River drainage. Dutch pushed on ahead in this new white powder, his skis and sled gliding along through the early November snow. Carl pushed, puffed, and fought the funny, confounded webbed instruments that were lashed to his feet, as the horse followed its lead-rope behind him. Both young men sweated in the cold winter setting that stretched out as far as they could see. It was the natural route to the Tungsten Mine, and the boys turned up Horseshoe Creek to gain what they thought was a gradual elevation up the steep mountain before them. What they found out was, in fact, they were a bit lost, and in a tight gorge with a heavy creek running through it. The two found themselves in an old camp. It was Frank Arnold's old camp on Horseshoe Creek. It is because these two trappers fell by chance on Frank's last camp that we can fit together a few more pieces to the puzzling death of the tough Englishman who laid covered-over in his grave somewhere at their feet.

Dutch remembers cutting a heavy rope that was wrapped around a leaning fir.

"It wasn't a light rope, either; it was like 3/4 inches. I cut about 10 to 12 feet from the tree and put it on the sled I was pulling."

Carl also spoke of the long rope, but thought it was no more than 1/2 inch in diameter. If Dutch had known that the rope he held in his hand for the rest of that winter had once held the swinging body of a fellow trapper, he would have avoided it like the black plague. But the two never gave it a thought, nor did they know the significance of where they were. It was only years later that Dutch and Carl learned that this cold, sunless camp, and the rope they cut down, once held the body of the leading citizen of the place they were going, the famous trapper, Frank Arnold of the Tungsten Mine.

They only considered it a lucky find when they stumbled into Frank's old camp. Here was some rope they needed, and Dutch cut it off, leaving just the tied part on the tree trunk. Both Carl and Dutch agreed that the rope really was not tied to a limb but may have laid over a limb. It is not clear just how it was tied, or why it was so long. All they knew was that there was a whole lot of rope in the tree, and it was heavy rope, too. George Honey, who cut out the last of the rope the next fall, 1937, also indicated that it was around the tree trunk and not tied to a limb, though it probably laid over a limb.

Carl found some jump-traps and fur-stretchers laying on the table. There was also an old catalog of some kind, probably a Sears and Roebuck. It was an old catalog even at that time. Dutch came up with some knot hole traps, some liquid cat bait in a bottle that was still good that he used that year trapping. He called it "Cat Nip." There was also some bedding in the lean-to, but Dutch's most important find was two marten hides laying on the table. Yes, two marten hides! Dutch looked them over really well in hopes he could sell them. They weren't that bad, but they weren't that good, either. They were a bit wormy, so he left them.

These two marten skins speak in a loud voice! They certainly do not help or back up the rogue trapper story as told by Iron, Lefty and Pete whatsoever. The mute marten hides dump cold water on the theory that Frank was killed and robbed for his furs, as the three men portrayed. The person or persons who left them weren't interested in the $40.00 or $50.00 they were worth in town. The two marten hides also sober us to the actuality of Frank's body becoming nothing but bones in just 21 months in the high mountains where half the months are all snow and freezing ice. But what they tell us is the fact that Frank Arnold was indeed out on his trap-line that winter of 1935 when he was killed, working his fur-lines as was normal, before he died.

How much snow, if any, was on the ground in the river canyon at 4,750 feet, that late November when Carl and Dutch came through, is hard to say, but there couldn't have been that much, or they wouldn't have found what they found, The two trappers didn't notice Frank's grave, which wasn't marked as it is today with rocks. The rocks were laid over the remains by Lloyd Ford years later, probably in the late 1950's. They walked all over the grave while cutting the rope out of the tree. They do not remember seeing the large 5 to 7-gallon kettle with holes in the bottom, that should have been laying right by the tree. The boys took the traps and possibly some stretchers, and were off, after finding Pete and Lefty's new trail across the creek, headed again for the Tungsten Mine. These two men were the first to visit the hanging site on Horseshoe Creek since Art Mitchell, Frank Maron and Pete were there just two months before.

Pete's Unanswered Questions

Pete's son said this about his dad: "Dad never liked to talk about someone who died. When he was dead, he was dead, and not to be dwelled upon, or talked about."

Pete died an early death sometime in the late 1950s, but his stories lived on. When he died, as far as I'm concerned, he left too many unanswered questions. Here are the overlooked facts as I see them, the questions, the loose ends, the pieces to the puzzle that can't be pounded into place by the simple suicide conclusion. These questions surround Pete's story and his deep involvement with the hanging of Frank Arnold.

(1) Why was Pete alone, so interested in finding Frank? He was the only one who went to such great length and expense, making a real display of trying to find Frank Arnold? He, alone, hired men to look for Frank Arnold, namely Clarence Landergreen and Johnny Bell. And

then, just short of 2 years later, he spent maybe two days, driving 300 miles, making a special trip to Medical Lake hospital just to bring back Frank Maron to go up and look some more. This seems inconsistent for "a man who didn't like to talk about someone that died," or "to dwell on the subject."

(2) How long did Pete want Maron to be gone? The idea was for him to travel all through Frank's old trapping zone. But Maron was lightly loaded, he did not have a pack horse or two loaded with weeks' worth of groceries, which he absolutely would have needed if he was going to mount an extensive search through all of the old trapper's stocking grounds. Understanding that Pete could very easily have provided him with these needed horses and gear from his own stock. But Pete didn't do this. Frank E. Maron left Thirty Mile Ranger Station that September morning with no more than a small pack on his back and a strong suggestion that he look in so and so camp, essentially directions where to look first "at the mouth of Horseshoe Creek." And he was back within the day. And Pete was waiting.

(3) It seems a bit coincidental that Pete, a busy family man, was still at the Thirty Mile Ranger Station that late Saturday night, when "lo-and-behold" back out comes Maron, after a 13-mile hike with a super strange story about finding 'a man hung in a tree' that Pete said had to be Frank Arnold, even though Maron knew it wasn't. All this circumstantial evidence points to Pete wanting Maron to find this camp first — and look no further.

(4) Why did Pete encourage Maron to look along the Chewack River where a lot of people had already looked? It is said they discussed the supposedly unknown camp there on Horseshoe Creek. Pete said later he "felt there could be a camp in the area that nobody knew about." But the facts were, that there was a trail that went right to it, up the east side of Horseshoe Creek, the trail Dutch Wasifurth and Carl Gibbons followed easily into his camp.

Foul Play on Horseshoe Creek

(5) Later in life, Pete told a different story of the route into Horseshoe Creek as Bob Curtis related. Pete told the same basic story of the hanging man, but said that he took Maron up to Long Swamp from Loomis (the east side of the mountains), and there let him off, then left Long Swamp and went back down the mountain to town, leaving Maron in the hills. Of course, this isn't the way it happened, for Pete didn't even live in the town of Loomis anymore, in 1936 when Maron found Arnold; he lived in Okanogan, Washington, 45 miles away. As he changed his story, he told of Maron finding Arnold, and then turning around, and coming back out east to Long Swamp, where Loy McDaniel just happened to pick him up in the mountains, on the Toats Coulee Road that same day he went in, and then came out. This was the story Pete told Bob Curtis, his last story, when he came back to Loomis for a visit, not long before he died.

But Loy McDaniel said he never picked Maron up on any road! Frank Maron's account counters this later story. Also countering Pete's story, is the story Pete told his own sons who said Maron and Pete went in by Thirty Mile on the Chewack River, and Maron came back out the same way he went in, with Pete waiting for him. So why would Pete tell such a different story latert? And, here is another question: Pete always said it was in the spring that Frank had been found, yet the paper stated that Frank was found in the fall. However, Pete's statements of finding Frank in the spring does indeed add support to George Miller's account of finding Frank in the spring shot in the head.

(6) Why did Pete not ask Shorty Fairbrother to go in and look for the lost trapper? If anybody was the man to find Frank, Shorty was the man. He knew most of Frank's layouts for they had trapped side by side for some 10 years, and Shorty absolutely knew of Frank's camp on Horseshoe Creek. For the facts are, he went through this camp in the fall of 1935 when he went looking for Frank on his own. He testified to this. Frank was not there in 1935! There was no body in the tree in 1935!

Shorty told Clyde Paul, years later, that he had been through Frank's camp on Horseshoe Creek, looking for him, and found, not Frank Arnold hanging, but three small lodge-pole pines pulled together and wired, making a sort of tepee. Again, this was summer or fall of 1935. It was years later, though, after that year of 1935, before Shorty was finally told where Arnold had been found. It turned out to be the very camp that he had searched. When Shorty heard that Frank Arnold had been found on Horseshoe Creek at that very camp where he remembered seeing three lodge-pole pines pulled together, he surmised that these had been used to hold up and hang Frank on.

Shorty moved to the west coast sometime after he quit trapping that last winter of 1935-1936 and didn't come back to the Oroville area until the late 1950's or early 1960's. Shorty left this curious question unanswered: Why was Frank "not there in 1935" and then "there in 1936." It must be remembered that Shorty was his own man, as was Frank Arnold. Shorty was not one who Frank looked up when he came to town, probably because he didn't drink. Shorty didn't look Frank up, per-se, when he went into the mountains. But Shorty did know Frank was missing, and he was checking that summer in 1935 to see if Frank was to be found adjacent to his old line. Shorty had left his western trap-line and moved further east. Being an honorable man, Shorty did not touch any of Frank's things in that Horseshoe camp, the things Pete, Maron, Deputy Art Mitchell, Dutch, and Carl Gibbons found the next year in this camp. For in Shorty's mind, Frank might come home to the Tungsten Mine. When George Miller and Pete, who were there even before Shorty Fairbrother, coming into the camp in the spring of 1935 and finding Frank shot, did they pass on the 30-30 Winchester rifle leaning against the tree in his camp? The one brought out by Art Mitchell? Did they pass on taking Frank's so-called backpack with the .22 Woodsman Colt automatic pistol in it. All this leads one to believe that most all of what was there in the fall of 1936 WAS PLANTED

Foul Play on Horseshoe Creek

THERE THAT SAME YEAR! Just as nothing was found by Emmet Smith in Frank's cabin that spring of 1935, but later the next year, in the summer of 1936, a good number of Frank's things were put back in the cabin. How could this have that happened? Somebody put a lot of Frank's things back in his cabin! Of course, Pete was always there and involved in these mysteries.

(7) Perhaps one of the most striking mystery of the whole crime, is how Pete knew for sure that Frank was gone in the early spring of 1935? In May of 1935, before the date his packer wanted to go in and see Frank Arnold on the 28th of that month, Pete said Fran was gone. Frank normally didn't come out until sometime in the spring. But Pete knew he was gone already before winter was over. It is true Frank did not come out that December, early winter of 1934/1935 like he normally did, but then there were other winters when he didn't come out and Pete didn't proclaim he "was gone," or that "he wasn't up there!" Pete did know that Frank had been over to the C.C.C. camp in Beaver meadows that winter. So, if Frank was alive that winter in Beaver Meadows, why wasn't he alive that next May? Keep in mind Pete knew Frank was gone in January, because he told the sheepherder Emmet Smith that Frank was missing as early as *JANUARY*. Emmet said that Pete said, "Arnold had failed to come to his place as scheduled in January." Meaning Pete's home place in Loomis. So according to this statement of Pete's, Frank was to meet Pete at his ranch in Loomis in January, but Frank didn't show. Of course, Pete did not tell Al Smith (or anyone else) about Frank standing him up on their January meeting, instead he told Al Smith yet another story.

(8) Who were the mysterious "snowshoers" that had told Pete, Frank was "gone" that winter? Who were they? Pete told his packer kid that some snowshoers had gone back to the Tungsten Mine and found that Frank was gone! Gone for good! This begs the question: Who were these *strange, unnamed snowshoers* that Pete knew personally and trusted

apparently? For they talked to him that winter, telling him Frank was gone." They knew for sure Frank was gone. And now Pete knew Frank was gone.

(9) How did these snowshoers know Frank Arnold was gone...gone for good? Did they wait around at the Tungsten Mine all winter for Frank to return?

(10) Why did Pete and George Miller not go right to the police when they had found Frank "shot in the head" that early spring — probably June 16, 1935 when Pete went in to do his mine assessment work? Why did they cover up a terrible death by gunshot?

(11) Why did Pete tell Emmet Smith that nobody had been back to the Tungsten Mine that spring, when he and George Miller had been? This is not only a lie, but it shows Pete putting on a very worried front about the missing Frank Arnold. George Miller "testified" to the fact that he and Pete both went into the mine that spring of 1935 to do Pete's assessment work. (And I suspect that the cabins were stripped of all goods, even at that time.}

(12) Why, when Emmet went back to the mine in late June of 1935, did he find the cabin completely cleaned out? What happened to all of Frank's many years of collected items? Frank had been there for 20 years. There could easily have been a 1,000 to 1,500 pounds worth of hardware, clothes, guns, ammunition, radios and parts, chemicals, cameras, development equipment, traps, cooking material, money and etc. Where did it go? Who could have taken so many things? Was it really Bud Shaffer who took it all? That along with Romie and Clent Hank's 225 pounds of traps as Lefty said? And if so, why would Bud take every scrap down to the bare floor? Would some half-crazed rogue trapper want trifle items like cameras and developing paraphernalia along with absolutely all of Frank's possessions? If so, the man now has over 1500 pounds of pilfered "stuff" on his back and on his sled. Giant packrats couldn't have done such a thorough job of cleaning out Frank's stuff

(though rats may have been involved). That period of 6 months, January to June 1935, was the only time open for the cabins to be stripped.

(13) Why were some of Frank Arnold's things back in his cabin a year later, in the early spring of 1936, when the miners came up to mine tungsten? The act of replacement would have to have been done in late 1935. Emmet's eyes weren't playing tricks on him. Who put Frank's many things back in the cabin? And where did they go in the first place? Somebody(s) did a lot of moving. The most logical person — in fact the only person — is the only man who was in there so much that year... **PETE!**

(14) How did Pete really end up with Frank's "good things?" (Because this is a mystery story, I have held back this important fact until now.) Pete had the good things that had belonged to Frank, like his cameras, development equipment, radio, a nice big black wood cargo chest, and a good number of pictures. Al Smith, Bob Curtis and Pete's sons testified to the fact that Pete had many of Frank's things.

Here is how Pete said he came by Frank Arnold's things. He found Frank's things in a cave just 100 feet or so above the Tungsten cabins. Why is it that he is the only one to report ever found this cave despite the fact that thousands of people have combed over that mountain, looking for firewood and tungsten ore, and more than one person has looked specifically for that mysterious lost cave. There was never an ore body up above the cabins in the first place. Pete said he found the items in 1937, two and a half years after Frank went missing. Given the nature of that mountain side, and a climate with some 30 inches of rain, wouldn't a camera, development equipment, pictures, gun, and a nice clean cargo chest, be rusted up and all but destroyed in a damp cave two and a half years after Frank's death? The fact is, there is a lot of moisture on that mountainside above the cabins. But the camera and valuables that Pete had were in excellent condition and were for many years thereafter. Did he really find Frank's things in an unfindable lost cave, as he said, or did he take Frank's belongings that winter of 1934/1935, or in early June of 1935, when he and George Miller went in there to do assessment work? Is it possible that he, Lefty and Iron were the *"mysterious snowshoers"* who went into the Tungsten Mine that winter and knew for sure that Frank was gone?

(15) Pete knew Fran was from New Brunswick, Canada. Did Pete find something in Frank's possessions that would have told him that Frank was from New Brunswick? Because Frank Arnold sure would not have told him that! Where he was from was one of the curious mysteries about Frank. For years, people in the small town of Loomis wondered where Frank Arnold had come from, and up till this book, still did.

(16) Why did Pete always say Frank was short on food that year, when he knew that both his packer and Clarence Landergreen helped him get in plenty, by Frank's standards, of food that winter.

(17) Was it really just a coincidence that the C.C.C. or Forest Service, with Pete and Lefty as the main crew members (Iron had bought his restaurant), were building a new trail up Horseshoe Creek, not a stone's throw from where Frank Arnold was found hung? Lefty, in a round-about way, admitted he had been to the hanging site by telling his own story of finding Frank Arnold hung.

(18) How could Frank Arnold have been only a sack of bones, like both Pete and Frank Maron said? Even Dutch Washifurth's two marten hides that he found in Frank's camp two months later, were in "good shape!" They both were dead supposedly for the same amount of time, yet the skinned marten had fur and hide. Frank, on the other hand, did not have any skin or hide at all. None! Would Frank Arnold really have been just a sack of dry bones with no other bodily material, while his cotton clothes were still strong and sound and in place? Logic tells us this was all a stage-show.

(19) Why did Pete take Art Mitchell, the Deputy Sheriff, up to Frank's camp in the black of night? It was another coincidence that Art

was newly recruited to the force, and Pete was able to convince him to bury the body that same night.

(20) The T-1 that was written in the notebook found on the body was in fact, an old Forest Service fire number. Was S-C a Forest Service number too? What was Frank doing with a Forest Service fire number in his notebook with the date of January 1935, in it? Frank was not known to keep a diary. He did not keep notes of any of his activities. This notebook points again to the site being stage and the notebook planted by somebody like Pete. Pete was the one who worked for the Forest Service and C.C.C. and had to keep notes.

(21) Which body is the true body of Frank Arnold? George Miller and Pete buried a Frank Arnold in the spring, June of 1935. Pete went back to Horseshoe Creek with the Deputy Sheriff in September 1936 and buried another body that was just bones, and a skull with teeth. Are two bodies buried up there? Keep in mind that there was no body in the tree when Shorty Faribrother's went through the camp in 1935.

22. Who put the bullet in poor Frank Arnold's head? This big question refers back to George Miller's account that Frank had been shot in the head when Pete and he found Frank in June of 1935 and buried him "down by the creek...in the soft-enough dirt." Someone had put a bullet in Frank's head.

(23) Perhaps the strangest question of all is "Where did the second body, the one that Maron found, the hanging one with the teeth come from? Who was it? Was coming up with a replacement skeleton a problem for Pete?

(24) This question involves the details of what was found on Horseshoe Creek at the grave site, as told mainly by Pete, and a little by Frank Maron and Art Mitchell. Frank was found hanging one 5- to 7-gallon pot and one block of wood high. If Frank had set up this pot and a block of wood in mid-winter, with say 2 to 4 feet of snow on the ground as was usual for winter conditions in the area, then Frank should

have been at least 4 ½ feet, and as much as 6 feet off the ground when he was found. But when found, Frank's feet couldn't have been over 3 feet off the ground and probably no more than 1 or 2 feet as implied by Maron using a stick to lift up the mask so he wouldn't have to touch a long dead corpse. After lifting the mask up, he could plainly see teeth. Carl Gibbons said the rope wasn't tied very high, only about 7 feet up where he and Dutch cut it off. This short distance off the ground indicates a hanging, not in mid-winter, when Frank was killed, but a hanging in say, the month of September!

More Non-Logical Events

Another thing that is not logical about Pete and Maron's account of the scene of Frank's death is the fact that the small bank that Frank supposedly jumped off of would not really be a good enough bank under the leveling effect of 3 feet of snow. If this 3-foot rise is added to the height of the big pot and the block of wood, Frank is hanging even higher up than he was found. The fact that there were no snowshoes found at the site and the corpse had on short, open-top rubber boots also indicates there was no snow on the ground when he died.

As everyone said and all pictures of him show, Frank never wore a stocking cap, though Lefty did. Maron knew this too. The stocking cap was further proof to him, that the man in the tree was not Frank Arnold. Frank religiously wore his city hat like a priest with his beads. Frank sure never wore the full-sleeved coveralls that the hanging man was said to have had on either. Frank wore bib-coveralls, even in New Brunswick, where he probably was a farmer. Frank either wore a wool mackinaw shirt with wool button pants and suspenders, or bibs. One version of the hanging from Pete put it like this: "his clothes were all sewed together like a big bag." Pete contradicted himself when he told his packer, Al Smith, what Frank had on when he found him. He told Al that Frank was wearing some clothes he had given him himself that

Foul Play on Horseshoe Creek

fall. They consisted of a wool shirt and a pair of wool button pants. Pete did not tell his packer that Frank wore full-suit coveralls because the packer knew Frank too well and would have known that he never would have worn those full-suit coveralls.

That brings up the question, "Who sewed the clothes together?" How could Frank have hung there until his bones rattled in the wind without his coveralls rotting away too? For all that was misplaced was a leg bone with its boot, showing the bones were indeed dry. Could Frank really have hung there for 21 months, half of which are cold, freezing winter months, and rotted away to absolutely nothing but dry bones but his clothing remain intact? Where did all the skin, cartilage, muscle and inside organs go? If he was really hanging there for that long of time, why didn't foxes, coyotes, marten, weasels, bears and birds tear up the body and the clothes? Magpies and crows are always the first to exploit and shred a dead carcass that smells of blood. They find these dead carcasses amazingly quickly. The lack of damage caused by predators points to the conclusion that the bones were already "dry" when they were sewn into the coveralls.

We cannot forget about the bizarre way the mask, gloves, and boots were tied on. They were tied with a light rope that, like the coveralls, should not have lasted any longer than the body. Both Maron and Pete said that the mask, gloves and boots were also sown on, though one said that they were also wired together. Paradoxically, the stocking cap was tied down around the neck and knotted in the back. How could Frank tie on the gloves and rubber boots so tight that they were still on the body after it had turned to dust and bones 21 months later? Without muscle and sinew, could the body have hung by just a neck bone for all that time swinging in the wind? It was nothing but bones when Frank Maron first found him and lifted up the stocking cap and the mustache fluttered out. When he came back a week or so later with Pete and Art

Mitchell, he said how the bones, lose as they were, rattled in the wind as the body swung back and forth, calling out its morbid death-rattle.

Guilty

If the circumstantial evidence presented so far makes Pete look bad, it should. There is more. Maron was befuddled from looking at a mouth with teeth when he pulled up the stocking face mask on the hanging man. When the body was exhumed, ten teeth were found, all in the front. Frank Arnold did not have teeth. The man found on Horseshoe Creek had a mouth full of good teeth. Frank Maron had every right to be perplexed. The man hanging on Horseshoe Creek was not Frank Arnold! (Though in this book, and probably for a long time to come, he will be called Frank Arnold.)

What was found in the exhumed grave of the poor man on Horseshoe Creek? First, a body was found buried about 16 to 20 inches deep, and all the small bones of the body were gone. Only ten bones, counting the skull were there, and they were badly decomposed. Two rubber boots about 8 inches high, and around a size 10 were found, plus a pair of plastic-rubber type rimmed sunglasses, metal buttons, two jack knives, a nice silver pocket watch, and a small purse, which was well deteriorated. But surprisingly, most of the contents were in good condition. In the purse was about $2.50 worth of silver coins, with no coin dating later than 1927. The purse contained a small magnifying glass the size of a nickel with a brass rim. There was what looked like an old recipe on paper that was all but gone. Possibly, the most interesting of the finds was a receipt from "Prince's Grocery Store." It measured, when new, around 4 by 7 inches, but only about half or less was there. What was there could still be read. It listed about twelve items of supplies, which were mostly, if not all, large quantities of groceries: 10 pounds of coffee, 20 pounds of flour, 20 pounds sugar, and the like. Interesting, too, The receipt had a name that looked like "FRANK" written in where it said purchaser.

Foul Play on Horseshoe Creek

How the Deputy Sheriff missed this stuff is understandable seeing that it was all done very late at night... and Art Mitchell was green to law enforcement and was shook up at being out of his element at a strange hanging man's death site. Inexperience, darkness, a powerful personality covering things up led to what can only be surmised as "skull-drudgery" and "murder" on Horseshoe Creek!

If a crime went unnoticed, it wasn't because of a lack of evidence, for up on that creek bank, Pete came up with Frank Arnold's old "Trapper-Nelson" knap-sack (the "pack" for all mountain men pre-1950's), his faithful pack that had seen so many thousands of miles of wilderness travel. But it was Pete's description of what was found in Frank's pack that is the clincher. It is what I can only believe is the "smoking-gun," the toe trap that caught the trapper," and the sad revelation of who really killed the lone trapper. In the Trapper-Nelson pack was some of the same kind of rope that was used to tie on the gloves, boots and mask. The pack contained a small bottle or two of medicine (kind unknown), two jack knives were in the pack, a bag or two of tea, some salt and pepper, sugar, one or two candles with matches, and a gun, the .22 Colt, Woodsman Automatic. The gun was well-oiled and clean. It was tucked in a wool, oily sock. There was a shell in the chamber, maybe live, or maybe spent, and a full bullet clip in the gun. There might have been an extra full shell clip, too, in the pack, along with some loose .22 shells. The contents of this pack was Pete's undoing. Just what kind of medicine it was never known. The two jack-knives make sense, but the tea doesn't fit Frank Arnold. Even though he was called an Englishman, and a teapot was found at the grave site, Frank was not a tea drinker. Frank packed in a lot of coffee in the fall, and it was one of the things his packer remembered well about his old friend. When asked about Frank drinking tea, he said, "It wasn't Frank that drank tea, but Pete." Yes, Pete and his family drank tea, not Frank Arnold. Others also remembered Frank drinking lots of coffee, such as Bob at the Curtis home. The salt and pepper, sugar, and the candles would be something Frank would use, but the GUN, the gun was Pete's undoing. Frank was never known to use a .22 auto of any kind, let alone a .22 Woodsman Colt Automatic. The last fall in 1934 when Frank was packed into the mine, when he shot the small deer that fall, he used his .22 *long barreled REVOLVER!* There is a big difference between a .22 automatic, which are normal size pistols with about a 5-inch barrel, and a "Butt-line," long-barrel revolver, where the bullet cylinder spins and the pistol barrel is 12 inches or a little longer. His long-barreled pistol was as famous as he was. Frank did not use a .22 Woodsman automatic, but Pete did. Before Frank Arnold was found dead on Horseshoe Creek in 1936, Pete's packer Al Smith, remembers Pete having a .22 Colt, Woodsman Automatic before Frank Arnold was found hung

    Al as a young man stayed with Pete for a number of years before Frank was found dead. His mother was the family's cook and housekeeper. He saw and handled the gun, and actually shot it somewhere around Pete's home on one of those years in the early 1930's. Al knew the gun very personally, a little too well, as anyone who owns one of these guns can warn you. The sliding block, firing, and ejecting mechanism is thrown back by the gasses of the explosion of the bullet and flies back in the blink of an eye and takes a patch of skin off your thumb knuckle if you don't know what you're doing. Al found out the hard way that your thumb to be safe has to be in its proper place on the handle. Al knew that gun all too well. He had a scab on his thumb for a few days to prove it. Al lost his home when Pete moved to Okanogan later in 1935 or early 1936. But knew Pete owned the gun before Frank's death. It was his own gun that Pete talked Art Mitchell into letting him keep. That gun stayed in the family for years after Frank's death as a novelty. Bob Curtis testified to seeing the gun in later years himself, calling it "Frank Arnold's .22 Woodsman Automatic" that Pete proudly showed off to him as being Frank's gun. Pete didn't even lose his gun in the ordeal of what looks like nothing but a dirty killing from all angles! Frank's real pistol, his "butt line" seven-shot .22 has never been accounted for.

When word got out to Al Smith that Frank Maron had found Frank Arnold that September, Al was with Roy Beeman and running a remount station up Black Canyon. Hearing the news, he wanted to go right in, right then, at that time, and bring Frank out, which was the natural thing anyone would have wanted to do, but not Pete. Al wanted to go in and get his friend right then, but who stopped him? Pete! Pete insisted that he had better do it. He took care of Frank Arnold's body a week later!

The Time of Frank's Death

Now we should cover at this stage the most probable time of Frank's death. It could have been in January, as the notebook found on Frank indicated, but the mitigating circumstances seem to place his death a little earlier than that date. Of course, at this time and place, to argue for a "time of death" the reader has to have reached a "probable cause" of death. This presentation works off the assumption that George Miller's account of riding in that spring of 1935 when Frank was found "shot in the head" is the one true account. The fact that he did not come out that year "in early winter," when for years before the 1929 forest fire, Frank did come out before Christmas to sell a few of his furs and buy a big turkey for Shorty and himself for a Christmas dinner. Even though after the 1929 fire, "Shorty" Lester Fairbrother probably moved too far west to come back as far as the Horseshoe Basin for Christmas, and Frank moved too far south, east, or north to find his furs, still, out of habit, and maybe by arrangement, he and Shorty might still have met up on one of those years for a winter Christmas dinner. Remember, that the first 2 years after the smoke had cleared, Frank E. Maron was trapping with Frank Arnold. Maron never mentioned Lester Fairbrother meeting up with them at all (though this doesn't mean much).

Grace Eastman, a friend of Frank Arnold said, "He usually came out the 40 miles during the early winter and took in more food after catching some fur bearing animals…." It seems that he kept this tradition up, coming out before Christmas, even after the fire, probably celebrating with Frank Maron after Shorty moved east. Frank came out late in the fall of 1934 to have his teeth pulled as Bob Curtis said, probably late October or early November, making Frank alive and well at that time. Then he had his picture taken in Beaver Meadows. From the picture scene, it looks like there was about a foot or two of snow on the ground. Winter sports enthusiast will tell you this places the date of the photo at least into the end of December. Finally, Frank was found dead on Horseshoe Creek in June of 1935 by George Miller.

On top of that, we have Pete knowing Frank was dead in May of 1935 a month earlier. He might have known even sooner than that date, seeing that "snowshoers" knew Frank Arnold was gone, (dead) that winter, which all shows that Frank had come back to his home grounds on the Chewack River before he was killed. Sometime after "later December," but before the month of May 1935.

Now if we believe the notebook found in the hanging man's pocket or pack, assuming it was Arnold that wrote it (which I cannot do), then Frank was still alive in January of 1935, and had no intention of coming out that early winter. For he was out, so to speak, by being 40 miles away in the company of the men at the C.C.C. camp. And if this was the way it went, then he fell on hard times sometime after he had his picture taken at Beaver Meadows, but it seems very unlikely to me that Frank stayed very long at the C.C.C. camp. At 65 years of age, he wasn't working on that job unless he was a cook. But this too is highly unlikely because he was in Loomis that late fall, early winter of 1934. Also, nobody figured him as being there, namely George Honey, Harold MacWilliams, or even Pete, Iron, or Lefty, which means he just slipped

Foul Play on Horseshoe Creek

in for a day or two, picked up a free meal, and then slipped back out, following his trap-lines that far south.

As said, I believes only George Miller's story is solid, and being George found frank 'shot in the head,' on or about the 16th of June. At that time, Frank;s body, though dead, was "in good shape." Some may take this, along with other parts of Pete's story, to say that Frank may not have been dead for very long. That is, if a person were to combine parts of George's story with parts of Pete's story. For it would seem that he could not have laid out there all winter in the snow without ravens or other scavengers, like weasels, foxes, coyotes or martens finding him. But, it is the ravens that always find death first. On the other hand, if Frank wasn't exposed, either by his being in his bedding, covered with canvas, in his lean-to, or even covered with deep snow, the body would have been preserved. His good condition as George and Pete found him; though his death may have been in mid-winter, is not overly surprising; but an important fact.

To be remembered also is that his Horseshoe camp sets in a very tight draw, with seep sides going into 7,000-foot mountains, giving little sun until the day was well along, and then for not many hours. This would help explain the ravens not finding a frozen body. As for the martins, foxes, bears and such, Frank probably had them trapped out on this stretch of the river. Remember that Dutches' two marten hides were not picked over or hauled off by scavengers, either, making the evidence suggest that they were indeed there at the camp for the full 22 months. (These 22 months though would be called into question if it was all a September "setup.")

So, could Frank have died that early spring of 1935, at a time with little or no snow? Perhaps. The later date of death relies pretty much on Frank's good condition when George found him. For the situation of the hanging body the next year, when Maron found a body, cannot be applied to George Millers find. The same is true for other facts and stories, like Pete saying that Frank had missed a meeting with him in January. If Frank was found in "good condition" with a bullet-hole in his head, and un-frozen in the month of June, then a death of only a few days or weeks before is in the realm of possibilities, being that snow lays heavy well into May along the Chewack River.

However, if he was just shot that spring at such a late date, before May, this would not have left enough time for the Tungsten cabins to be searched and emptied and the raider(s) time to figure out what to do next — that is to cover their tracks. For it sure wasn't Bud Shaffer that took all of Frank's things down to the bare floor. For the raider(s) trail of footprints would have been clearly seen by George in the mud, dirt and snow over the 15 miles he traveled up to the mine and at the mine. Such activity would have been hard to hide. And George if he had seen evidence of all that activity that early spring by the raider(s), would have wondered even more than he did about this mysterious case he found himself mixed-up in. Of course, if George had seen any signs and tracks, Pete could have told him about Bud Shaffer just being in there that very spring, "raising hell." For again, George Miller was thoroughly convinced it was Bud Shaffer's "dirty-work" that winter based on the testament of three witnesses. And for what it's worth, Lefty did say that Shaffer had stayed late, into early spring, running out of snow at Thirty Mile Station and leaving his sled and traps there. It would have been the case in the month of April. But George saw no other tracks that spring when he visited the Tungsten mine, or it would have been heavy on his mind. So, though it is possible Frank could have been killed that spring of 1935 in April or earlier, the idea of a spring killing does not fit all of the known facts and testimonies in my opinion. It should also be remembered that spring travel on snowshoes in March through May when the snow is melting is by no-means easy travel. The traveler is often forced to travel at night when the snow is again frozen over and crusted and not wet, soft and heavy.

Foul Play on Horseshoe Creek

So there is a very high probability, as I see it, that Frank was frozen on the ground for six months, fitting in with Pete telling Al Smith that "snowshoers" had gone into the Tungsten, and they knew Frank was gone that very winter. Add this Pete's statement to Emmet Smith that Frank had missed a meeting with him in January, makes it an easy assumption that Pete knew Frank was "DEAD" those cold winter months of 1934/1935 when he didn't come out. That said, a date of death in late December, or early January is the best guess and conclusion.

Time, has not changed the fact that the loose ends of the rope have always pointed to Pete. For his involvement in the whole affair was far too deep, and far from smooth, though he tried hard to make it smooth. Back in the crowd of people from Loomis and the Methow there were those who pointed their finger at him as a probable killer of Frank Arnold. This may have contributed to his moving out of town in 1935, and out of the state in 1940. Tom Bean and Bill Briley were two who suspected his involvement from the first. Hans Richter was another and said out right, "...Pete probably killed Frank Arnold!"

The subject of Pete killing Frank was talked about by more than one person back at that time, and still is today. The old Forest Service hand, Ted Bolin, told me that it was rumored that Pete could have done it. Bill Briley an old timer from Nighthawk, was quoted as saying; "He sure could have!" when Tom Bean, a bit of a mountain man himself, said to Bill; "Pete probably killed Frank Arnold."

Pete had the personality to be a killer, though many thought he was a nice man. Pete had a bad problem! Dick Loudon said of the man: "Pete could be the nicest man in the world, but when he *drank*, he would get so mean he could kill!" Pete's inner dark personality goes along with the twisted, bizarre, strange, and mysterious death of our man, Frank Arnold. In fact, Pete has more deaths to answer for than that of just Frank Arnold. Was this man a cold-blooded killer?

Harry Forde was found shot on Pete's very property. Did Harry Forde, a relative of Pete's, really "shoot himself" to death on Pete's ranch, or did Pete help him with the gun? George Bowers was an old miner and trapper who had a mountain lake named after him on Chapaka Mountain where he lived for years and years. Did George Bowers, whom Pete befriended, as he did Frank Arnold, really hang himself, in Pete's barn? Or did he get too close to Pete and was given a hand with the rope? (This most likely was Pete's first hanging. Frank Arnold was his second.) Another trapper, George Dunkin, who lived on the North Fork of the Toats Coulee went missing in 1928 after selling his furs and cashing his big check in Loomis. The 50-year-old man was never seen or found after that. Was Pete around? This George Dunkin also lived year around in the mountains far up the North-fork of the Toats Coulee, his cabin is believed to be just east of "cow-camp," between Good-enough Mountain and Snowshoe Mountain, on Olive Creek, at one time a very large and nice cabin.

There was also a sad event that happened in the town of Loomis? In 1940, about the time Pete left the state, an older woman relative of Pete's was also found "HUNG" also! This poor lady was found hanging by her neck from the "bathroom door hinge." She was hung with a small, light, electrical cord around her neck. The poor woman hung there just 2 inches off the bathroom floor! She "hung herself because she wanted to," they said. Another suicide that happened when Pete wasn't very far away! A third hanging to ask him about. Can these other five deaths be explained away as "coincidences" and "suicides" (forgetting that four of them involved close association with Pete)? Can they be passed off? Frank Arnold cannot be passed off! Pete could not have acted alone this time though. Frank, even at 65, was tough, quick, and cautious, and Pete knew this. One man coming into Frank's camp alone would have only a small chance of gaining the upper hand on the wiry old trapper, who had senses like the animals he caught. For like Bob Curtis said,

Foul Play on Horseshoe Creek

"No one man coming into Frank's camp alone (thinking of Bud Shaffer) was going to get the jump on Frank Arnold." And, Bob was so right in concluding this about his lost hero. But friends, on the other hand, are supposed to be friends so your guard might be down.

How Frank's Death Came About

Pete went up the Chewack River that winter of 1934 from the Methow Valley, with his two "snowshoe-in' side-kicks." They had some time off from their C.C.C. job that winter of 1934/1935. They could have, and probably did make arrangements with Frank up at the C.C.C. camp, to meet him a little later, in a few days, at his Horseshoe Creek camp, just before, or during the holidays, Christmas, most likely, or New Year's Day. It was holiday time when all the men at the camp were probably given 2 weeks off. Frank had tramped into Beaver Meadows on his snowshoes, so they had just talked to him. It was there in their friendly government gathering that they made arrangements to bring him in some food, check their own trap-lines, and say a holiday hello. However, these men had other motives in mind. For on that neighborly trip in to say "Hello," in their coat pockets bounced a couple bottles of booze. Pete knowing too well what Frank's one weakness was. Two bottles of booze along with two scummy scalawags should be enough to get the old man's tongue working right, and his old feeble mind around to Pete's way of thinking, Pete needed this man of the woods to talk. He needed two questions answered:

"Where did you get your gold at, Frank old buddy?... The stuff Maron seen?"

"Where is your puke at, the one that's full of 25 years of trapping money... old man? We know you have been making a killing on martens up here for way too many years, ya-old-buzzard... You should have enough "green-backs" and "bat-wings" by now to share with US!"

To share with us? Did he mean Lefty and Iron? Why can't they get it straight? Why so many wild, twisted and changed stories? More questions:

1. Was it just another coincidence that Lefty was working with Pete on that *same trail*, at that *same time*; at that *same place*, when Frank Arnold was found hung just a Sabbath walk away? Just another coincidence, one of dozens?

2. Why couldn't Lefty or Pete remember it was in September of 1936 that they found Frank Arnold? They were both working on the Horseshoe Creek trail on that very date, and it was the same year the miners were in there. They just couldn't remember that year 1936, though. The two, for some dark reason, gave every other date but the right one.

3. Why did Lefty also tell so many conflicting stories (some of them "cock-and-bull" to be sure) through the years about he himself finding Frank Arnold? Lefty wasn't even there with Art Mitchell the Deputy and Maron and Pete. He couldn't hold back from telling a story about himself finding Frank Arnold. So how probable is it that he and Pete "set-up" the whole scene that fall, on government time, the staged hanging there on Horseshoe Creek for Art Mitchell and Frank E. Maron to find? All the while under the deception of working on a trail for the Forest Service? If true, then Lefty was there as he testified and getting paid for it by the government at the same time.

4. And why the wild lie: Who was this unknown "*prospector*" Lefty told me had found Frank Arnold? It wasn't Frank Maron. He said he knew that for sure. How did he know the prospector wasn't Frank Maron? And, why is he the only one exclusively who has this story about a wandering prospector who found Frank Arnold? Perhaps, this was just one more of Lefty's diversions and covering stories.

5. Why did Lefty tell me over the phone that he had "seen Frank Arnold" that winter he died? He claimed that Frank "looked awful rough." Then, later, he denied telling me this, in another personal, face-to-face interview at his home. Over the phone testifying that he was the last one to see Frank alive (with the exception of possibly Bud Shaffer if you believe that story).
6. Why did Lefty tell me over the phone that he had seen Bud Shaffer that winter, but denied that later, too, in our home interview?
7. Why did he tell me over the phone that he "...went up a switchback... looked back into the creek... and saw Frank Arnold hanging in the tree?" You can't do this because you can't see Frank's camp from any switchback on that trail. But he changed that version, too. More lies and stories.
8. Why would Lefty say Iron had seen the rogue trapper on Fox Creek, and spoke to the man even? Iron never mentioned such a thing when he told his "Bud Shaffer" story. Why would Iron have omitted such an important meeting with Bud Shaffer, not even mentioning he had seen him or talked to him like Lefty said he did?
9. Iron said Ben Prince, the grocery store owner of Oroville, dealt with the rogue trapper and bought his furs that were stolen from Frank Arnold. Yet both Ben and Louie Prince said they had never even heard of this story of a "Bud Shaffer with the Frank Arnold furs" when asked by Bob Curtis, a few years later. Ben Prince also never mentioned the tale to Bruce Jr. McPherson, who was a friend of his, and had talked more than once to Ben about the Tungsten Mine. Ben "in-no-way" collaborated Iron's story. So why did Iron concoct such a wild story out of his own imagination? There is only one true answer — to throw the blame — and cover himself for a dastardly crime committed.

10. Why would Lefty appear to lie about so many big things, like when he said that he had never seen Frank Arnold in his life. And yet, a surviving picture shows the two together at Beaver Meadows and Lefty wearing a stocking cap proves the contrary. Lefty and Iron were the closest of friends for all those years, living next to each other and working together just about every year, and yet Lefty claims he never ever saw Frank Arnold, and, contrarily, Iron knew him well. One old timer said Iron and Lefty even took Frank Arnold in some food for one or two of those winters. Lefty did say over the phone he had indeed seen Arnold that last year and said he had been to the Tungsten Mine too. The old timers who knew them, if asked if Lefty had ever met or seen, or knew Frank Arnold would say the answer would always be yes.

11. Again I ask, "who were the "snowshoeres" (plural) Pete was friends with, who had snowshoed into the Tungstne Mine that winter of 1934-1935 and knew Frank Arnold wasn't coming back?' EVER! Could it have been his close buddies Lefty *and* Iron? Pete and those snowshoers knew Frank Arnold was gone for good — as in cold DEAD!

12. Lefty said that Bud Shaffer's sled was left in the "garage" at Thirty Mile Ranger Station holding Romie Johnson's and Clent Hank's traps. However, Iron never mentioned this. Instead, Iron was more interested in telling why they figured the sled had been left at "Sled Camp," a camp just off the Chewack drive-way trail. ("Sled Camp" being so named because of the sled being left right there, 3 miles upriver from the Thirty Mile Ranger Station Garage. It was always some 3 miles up from the Ranger Station, because the miners of 1936 rode by it every other day, with George Honey stopping to look at the belting.

13. Now Lefty and Iron, answer this: "How did Romie's and Clent Hank's traps get left on Shorty Fairbrother's Sled anyway? The sled at "Sled-Camp" was left by the trapper, Shorty Lester Fairbrother, not Bud Shaffer. Shorty told Bob Curtis he left it (the sled) at the bottom of the Chewack dirve-way his last year trapping, 1935/1936 with his trapping partner Bill Higginbotham. Shorty said he left his traps in the mountains, too, probably on the sled. The sled that was never at the Thirty Mile Ranger Station was Shorty Fairbrother's sled. It did not belong to the phantom, renegade, rogue-trapper, Bud Shaffer, blowing Left and Iron's whole story to pieces!

14. Backing up, if this Bud Shaffer story could somehow be true, just why didn't Shorty Fairbrother himself run into him over on the Pasayten River? Shorty was right in the middle of where Shaffer was supposedly trapping. And it's no doubt that Lefty and Iron wondered at whose snowshoe tracks they saw from time to time east of their area. For 5 years, 1930-1935, Shorty trapped Island Mountain, the East Fork of the Pasayten River and along the Canadian border. Again, right in the middle of where Bud Shaffer was said to have tromped on his "bear-paw" snowshoes. But Shorty, by being in those mountains east of Lefty and Iron's lines, was almost surely the "inspiration" for the convoluted rogue-trapper story.

15. Why is it that every place Pete, Lefty and Iron crossed, coincidentally had also been crossed by Bud Shaffer? Bud Shaffer happily left his name on signposts all over that country. Was Shaffer really so dumb as to have written his name at every place he ravaged, pillaged, and killed? Or could his name have just been planted in these places by Frank's real killers, who just happen to be in the same areas working for the Forest Service?

16. Lefty: How could anyone come "busting down off Black Lake Ridge" when it is a solid cliff wall for miles, miles before and after the Fox Creek trail? Did he fly down? (Rolling down like a snowball might work.)

17. Lefty: How did Bud Shaffer pack on his back 225 pounds of traps, or pull (after he somehow made a sled at Romie and Clent's cabin) a sled with "bear-paw" snowshoes on? How did he even cross the Pasayten with "bear-paws" on? Bear-paw snowshoes are commonly the smallest kind made. They are not designed to be used in deep powder, mid-winter snows, and will drag the trapper down in a matter of hours in 4 to 6 feet of snow, which is what the high mountains of the Pasayten get. If Shaffer was wearing "bearpaws," he could not have crossed the Pasayten even if he wanted to. This is a fact, just find an old trapper and ask him. Harold MacWilliams told the story of almost dying of fatigue by trying to cover just 12 miles of the Pasayten in bear-paw snowshoes. It was one of the most exhausting things he had ever done.

18. How did this rogue trapper know where he was going? Did he have a map that showed Romie's and Clent's cabin, the Tungsten Mine, the Fox Creek trail, two or three look-outs that are on the very tops of two or three, very high mountains, Peepsight Lake, Pasayten River, Robinson Creek cabins, and Frank's Horseshoe Creek camp, all under 4 feet and more of snow? As the story goes: Bud Shaffer is traveling in mid-winter, with bear-paw snowshoes on, in the middle of a vast wilderness, with all the trails covered with snow, all area trappers working on a C.C.C job, all but Frank Arnold and Shorty Fairbrother. How did Bud Shaffer know where to go? It is hard to keep track of where to go in the summertime up there, even with all the trails marked and cut-out. It certainly appears that the rogue trapper was not

Foul Play on Horseshoe Creek

named Bud Shaffer at all, but persons who indeed knew the area well. Because no man, let alone a stranger to the country, would take off across a mountainous wilderness with no map, without the proper snowshoes on, and a sled load of provisions. Bud Shaffer had none of these provisions.

19. How did Iron end up with many of Frank Arnold's pictures in later years? He had to have gotten them before the spring of 1936 when the miners came in and threw what was left of Frank's things out. Iron told Clyde Paul he had a good number of Frank's pictures. When did he get them? For Iron bought a restaurant in town in 1935 and did not go back to trapping until 1939/1940.

20. Why and when did Iron write the two different dates of Frank's death on the Tungsten Mine walls, and both of them were the wrong dates according to Art Mitchell's newspaper report. This proves that Iron had visited the Tungsten Mine after Frank Arnold was found. And if Iron was there, Lefty was there!

21. Why, like Pete, was Iron so concerned about Frank Arnold that he wanted to make sure that Frank's grave site was not misplaced? He marked the grave under the tree with a big lid he toted all the way from the Tungsten Mine. He wrote the date of Frank's death on the lid and wired it to the grave in about 1950. I found, 35 years later, that his writings are no longer legible. Could Iron have been worried someone might find two graves and bodies up there, one with a bullet in its head without teeth? If true, and found, this would be our man, Arnold.

22. And the big question which basically proves Lefty and Iron's stories are all just a big cover-up and diversion is If Lefty and Iron were on the road/trail crew with the C.C.C along with Romie Johnson, Clent Hanks and Pete at Beaver Meadows, which they were that winter of 1934/1935, as George Honey

said, then how could they have been trapping on their trap-line, 35 miles away, at Black Lake that same year? Romie Johnson, Clent Hank, Lefty and Iron, weren't in the Pasayten trapping in 1934/1935, the year Frank died, because they were on the C.C.C. Beaver Meadows road job that winter. So was Pete! And neither they, nor Bud Shaffer would likely have trapped later on that year in the soft, wet, March through May snow, as Lefty said Bud Shaffer did, saying he came back through their lay-out later that year.

23. And why did a picture, showing plainly that Frank did not have teeth, strangely disappear after a visit by Lefty? This just after our interview about Frank. Della Northcott said Lefty had come by after I had been to her home, and looked at the very same photos, those that came from Iron. And Frank's no-teeth picture was gone after his visit.

24. And last but not least, How did Iron and Lefty get all their wealth and prosperity in 1935? Iron made enough money somehow to buy a restaurant and a car, as well as get married by 1938. And Lefty made enough for a good car and to court the prettiest girl in town; he was married in 1937. This was done in the greatest depression years the country had ever seen, and just after the worst forest fire in hundreds of years, a forest fire that devastated all their trapping grounds. Trapping was so bad in the Pasayten that the Game Department soon closed down marten trapping up there. But our boys had "money" when they should have been poor as hungry coyotes. Pete always did seem to have money, and one reason for it was he boot-legged up until 1933 when prohibition ended. But still, you would have thought he would be a little on the lean side that December of 1934, but Pete soon drove away in a new, bright red 1935 Dodge. You don't buy that on C.C.C. wages.

Foul Play on Horseshoe Creek

These are the cold hard facts and questions that surround Pete, Lefty, and Iron. Nobody wanted to, cared to, or took the time to gather up and bring these out to the public. There was indeed, "foul play" on Horseshoe Creek that winter of 1934/1935.

CHAPTER 24

Hopefully not the Closing Chapter on the Tungsten Mine

BRUCE MCPHERSON, AS A YOUNG 15-year-old teenager, had worked up there on Wolframite Mountain in 1936 with his father, " Mac." He could never quite get the high mountain mine out of his mind. Beginning in the 1950's, Bruce started watching the County Courthouse Record books to see if the mine would come open for claim staking. On chance, during a check in 1963, Bruce found the mine open after the claim changed hands about four times.

He brought in two friends from Seattle, Lee Brackett and Frank Monahan. He called on Hank Dammann, Jr., now a Winthrop packer, to take them into the mine on his horses to drive-in some claim stakes. Bruce and Hank Dammann were still friends from their happy days together back in 1936, when Mac (Sr.) and Harold Dardier worked up 30 tons of tailings with the help of Henry Dammann (Sr.). By the time they had ridden into the mine — "what the heck" — Hank was a fourth partner. The new claim was called the "Wolframite Mountain Mine," which consisted of only one claim by the time the city boys walked up and down the mountain a few times. Bruce McPherson and Hank Dammann held this one claim until the Forest Service got mean in 1988.

Loy McDaniel was still involved, too, and never gave up on the Tungsten Mine. He kept an interest and some claims until he died in the 1980's. Jim McDaniel, his son, then took them over. Jim held them until the big court fight between the Tungsten Mine claim holders and the Forest Service. These men spent thousands of dollars against the bulging, bottomless money pocket of the U.S. Forest Service, trying to hold on to a traditional freedom that three generations of his family had loved, enjoyed, and worked for, the free right to hold, live on and work a valid mining claim. By 1988, Jim held four claims, two on Apex Mountain and two on Wolframite. Though many claims had come and gone from 1951 through 1988, it seems that only five or so claims remained when the Forest Service struck. Private mining claims have always been a thorn in the side of the Forest Service. It is one of the last good outdoor freedoms still on the books for the American people. It is a wonderful law for the people and should be strongly upheld in the years to come, though this right is being cut to pieces.

The Forest Service, however, does not see it this way, and would like to do away with this basic freedom given to the American people. They would selfishly put everybody in their nice neat line and work the people like a bunch of sheep headed to the market. No black sheep and no personal freedoms, like a private mining claim, on "THEIR" land. This is the Forest Service's attitude toward the individual miner and claimholder. Just ask a miner or take the time to go through the Forest Service records.

To understand fully why the Forest Service dealt the way they did with the Tungsten Mine, the whole mining issue has to be looked at from the top down. It is true that the Forest Service, and other government agencies have a responsibility to protect the people's forested land, but

Hopefully not the Closing Chapter on the Tungsten Mine

are they really doing this? This land use issue has turned into a great big "strain-out-the-gnat, gulp down-the-camel" type scenario. A person is extremely hard-pressed to find just one place in the Forest Service controlled land, where the dirt has not been turned over by a logger.

Thousands of square miles of land are tromped on, dug up, beaten down, turned over and vegetation stripped. Wildlife has been killed off and chased off and their homes ruined. Complete ecosystems have been cut-up and destroyed by loggers. Millions of beautiful acres of virgin, timbered land have been turned ugly and de-timbered by this government agency called the Forest Service! They spend billions of dollars annually, pay for millions of man hours, and have built millions of miles of roads over every wilderness mountain to make logging possible. Now stop and think. Let Jim McDaniel, Bruce McPherson, or some other miner go up into the woods and try to move two shovels full of dirt on a piece of ground, where in the extreme likelihood, no more than an acre of mineable ore sits, and watch these selfish paper pushers start jumping. And, what's their reasoning for this involvement, and heavyhanded dealing, if asked? You guessed it. They say they are protecting the woods. Did you get that? "To protect the woods!" Of course, this is not true or logical. The main reason is money, something they don't get from a miner. There is also the human factors: greed, jobs, jealousy, and selfish government powerplays. Nobody wants to see another person find a rich mine and sit on their land while they try to do so, enjoying the chaste and rich beauty of the land in the process. This land use freedom is too much for the government, the Forest Service or the Bureau of Land Management. There is not private land on "their" land.

The list is long of the Forest Service's harassment of the small miner, and the Tungsten Mine is a gem of a case. What place is more loved by the people and its miners than the old cabins, workings, and nostalgic history of the Tungsten Mine? Yet the Forest Service would like to see it gone forever, wiped off the face of Wolframite Mountain, and the last miner run out of the country. This they have all but done, and the last axe is ready to fall. The Tungsten Mine at this writing sits on the edge of oblivion, teetering back and forth on the desk of the "Bull-of-the-Woods." It's a bit of a hot potato now that they have taken it away from the miners, for to burn it down, like they would like to do, or tear it down, which they have ideas of doing, is to cut the people who love the mine like an assassin with a knife. But to preserve it as it sits is to totally defeat their purpose of taking it away from the miners in the first place. Another ploy of theirs is to put a "No Trespassing" sign on a cabin, and then let the cabin fall by natural decay. Yet not one of the thousands of backpackers or horsemen who have ever seen this mine and enjoyed its place on the mountain, would see this as anything but another government crime.

It started long ago, of course. Herb Curtis fought with the Forest Service over where they should put in the road to the Tungsten Mine back in 1916-1920. It wasn't until the ecology movement of the 1970's, when many young people realized that "progress" was no longer "progress," but "destruction!" The Forest Service, though powerfully destructive in their own right (a million times more so than all the miners put together), realized that the small miner was not really needed anymore because all the easy ore had been taken by their forefathers, and only the big companies with their hundreds of thousands of dollars could realistically bring a mine into production. Therefore, the little guy was just a nuisance — a thorn — with rights above the norm, on "their" land! To them, he was just in the way of their master scheme of things — logging in the main, with some outdoor camping thrown in. Now it is true that for the most part, the small miner will have trouble bringing into production an ore body. Still, the little guy can find and sell these low/high grade surface ore bodies just about as well as the big mining companies can. In fact, the small miner is responsible for many large strikes.

Hopefully not the Closing Chapter on the Tungsten Mine

After a mining claim is filed, the law says that the land can not only be used for mining but ENJOYED! This one fact, the people's right to enjoy the land, under the covenants and laws of mining, the Forest Service has not been able to hold still for.

What was the reason why the Forest Service took the Tungsten Mine away from the miners? Was it being abused? No. What was it hurting? Nothing. But it was being visited and *enjoyed*. Yes! The claimholders were content to let the public use the cabins and ride across the property to "enjoy" the Tungsten Mine as the law specifically states. And, herein lies the meat of the problem. That is, as far as the Forest Service was concerned, the Tungsten Mine, being on a popular trail, was just too much of a "mecca," and they couldn't stand seeing the people enjoy this historical piece of land. It was a piece of land that they did not have control over. What the people or the miners were hurting on that few acres of ground is far from clear, but the Forest Service could not stand the cabins being used by the people. Their enjoyment of having a roof over their heads, and a panoramic view of Apex Mountain, with historical nostalgia thrown in at the same time, was just too much for the paper pushers down in town. So, they hatched their plan to pull the Tungsten Mine out from underneath the claimants.

The Forest Service was quite good at this by 1988, having vast experience in the right maneuvers to take, and buffalo a claim from a poor citizen. They have the procedure down to a science. It basically works like this: first they know that most claim holders do not know what their rights as miners are, and most town lawyers don't, either. Mining law is a vast field all its own and takes a specialized, experienced lawyer. The laws are easily understood though scattered out in many law books, badly misconstrued by the Forest Service, and often by the courts. Second, few claimholders are really full time miners, just claim holders. With this in mind, the Forest Service approaches the miner (by letter) and asks the claimholder if they can come in and "evaluate"

TALES OF THE TUNGSTEN MINE

his claim, come in, take some samples, look things over, and give them a finding. "Boy! This is probably a good idea," says the claim holder. A free "evaluation." He little dreams he has just fallen into a trap. In the Tungsten Mine case, the adits and veins have been evaluated many times in the past by honest and professional people in 1905, 1938, 1942, 1952, 1965, and a few times in between. Most all these reports were very favorable. But the Forest Service was not happy with these. They wanted to look again in 1988 with the absolute purpose (for they themselves have many reports on the mine) of squelching the claims of Bruce McPherson and Jim McDaniel. And herein is what can only be a "wrong" by the Forest Service:

(1) The "DESIRE" to take away a citizen's mining claim.

(2) The Forest Service does not come in and make a thorough "professional evaluation" like a good mining company would do. For one thing, they might find something good under that ground. For another, it would cost too much, to spend all that money on just a "little-ole" mining claim. They are just not going to do it in any thorough way. It would cost hundreds of thousands of dollars to do it right. The Forest Service isn't going to evaluate in a professional manner because they don't have to. For an easy "quicky" on-the-surface evaluation has worked well enough so far. Of course, once the citizen has allowed the Forest Service's Mining Engineer to set foot on his mining property and make his "evaluation," this educated man now has the clout and knowledge to prove the claim does not have the needed "valuable mineral discovery" that the law says the claim must have. The judge in that court room will rule against the claimholder every time. The exception would be if the assayer who evaluates the ore sample sends back a good value for the ore. That would make your mine a profitable operation.

In the Tungsten Mine's case, with the claim holders living miles away, and the diggings having been caved in, a quick, slip-shod evaluation of a few quartz rocks laying on the surface gave the Forest Service all the

Hopefully not the Closing Chapter on the Tungsten Mine

evidence they needed to disprove a "valuable mineral discovery." So, the judge ruled the claims invalid on the basis of the poor evaluation by the Forest Service. "They didn't even go into the mining shafts!" The miners of 1936 had lapped up every good surface rock for hundreds of feet in all direction, trying to make an easy buck.

So the Tungsten Mine was plotted against by the Forest Service, and not given a fair shake in that courtroom in 1988. The Tungsten Mine sits in the Wilderness Reserve, so no new claims can be filed, as planned by the Forest Service. At this writing, through perseverance and the great interest shown by the local Oroville horsemen and women, the Forest Service has bent "their rules" for the time-being and allowed the cabins to be used and maintained. Hopefully, this cooperation will continue....

So the far away mountain mine, the home of Frank Arnold with its exciting, interesting, sad, and wonderful history, the place where few can go and not get struck by its intriguing fever sits today, preserved by local Oroville horsemen and women.

That is the way it happened as brought down to me. May the enjoyment and freedoms not die because of a government agency and may the Tungsten Mine be preserved and protected for the people who enjoy the Pasayten Wilderness.

The End

G. A. Henderson

Summary

THE WRITER CAME INTO THIS story now, many years ago, with an open mind. What he knew about the history of the Tungsten Mine and the man called Frank Arnold you could put on the head of a pin. But like many others, he had ridden his horses, in this case, since the age of ten, to that far-away mine many times. In digging into this story, he really found out a little more than he wanted to know, as surely some of the readers will, too. However, there is also the feeling of satisfaction that a story has been told with very few loose ends. The Tungsten Mine history and the life of Frank Arnold are now told and preserved in these pages of history. Frank can now roll-over in peace and wait for a greater judge than the writer.

True, some may feel he has gone too far digging up the past and accusing Pete, Lefty and Iron of killing poor Frank. Yet how could he have done it any other way without also being guilty of covering up what he believes to be the brutal killing of a unique and interesting man? In the writers mind, it was *tell all or nothing*, and, at one time, after coming to the reality of what happened up on that creek bank, the pen did rest for a time. But the story of this place and man were much too important to let die in the fading shadow of time.

In analyzing Frank's death, you find:

Motive: A time honored motive, one there has always been: poor, wicked people wanting an easy target's money and rumored gold.

Scene: What better place to commit a crime? A place where the policeman never walks a beat and in a time when few men wandered its breadth.

Characters: You have men who were capable of such a deed. Pete, the man who could "get so mean he could kill," had already a history of involvement with more than one close "friend" who committed *suicide*. Two of them were hangings. And Iron, strongly disliked by many, was a strange, cold, taciturn man. Lefty was just poor, raised with little supervision, young, and greedy!

Plot: These men were very closely tied to Frank at the time he went missing. Lefty and Iron trapped beside him and worked with him that last year. They came up with a big "cock-and-bull" story about Bud Shaffer being the prime suspect after Frank was found hung. Perpetrating this story as a cover-up, the story even made the newspapers, being reported in the Wenatchee World in the 1950s.

Climax: The many "so-called" coincidences that surrounded this hanging death.

Climax: The known lies that the three men told.

Conclusion: All three men prospered right after Frank's death.

Conclusion: Two of them were known to have had the murdered victim's possessions; Pete having a heck-of-a-lot of Frank's good things.

Conclusion: The final true confession, of sorts, by George Miller, of finding Frank shot in the head. This turned out to be the only logical and most realistic death story. And, the fact that he kept it secret for so long for Pete's sake. George really wanted to believe that Bud Shaffer

Summary

had caused Frank's death. This story also means that there are two bodies up there.

Conclusion: The time was perhaps the worst in the history of this nation: the Great Depression of the 1930's. It took the war in Europe to really pull the country out of the hard times. Frank Maron went to work with a lot of other men on the Grand Coulee Dam, where he hurt his back and was put in a wheelchair. The Thirties were the desperate times when Frank disappeared and then was found, and the story of a lone trapper who never spent any of his (big) money for 25 years was certainly bait to a thief. Add to this the story of gold that popped up at that same time and was real and came out with Frank Maron and others. It was just too much for the hardened men of the times. Frank Arnold could make them all wealthy with some persuasion to talk. Frank wasn't going to and did not talk. And being tough as nails, they couldn't beat it out of him, though I'm sure they tried. They had only one option left, a bullet into the cold blue eyes that stared back at them. The fact is that the men never grew greatly wealthy, and they had to remove all of Frank's things from his cabin to find his money puke from his years of trapping. Their lack of great, long-lasting wealth and any later mining activity proves Frank never talked. George Miller and Pete rode in that next spring and buried the real Frank Arnold. Pete felt the need to go back to the crime-scene and take better care of the incriminating body before somebody else found it. He couldn't let somebody else find him shot.

There was just too much action taking place up there in those years. Miners were up and down that trail much too often for comfort, and more trappers would come. With George Miller now involved, knowing of Frank's death, could he be trusted to sit-on-it with his mouth shut? George would have gone to the police eventually — I think — if Pete didn't. This forced Pete and Lefty to come up with another body without a bullet hole in it and to drum-up the concocted story of the wild trapper named Bud Shaffer, who, coincidentally, did get into some trouble over in the Loomis area. George Miller thought he knew what was going on, and three of his working friends swore that Bud Shaffer did it! So, George knew who killed Frank. But no one could find Bud Shaffer. George was just a little short on the truth by saying that he found Frank "hung" on Horseshoe Creek. How could he say, "shot in the head on Horseshoe Creek" while Pete was around?

Conclusion: It's obvious that Pete and Lefty planted the body they called Frank Arnold. The body had teeth. Frank did not have teeth. They had to have used another body, long dead, that was just bones, from some poor, dug-up person. So, it is a good bet that there are indeed two bodies buried up there. As to what was found at the Horseshoe camp, you can bet that most of what Art Mitchell saw was planted. Only the canvas lean-to and the wood table nailed to a tree could be said to have been untouched by Pete and Lefty. Shorty, Lester Fairbrother told Clyde Paul what he found in this camp when he scouted through it in the late fall of 1935. And there was nothing worth mentioning: only three small pine trees pulled together and tied. He wouldn't have taken anything, knowing that Frank just might show back up. What Shorty did not find was the man that he looked for, Frank Arnold. Frank was not in this camp that fall of 1935.

Conclusion: The Colt .22 Woodsman semi-automatic was a plant. It was a gun of Pete's that he had before it was found by himself, Frank Maron and Art Mitchell in 1936, when Pete claimed it was Frank Arnold's gun. Frank did not own this gun. He owned the famous .22 long-barrel revolver.

Conclusion: Art Mitchell has repeated what a thousand new law enforcement officers have done from time immortal. Through inexperience, Art "muffed it." With just a little extra work, he could have come to a different conclusion than "suicide," Pete himself said in later years that Art was "shook" when he was in there investigating the strange death. Deputy Jim Vandiver later, under Art Mitchell who became

Summary

County Sheriff a year or two later, was not impressed with Art. He said he probably did act as told in the story, for he just wasn't the outdoors type; in fact, he said Art had a hard time getting out of the office.

It is my belief that Pete, Lefty and Iron snowshoed in to the mine and cleared out Frank's cabin that winter, leaving Frank bleeding on the ground at Horseshoe Creek, beaten-up and with a bullet hole in his head as they snowshoed passed him with his worldly goods. But one of them must have covered Frank up in some way to protect him from the few remaining scavengers that might have escaped his traps. Or it might have just snowed heavily, covering him in just the right amount of snow to bring him forth "in good shape" that next spring, as George Miller said.

The three, after killing Frank, took all of Frank's things out of his cabin up at the Tungsten looking for his puke, 25 years of trapping money, probably in the neighborhood of at least $30,000 or $50,000, which they **did** find and divided like lions and pirates three ways. Taking home what they wanted and stashing the rest around the mine somewhere. Pete put most of the discarded things back in the cabins later that year. When Pete, with George Miller came back that spring in 1935, they were the ones who put the empty coffee can on the floor that June day when Emmet Smith rode in, to catch the water from a leaky roof; one of the things not quite right that day. This is also why George Miller knew Bud Shaffer had stolen "all" of Frank's provisions. There just wasn't anything of Frank's left at the mine! Bud Shaffer left Frank with nothing, so poor Frank had to either shoot himself, or starve to death. This made sense to George, as he was sucked into the killer's evil cover-up. Thus again, the cabin was empty before Emmet Smith, the sheepherder got there a few days later in late June. But Pete made a mistake in the final run by putting some of the things back for the miners in 1936 to find..

The "Pasayten Wilderness" can be as deadly as its name implies. Not only was Frank cheated out of 20 years of life, but we who could have known him were cheated also. Herb Curtis, who was just 2 years younger than Frank Arnold, lived clear into the mid 1960's. If Frank had lived until he was 85, which many men of the times and place did, it would have placed Frank into the mid-fifties, and into the memory of a lot of people alive today, maybe even mine. And what stories the old bird could have told if a person could have just gotten him to talk. But dead men don't talk!

The Tungsten Mine, despite this sad death, is a wonderful place to visit still, and it puts you back in time 100 years. Its history tells a lively tale, and hopefully the Forest Service gets smart enough to work to save it, not destroy it now that they have taken it away from the miners. For it is a sad fact that the Forest Service has had a policy, from about the mid 1960's on, of selfishly tearing down, and burning down old historical cabins. They had in those years a crew of young workers who did nothing but take apart old miner, trapper, and cattlemen's cabins. Public pressure is one of the only things the Forest Service understands.

This book is going to ruffle a few feathers, but hopefully those who might take offense, will broaden their thinking capacity to encompass all the facts that surround the death of Frank Arnold and the Tungsten Mine. The writer had only the words and stories of those who were there, and those who are left, those who personally experienced the history of this person and mine.

Our vision and knowledge of Frank Arnold is the one from 1910 on, which leaves 40 years of this man's life pretty much open to our imagination. Perhaps there is some "poetic-justice" in the death or murder of this mysterious man. What do we know of his past? Frank Arnold just had to have been on the run from the long arm of the law! Almost assuredly, he was on the run from the Canadian law. It is the only logical reason he would never disclose where he had come from, or speak of past family, and lived the recluse life that he did. The ironic part is that the world found him anyway! The man was too exceptional!

Summary

Who else has ever raised two moose and taught them to pull, a wagon? Only the young man from Fredericton, New Brunswick. Yes, though he was disciplined well with a tight lip that never faltered even to his death, his past, has at last, just about caught up with him. But it won't come from this writer. Not this time. For he is not so sure he wants to know about Frank's past. For he has already shattered enough heroes for one book. So, we will just always have to keep wondering if his great skill with a six-gun was only for protection against wild animals. Could it be that his many hours on a lonesome drunk, would, and just might, pull the string on the coldest of hearts, if his past affairs were really to be known? If he was wanted by the law, he beat it. The answer could well be in the "Fredericton Daily Gleaner," that goes clear back to the year 1889. And there, on one of its pages you will find a story about a young man "…that was not your average sort of human being.…"

This man called "Frank Arnold" does have one other "champion" to remind us of him, the beautiful mountain in the Horseshoe Basin where so many times in the past this same Englishman, in his city hat and bib-overalls, walked alone, all by himself; it is called: "Arnold-Peak."

Whether the mentioned people in this book agree or disagree with its contents (for the writer wrote freely and unbiased), each of them added and helped put this story together, and they are all thanked now by the writer, and I hope the readers.

Jim McDaniel, Harry Sherling, George Honey, and others, were powerful players in this story. But Bob Curtis was a special player. His life span was just right to save this interesting tale of the Tungsten Mine, and no one man living was closer, or remembered more than he. The fever of the Tungsten Mine still ran hot in his blood. Bob was a special class of observer because of his Dad's long involvement with the Tungsten Mine, because of his own exceptional memory, because of his early interviews and research, and most of all, because of his firsthand conversations with, the man Frank Arnold and with those who knew

Frank Arnold well. However, that special "thanks" that goes to him, comes not from all of this, but from his willingness to share a story, that was almost all his — with us. It is because of Bob's unselfish desire to see this amazing story told and not lost forever, that the writer thanks him. For there are today, and there have been ever since that fateful day in 1903, a handful of people whose lives and souls have been caught up in... The Tungsten Mine!

MARY ROBERTS RINEHART'S PARTY WITH HER YOUNGER SON, WATCHING HER PACKER OVERLOAD HIS HORSE.

JIM DODD WITH A GOOD $1500 WORTH OF FURS; THOUGH THE WRITER BELIEVES HE HAD EARL ERWIN TO HELP HIM WITH THIS CATCH. NOTE THE LARGE WOLF HIDES AND HIS BUMPER CROP OF MARTIN. CRITERIA: BEFORE THE BIG '29 FIRE.

JOHNNY BELL OF LOOMIS - WENT ON TWO LONG MOUNTAIN TRIPS FOR FRANK'S BENEFIT - PHOTO EARLY 1960'S.

JOHNNY BELL'S NORTH-FORK TOATS COULEE CRAWL-IN-CABIN.

FRANK'S HOME FOR TWENTY YEARS. WINTER SCENE 1920. CABIN STILL STANDING; NOTE THE POWER LINES.

PULLING OUT AND HEADING EAST - AND IT HAD TO BE TO LOOMIS. THESE PICTURES HAD TO HAVE BEEN TAKEN IN 1921 OR '22, FOR THERE IS STILL TAR-PAPER ON THE ROOF OF THE BIG COOKHOUSE - AND THERE WASN'T A YEAR OR TWO LATER.

FRANK ARNOLD ... HIS LAST WINDER 1934/35

THE RINEHART COWBOYS - SOME OR ALL COULD BE FROM THE LOCAL AREA - THESE FOUR ARE OF THE TEN OR MORE IN THE PARTY AND FIVE OF THE FIFTEEN OR MORE HORSES. NOTE THE MILL BUILDINGS AND CABIN IN THE BACKGROUND.

CLARENCE LANDERGREEN (PICTURE CUT TOO LOW), HELPING FRANK AT ONE OF HIS CATCHES "THE-CAVE-MAN OF LOOMIS" AS HE WAS CALLED IN THE BOXING CIRCLES, AND A GOOD DRINKING BUDDY OF FRANK'S ... AND THE LAST MAN TO SEE FRANK ALIVE! ... ALMOST. NOTE STOVE-PIPE LEGS, AND THE CANVAS TARPPED ROOF.

OLD TIN-TYPE FOUND IN FRANK'S CABIN AFTER HIS DEATH, BELIEVED TO BE FRANK IN HIS BETTER DAYS, IF NOT, IT SURLY WOULD BE HIS FATHER

APEX MOUNTAIN - SHOT FROM TOPE OF WOLFRAMITE MOUNTAIN. AUTHORS PHOTO

FERRIS FORD HAD DEALINGS WITH FRANK FOR YEARS - ON ANOTHER SUCCESSFUL HUNT ... UNKNOWN "CLOWN" ON THE RIGHT.

"CATHEDRAL PEAK", CROWN OF THE EASTER PASAYTEN WILDERNESS, FOUR MILES DUE WEST FROM THE TUNGSTEN MINE. AUTHORS PHOTO

HANS RICHTER SAID THAT PETE COULD HAVE KILLED FRANK; LOVED RACING HORSES; HERE HE IS BEING HONORED AT A RACE STADIUM.

FRANK SHELLY, JUST OUT OR JUST IN LOOMIS.

SHORTY FAIRBROTHER ... NOTE THAT THE LYNX HE IS HOLDING IS AS LARGE AS HE IS. $2,000 OF FURS HANG ON THAT WALL - FAR, FAR MORE THAN A UNION LABOR COULD MAKE ALL YEAR-LONG IN THAT SAME ERA: 1928.

TAMING AND BRAKING A HORSE IS HARD ENOUGH, BRAKING A MOOSE IS A WHOLE NEW EXPERIENCE.

JIM MCDANIEL AT THE DUNKIN JAMES CABIN; CRITERIA 1960'S.

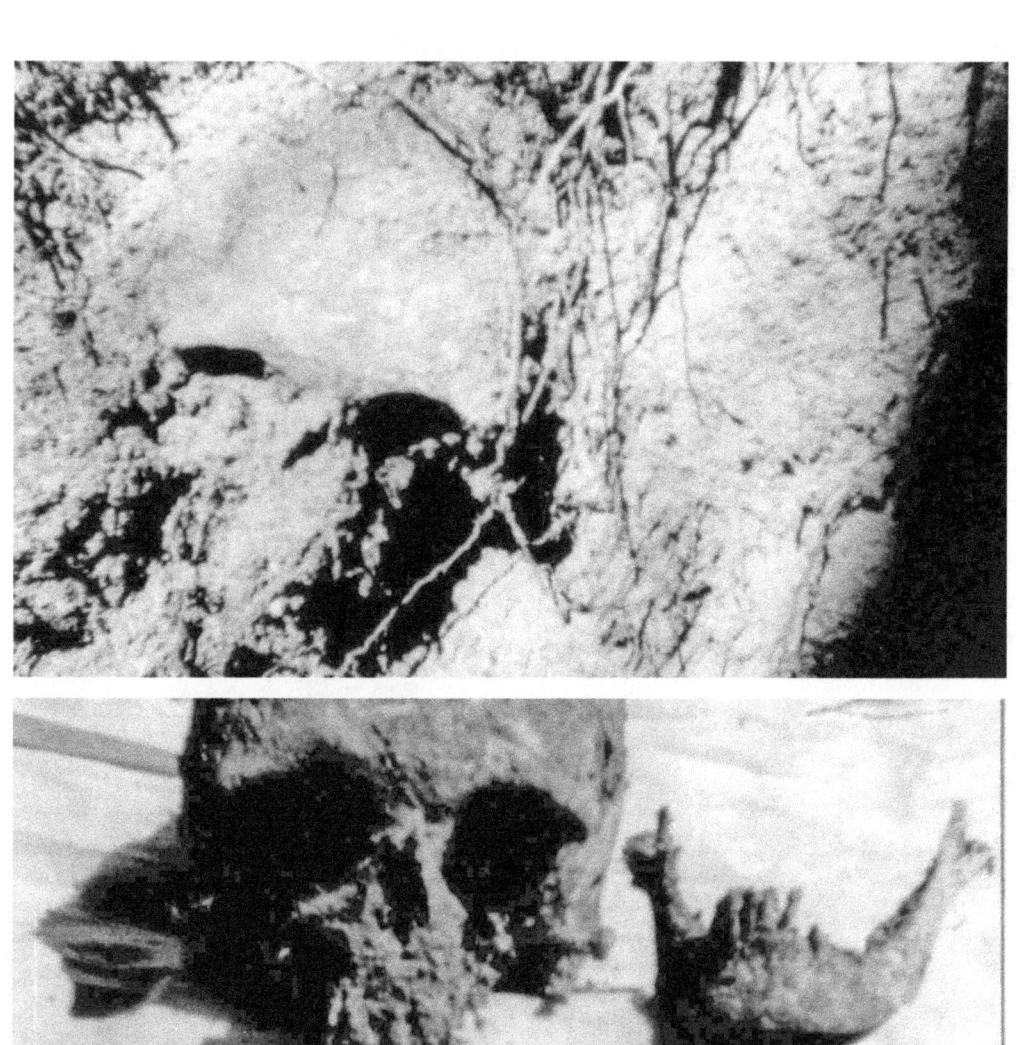

FRANK SHELLY, JUST OUT OR JUST IN LOOMIS.

SHORTY FAIRBROTHER ... NOTE THAT THE LYNX HE IS HOLDING IS AS LARGE AS HE IS. $2,000 OF FURS HANG ON THAT WALL - FAR, FAR MORE THAN A UNION LABOR COULD MAKE ALL YEAR-LONG IN THAT SAME ERA: 1928.

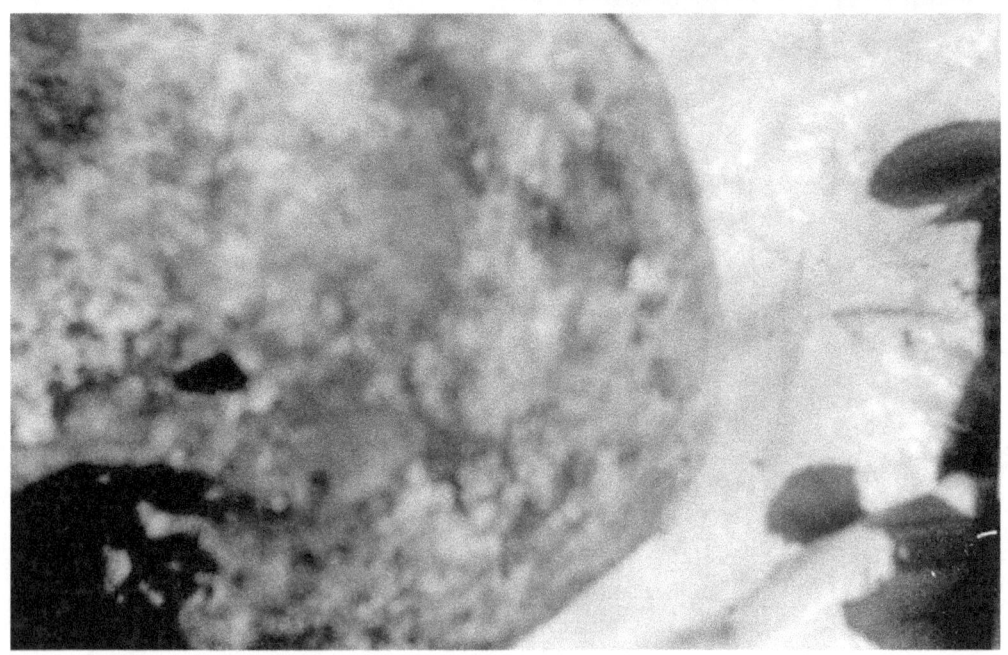

THE HORSESHOE CREEK GRAVE - DUGOUT ABOUT 20 INCHES - DOWN TO THE SKULL AND BONES.

THE GRAVE SKULL HAS A BULLET-HOLE ABOVE THE LEFT EAR. BUT BECAUSE THE PERSON ALSO HAD TEETH, IT CAN'T BE THE SKULL OF FRANK ARNOLD'S.

THE BODY, OR WHAT'S LEFT OF IT.

TALES OF THE TUNGSTEN MINE

Appendix 1

196161
Herbert Curtis et al to W.H. Rowe

OPTION AGREEMENT

For and in consideration of the sum of One Hundred Ninety-nine Thousand, Nine Hundred and Sixty ($199,960) Dollars, lawful money of the United States of America to me in hand paid by the Tungsten Mines Company, a corporation, duly organized and existing under the laws of the State of Washington, the receipt of which is hereby acknowledged, I do hereby sell, assign, transfer and set over unto the said Tungsten Mines Company the within and hereto attached contract and all my right, title and interest therein and thereto.

The contract referred to herein and assigned by this instrument is that certain contract made and entered into upon the 29th day of September 1915, by and between Herbert Curtis, W.H. McDaniel and Jacob Kast of Ruby, Washington and George W. Loudon and Paul F. Loudon of

Ruby, Washington, parties of the first part and the undersigned as party of the second part, relating to the following described Tungsten Mining Claim, situated in Okanogan County Washington, to-wit:

"Republic," "Mountain Dew," "Tungsten," "Blue Grouse," "Cathedral Number 1," and "Cathedral Number 2."

IN WITNESS WHEREOF, I have hereunto set my hand and seal this 3rd day of November 1915.

W.H. Rowe.... (seal)

STATE OF WASHINGTON
SS.
County of king

On this 3rd day of November, 1915, before me, a Notary Public in an for the State of Washington, duly commissioned and qualified, personally appeared W.H. Rowe, to me know to the individual described in and who executed the within and foregoing instrument and acknowledged to me that he signed and sealed the same as his free and voluntary act and deed, for the uses and purposes therein mentioned.

Witness, my hand and OFFICAIAL SEAL the day and year in this certificate first above written.

Edwin P. Whiting
Notary Public in and for the State
of Washington, residing at Seattle.
Notary Seal, Com. Exp. Nov. 29,1916

THIS AGREEMENT made and entered into this 29th day of September, 1915, by and between Herbert Curtis and W.H. McDaniel and Jacob Kast, of Loomis, Washington and George Loudon and Paul F.

Appendix 1

Loudon of Ruby, Washington, parties of the first part and W.H. Rowe, of Seattle, Washington, part of the second part, W I T N E S S E T H:

THAT WHEREAS, the parties of the first part are the owners of certain unpatented Tungsten mining claims, situated in Okanogan County, Washington, and known and described as follows, to-wit:

Republic," "Mountain Dew," "Tungsten," " Blue Grouse," "Cathedral Number 1," "Cathedral Number 2."

Notices of the location all of which said mining claims have been duly recorded in the office of the County Auditor of Okanogan County, Washington, to which said notices of location reference is hereby made for a more particular description of said property.

AND WHEREAS, the said parties of the first part are desirous of selling and disposing of the same and the said party of the second part is desirous of acquiring the same.

NOW THEREFORE, in consideration of the sum of One Dollar and other good and valuable considerations in hand paid by the said party of the second part to the said parties of the first part, the receipt of which is hereby acknowledged, the said parties of the first part do hereby give and grant unto the said party of the second part and exclusive option to purchase the above described mining claims, within the time and upon the terms and conditions herein after stated, to wit:

The purchase price of said mining property shall be the sum of Seventy-five Thousand Dollars.

The said sum shall, in the event that the said party of the second part shall elect to exercise this option, be due and payable as follows: Ten Thousand Dollars, on or before the First day of October 1916. Thirty Thousand Dollars on or before the first day of October 1917, and the sum of Thirty-Five Thousand Dollars on or before the first day of October 1918.

The said party of the second part shall within fifteen days from and after the execution of this instrument commence operations, with a crew of a least three men, continuously, during working days during the life of this option, and such operations shall not be discontinued for more than thirty days in any one year, barring unavoidable accident, strikes, acts of God, or weather conditions making such operations impossible or impracticable. Work done on trails or on about said property tending to the opening up or development of the same shall be deemed to be work upon said property within the meaning of this paragraph.

The said party of the second part shall be entitled to the immediate possession of said property, together with all machinery, tools and equipment now upon said property, all of which personal property is hereby included in this option; said second party shall also have the right to remove ore from said mining property, at any time during the life of this option, provided, however, that said second party shall pay to the parties of the first part the net value of said ore, or ore products at the nearest Railroad station, after deducting all the cost of transportation and smelter treatment, said value to be ascertained and estimated upon the then market value for Tungsten concentrates, which said payment shall be made within thirty days from and after the date of shipment from said Railroad station, all of which said payment shall be credited and applied upon the purchase price of said property.

That parties of the first part shall not in any manner be liable for any debts, obligations or liabilities that may be incurred by the party of the second part, during the life of this option or shall any such items be or become a lien or charge upon said property, and the said party of the second part shall not suffer or permit any liens or claims to be filed against said property, during the life on this option, and the said parties of the first part shall have the right to post notices upon said property, if they shall deem it necessary or proper, for the purpose of carrying out the provisions of this paragraph.

The said party of the second part shall on or before the first day of October 1916 build and establish upon or adjacent to said property a

Appendix 1

concentrating plant, for the purpose of concentrating the ore produced from said property, the capacity and character of said plant to be solely within the determination and discretion of the said party of the second part.

In the event that the party of the second part shall elect to exercise this option, and shall pay the sum of Ten Thousand Dollars on or before the first day of October, 1916 build and establish upon or adjacent to said property a concentration plant, for the purpose of concentrating the ore produced from said property, the capacity and character of said plant to be solely within the determination and discretion of the said party of the second part.

In the event that the party of the second part shall elect to exercise this option, and shall pay the sum of Ten Thousand Dollars on or before the first day of October 1916 as herein provided, the said parties of the first part shall, if the party of the second part so desires enter into a contract for the sale of said property, upon payment of the said sum of Thirty Thousand Dollars, upon the first day of October 1917, the said parties of the first part shall, at the election of second party, make, execute and deliver to said party of the second part a good and sufficient deed to said property, vesting in said Rowe the title to said property, and the said party of the second part shall thereupon make execute and deliver to said first parties a mortgage to secure the payment of the balance of the purchase price of said property then due.

Said parties of the first part shall, prior to the payment of the sum of Ten Thousand Dollars, as herein provided, and prior to the erection of said concentrating plant furnish second party with such evidence of title to said property as may be necessary or proper to show the validity of said title, and the right of first parties to a patent to said property, subject to the mining laws of the United States .

Said party of the second part shall do all necessary assessment work, required by the laws of the United State of America or the State of

Washington, to protect and preserve the title to said property, and shall file as necessary proofs of such work.

All further notices of location of said property, and any and all amendments of notices of location which may be hereafter filed by first parties shall be deemed to be in further assurance to the party of the second part of a good and valid title to said property, and the said parties of the first part shall at any time furnish such other and further papers, conveyances and evidences of title as may be necessary and proper to carry out the purposes and intention of this agreement.

The said party of the second part may at any time during the life of this option elect to abandon the same, and in the event that he shall so elect to abandon this option, or in the event the said party of the second part shall fail to make any of the payments herein specified, or shall fail to do or perform any of the conditions herein contained, by him to be performed, then this option shall be null and void and of no further force and effect and the said parties of the first part shall retain all sums paid herein and all improvements made upon such property, as an for their damages for the use and occupation of said property, provided, however, that no forfeiture shall be declared by the parties of the first part, except by thirty days written notice served upon the party of the second part, or deposited in the mail, registered and postage prepaid, and addressed to said second party, and upon make performance within the period of said notice, all claims of said second party in an to said property shall cease and determine, and the parties of the first part may there upon re-enter and take possession of said property.

This agreement shall bind and inure to the benefit of the heirs, executors, administrators, and assigns of the parties hereto as fully as though specifically mentioned herein.

IN WITNESS WHEREOF, the parties hereto have hereunto set their hands and seals the day and year in this instrument first above written.

Appendix 1

Herbert Curtis   (seal)

W. H. McDaniel   (seal)
George W. Loudon   (seal)
W.H. Rowe   (seal)
Jacob Kast by
Herbert Curtis historical
Attorney in Fact
Paul F. Loudon

STATE OF WASHINGTON)
ss.
COUNTY OF OKANOGAN)

On this 21st day of October, 1915, before me, a Notary Public in and for the State of Washington, duly commissioned and qualified, personally appeared Herbert Curtis, W. H. McDaniel and George W. Loudon, and Herbert Curtis, Attorney in fact for Jacob Kast, and Paul F. Loudon, to me known to be the individuals described in and who executed the within and foregoing instrument, and acknowledged to me that they signed and sealed the same as their free and voluntary act and deed for the uses and purposes therein mentioned.

WITNESS, my hand and OFFICIAL SEAL the day and year in the certificate first above written.

Geo. J. Hurly
Notary Public

STATE OF WASHINGTON)
ss.
COUNTY OF OKANOGAN)

On this 29th day of September, 1915, before me a Notary Public in and for the State of Washington, duly commissioned and qualified, personally appeared W.H. Rowe, to me known to be the individuals described in and who executed the within and foregoing instrument and acknowledged to me that he signed and sealed the same as his free and voluntary act and deed for the uses and purposes therein mentioned.

WITNESS, my hand and official seal the day and year in this certificate first above mentioned.

Edwin P. Whiting

Notary Public (Seattle)

Filed for record Nov. 12, 1915, at 9:11 A.M. Request Tungsten Mines Com. Recorded Nov. 12, 1915."

www.ingramcontent.com/pod-product-compliance
Lightning Source LLC
Chambersburg PA
CBHW020239030426
42336CB00010B/534